POLITICAL
LIBERALISM

The John Dewey Essays
in Philosophy

Number Four

Political Liberalism

The John Dewey Essays
in Philosophy

W. V. Quine, *Ontological Relativity and Other Essays* (1969)

A. J. Ayer, *Probability and Evidence* (1972)

Ernest Nagel, *Teleology Revisited and Other Essays in the
Philosophy and History of Science* (1979)

POLITICAL
LIBERALISM

John
Rawls

Columbia
University
Press

New York

COLUMBIA UNIVERSITY PRESS
NEW YORK   CHICHESTER, WEST SUSSEX

"Reply to Habermas" first appeared in
The Journal of Philosophy 92:3 (March 1995).

Library of Congress Cataloging-in-Publication Data

Rawls, John, 1921–
    Political liberalism / John Rawls.
        p.   cm. — (John Dewey essays in philosophy : no. 4)
    Includes index.
    ISBN 0–231–05248–0 (alk. paper)
    ISBN 0–231–05249–9 (pbk.)
    1. Justice.   2. Liberalism.   3. Political stability.   I. Title.
II. Series.
JC578.R37   1993   92–43224
320.5'1—dc20   CIP

Casebound editions of
Columbia University Press books
are printed on permanent and
durable acid-free paper.
Printed in the United States of America

c 10 9 8 7 6 5 4
p 10 9 8 7 6 5 4 3 2 1

For
Anne,
Lee,
Alec,
and
Liz

Contents

Contents

Contents

Contents

Introduction

The contents of this work are as follows. The first three lectures more or less cover the ground of three lectures I gave at Columbia University in April of 1980 and which appeared considerably revised in the *Journal of Philosophy* in September of that year under the title "Kantian Constructivism in Moral Theory." In the more than ten years since they have again been recast and further revised. I think they are much clearer than before, which is not to say they are now clear. I continue to call lectures what might be called chapters, since they were all given as lectures and I try to preserve, perhaps unsuccessfully, a certain conversational style.

When the original lectures were given I planned to publish them with three additional lectures. One, "Basic Structure as Subject" (1978), was already given and in print, the other two, "Basic Liberties and Their Priority" (1982) and "Social Unity and Primary Goods" (1982), were either drafted or near completion. But when these three additional lectures were finally done, they lacked the kind of unity I wanted, either with themselves or with the three preceding lectures.[1] I then wrote three further lectures on political liberalism,[2] as I now refer to it, beginning with "Political not Metaphysical" (1985), much of which is included in the first lecture, followed by "Overlapping Consensus" (1987), "Ideas of the Good" (1988), and "Domain of the Political" (1989). The last three, considerably redone and combined, together with "Public Reason," which appears here for the first time, make up the second three lectures.

The first six lectures are related this way: the first three set out the general philosophical background of political liberalism in practical reason, especially §§1, 3, 7, 8 of II and all of III, while the second three lay out in more detail several of its main ideas: the idea of an overlapping consensus, the idea of the priority of right and its relation to ideas of the good, and the idea of public reason. The lectures now have the desired unity both among themselves and with the spirit and content of *A Theory of Justice*,[3] a unity given by their topic: the idea of political liberalism.

To explain this last remark: the aims of *A Theory of Justice* were outlined in its preface (paragraphs 2–3). To paraphrase, I began by noting that during much of the modern period of moral philosophy the predominant systematic view in the English-speaking world had been some form of utilitarianism. One reason for this was that it had been represented by a long line of brilliant writers, from Hume and Adam Smith to Edgeworth and Sidgwick, who built up a body of thought truly impressive in its scope and depth. Those who criticized it often did so on a narrow

1. The first two of these additional lectures are now reprinted here unchanged as Lectures VII and VIII.
2. This term is used in "Overlapping Consensus," *Oxford Journal of Legal Studies* 7 (February 1987):23f., and "The Priority of Right and Ideas of the Good," *Philosophy and Public Affairs* 17 (Summer 1988):271, 273, 275.
3. *A Theory of Justice* (Cambridge, Mass.: Harvard University Press, 1971.)

front. They noted difficulties with the principle of utility and pointed out serious apparent discrepancies between its implications and our ordinary moral convictions. Yet I thought these critics failed to elaborate a workable and systematic moral conception that could successfully oppose it. The outcome was that we were often forced to choose between utilitarianism and rational intuitionism and were likely to settle for a variant of the principle of utility circumscribed and restricted by seemingly ad hoc intuitionistic constraints.

The aims of *Theory* (still to paraphrase) were to generalize and carry to a higher order of abstraction the traditional doctrine of the social contract. I wanted to show that this doctrine was not open to the more obvious objections often thought fatal to it. I hoped to work out more clearly the chief structural features of this conception—which I called "justice as fairness"—and to develop it as an alternative systematic account of justice that is superior to utilitarianism. I thought this alternative conception was, of the traditional moral conceptions, the best approximation to our considered convictions of justice and constituted the most appropriate basis for the institutions of a democratic society.

The aims of these lectures are quite different. Note that in my summary of the aims of *Theory,* the social contract tradition is seen as part of moral philosophy and no distinction is drawn between moral and political philosophy. In *Theory* a moral doctrine of justice general in scope is not distinguished from a strictly political conception of justice. Nothing is made of the contrast between comprehensive philosophical and moral doctrines and conceptions limited to the domain of the political. In the lectures in this volume, however, these distinctions and related ideas are fundamental.

Indeed, it may seem that the aim and content of these lectures mark a major change from those of *Theory*. Certainly, as I have indicated, there are important differences. But to understand the nature and extent of the differences, one must see them as arising from trying to resolve a serious problem internal to justice as fairness, namely from the fact that the account of stability in part III of *Theory* is not consistent with the view as a whole. I believe all differences are consequences of removing that inconsistency. Otherwise these lectures take the structure and content of *Theory* to remain substantially the same.[4]

To explain: the serious problem I have in mind concerns the unrealistic idea of a well-ordered society as it appears in *Theory*. An essential feature of a well-ordered society associated with justice as fairness is that all its citizens endorse this conception on the basis of what I now call a comprehensive philosophical doctrine. They accept, as rooted in this doctrine, its two principles of justice. Similarly, in the well-ordered society associated with utilitarianism citizens generally endorse that view as a comprehensive philosophical doctrine and they accept the principle of utility on that basis. Although the distinction between a political conception of justice and a comprehensive philosophical doctrine is not discussed in *Theory,* once the question is raised, it is clear, I think, that the text regards justice as fairness and utilitarianism as comprehensive, or partially comprehensive, doctrines.

Now the serious problem is this. A modern democratic society is characterized not simply by a pluralism of comprehensive religious, philosophical, and moral doctrines but by a pluralism of incompatible yet reasonable comprehensive doctrines. No one of these doctrines is affirmed by citizens generally. Nor should one expect that in the foreseeable future one of them, or some other reasonable doctrine, will ever be affirmed by all, or nearly all, citizens. Political liberalism assumes that, for political purposes, a plurality of reasonable yet incompatible comprehensive doctrines is the normal result of the exercise of human reason within the framework of the free institutions of a constitutional democratic regime. Political liberalism also supposes that a reasonable comprehensive doctrine does not reject the essentials of a democratic regime. Of course, a society may also contain unrea-

---

4. Of course, a number of errors and revisions need to be made in the way the structure and content of justice as fairness was presented in *Theory*. Some of these are discussed herein but to rectify these matters is not my concern in these lectures.

sonable and irrational, and even mad, comprehensive doctrines. In their case the problem is to contain them so that they do not undermine the unity and justice of society.

The fact of a plurality of reasonable but incompatible comprehensive doctrines—the fact of reasonable pluralism—shows that, as used in *Theory,* the idea of a well-ordered society of justice as fairness is unrealistic. This is because it is inconsistent with realizing its own principles under the best of foreseeable conditions. The account of the stability of a well-ordered society in part III is therefore also unrealistic and must be recast. This problem sets the stage for the later essays beginning in 1980. The ambiguity of *Theory* is now removed and justice as fairness is presented from the outset as a political conception of justice (I:2).

Surprisingly, this change in turn forces many other changes and calls for a family of ideas not needed before.[5] I say surprisingly because the problem of stability has played very little role in the history of moral philosophy, so it may seem odd that an inconsistency of this kind should turn out to force such extensive revisions. Yet the problem of stability is fundamental to political philosophy and an inconsistency there is bound to require basic readjustments. So perhaps it is not surprising after all that besides the ideas already mentioned—the ideas of a political conception of justice as opposed to a comprehensive doctrine, and of an overlapping consensus and of public reason—others are also needed. Here I mention that of a political conception of the person (I:5) and of reasonable as opposed to simple pluralism. Further, the idea of political constructivism is connected with these matters and raises questions about the truth of moral judgments, commented on below.[6]

The main conclusion to draw from these remarks—a conclu-

5. One apparent exception is the idea of an overlapping consensus. Yet its meaning in *Theory,* pp. 387f., is quite different.

6. The changes in the later essays are sometimes said to be replies to criticisms raised by communitarians and others. I don't believe there is a basis for saying this. Of course, whether I am correct in this belief depends on whether the changes can be satisfactorily explained by an analytic view of how they fit into the revised account of stability. It is certainly not settled by my say so.

sion to which I return in a moment—is that the problem of political liberalism is: How is it possible that there may exist over time a stable and just society of free and equal citizens profoundly divided by reasonable though incompatible religious, philosophical, and moral doctrines? Put another way: How is it possible that deeply opposed though reasonable comprehensive doctrines may live together and all affirm the political conception of a constitutional regime? What is the structure and content of a political conception that can gain the support of such an overlapping consensus? These are among the questions that political liberalism tries to answer.

For orientation, a few comments about political liberalism. Sometimes one hears reference made to the so-called Enlightenment project of finding a philosophical secular doctrine, one founded on reason and yet comprehensive. It would then be suitable to the modern world, so it was thought, now that the religious authority and the faith of Christian ages was alleged to be no longer dominant.

Whether there is or ever was such an Enlightenment project we need not consider; for in any case political liberalism, as I think of it, and justice as fairness as a form thereof, has no such ambitions. As I have said, political liberalism takes for granted not simply pluralism but the fact of reasonable pluralism; and beyond this, it supposes that of the main existing reasonable comprehensive doctrines, some are religious. The conception of the reasonable (II:3) is characterized so as to allow this. The problem of political liberalism is to work out a conception of political justice for a constitutional democratic regime that the plurality of reasonable doctrines—always a feature of the culture of a free democratic regime—might endorse. The intention is not to replace those comprehensive views, nor to give them a true foundation. Indeed, that intention would be delusional, but that is not the point. Rather, doing that is not the business of political liberalism.

Part of the seeming complexity of political liberalism—shown, say, in its having to introduce a further family of ideas—arises from accepting the fact of reasonable pluralism. For once we do this, then we assume that, in an ideal overlapping consensus, each citizen affirms both a comprehensive doctrine and the focal political conception, somehow related. In some cases the political conception is simply the consequence of, or continuous with, a citizen's comprehensive doctrine; in others it may be related as an acceptable approximation given the circumstances of the social world (IV:8). In any case, since the political conception is shared by everyone while the reasonable doctrines are not, we must distinguish between a public basis of justification generally acceptable to citizens on fundamental political questions and the many nonpublic bases of justification belonging to the many comprehensive doctrines and acceptable only to those who affirm them.

Similarly, there will be many parallel distinctions. For the elements of the political conception of justice must be separated from the analogous elements within comprehensive doctrines. We must keep track of where we are. Thus, ideas of the good in the political conception have to be appropriately political and distinct from those in more extensive views. The same holds for the political conception of persons as free and equal.

Given the fact of the reasonable pluralism of democratic culture, the aim of political liberalism is to uncover the conditions of the possibility of a reasonable public basis of justification on fundamental political questions. It should, if possible, set forth the content of such a basis and why it is acceptable. In doing this, it has to distinguish the public point of view from the many nonpublic (not private) points of view. Or, alternatively, it has to characterize the distinction between public reason and the many nonpublic reasons and to explain why public reason takes the form it does (VI). Moreover, it has to be impartial (in ways that need to be explained) between the points of view of reasonable comprehensive doctrines.

This impartiality is shown in various ways. For one thing, political liberalism does not attack or criticize any reasonable view. As part of this, it does not criticize, much less reject, any particular theory of the truth of moral judgments.[7] In this regard, it simply supposes that judgments of such truth are made from the point of view of some comprehensive moral doctrine. These doctrines render a judgment, all things considered: that is, taking into consideration what they see as all relevant moral and political values and all relevant facts (as each doctrine determines). Which moral judgments are true, all things considered, is not a matter for political liberalism, as it approaches all questions from within its own limited point of view. There are, however, occasions when it must say something here to strengthen its own case. This is attempted in III:8 and V:8.

Further, political liberalism, rather than referring to its political conception of justice as true, refers to it as reasonable instead. This is not merely a verbal matter but does two things. First, it indicates the more limited point of view of the political conception as articulating political and not all values, while providing at the same time a public basis of justification. Second, it indicates that the principles and ideals of the political conception are based on principles of practical reason in union with conceptions of society and person, themselves conceptions of practical reason. These conceptions specify the framework within which principles of practical reason are applied. The meaning of all this is given in the account of political (as opposed to moral) constructivism in III.

The idea of political constructivism will be familiar to anyone acquainted with the original position of justice as fairness, or with some similar framework. The principles of political justice are the result of a procedure of construction in which rational persons (or their representatives), subject to reasonable conditions, adopt the principles to regulate the basic structure of society. The principles that issue from a suitable procedure of construction, one that properly expresses the requisite principles and conceptions of practical reason, I think of as reasonable. The judgments those principles support are also reasonable. When

---

7. See IV:4.1, repeating verbatim the matching paragraph from "The Idea of an Overlapping Consensus."

citizens share a reasonable political conception of justice, they have a basis on which public discussion of fundamental political questions can proceed and be reasonably decided, not of course in all cases but we hope in most cases of constitutional essentials and matters of basic justice.

The dualism in political liberalism between the point of view of the political conception and the many points of view of comprehensive doctrines is not a dualism originating in philosophy. Rather, it originates in the special nature of democratic political culture as marked by reasonable pluralism. This special nature accounts, I believe, at least in good part, for the different problems of political philosophy in the modern as compared with the ancient world. To explain this I state a conjecture—I shouldn't say it is more than that—about the historical contexts that accounts for characteristic problems of the ancients and the moderns respectively.

When moral philosophy began, say with Socrates, ancient religion was a civic religion of public social practice, of civic festivals and public celebrations. Moreover, this civic religious culture was not based on a sacred work like the Bible, or the Koran, or the Vedas of Hinduism. The Greeks celebrated Homer and the Homeric poems were a basic part of their education, but the Iliad and the Odyssey were never sacred texts. As long as one participated in the expected way and recognized the proprieties, the details of what one believed were not of great importance. It was a matter of doing the done thing and being a trustworthy member of society, always ready to carry out one's civic duties as a good citizen—to serve on juries or to row in the fleet in war—when called upon to do so. It was not a religion of salvation in the Christian sense and there was no class of priests who dispensed the necessary means of grace; indeed the ideas of immortality and eternal salvation did not have a central place in classical culture.[8]

Greek moral philosophy begins, then, within the historical

---

8. In this paragraph I follow Walter Burkert, *Greek Religion* (Cambridge, Mass.: Harvard University Press, 1985), pp. 254–60, 273–75.

and cultural context of a civic religion of a polis in which the Homeric epics, with their gods and heroes, play a central part. This religion contains no alternative idea of the highest good to set against that expressed by the Homeric gods and heroes. The heroes are of noble birth; they openly seek success and honor, power and wealth, social standing and prestige. They are not indifferent to the good of family, friends, and dependents, yet these claims have a lesser place. As for the gods, they are not, morally speaking, very different; though being immortal, their lives are relatively happy and secure.

So in rejecting the Homeric ideal characteristic of a way of life of the warrior class of a bygone age, Greek philosophy had to work out for itself ideas of the highest good for human life, ideas acceptable to the citizens of the different society of fifth century B.C. Athens. Moral philosophy was always the exercise of free, disciplined reason alone. It was not based on religion, much less on revelation, as civic religion was neither a guide nor a rival to it. Its focus was the idea of the highest good as an attractive ideal, as the reasonable pursuit of our true happiness, and addressed a question civic religion left largely unanswered.[9]

Turning to the modern period, three historical developments deeply influenced the nature of its moral and political philosophy.

The first is the Reformation in the sixteenth century. It fragmented the religious unity of the Middle Ages and led to religious pluralism, with all its consequences for later centuries. This in turn fostered pluralisms of other kinds, which were a permanent feature of culture by the end of the eighteenth century.

The second is the the development of the modern state with its central administration, at first ruled by monarchs with enormous if not absolute powers. Or at least by monarchs who tried to be as absolute as they could, only granting a share in power to the aristocracy and the rising middle classes when they had to, or as suited their convenience.

---

9. In these last two paragraphs I follow Terence Irwin, *Classical Thought* (New York: Oxford University Prtess, 1989), esp. chap. 2.

The third is the development of modern science beginning in the seventeenth century. By modern science I mean the development of astronomy with Copernicus and Kepler and Newtonian physics; and also, it must be stressed, the development of mathematical analysis (calculus) by Newton and Leibniz. Without analysis, the development of physics would not have been possible.

I note first, the obvious contrast with the classical world in regard to religion. Medieval Christianity had five characteristic features that civic religion lacks:

It tended towards an authoritarian religion: its authority—the Church itself headed by the papacy—was institutional, central, and nearly absolute, although the supreme authority of the pope was sometimes challenged, as in the conciliar period of the fourteenth and fifteenth centuries.

It was a religion of salvation, a way to eternal life, and salvation required true belief as the Church taught it.

Hence, it was a doctrinal religion with a creed that was to be believed.

It was a religion of priests with the sole authority to dispense means of grace, means normally essential to salvation.

Finally, it was an expansionist religion of conversion that recognized no territorial limits to its authority short of the world as a whole.

The Reformation had enormous consequences. When an authoritative, salvationist, and expansionist religion like medieval Christianity divides, this inevitably means the appearance within the same society of a rival authoritative and salvationist religion, different in some ways from the original religion from which it split off, but having for a certain period of time many of the same features. Luther and Calvin were as dogmatic and intolerant as the Roman Church had been.

There is a second, if less obvious, contrast with the classical world, this time with regard to philosophy. During the wars of religion people were not in doubt about the nature of the highest good, or the basis of moral obligation in divine law. These things they thought they knew with the certainty of faith, as here their moral theology gave them complete guidance. The problem was rather: How is society even possible between those of different faiths? What can conceivably be the basis of religious toleration? For many there was none, for it meant the acquiescence in heresy about first things and the calamity of religious disunity. Even the earlier proponents of toleration saw the division of Christendom as a disaster, though a disaster that had to be accepted in view of the alternative of unending religious civil war.

Thus, the historical origin of political liberalism (and of liberalism more generally) is the Reformation and its aftermath, with the long controversies over religious toleration in the sixteenth and seventeenth centuries.[10] Something like the modern understanding of liberty of conscience and freedom of thought began then. As Hegel saw, pluralism made religious liberty possible, certainly not Luther's and Calvin's intention.[11] Of course, other controversies are also of crucial importance, such as those over limiting the powers of absolute monarchs by appropriate principles of constitutional design protecting basic rights and liberties.

Yet despite the significance of other controversies and of principles addressed to settling them, the fact of religious division remains. For this reason, political liberalism assumes the fact of reasonable pluralism as a pluralism of comprehensive doctrines, including both religious and nonreligious doctrines. This pluralism is not seen as disaster but rather as the natural outcome of the activities of human reason under enduring free institutions. To see reasonable pluralism as a disaster is to see the exercise of reason under the conditions of freedom itself as a

10. Judith Shklar, in her *Ordinary Vices* (Cambridge, Mass.: Harvard University Press, 1984), speaks of the liberalism of fear, represented by Montaigne and Montesquieu, and described in that work as born out of the cruelties of the religious civil wars. See p. 5.

11. See *Grundlinien der Philosophie des Rechts* (1821), §270, near the end of the long comment.

disaster. Indeed, the success of liberal constitutionalism came as a discovery of a new social possibility: the possibility of a reasonably harmonious and stable pluralist society.[12] Before the successful and peaceful practice of toleration in societies with liberal institutions there was no way of knowing of that possibility. It is more natural to believe, as the centuries-long practice of intolerance appeared to confirm, that social unity and concord requires agreement on a general and comprehensive religious, philosophical, or moral doctrine. Intolerance was accepted as a condition of social order and stability. The weakening of that belief helps to clear the way for liberal institutions. Perhaps the doctrine of free faith developed because it is difficult, if not impossible, to believe in the damnation of those with whom we have, with trust and confidence, long and fruitfully cooperated in maintaining a just society.

As I noted earlier, then, the problem of political liberalism is: How is it possible that there may exist over time a stable and just society of free and equal citizens profoundly divided by reasonable religious, philosophical, and moral doctrines? This is a problem of political justice, not a problem about the highest good. For the moderns the good was known in their religion; with their profound divisions, the essential conditions of a viable and just society were not. The problem of understanding these conditions moves to the center of the stage. Part of this problem is: What are the fair terms of social cooperation between citizens characterized as free and equal yet divided by profound doctrinal conflict? What is the structure and content of the requisite political conception, if, indeed, such a conception is even possible? This is not the problem of justice as it arose in the ancient world. What the ancient world did not know was the clash between salvationist, creedal, and expansionist religions. That is a phenomenon new to historical experience, a possibility realized by the Reformation. Of course, Christianity already made possible

---

12. Hume remarks on this in par. 6 of "Liberty of the Press" (1741). See also A. G. Dickens, *The English Reformation* (London: Fontana Press, 1967), pp. 440f.

the conquest of people, not simply for their land and wealth, and to exercise power and dominion over them, but to save their souls. The Reformation turned this possibility inward upon itself.

What is new about this clash is that it introduces into people's conceptions of their good a transcendent element not admitting of compromise. This element forces either mortal conflict moderated only by circumstance and exhaustion, or equal liberty of conscience and freedom of thought. Except on the basis of these last, firmly founded and publicly recognized, no reasonable political conception of justice is possible. Political liberalism starts by taking to heart the absolute depth of that irreconcilable latent conflict.

On the relation between political liberalism and the moral philosophy of the modern period, while moral philosophy was, of course, deeply affected by the religious situation within which it developed after the Reformation, by the eighteenth century leading writers hoped to establish a basis of moral knowledge independent of ecclesiastical authority and available to the ordinary reasonable and conscientious person. This done, they wanted to develop the full range of concepts and principles in terms of which to characterize the requirements of moral life. To this end they studied basic questions of moral epistemology and psychology, such as:

Is the knowledge or awareness of how we are to act directly accessible only to some, or to a few (the clergy, say), or is it accessible to every person who is normally reasonable and conscientious?

Again, is the moral order required of us derived from an external source, say from an order of values in God's intellect, or does it arise in some way from human nature itself (either from reason or feeling or from a union of both), together with the requirements of our living together in society?

Finally, must we be persuaded or compelled to bring ourselves in line with the requirements of our duties and obligations by some external motivation, say, by divine sanctions or by those of the state; or are we so constituted that we have in our nature sufficient motives to lead us to act as we ought without the need of external threats and inducements?[13]

Each of these questions first arose out of theology. Of the writers we usually study, Hume and Kant, both in their different ways, affirm the second alternative in each of these three questions. They believe that the moral order arises in some way from human nature itself, as reason or as feeling, and from the conditions of our life in society. They also believe that the knowledge or awareness of how we are to act is directly accessible to every person who is normally reasonable and conscientious. And finally, they believe that we are so constituted that we have in our nature sufficient motives to lead us to act as we ought without the need of external sanctions, at least in the form of rewards and punishments imposed by God or the state. Indeed, both Hume and Kant are about as far as one can get from the view that only a few can have moral knowledge and that all or most people must be made to do what is right by means of such sanctions.[14] In this their beliefs belong to what I refer to as comprehensive as opposed to political liberalism.

Political liberalism is not comprehensive liberalism. It does not take a general position on the three questions above but leaves these to be answered in their own way by different comprehensive views. However, political liberalism does affirm the second alternative in each case with respect to a political conception of justice for a constitutional democratic regime. Affirming

13. The last two paragraphs above follow J. B. Schneewind, *Moral Philosophy from Montaigne to Kant: An Anthology*, 2 vols. (Cambridge: Cambridge University Press, 1990). See the introduction to the first volume, p. 18. I am much indebted to these volumes and to Schneewind's many essays, among them in particular: "Natural Law, Skepticism, and the Method of Ethics," *Journal of the History of Ideas* 52 (1991):289–308.

14. Schneewind says this of Kant, *Moral Philosophy*, p. 29, but I believe it holds of Hume as well.

those alternatives in this fundamental case is part of political constructivism (III). The general problems of moral philosophy are not the concern of political liberalism, except insofar as they affect how the background culture and its comprehensive doctrines tend to support a constitutional regime. Political liberalism sees its form of political philosophy as having its own subject matter: how is a just and free society possible under conditions of deep doctrinal conflict with no prospect of resolution? To maintain impartiality between comprehensive doctrines, it does not specifically address the moral topics on which those doctrines divide. On occasion this appears to raise difficulties and these I try to answer as they arise, for example in V:8.

It may seem that my emphasis on the Reformation and the long controversy about toleration as the origin of liberalism is dated in terms of the problems of contemporary political life. Among our most basic problems are those of race, ethnicity, and gender. These may seem of an altogether different character calling for different principles of justice, which *Theory* does not discuss.

As I noted earlier, that work set out to offer an account of political and social justice that is more satisfactory than the leading familiar traditional conceptions. To this end it limited itself—as the questions it actually discusses make clear—to a family of classical problems that had been at the center of the historical debates concerning the moral and political structure of the modern democratic state. Hence it treats the grounds of the basic religious and political liberties, and of the basic rights of citizens in civil society, including here freedom of movement and fair equality of opportunity, the right of personal property, and the protections of the rule of law. It also takes up the justice of economic and social inequalities in a society in which citizens are viewed as free and equal. But *Theory* leaves aside for the most part the question of the claims of democracy in the firm and the workplace, as well as that of justice between states (or peoples as I prefer to say); it barely mentions retributive justice and the protection of the environment or the preservation of wildlife.

Other major matters are omitted, for example, the justice of and in the family, though I do assume that in some form the family is just. The underlying assumption is that a conception of justice worked up by focusing on a few long-standing classical problems should be correct, or at least provide guidelines for addressing further questions. Such is the rationale of focusing on a few main and enduring classical problems.

Of course, the conception of justice so arrived at may prove defective. This underlies much of the criticism of *Theory*. This criticism holds that the kind of liberalism it represents is intrinsically faulty because it relies on an abstract conception of the person and uses an individualist, nonsocial, idea of human nature; or else that it employs an unworkable distinction between the public and the private that renders it unable to deal with the problems of gender and the family. I believe that much of the objection to the conception of the person and the idea of human nature springs from not seeing the idea of the original position as a device of representation, as explained in I:4. I believe also, though I do not try to show in these lectures, that the alleged difficulties in discussing problems of gender and the family can be overcome.

Thus, I still think that once we get the conceptions and principles right for the basic historical questions, those conceptions and principles should be widely applicable to our own problems also. The same equality of the Declaration of Independence which Lincoln invoked to condemn slavery can be invoked to condemn the inequality and oppression of women. I think it a matter of understanding what earlier principles require under changed circumstances and of insisting that they now be honored in existing institutions. For this reason *Theory* focused on certain main historical problems in the hope of formulating a family of reasonable conceptions and principles that might also hold for other basic cases.

To conclude, in the remarks above I have tried to set out how I now understand justice as fairness as a form of political liberalism and why changes in it were necessary. These remarks emphasize the serious internal problem that forced those changes. I do not mean, however, to give an account of how and why those changes were actually made. I don't think I really know why I took the course I did. Any story I would tell is likely to be fiction, merely what I want to believe.

My first use of such ideas of a political conception of justice and of an overlapping consensus were misleading and led to objections I initially found puzzling: how could such simple ideas as those of a political conception of justice and of an overlapping consensus be misunderstood? I had underestimated the depth of the problem of making *Theory* consistent and had taken for granted a few missing pieces essential for a convincing statement of political liberalism. Central among these missing pieces are:

1. the idea of justice as fairness as a freestanding view and that of an overlapping consensus as belonging to its account of stability;

2. the distinction between simple pluralism and reasonable pluralism, together with the idea of a reasonable comprehensive doctrine; and

3. a fuller account of the reasonable and the rational worked into the conception of political (as opposed to moral) constructivism, so as to bring out the bases of the principles of right and justice in practical reason.

With these pieces in place, I now believe the obscurities are cleared up. I have many debts, most of which are indicated in footnotes throughout. To those with whom I had instructive discussions about the missing pieces described above, and from whom I have also learned much, I acknowledge a special debt.

To T. M. Scanlon for numerous instructive discussions from the beginning about political constructivism, and constructivism more generally, so that this view as given in III is now more clear than first sketched in 1980; and also for discussions about the distinction between the reasonable and the rational, and how to specify the reasonable for the purposes of a political conception of justice (II:1–3).

To Ronald Dworkin and Thomas Nagel for many conversations while taking part in seminars at New York University during 1987–1991; and in connection with the idea of justice as fairness as a freestanding view (I:5), a rare illuminating midnight conversation in the deserted bar of the Santa Lucia Hotel in Napoli in June 1988.

To Wilfried Hinsch for the need for an idea of a reasonable comprehensive doctrine, as opposed to a comprehensive doctrine simpliciter (II:3), and for instructive discussions about this in May and June of 1988.

To Joshua Cohen, who stressed the significance of the distinction between reasonable pluralism and simple pluralism (I:6.2), and for many valuable discussions about the idea of the reasonable in 1989–90, all summed up in his paper of May 1990.

To Tyler Burge for two long letters in the summer of 1991 that queried and criticized an earlier version of III. He persuaded me that not only had I failed to give a clear sense of the ways in which both Kant's moral constructivism and my political constructivism provide an account of either moral or political autonomy, but that I had exceeded the limits of a political conception of justice in making the contrast between political constructivism and rational intuitionism. In an effort to correct these serious faults, I have entirely rewritten §§1, 2, and 5.

As the dates above indicate, I reached a clear understanding of political liberalism—or so I think—only in the past few years. Although many of the earlier essays appear here with the same or a similar title, and much the same content, they have all been considerably adjusted so that together they express what I now believe is a consistent view.

I have tried to acknowledge other debts in the footnotes. The following debts, however, extend over a long period of time and for one reason or another cannot be properly acknowledged in that way.

To Burton Dreben, with whom I have discussed the questions of these lectures at length beginning in the late 1970s when the idea of political liberalism began to take shape in my mind. His firm encouragement and severe talmudic criticism have done me immense good. My debt to him is beyond accounting.

To the late David Sachs, with whom I have discussed, since 1946 when we first met, many of the questions the text considers, particularly those concerning moral psychology. In regard to the topics of this volume, Sachs and I had lengthy discussions, very valuable to me, in Boston three times in the 1980s. In the spring and summer of 1982 we discussed various of the difficulties we found in the lectures I gave at Columbia in 1980; in the summer of 1983 he helped me prepare a considerably improved version of "Basic Structure as Subject," as well as a much better version of §6 of "The Basic Liberties and Their Priority," dealing with the idea of society as a social union of social unions. Both of these I hope to use at some later date. In the summer of 1986 we reworked the lecture I gave at Oxford the previous May in honor of H. L. A. Hart. This improved version appeared in February 1987 in the *Oxford Journal of Legal Studies,* and much of it reappears here in IV.

To the late Judith Shklar, I am indebted for innumerable instructive discussions since we met over thirty years ago. While never a student of hers, I learned from her as a student might and I am the better for it. With regard to this work, she was especially helpful in pointing out directions that should be pursued; and I have always relied on her in matters of historical interpretation, crucial at a number of places in the text. Our last discussion concerned such matters.

To Samuel Scheffler, who in the fall of 1977 sent me a short paper, "Moral Independence and the Original Position," in which he argued that there was a serious conflict between the third part of my paper "The Independence of Moral Theory" (1975), which took up the relation between personal identity and moral theory, and my arguments against utilitarianism in *Theory.*[15] I remember this as the moment (I was on leave that year) when I started thinking about whether and how far the view of *Theory* needed

15. Scheffler's paper later appeared in *Philosophical Studies* 35 (1979):397–403.

to be recast. The decision to pursue this problem and not another topic led eventually to the Columbia lectures of 1980 and
to the later essays elaborating the idea of political liberalism.

To Erin Kelly, who for the past two years or so has read the
drafts of the manuscript, pointing out places where the text was
obscure and suggesting clarifications; she indicated ways in which
the argument could be reorganized to give it greater force; and
by asking questions and raising objections she has led me to
reshape the text throughout. It would be impossible to list all the
revisions to which her comments have led but they sometimes
led to important changes. The more basic of these I have tried to
acknowledge in footnotes. The merits of this work, such as they
are, arise to an important extent from her efforts.

Finally, I would like to thank the following persons for their
written comments on the manuscript.

Dennis Thompson gave me several pages of extremely valuable suggestions, all but a few of which led to corrections or
revisions in the text; and I have indicated where a few of these
have been made, or conveyed his comments, in the footnotes.

Frank Michelman's many penetrating comments I reluctantly
felt I could not respond to usefully without making far-reaching
and substantial changes at this time. At only one place (in VI:6.4)
have I been able to address his concerns.

Robert Audi, Kent Greenawalt, and Paul Weithman sent me
instructive suggestions on VI, some of which I managed to include, several at the last moment.

Alyssa Bernstein, Thomas Pogge, and Seana Shiffrin gave me
extensive written comments but unhappily I have not been able
to take them all into account. I regret they won't see their
comments dealt with here as they should have been. I regret also
that in reprinting unchanged "Basic Liberties and Their Priority
(1982), I have not replied to Rex Martin's probing criticisms
expressed in his *Rawls and Rights,* esp. chaps. 2, 3, 6, and 7.[16]

For the hapless work of helping me correct and edit the galleys

---

16. *Rawls and Rights* (Lawrence: University of Kansas Press, 1985).

and page proofs, I thank my wife Mard and our daughter Liz, and Michelle Renfield and Matthew Jones.

John Rawls
October 1992

Introduction to the
Paperback Edition

In this introduction to the paperback edition, I give a Reader's Guide to the leading ideas of the book.[1] A main aim of *Political Liberalism* (= PL) is to say how the well-ordered society of *justice as fairness*[2] (set out

1. I should like to thank several people for helping me with this second introduction: Percy Lehning for many fruitful discussions as to how to approach it and for correcting several of my false starts; Norman Daniels for instructive conversations about the role of stability in political liberalism; Erin Kelly, T. M. Scanlon, and Dennis Thompson gave me a great many valuable suggestions, which I have gladly accepted; and finally, Burton Dreben, with whom I have had long conversations and to whom I owe much for his seemingly innumerable thoughts and criticisms about how to organize and improve the final text. Without their aid and efforts, and that of others mentioned below, I would not have been able to write this introduction.

2. I put this phrase in italics because it is the proper name of a particular account of justice and it is always to be so understood. I shall use the term *doctrine* for comprehensive views of

in *A Theory of Justice* [1971] [= *Theory*]) is to be understood once it is adjusted to the fact of reasonable pluralism (3ff., 36ff.)[3] and regulated by a political conception of justice. I start with the idea of the domain of the political together with the idea of a political conception of justice, using as an example the conception of justice as fairness. These ideas and their distinction from comprehensive[4] doctrines of all kinds, are, I believe, among the most crucial ideas of political liberalism. All of part I and lecture V of part II of PL set out those ideas and definitions for other needed conceptions. Another main aim of PL is to say how a well-ordered liberal society containing a number of reasonable political conceptions is to be understood. In this case there is both the fact of reasonable pluralism and a family of reasonable though differing liberal political conceptions; I ask what is the most reasonable basis of social unity given these two conditions. These things are done in discussing the leading ideas of part II as they appear in lectures IV and VI. I shall focus on the idea of citizenship in a democratic regime and how it is connected with the ideas of political legitimacy and public reason. I emphasize that the ideas of the domain of the political and a political conception of justice are normative and moral ideas in their own right, that is, their "content is given by certain ideals, principles, and standards, and these norms articulate certain values, in this case political values" (11*n*). I also take note of the place of justice as fairness in both *Theory* and PL.

1. Before going into these matters, I should note that an obstacle to reading PL is its failing to identify explicitly the

---

all kinds and the term *conception* for a political conception and its component parts, such as the conception of the person as citizen. The term *idea* is used as a general term and may refer to either as the context determines. References to *Theory* and PL are given by lecture, section, or page numbers in parentheses.

3. This is the fact that a plurality of reasonable comprehensive doctrines, religious, philosophical, and moral, is the normal condition of democratic culture given its free institutions.

4. A comprehensive doctrine is defined (13). It is distinct from a political conception of justice, since it applies to all subjects and its virtues cover all parts of life.

philosophical question it addresses. There is no such obstacle in reading *Theory:* it explicitly attempts to work out from the idea of the social contract, represented by Locke, Rousseau, and Kant, a theory of justice that is no longer open to objections often thought fatal to it, and that proves superior to the long dominant tradition of utilitarianism. *Theory* hopes to present the structural features of such a theory of justice so as to make it the best approximation to our considered judgments of justice and hence to give the most appropriate moral basis for a democratic society (p. viii). This is a recognized philosophical question, academic though it may be.

The obstacle in identifying the philosophical question PL primarily addresses is that this question is not clearly explained by the opening to lecture I, where it asks (p. 4): How is it possible for there to exist over time a just and stable society of free and equal citizens who remain profoundly divided by reasonable religious, philosophical, and moral doctrines? If the problem is how is this society to be stable for the right reasons (143ff.)— always the relevant idea of stability[5]—then why should there be any fundamental problem with conflicting comprehensive liberalisms such as those of Kant and Mill, which already (let's suppose) endorse a just democratic regime, even if they do so for different reasons? Indeed, this seems an easy case. Thus, the question should be more sharply put this way: How is it possible for those affirming a religious doctrine that is based on religious authority, for example, the Church or the Bible, also to hold a reasonable political conception that supports a just democratic regime?

The point is that not all reasonable comprehensive doctrines are liberal comprehensive doctrines; so the question is whether they can still be compatible for the right reasons with a liberal political conception. To do this, I contend, it is not sufficient that these doctrines accept a democratic regime merely as a *modus vivendi*. Rather, they must accept it as members of a reasonable

---

5. The phrase "stability for the right reasons" does not occur in the text of PL, but "stability" should usually be given that meaning in both *Theory* and PL, as the context determines.

overlapping consensus (IV:3). Referring to citizens holding such a religious doctrine as citizens of faith, we ask: How is it possible for citizens of faith to be wholehearted members of a democratic society when they endorse an institutional structure satisfying a liberal political conception of justice with its own intrinsic political ideals and values, and when they are not simply going along with it in view of the balance of political and social forces?

To sketch an answer, the original introduction to PL makes these points. Political liberalism is not a form of Enlightenment liberalism, that is, a comprehensive liberal and often secular doctrine founded on reason and viewed as suitable for the modern age now that the religious authority of Christian ages is said to be no longer dominant. Political liberalism has no such aims. It takes for granted the fact of reasonable pluralism of comprehensive doctrines, where some of those doctrines are taken to be nonliberal and religious. The problem of political liberalism is to work out a political conception of political justice for a constitutional democratic regime that a plurality of reasonable doctrines, both religious and nonreligious, liberal and nonliberal, may freely endorse, and so freely live by and come to understand its virtues. Emphatically it does not aim to replace comprehensive doctrines, religious or nonreligious, but intends to be equally distinct from both and, it hopes, acceptable to both. These remarks paraphrase and abbreviate (p. xviii).

In addition, the pages (xxi–xxvi) spell out what PL sees as the contrast between ancient and modern political philosophy. For the ancients the central problem was the doctrine of the good and for the moderns the central problem was the conception of justice. PL conjectures as to why this was so. For the ancients, religion was civic religion, and it was left for philosophy to work out a doctrine of the good. For the moderns, religion was the salvation religions of Christianity, which, as Catholic and Protestant, clashed in the Reformation; and these already included a doctrine of the good—the good of salvation. But resting on the conflicting authorities of Church or Bible, there was no resolution between them, as their competing transcendent elements do not admit of compromise. Their mortal combat can be moderated only by circumstance and exhaustion, or by equal liberty of conscience and freedom of thought. Circumstance and exhaustion lead to a *modus vivendi;* equal liberty of conscience and freedom of thought, as IV:6–7 suggests, may sometimes lead to the more hopeful possibilities of a constitutional, and then to an overlapping, consensus.

Thus, to repeat, the problem of political liberalism is to work out a political conception of political justice for a (liberal) constitutional democratic regime that a plurality of reasonable doctrines, both religious and nonreligious, liberal and nonliberal, may endorse for the right reasons. A fundamental difficulty is that since under reasonable pluralism the religious good of salvation cannot be the common good of all citizens, the political conception must employ, instead of that good, political conceptions such as liberty and equality together with a guarantee of sufficient all-purpose means (primary goods [IV:3–4]) for citizens to make intelligent and effective use of their freedoms. These are long recognized questions, though to some they may seem more political than philosophical. It doesn't matter which we say, so long as we recognize the nature of the questions. I view them as philosophical, because a political conception of justice is a normative and moral conception, and so is the domain of the political, as well as all the other political conceptions. PL discusses, from the point of view of the political, the main moral and philosophical conceptions of a constitutional democratic regime: the conceptions of a free and equal citizen, of the legitimacy of the exercise of political power, of a reasonable overlapping consensus, of public reason with its duty of civility, and of stability for the right reasons. It also looks for the most reasonable basis of social unity available to citizens of a modern democratic society. In sum, PL considers whether in the circumstances of a plurality of reasonable doctrines, both religious and nonreligious, liberal and nonliberal, a well-ordered and stable democratic government is possible, and indeed even how it is to be conceived as coherent.

2. Given this background, I now turn to the Reader's Guide. In part III, *Theory* supposes that the well-ordered society of justice as fairness is possible and somehow comes about. It then asks whether that society is stable. It argues that the laws of nature and human psychology would lead citizens who grow up as members of that well-ordered society to acquire a sense of justice sufficiently strong to uphold their political and social institutions over generations. The whole argument culminates in chapters 8 and 9 with a sketch of the stages of moral learning and of stability. As always, stability means stability for the right reasons. This implies that the reasons from which citizens act include those given by the account of justice they affirm—in this case the comprehensive doctrine of justice as fairness[6]—which characterizes their effective sense of justice.

However, since the principles of justice as fairness in *Theory* require a constitutional democratic regime, and since the fact of reasonable pluralism is the long-term outcome of a society's culture in the context of these free institutions (p. xvi), the argument in *Theory* relies on a premise the realization of which its principles of justice rule out. This is the premise that in the well-ordered society of justice as fairness, citizens hold the same comprehensive doctrine, and this includes aspects of Kant's comprehensive liberalism, to which the principles of justice as fairness might belong. But given the fact of reasonable pluralism, this comprehensive view is not held by citizens generally, any more than a religious doctrine, or some form of utilitarianism.

In this situation, what political conception of justice can provide the common basis of principles and ideals to guide public political discussion on which citizens affirming conflicting religious and nonreligious yet reasonable comprehensive doctrines can agree? It is easy to see how there might be a reasonably just *modus vivendi* between a plurality of conflicting comprehensive doctrines. We simply suppose that historical circumstances have

---

6. As a comprehensive moral doctrine, it suggested that justice as fairness is part of rightness as fairness (*Theory*, 17, 111).

so turned out that for the time being at least, the balance of forces keeps all sides supporting the current arrangements, which happen to be just to each of them. However, when two salvation religions clash, can there be any resolution of the conflict that goes beyond that? I have noted (§1 above) that sometimes a *modus vivendi* might develop into an overlapping consensus of reasonable doctrines (IV:6–7). As explained in IV:3, the idea of an overlapping consensus is moral in its object and motivation, rendering the consensus stable over the distribution of doctrines. This gives stability for the right reasons (143ff.), and this distinguishes the idea of such a consensus from a *modus vivendi*.

3. Thus, a main aim of PL is to show that the idea of the well-ordered society in *Theory* may be reformulated so as to take account of the fact of reasonable pluralism. To do this it transforms the doctrine of justice as fairness as presented in *Theory* into a political conception of justice that applies to the basic structure of society.[7] Transforming justice as fairness into a political conception of justice requires reformulating as political conceptions the component ideas that make up the comprehensive doctrine of justice as fairness.[8] Some of these components may seem in *Theory* to be religious, philosophical, or moral, and indeed may actually be so, since *Theory* does not distinguish between comprehensive doctrines and political conceptions. This transformation is done in all of part I of PL and in lecture V of

7. By the basic structure is meant society's main political, constitutional, social, and economic institutions and how they fit together to form a unified scheme of social cooperation over time (11f). This structure lies entirely within the domain of the political.

8. Not very much of the content of the doctrine of justice as fairness needs to be changed. For example, the meaning and content of the two principles of justice and of the basic structure are much the same except for the framework to which they belong. On the other hand, as I note later in the text above, PL stresses the difference between political autonomy and moral autonomy (II:6) and it is careful to emphasize that a political conception of justice covers only the former. This distinction is unknown to *Theory*, in which autonomy is interpreted as moral autonomy in its Kantian form, drawing on Kant's comprehensive liberal doctrine (*Theory*, §§40, 78, 86).

Pt. II. A political conception of justice is what I call freestanding (pp. 10, 12) when it is not presented as derived from, or as part of, any comprehensive doctrine. Such a conception of justice in order to be a moral conception must contain its own intrinsic normative and moral ideal.

One such ideal can be set out this way. Citizens are reasonable when, viewing one another as free and equal in a system of social cooperation over generations, they are prepared to offer one another fair terms of social cooperation (defined by principles and ideals) and they agree to act on those terms, even at the cost of their own interests in particular situations, provided that others also accept those terms. For these terms to be fair terms, citizens offering them must reasonably think that those citizens to whom such terms are offered might also reasonably accept them. Note that "reasonably" occurs at both ends in this formulation: in offering fair terms we must reasonably think that citizens offered them might also reasonably accept them. And they must be able to do this as free and equal, and not as dominated or manipulated, or under the pressure of an inferior political or social position. I refer to this as the criterion of reciprocity (49f, 54).[9] Thus, political rights and duties are moral rights and duties, for they are part of a political conception that is a normative (moral) conception with its own intrinsic ideal, though not itself a comprehensive doctrine.[10]

For an example of the difference between the moral values of a comprehensive doctrine and the (moral) political values of a political conception, consider the value of autonomy. This value may take at least two forms. One is political autonomy, the legal independence and assured political integrity of citizens and their sharing with other citizens equally in the exercise of political power. The other form is moral autonomy expressed in a certain mode of life and reflection that critically examines our deepest

9. In emphasizing that "reasonably" occurs at both ends, so to speak, the criterion of reciprocity is stated more fully than in PL, as it needs to be.

10. See, for an example, the third view described on p. 145.

ends and ideals, as in Mill's ideal of individuality,[11] or by following as best one can Kant's doctrine of autonomy.[12] While autonomy as a moral value has had an importance place in the history of democratic thought, it fails to satisfy the criterion of reciprocity required of reasonable political principles and cannot be part of a political conception of justice. Many citizens of faith reject moral autonomy as part of their way of life.

In the transformation from the comprehensive doctrine of justice as fairness to the political conception of justice as fairness, the idea of the person as having moral personality with the full capacity of moral agency is transformed into that of the citizen. In moral and political philosophical doctrines, the idea of moral agency is discussed, along with agents' intellectual, moral, and emotional powers. Persons are viewed as being capable of exercising their moral rights and fulfilling their moral duties and as being subject to all the moral motivations appropriate to each moral virtue the doctrine specifies. In PL, by contrast, the person is seen rather as a free and equal citizen, the political person of a modern democracy with the political rights and duties of citizenship, and standing in a political relation with other citizens. The citizen is, of course, a moral agent, since a political conception of justice is, as we have seen, a moral conception ($11n$). But the kinds of rights and duties, and of the values considered, are more limited.

The fundamental political relation of citizenship has two special features: first, it is a relation of citizens within the basic structure of society, a structure we enter only by birth and exit only by death (p. 12);[13] and second, it is a relation of free and equal citizens who exercise ultimate political power as a collective body. These two features immediately give rise to the question of how, when constitutional essentials and matters of basic justice are at stake, citizens so related can be bound to honor the

11. See *On Liberty*, ch. 3, esp. paras. 1–9.
12. Recall here what was said in footnote 8 concerning Kant's doctrine of autonomy.
13. For concerns about exiting only by death, see p. 136, n 4.

structure of their constitutional regime and to abide by the statutes and laws enacted under it. The fact of reasonable pluralism raises this question all the more sharply, since it means that the differences between citizens arising from their comprehensive doctrines, religious and nonreligious, are irreconcilable and contain transcendent elements. By what ideals and principles, then, are citizens as sharing equally in ultimate political power to exercise that power so that each of them can reasonably justify their political decisions to each other?

The answer is given by the criterion of reciprocity: our exercise of political power is proper only when we sincerely believe that the reasons we offer for our political action may reasonably be accepted by other citizens as a justification of those actions.[14] This criterion applies on two levels: one is to the constitutional structure itself, and the other is to particular statutes and laws enacted in accordance with that structure. Political conceptions to be reasonable must justify only constitutions that satisfy this principle. This gives what may be called the liberal principle of legitimacy (p. 137) as it applies to the legitimacy of constitutions and statutes enacted under them.[15]

In order to fulfill their political role, citizens are viewed as having the intellectual and moral powers appropriate to that role, such as a capacity for a sense of political justice given by a liberal conception and a capacity to form, follow, and revise their individual doctrines of the good,[16] and capable also of the political virtues necessary for them to cooperate in maintaining a

---

14. I note that there is, strictly speaking, no argument here. The preceding paragraph in the text simply describes an institutional context in which citizens stand in certain relations and consider certain questions, and so on. It is then said that from that context a duty arises on those citizens to follow the criterion of reciprocity. This is a duty arising from the idea of reasonableness of persons as characterized at pp. 49f. A similar kind of reasoning is found in T. M. Scanlon's "Promises and Practices," *Philosophy and Public Affairs* 19:3 (Summer 1990). Of course, the particular cases and examples are entirely different.

15. The last two paragraphs summarize pp. 135ff.

16. The terminology here follows footnote 2 above. Both *Theory* and PL speak of a (comprehensive) conception of the good. From here on, it is referred to as a doctrine.

just political society. (Their capacity for the other virtues and moral motives beyond this is not of course denied.)

4. Two ideas that are not found in *Theory* are needed to meet the fact of reasonable pluralism, namely, the ideas of a reasonable overlapping consensus (15, 39ff., IV:3) and of public reason (VI:4, 7, 8). Without these ideas we do not see the role a political conception of justice has (or, as we shall see, a family thereof has) in specifying the public reason of a well-ordered society when it is regulated by a political conception. In carrying out this conceptual task, justice as fairness (as now transformed) is used as the main example.

I shall not try to describe here the idea of an overlapping consensus beyond what I have occasionally said. I note instead two points related to it. One is that it is the fact of reasonable pluralism that leads—at least me—to the idea of a political conception of justice and so to the idea of political liberalism. For rather than confronting religious and nonliberal doctrines with a comprehensive liberal philosophical doctrine, the thought is to formulate a liberal political conception that those nonliberal doctrines might be able to endorse. To find this political conception we do not look at known comprehensive doctrines with the aim of striking a balance or average between them, nor do we attempt to strike a compromise with a sufficient number of those doctrines actually existing in society by tailoring the political conception to fit them. Doing that appeals to the wrong idea of consensus and makes the political conception political in the wrong way (39ff.).[17] Rather, we formulate a freestanding political conception having its own intrinsic (moral) political ideal expressed by the criterion of reciprocity. We hope in this way that reasonable comprehensive doctrines can endorse for the right reasons that political conception and hence be viewed as belonging to a reasonable overlapping consensus.

The other point about a reasonable overlapping consensus is that PL makes no attempt to prove, or to show, that such a

17. Also see IX: 2:389.

consensus would eventually form around a reasonable political conception of justice. The most it does is to present a freestanding liberal political conception that does not oppose comprehensive doctrines on their own ground and does not preclude the possibility of an overlapping consensus for the right reasons. PL does note certain historical events and processes that seem to have led to consensus, and others that may take place (IV:6–7), but observing these commonsense facts of political sociology does not constitute proof.

In addition to conflicting comprehensive doctrines, PL does recognize that in any actual political society a number of differing liberal political conceptions of justice compete with one another in society's political debates (6f.). This leads to another aim of PL: saying how a well-ordered liberal political society is to be formulated given not only reasonable pluralism but a family of reasonable liberal political conceptions of justice. The definition of liberal conceptions is given by three conditions[18] (p. 6): first, a specification of certain rights, liberties, and opportunities (of a kind familiar from democratic regimes); second, a special priority for these freedoms; and third, measures assuring all citizens, whatever their social position, adequate all-purpose[19] means to make intelligent and effective use of their liberties and opportunities. Note that I am here talking about liberal political conceptions and not about liberal comprehensive doctrines.

Justice as fairness—its two principles of justice, which of course include the difference principle—I believe to be the most reasonable conception because it best satisfies these conditions.[20]

18. The text of PL refers to these as features. The term *conditions* is better than *features,* since they define a liberal political conception, as I understand it.

19. This term refers to primary goods, as defined in V:4.

20. This is not to deny that certain changes must be made in justice as fairness. For example, lect. VIII revises the account of the basic liberties in view of H. L. A. Hart's criticisms. Lecture V:3–4 revises the account of primary goods to meet the criticisms of K. J. Arrow and Amartya Sen, Joshua Cohen and T. M. Scanlon, and others. Also I would revise the just savings principle and its derivation, as suggested by Thomas Nagel and Derek Parfit, and Jane English (VII:274n). I believe that these and other changes leave justice as fairness substantially intact, since its basic ideals

But while I view it as the most reasonable (even though many reasonable people seem to disagree with me), I shouldn't deny that other conceptions also satisfy the definition of a liberal conception. Indeed, I would simply be unreasonable if I denied that there were other reasonable conceptions satisfying that definition, for example, one that substitutes for the difference principle, a principle to improve social well-being subject to a constraint guaranteeing for everyone a sufficient level of adequate all-purpose means. Any conception that meets the criterion of reciprocity and recognizes the burdens of judgment (II:2) is a candidate. These burdens have a double role in PL: they are part of the basis for liberty of conscience and freedom of thought founded on the idea of the reasonable (60ff.). And they lead us to recognize that there are different and incompatible liberal political conceptions.

PL is also concerned with what is the most reasonable basis of social unity (133ff.) available to citizens of a modern liberal democracy, although this concern is not pursued as far as it might be. This basis of social unity is the following:[21]

> a. The basic structure of society is effectively regulated by one of a family of reasonable liberal conceptions of justice (or a mix thereof), which family includes the most reasonable conception.
>
> b. All reasonable comprehensive doctrines in society endorse some member of this family of reasonable conceptions, and citizens affirming these doctrines are in an enduring majority with respect to those rejecting each of that family.
>
> c. Public political discussion, when constitutional essentials and matters of basic justice are at stake, are always, or nearly always, reasonably decidable on the basis of reasons

---

and principles remain and only their finer formulation has been, and no doubt will continue to be, revised and adjusted.

21. This definition and suggested basis of unity is not spelled out in PL. I mention it here explicitly for the first time and in "Reply to Habermas," XI: 2:1.

specified by one of a family of reasonable liberal conceptions of justice, one of which is for each citizen the most (more) reasonable.

Clearly this definition may be varied in several ways. For instance, this basis would be ideally the most reasonable if society is effectively regulated by the most reasonable conception and citizens are in wide and general reflective equilibrium about this. Practically, the most reasonable basis, one that might actually come about, is one in which all citizens agree that the regulative political conception is reasonable and some think it the most reasonable. This is sufficient for political society to be stable for the right reasons: the political conception can now be honored by all citizens as at least reasonable and for political purposes that usually is the most we can expect.

5. I now consider the idea of public reason and its ideal, and supplement what is said in VI:4, 7, 8. The reader should be careful to note the kinds of questions and forums to which public reason applies (pp. 213–16, 252ff.)—for example, the debates of political parties and those seeking public office when discussing constitutional essentials and matters of basic justice—and distinguish them from the many places in the background culture (p. 14) where political matters are discussed, and often from within peoples' comprehensive doctrines.[22] This ideal is that citizens are to conduct their public political discussions of constitutional essentials and matters of basic justice[23] within the framework of what each sincerely regards as a reasonable political conception of justice, a conception that expresses political values that others as free and equal also might reasonably be expected reasonably to endorse (pp. 226, 241). Thus each of us must have principles

22. Public reason in political liberalism and Habermas's public sphere are not the same thing. See IX: 1:382n.

23. Constitutional essentials concern questions about what political rights and liberties, say, may reasonably be included in a written constitution, when assuming the constitution may be interpreted by a supreme court, or some similar body. Matters of basic justice relate to the basic structure of society and so would concern questions of basic economic and social justice and other things not covered by a constitution.

and guidelines to which we appeal in such a way that the criterion of reciprocity is satisfied. I have proposed that one way to identify those political principles and guidelines is to show that they would be agreed to in what in PL is the original position (I:4). Others will think that other ways to identify these principles are more reasonable. While there is a family of such ways and such principles, they must all fall under the criterion of reciprocity (226ff.).

To make more explicit the role of the criterion of reciprocity as expressed in public reason, I note that its role is to specify the nature of the political relation in a constitutional democratic regime as one of civic friendship. For this criterion, when citizens follow it in their public reasoning, shapes the form of their fundamental institutions.[24] For example—I cite easy cases—if we argue that the religious liberty of some citizens is to be denied, we must give them reasons they can not only understand—as Servetus could understand why Calvin wanted to burn him at the stake—but reasons we might reasonably expect that they as free and equal might reasonably also accept. The criterion of reciprocity is normally violated whenever basic liberties are denied. For what reasons can both satisfy the criterion of reciprocity and justify holding some as slaves, or imposing a property qualification on the right to vote, or denying the right of suffrage to women?

When engaged in public reasoning may we also include reasons of our comprehensive doctrines? I now believe, and hereby I revise VI:8, that reasonable such doctrines may be introduced in public reason at any time, provided that in due course public reasons, given by a reasonable political conception, are presented

24. It is sometimes said that the idea of public reason is put forward primarily to allay the fear of the instability or fragility of democracy in the practical political sense. That objection is incorrect and fails to see that public reason with its criterion of reciprocity characterizes the political relation with its ideal of democracy and bears on the nature of the regime whose stability or fragility we are concerned about. These questions are prior to questions of stability and fragility in the practical political sense, though of course no view of democracy can simply ignore these practical questions.

sufficient to support whatever the comprehensive doctrines are introduced to support.[25] I refer to this as the proviso[26] and it specifies what I now call the wide view of public reason. It is satisfied by the three cases discussed at pp. 249ff. Of special historical importance are the cases of the Abolitionists and the civil rights movement. I said that they did not violate what in VI:8 I had called the inclusive view of public reason. Both the Abolitionists' and King's doctrines were held to belong to public reason because they were invoked in an unjust political society, and their conclusions of justice were in accord with the constitutional values of a liberal regime. I also said that there should be reason to believe that appealing to the basis of these reasons in citizens' comprehensive doctrines would help to make society more just. I now see no need for these conditions so far as they go beyond the proviso and drop them. The proviso of citizens' justifying their conclusions in due course by public reasons secures what is needed.[27] It has the further advantage of showing to other citizens the roots in our comprehensive doctrines of our allegiance to the political conception, which strengthens stability in the presence of a reasonable overlapping consensus. This gives the wide view and fits the examples in VI:8.

It is crucial that public reason is not specified by any one political conception of justice, certainly not by justice as fairness

25. This is more permissive than PL VI:8, which specifies certain conditions on their introduction in what it refers to as the inclusive view. The wide view (as I call it) is not original with me and was suggested to me by Erin Kelly (summer 1993). A similar view is found in Lawrence Solum, whose fullest statement is "Constructing an Ideal of Public Reason," *San Diego Law Review* 30:4 (Fall 1993), with a summary at pp. 747–751. There is a more recent statement in the *Pacific Philosophical Quarterly* 75:3 and 4 (Sept.–Dec. 1994).

26. Many questions may be asked about satisfying this proviso. One is: when does it need to be satisfied, on the same day or some later day? Also, on whom does the obligation to honor it fall? There are many such questions—I only indicate a few of them here. As Thompson has urged, it ought to be clear and established how the proviso is to be appropriately satisfied.

27. I do not know whether the Abolitionists and King ever fulfilled the proviso. But whether they did or not, they could have. And, had they known the idea of public reason and shared its ideal, they would have. I thank Paul Weithman for this point.

alone. Rather, its content—the principles, ideals, and standards that may be appealed to—are those of a family of reasonable political conceptions of justice and this family changes over time. These political conceptions are not of course compatible and they may be revised as a result of their debates with one another. Social changes over generations also give rise to new groups with different political problems. Views raising new questions related to ethnicity, gender, and race are obvious examples, and the political conceptions that result from these views will debate the current conceptions. The content of public reason is not fixed, any more than it is defined by any one reasonable political conception.

One objection to the wide view of public reason is that it is still too restrictive. However, to establish this, we must find pressing questions of constitutional essentials or matters of basic justice (IV:5) that cannot be reasonably resolved by political values expressed by any of the existing reasonable political conceptions, nor also by any such conception that could be worked out. PL doesn't argue that this can never happen; it only suggests it rarely does so. Whether public reason can settle all, or almost all, political questions by a reasonable ordering of political values cannot be decided in the abstract independent of actual cases. We need such cases carefully spelled out to clarify how we should view them. For how to think about a kind of case depends not on general considerations alone but on our formulating relevant political values we may not have imagined before we reflect about particular instances.

Public reason may also seem too restrictive because it might seem to settle questions in advance. However, it does not, as such, determine or settle particular questions of law or policy. Rather, it specifies the public reasons in terms of which such questions are to be politically decided. For example, take the question of school prayer. One might suppose that a liberal position on this would reject their admissibility in public schools. But why so? We have to consider all the political values that can be invoked to settle this question and on which side the decisive reasons fall. The famous case of the debate in the Virginia House of Delegates in 1785 between Patrick Henry and James Madison over the establishment of the Anglican Church and involving religion in the schools was argued almost entirely by reference to political values alone.[28]

Perhaps others think public reason is too restrictive because it may lead to a stand-off[29] and fail to lead to agreement of views among citizens. It is alleged to be too restrictive since it doesn't supply enough reasons to settle all cases. This, however, happens not only in moral and political reasoning but in all forms of reasoning, including science and common sense. But the relevant comparision for public reasoning is to those cases in which some political decision must be made, as with legislators enacting laws

---

28. The most serious opposition to Jefferson's "Bill for Establishing Religious Freedom," which was adopted by the Virginia House of Delegates in 1786, was provided by the popular Patrick Henry. Henry's argument for keeping the religious establishment was based on the view that "Christian knowledge hath a natural tendency to correct the morals of men, restrain their vices, and preserve the peace of society, which cannot be effected without a competent provision for learned teachers." See Thomas J. Curry, *The First Freedoms* (New York: Oxford University Press, 1986), with ch. 4 on the case of Virginia. Henry did not seem to argue for Christian knowledge as such but rather that it was an effective way to achieve basic political values, namely, the good and peaceable conduct of citizens. Thus, I take him to mean by "vices," at least in part, those actions violating the political virtues found in political liberalism (194f), and expressed by other conceptions of democracy. Leaving aside the obvious difficulty of whether prayers can be composed that satisfy all the needed restrictions of political justice, Madison's objections to Henry's bill turned largely on whether religious establishment was necessary to support orderly civil society—he concluded it was not. Madison's objection depended also on the historical effects of establishment both on society and on the integrity of religion itself. See Madison's "Memorial and Remonstrance" (1785) in *The Mind of the Founder*, ed. Marvin Meyers (New York: Bobbs-Merrill, 1973), pp. 7–16; and also Curry, pp. 142ff. He cited the prosperity of colonies that had no establishment, notably Pennsylvania and Rhode Island, the strength of early Christianity in opposition to the hostile Roman Empire, and the corruption of past establishments. With some care in formulation, many if not all of these arguments can be expressed in terms of political values of public reason. The special interest of the example of school prayer is that it shows that the idea of public reason is not a view about specific political institutions or policies, but a view about how they are to be argued for and justified to the citizen body that must decide the question.

29. I take the term from Paul Quinn. The idea appears in PL at VI:7.1–2.

and judges deciding cases. Here some political rule of action must be laid down and all must be able reasonably to endorse the process by which it is reached. Public reason sees the office of citizen with its duty of civility as analogous to that of judgeship with its duty of deciding cases. Just as judges are to decide them by legal grounds of precedent and recognized canons of statutory interpretation and other relevant grounds, so citizens are to reason by public reason and to be guided by the criterion of reciprocity, whenever constitutional essentials and matters of basic justice are at stake.

Thus, when there seems to be a stand-off, that is, legal arguments seem evenly balanced on both sides, judges cannot simply resolve the case by appealing to their own political views. To do that is for judges to violate their duty. The same holds with public reason: if when stand-offs occur, citizens invoke the grounding reasons of their comprehensive views,[30] then the principle of reciprocity is violated. The reasons deciding constitutional essentials and basic justice are no longer those that we may reasonably expect that all citizens may reasonably endorse, particularly those whose religious liberties, or rights to vote, or rights to fair opportunity are denied. From the point of view of public reason citizens should simply vote for the ordering of political values they sincerely think the most reasonable. Otherwise we fail to exercise political power in ways that satisfy the criterion of reciprocity.

However, disputed questions, such as that of abortion, may lead to a stand-off between different political conceptions, and citizens must simply vote on the question.[31] Indeed, this is the

30. I use the term *grounding reasons* since many who might appeal to these reasons view them as the proper grounds, or the true basis, religious or philosophical or moral, of the ideals and principles of public reasons and political conceptions of justice.

31. Some have quite naturally read the footnote (243f.) as an argument for the right to abortion in the first trimester. I do not intend it to be one. (It does express my opinion, but an opinion is not an argument.) I was in error in leaving it in doubt that the aim of the footnote was only to illustrate and confirm the following statement in the text to which the footnote is attached: "The only comprehensive doctrines that

normal case: unanimity of views is not to be expected. Reasonable political conceptions of justice do not always lead to the same conclusion (24ff.), nor do citizens holding the same conception always agree on particular issues. Yet the outcome of the vote is to be seen as reasonable provided all citizens of a reasonably just constitutional regime sincerely vote in accordance with the idea of public reason. This doesn't mean the outcome is true or correct, but it is for the moment reasonable, and binding on citizens by the majority principle. Some may, of course, reject a decision, as Catholics may reject a decision to grant a right to abortion. They may present an argument in public reason for denying it and fail to win a majority.[32] But they need not exercise

run afoul of public reason are those that cannot support a reasonable balance [or ordering] of political values [on the issue]." To try to explain what I meant, I used three political values (of course, there are more) for the troubled issue of the right to abortion, to which it might seem improbable that political values could apply at all. I believe a more detailed interpretation of those values may, when properly developed at public reason, yield a reasonable argument. I don't say the most reasonable or decisive argument; I don't know what that would be, or even if it exists. (For an example of such a more detailed interpretation, see Judith Jarvis Thomson's, "Abortion: Whose Right?" *Boston Review* 20:3 [Summer 1995]; though I would want to add several addenda to it.) Suppose now, for purposes of illustration, that there is a reasonable argument in public reason for the right of abortion but there is no equally reasonable balance, or ordering, of the political values in public reason that argues for the denial of that right. Then in this kind of case, but only in this kind of case, does a comprehensive doctrine denying the right of abortion run afoul of public reason. However, if it can satisfy the proviso of the wide public reason better, or at least as well as other views, it has made its case at public reason. A comprehensive doctrine can be unreasonable on one or several issues without being simply unreasonable.

32. For such an argument, see Cardinal Bernadin's view in "The Consistent Ethics: What Sort of Framework?" *Origins* 16 (Oct. 30, 1986), pp. 345, 347–50. The idea of public order the Cardinal presents includes these three political values: public peace, essential protections of human rights, and the commonly accepted standards of moral behavior in a community of law. Further, he grants that not all moral imperatives are to be translated into prohibitive civil statutes and thinks it essential to the political and social order to protect human life and basic human rights. The denial of the right to abortion he hopes to justify on the basis of those three values. I don't assess his argument here, except to say it is clearly cast in the form of public reason. Whether it is itself reasonable or not, or more reasonable than the arguments on the other side, is another matter. As with any form of reasoning in public reason, the reasoning may be fallacious or mistaken.

the right of abortion in their own case. They can recognize the right as belonging to legitimate law and therefore do not resist it with force. To do that would be unreasonable (60ff.): it would mean their attempting to impose their own comprehensive doctrine, which a majority of other citizens who follow public reason do not accept. Certainly Catholics may, in line with public reason, continue to argue against the right of abortion. That the Church's nonpublic reason requires its members to follow its doctrine is perfectly consistent with their honoring public reason.[33] I do not pursue this question since my aim is only to stress that the ideal of public reason does not often lead to general agreement of views, nor should it. Citizens learn and profit from conflict and argument, and when their arguments follow public reason, they instruct and deepen society's public culture.

6. In section 4 above we saw that a liberal conception combines and orders the two basic values of liberty and equality in terms of three features. The first two state the basic rights and liberties and their priority; the third is the assurance of sufficient all-purpose means to enable all citizens to make intelligent and effective use of their freedoms. This third feature must, of course, satisfy the criterion of reciprocity and thus enjoins a basic structure that prevents social and economic inequalities from being excessive as specified by that criterion. Without the institutions (a) to (e) listed below, or similar arrangements, reasonable political liberalisms hold that these excessive inequalities tend to develop. This is an application of common sense political sociology.

At three places PL briefly considers such an application. It does so in part II, lecture IV. It takes up in IV:6 how a constitutional consensus might gradually arise from an earlier period in

33. As far as I can see, this view is similar to Father John Courtney Murray's position about the stand the Church should take in regard to contraception in *We Hold These Truths* (New York: Sheed and Ward, 1960), pp. 157f. See also Mario Cuomo's lecture on abortion in his Notre Dame lecture of 1984 in *More Than Words* (New York: St. Martin's, 1993), pp. 32–51. I am indebted to Leslie Griffin and Paul Weithman for discussion and clarification about points involved in this and the two preceding footnotes and for acquainting me with Father Murray's view.

which constititutional principles such as liberty of conscience were adopted only with great reluctance as part of a *modus vivendi*. Next IV:7 goes over how a constitutional consensus might change into an overlapping consensus. And in VI:8 we see that a reasonable comprehensive doctrine supporting a reasonable political conception may be introduced with the hope of hastening the change to a just constitutional regime. The essential difference between a constitutional consensus and an overlapping consensus is that the former is a consensus on certain constitutional principles that guarantee various liberties. These principles—such as liberty of conscience—were expanded later to those included in the Declaration of Independence and the French Revolution's Declaration of the Rights of Man.

These guaranteed liberties taken alone are properly criticized as purely formal (VIII:7).[34] By themselves they are an impoverished form of liberalism, indeed not liberalism at all but libertarianism (VII:3).[35] The latter does not combine liberty and equality in the way liberalism does; it lacks the criterion of reciprocity and allows excessive social economic inequalities as judged by that criterion. In this case, we do not have stability for the right reasons, which is always lacking in a purely formal constitutional regime. An indication of institutions required for this stability is the following:

a. Public financing of elections and ways of assuring the availability of public information on matters of policy (VIII:12–13). The statement of these arrangements (and of those below) merely hints at what is needed for representatives and other officials to be sufficiently independent of particular social and economic interests and to provide the knowledge and information upon which policies can be formed and intelligently assessed by citizens using public reason.

34. Hegel, Marxist, and socialist writers have been quite correct in making this objection.
35. See also VII:4,9.

b. A certain fair equality of opportunity, especially in education and training. Without these opportunities, all parts of society cannot take part in the debates of public reason or contribute to social and economic policies.

c. A decent distribution of income and wealth meeting the third condition of liberalism: all citizens must be assured the all-purpose means necessary for them to take intelligent and effective advantage of their basic freedoms.[36] In the absence of this condition, those with wealth and income tend to dominate those with less and increasingly to control political power in their own favor.

d. Society as employer of last resort through general or local government, or other social and economic policies. Lacking a sense of long-term security and the opportunity for meaningful work and occupation is not only destructive of citizens' self-respect but of their sense that they are members of society and not simply caught in it. This leads to self-hatred, bitterness, and resentment.

e. Basic health care assured all citizens.

These institutions do not, of course, fully satisfy the principles of justice as fairness. But we are discussing not what those principles require but listing essential prerequisites for a basic structure within which the ideal of public reason, when conscientiously followed by citizens, may protect the basic liberties and prevent social and economic inequalities from being excessive. Since the ideal of public reason contains a form of public political deliberation, these institutions, most clearly the first three, are necessary for this deliberation to be possible and fruitful. A belief in the importance of public deliberation is essential for a reasonable constitutional regime, and specific institutions and arrangements need to be laid down to support and encourage it.

---

36. The requirement is far more than provision for food, clothing, and housing, or simply for basic needs. Basic freedoms are defined by the list of basic liberties and opportunities, and these include the political liberties and fair access to the political process.

The idea of public reason proposes how to characterize the structure and content of society's fundamental bases for political deliberations.

I conclude this section with a comment on the limits of reconciliation by public reason. There are three main kinds of conflicts: those deriving from citizens' conflicting comprehensive doctrines; those from their different status, class position, and occupation, or from their ethnicity, gender, and race; and finally, those resulting from the burdens of judgment. Political liberalism mitigates but cannot eliminate the first kind of conflict, since comprehensive doctrines are, politically speaking, unreconcilable and remain inconsistent with one another. However, the principles of justice of a reasonably just constitutional regime can reconcile us to the second kind of conflict. For once we accept principles of justice, or recognize them as at least reasonable (even though not as the most reasonable), and know that our political and social institutions conform to them, the second kind of conflict need no longer arise, or arise so forcefully. I believe that these sources of conflict can be largely removed by a reasonably just constitutional regime whose principles of political justice satisfy the criterion of reciprocity.[37] PL does not take up these conflicts, leaving them to be settled by justice as fairness (as in *Theory*), or by some other reasonable political conception of justice. Conflicts arising from the burdens of judgment always, however, remain and limit the extent of possible agreement.

7. Both *Theory* and PL attempt to say how a reasonably just and well-ordered democratic society might be possible, and why justice as fairness should have a special place among the political conceptions in its political and social world. Of course, many are prepared to accept the conclusion that a just and well-ordered democratic society is not possible, and even regard it as obvious. Isn't admitting it part of growing up, part of the inevitable loss of innocence? But is this conclusion one we can so easily accept?

---

37. I believe also that such a regime may also fairly deal with differences of culture and nationality (separating the latter idea from that of state). Here I follow Yael Tamir in her *Liberal Nationalism* (Princeton: Princeton University Press 1993), esp. ch. 3.

What is the effect of our doing so and what is the consequence for our view of the political world, and even the world as a whole?

Philosophy may study political questions at many different levels of generality and abstractness, all valuable and significant. It may ask why it is wrong to attack civilians in war either from the air by ordinary bombs or by atomic weapons. More generally, it may ask about just forms of constitutional arrangements and which kinds of questions properly belong to constitutional politics. More generally still, it may ask whether a just and well-ordered constitutional democracy is possible and what makes it so. I don't say that the more general questions are the more philosophical, nor that they are more important. All these questions and their answers, so far as we can find them, bear on one another and work together to add to the knowledge of philosophy.

The answer we give to the question of whether a just democratic society is possible and can be stable for the right reasons affects our background thoughts and attitudes about the world as a whole. And it affects these thoughts and attitudes before we come to actual politics, and limits or inspires how we take part in it. Debates about general philosophical questions cannot be the daily stuff of politics, but that does not make these questions without significance, since what we think their answers are will shape the underlying attitudes of the public culture and the conduct of politics.[38] If we take for granted as common knowledge that a just and well-ordered democratic society is impossible, then the quality and tone of those attitudes will reflect that knowledge. A cause of the fall of Weimar's constitutional regime was that none of the traditional elites of Germany supported its constitution or were willing to cooperate to make it work. They no longer believed a decent liberal parliamentary regime was possible. Its time had past. The regime fell first to a series of authoritarian cabinet governments from 1930 to 1932. When

38. I agree here with Michael Walzer in his review of Benjamin Barber's *The Conquest of Politics* in the *New York Review of Books*, February 2, 1989, pp. 42f.

these were increasingly weakened by their lack of popular support, President Hindenburg was finally persuaded to turn to Hitler, who had such support and whom conservatives thought they could control.[39] Others may prefer different examples.

The wars of this century with their extreme violence and increasing destructiveness, culminating in the manic evil of the Holocaust, raise in an acute way the question whether political relations must be governed by power and coercion alone. If a reasonably just society that subordinates power to its aims is not possible and people are largely amoral, if not incurably cynical and self-centered, one might ask with Kant whether it is worthwhile for human beings to live on the earth?[40] We must start with the assumption that a reasonably just political society is possible, and for it to be possible, human beings must have a moral nature, not of course a perfect such nature, yet one that can understand, act on, and be sufficiently moved by a reasonable political conception of right and justice to support a society guided by its ideals and principles. *Theory* and PL try to sketch what the more reasonable conceptions of justice for a democratic regime are and to present a candidate for the most reasonable. They also consider how citizens need to be conceived to construct (PL III) those more reasonable conceptions, and what their moral psychology has to be to support a reasonably just political society over time.[41] The focus on these questions no doubt explains in part what seems to many readers the abstract and unwordly character of these texts.

I do not apologize for that.

John Rawls
December 1995

---

39. See Carl Schmitt's *The Crisis of Parliamentary Democracy*, trans. Ellen Kennedy (Cambridge: MIT Press, 1988). See especially the preface to the second edition (1926) and ch. 2. On Weimar, see the instructive works by Detlev Peukert, *The Weimar Republic*, trans. Allen Lane (Boston: Penguin, 1991), esp. chs. 11–14; and Klaus Fischer, *Nazi Germany* (New York: Continuum, 1995), ch. 7 and conclusion, pp. 258–263.

40. "If justice perishes, then it is no longer worthwhile for men to live upon the earth" (*Rechtslehre*, in remark E following §49, Ak:VI:332).

41. For this psychology see *Theory*, Pt. III, esp. ch. 8 and PL:II:1–3.

POLITICAL
LIBERALISM

PART ONE

Political Liberalism: Basic Elements

Fundamental Ideas

Political liberalism, the title of these lectures, has a familiar ring. Yet I mean by it something quite different, I think, from what the reader is likely to suppose. Perhaps I should, then, begin with a definition of political liberalism and explain why I call it "political." But no definition would be useful at the outset. Instead I begin with a first fundamental question about political justice in a democratic society, namely what is the most appropriate conception of justice for specifying the fair terms of social cooperation between citizens regarded as free and equal, and as fully cooperating members of society over a complete life, from one generation to the next?

We join this first fundamental question with a second, that of toleration understood in a general way. The political culture of a democratic society is always marked by a diversity of opposing and irreconcilable religious, philosophical, and moral doctrines. Some of these are perfectly reasonable, and this diversity among reasonable doctrines political liberalism sees as the inevitable long-run result of the powers of human reason at work within the background of enduring free institutions. Thus, the second question is what are the grounds of toleration so understood and given the fact of reasonable pluralism as the inevitable outcome of free institutions? Combining both questions we have: how is it possible for there to exist over time a just and stable society of free and equal citizens, who remain profoundly divided by reasonable religious, philosophical, and moral doctrines?

The most intractable struggles, political liberalism assumes, are confessedly for the sake of the highest things: for religion, for philosophical views of the world, and for different moral conceptions of the good. We should find it remarkable that, so deeply opposed in these ways, just cooperation among free and equal citizens is possible at all. In fact, historical experience suggests that it rarely is. If the problem addressed is all too familiar, political liberalism proposes, I believe, a somewhat unfamiliar resolution of it. To state this resolution we need a certain family of ideas. In this lecture I set out the more central of these and offer a definition at the end (§8).

§ 1. Addressing Two Fundamental Questions

1. Focusing on the first fundamental question, the course of democratic thought over the past two centuries or so makes plain that there is at present no agreement on the way the basic institutions of a constitutional democracy should be arranged if they are to satisfy the fair terms of cooperation between citizens regarded as free and equal. This is shown in the deeply contested ideas about how the values of liberty and equality are best expressed in the basic rights and liberties of citizens so as to answer to the claims of both liberty and equality. We may think of this disagreement as a conflict within the tradition of democratic thought itself, between the tradition associated with Locke, which

gives greater weight to what Constant called "the liberties of the moderns," freedom of thought and conscience, certain basic rights of the person and of property, and the rule of law, and the tradition associated with Rousseau, which gives greater weight to what Constant called "the liberties of the ancients," the equal political liberties and the values of public life.[1] This familiar and stylized contrast may serve to fix ideas.

As a way to answer our first question, justice as fairness[2] tries to adjudicate between these contending traditions, first, by proposing two principles of justice to serve as guidelines for how basic institutions are to realize the values of liberty and equality; and second, by specifying a point of view from which these principles can be seen as more appropriate than other familiar principles of justice to the idea of democratic citizens viewed as free and equal persons. What must be shown is that a certain arrangement of basic political and social institutions is more appropriate to realizing the values of liberty and equality when citizens are so conceived. The two principles of justice (noted above) are as follows:[3]

> a. Each person has an equal claim to a fully adequate scheme of equal basic rights and liberties, which scheme is compatible with the same scheme for all; and in this scheme the equal political liberties, and only those liberties, are to be guaranteed their fair value.

1. See "Liberty of the Ancients Compared with that of the Moderns," (1819), in Benjamin Constant, *Political Writings,* translated and edited by Biancamaria Fontana (Cambridge: Cambridge University Press, 1988). The discussion in the introduction of the difference between the problem of political philosophy in the ancient and modern worlds illustrates the significance of Constant's distinction.

2. The conception of justice presented in *Theory.*

3. The statement of these principles differs from that given in *Theory* and follows the statement in "The Basic Liberties and Their Priority," *Tanner Lectures on Human Values,* vol. III (Salt Lake City: University of Utah Press, 1982), p. 5. The reasons for these changes are discussed on pp. 46–55 of that lecture. They are important for the revisions in the account of the basic liberties found in *Theory* and were made to try to answer the forceful objections raised by H. L. A. Hart in his critical review in the *University of Chicago Law Review* 40 (Spring 1973):535–55. In this volume, see VIII, pp. 291, 331–34, respectively.

   b. Social and economic inequalities are to satisfy two conditions: first, they are to be attached to positions and offices
open to all under conditions of fair equality of opportunity;
and second, they are to be to the greatest benefit of the
least advantaged members of society.

   Each of these principles regulates institutions in a particular
domain not only in regard to basic rights, liberties, and opportunities but also in regard to the claims of equality; while the
second part of the second principle underwrites the worth of
these institutional guarantees.[4] The two principles together, with
the first given priority over the second, regulate the basic institutions that realize these values.

   2. Much exposition would be needed to clarify the meaning
and application of these principles. Since in these lectures such
matters are not our concern, I make only a few comments. First,
I view these principles as exemplifying the content of a liberal
political conception of justice. The content of such a conception
is given by three main features: first, a specification of certain
basic rights, liberties and opportunities (of a kind familiar from
constitutional democratic regimes); second, an assignment of
special priority to those rights, liberties, and opportunities, especially with respect to claims of the general good and of perfectionist values; and third, measures assuring to all citizens adequate all-purpose means to make effective use of their liberties
and opportunities. These elements can be understood in different ways, so that there are many variant liberalisms.

   Further, the two principles express an egalitarian form of
liberalism in virtue of three elements. These are a) the guarantee
of the fair value of the political liberties, so that these are not
purely formal; b) fair (and again not purely formal) equality of
opportunity; and finally c) the so-called difference principle, which
says that the social and economic inequalities attached to offices
and positions are to be adjusted so that, whatever the level of

   4. The worth of these guarantees is specified by reference to an index of primary
goods. How this is done is mentioned in II:5 and discussed more fully in V:3–4.

6

those inequalities, whether great or small, they are to the greatest benefit of the least advantaged members of society.[5] All these elements are still in place, as they were in *Theory;* and so is the basis of the argument for them. Hence I presuppose throughout these lectures the same egalitarian conception of justice as before; and though I mention revisions from time to time, none of them affect this feature of it.[6] Our topic, however, is political liberalism and its component ideas, so that much of our discussion concerns liberal conceptions more generally, allowing for all variants, as for example when we consider the idea of public reason (in VI).

Finally, as one might expect, important aspects of the principles are left out in the brief statement as given. In particular, the first principle covering the equal basic rights and liberties may easily be preceded by a lexically prior principle requiring that citizens' basic needs be met, at least insofar as their being met is necessary for citizens to understand and to be able fruitfully to exercise those rights and liberties. Certainly any such principle must be assumed in applying the first principle.[7] But I do not pursue these and other matters here.

---

5. There are a number of questions that arise concerning the intended interpretation of the difference principle. For example, the least advantaged members of society are given by description and not by a rigid designator (to use Saul Kripke's term in *Naming and Necessity* [Cambridge, Mass.: Harvard University Press, 1972]). Further, the principle does not require continual economic growth over generations to maximize upward indefinitely the expectations of the least advantaged. It is compatible with Mill's idea of a society in a just stationary state where (real) capital accumulation is zero. What the principle does require is that however great inequalities are, and however willing people are to work so as to earn their greater return, existing inequalities are to be adjusted to contribute in the most effective way to the benefit of the least advantaged. These brief remarks are hardly clear; they simply indicate the complexities that are not our concern in these lectures.

6. I make this comment since some have thought that my working out the ideas of political liberalism meant giving up the egalitarian conception of *Theory.* I am not aware of any revisions that imply such a change and think the surmise has no basis.

7. For the statement of such a principle, as well as an instructive fuller statement in four parts of the two principles, with important revisions, see Rodney Peffer's *Marxism, Morality, and Social Justice* (Princeton: Princeton University Press, 1990), p. 14. I should agree with most of Peffer's statement, but not with his 3(b), which

3. I return instead to our first question and ask: How might political philosophy find a shared basis for settling such a fundamental question as that of the most appropriate family of institutions to secure democratic liberty and equality? Perhaps the most that can be done is to narrow the range of disagreement. Yet even firmly held convictions gradually change: religious toleration is now accepted, and arguments for persecution are no longer openly professed; similarly, slavery, which caused our Civil War, is rejected as inherently unjust, and however much the aftermath of slavery may persist in social policies and unavowed attitudes, no one is willing to defend it. We collect such settled convictions as the belief in religious toleration and the rejection of slavery and try to organize the basic ideas and principles implicit in these convictions into a coherent political conception of justice. These convictions are provisional fixed points that it seems any reasonable conception must account for. We start, then, by looking to the public culture itself as the shared fund of implicitly recognized basic ideas and principles. We hope to formulate these ideas and principles clearly enough to be combined into a political conception of justice congenial to our most firmly held convictions. We express this by saying that a political conception of justice, to be acceptable, must accord with our considered convictions, at all levels of generality, on due reflection, or in what I have called elsewhere "reflective equilibrium." [8]

---

appears to require a socialist form of economic organization. The difficulty here is not with socialism as such; but I should not include its being required in the first principles of political justice. These principles I see (as I did in *Theory*) as setting out fundamental values in terms of which, depending on the tradition and circumstances of the society in question, one can consider whether socialism in some form is justified.

8. See *Theory*, pp. 20f., 48–51, and 120f. One feature of reflective equilibrium is that it includes our considered convictions at all levels of generality; no one level, say that of abstract principle or that of particular judgments in particular cases, is viewed as foundational. They all may have an initial credibility. There is also an important distinction between narrow and wide reflective equilibrium, which is implicit in the distinction between the first and second kind of reflective equilibrium on pp. 49–50 (though the terms are not used). The terms *narrow* and *wide* were used first in §1 of

The public political culture may be of two minds at a very deep level. Indeed, this must be so with such an enduring controversy as that concerning the most appropriate understanding of liberty and equality. This suggests that if we are to succeed in finding a basis for public agreement, we must find a way of organizing familiar ideas and principles into a conception of political justice that expresses those ideas and principles in a somewhat different way than before. Justice as fairness tries to do this by using a fundamental organizing idea within which all ideas and principles can be systematically connected and related. This organizing idea is that of society as a fair system of social cooperation between free and equal persons viewed as fully cooperating members of society over a complete life. It lays a basis for answering the first fundamental question and is taken up below in §3.

4. Now suppose justice as fairness were to achieve its aims and a publicly acceptable political conception were found. Then this conception provides a publicly recognized point of view from which all citizens can examine before one another whether their political and social institutions are just. It enables them to do this by citing what are publicly recognized among them as valid and sufficient reasons singled out by that conception itself. Society's main institutions and how they fit together into one system of social cooperation can be assessed in the same way by each citizen, whatever that citizen's social position or more particular interests.

The aim of justice as fairness, then, is practical: it presents itself as a conception of justice that may be shared by citizens as a basis of a reasoned, informed, and willing political agreement. It expresses their shared and public political reason. But to attain such a shared reason, the conception of justice should be, as far as possible, independent of the opposing and conflicting philosophical and religious doctrines that citizens affirm. In formulat-

---

"Independence of Moral Theory," *Proceedings of the American Philosophical Association* 49 (1974).

ing such a conception, political liberalism applies the principle of toleration to philosophy itself. The religious doctrines that in previous centuries were the professed basis of society have gradually given way to principles of constitutional government that all citizens, whatever their religious view, can endorse. Comprehensive philosophical and moral doctrines likewise cannot be endorsed by citizens generally, and they also no longer can, if they ever could, serve as the professed basis of society.

Thus, political liberalism looks for a political conception of justice that we hope can gain the support of an overlapping consensus of reasonable religious, philosophical, and moral doctrines in a society regulated by it.[9] Gaining this support of reasonable doctrines lays the basis for answering our second fundamental question as to how citizens, who remain deeply divided on religious, philosophical, and moral doctrines, can still maintain a just and stable democratic society. To this end, it is normally desirable that the comprehensive philosophical and moral views we are wont to use in debating fundamental political issues should give way in public life. Public reason—citizens' reasoning in the public forum about constitutional essentials and basic questions of justice—is now best guided by a political conception the principles and values of which all citizens can endorse (VI). That political conception is to be, so to speak, political and not metaphysical.[10]

Political liberalism, then, aims for a political conception of justice as a freestanding view. It offers no specific metaphysical or epistemological doctrine beyond what is implied by the political conception itself. As an account of political values, a freestanding political conception does not deny there being other values that apply, say, to the personal, the familial, and the associational; nor does it say that political values are separate from, or discontinuous with, other values. One aim, as I have

9. The idea of an overlapping consensus is defined in §2.3 and discussed further in §6.3–4.
10. The context here serves to define the phrase: "political not metaphysical."

10

said, is to specify the political domain and its conception of justice in such a way that its institutions can gain the support of an overlapping consensus. In this case, citizens themselves, within the exercise of their liberty of thought and conscience, and looking to their comprehensive doctrines, view the political conception as derived from, or congruent with, or at least not in conflict with, their other values.

§ 2. The Idea of a Political Conception of Justice

1. To this point I have used the idea of a political conception of justice without explaining its meaning. From what I have said, one can perhaps gather what I mean by it and why political liberalism uses that idea. Yet we need an explicit statement thus: a political conception of justice has three characteristic features, each of which is exemplified by justice as fairness. I assume some but not much acquaintance with that view.

The first concerns the subject of a political conception. While such a conception is, of course, a moral conception,[11] it is a moral conception worked out for a specific kind of subject, namely, for political, social, and economic institutions. In particular, it applies to what I shall call the "basic structure" of society, which for our present purposes I take to be a modern constitutional democracy. (I use "constitutional democracy" and "democratic regime," and similar phrases interchangeably unless otherwise stated.) By the basic structure I mean a society's main political, social, and economic institutions, and how they fit together into one unified system of social cooperation from one generation to the next.[12] The initial focus, then, of a political conception of justice is the framework of basic institutions and the principles, standards, and precepts that apply to it, as well as

11. In saying that a conception is moral, I mean, among other things, that its content is given by certain ideals, principles and standards; and that these norms articulate certain values, in this case political values.

12. See *Theory,* §2 and the index, and also "The Basic Structure as Subject," in this volume, pp. 257–88.

11

how those norms are to be expressed in the character and attitudes of the members of society who realize its ideals.

Moreover, I assume that the basic structure is that of a closed society: that is, we are to regard it as self-contained and as having no relations with other societies. Its members enter it only by birth and leave it only by death. This allows us to speak of them as born into a society where they will lead a complete life. That a society is closed is a considerable abstraction, justified only because it enables us to focus on certain main questions free from distracting details. At some point a political conception of justice must address the just relations between peoples, or the law of peoples, as I shall say. In these lectures I do not discuss how a law of peoples might be worked out, starting from justice as fairness as applied first to closed societies.[13]

2. The second feature concerns the mode of presentation: a political conception of justice is presented as a freestanding view. While we want a political conception to have a justification by reference to one or more comprehensive doctrines, it is neither presented as, nor as derived from, such a doctrine applied to the basic structure of society, as if this structure were simply another subject to which that doctrine applied. It is important to stress this point: it means that we must distinguish between how a political conception is presented and its being part of, or as derivable within, a comprehensive doctrine. I assume all citizens to affirm a comprehensive doctrine to which the political conception they accept is in some way related. But a distinguishing feature of a political conception is that it is presented as freestanding and expounded apart from, or without reference to, any such wider background. To use a current phrase, the political conception is a module, an essential constituent part, that fits into and can be supported by various reasonable comprehensive doctrines that endure in the society regulated by it. This means that it can be presented without saying, or knowing, or hazarding

---

13. See my "Law of Peoples" (an Oxford Amnesty Lecture), to be published with the other Amnesty Lectures by Basic Books, 1993.

a conjecture about, what such doctrines it may belong to, or be supported by.

In this respect a political conception of justice differs from many moral doctrines, for these are widely regarded as general and comprehensive views. Utilitarianism is a familiar example: the principle of utility, however understood, is usually said to hold for all kinds of subjects ranging from the conduct of individuals and personal relations to the organization of society as a whole as well as to the law of peoples.[14] By contrast, a political conception tries to elaborate a reasonable conception for the basic structure alone and involves, so far as possible, no wider commitment to any other doctrine.

This contrast will be clearer if we observe that the distinction between a political conception of justice and other moral conceptions is a matter of scope: that is, the range of subjects to which a conception applies and the content a wider range requires. A moral conception is general if it applies to a wide range of subjects, and in the limit to all subjects universally. It is comprehensive when it includes conceptions of what is of value in human life, and ideals of personal character, as well as ideals of friendship and of familial and associational relationships, and much else that is to inform our conduct, and in the limit to our life as a whole. A conception is fully comprehensive if it covers all recognized values and virtues within one rather precisely articulated system; whereas a conception is only partially comprehensive when it comprises a number of, but by no means all, nonpolitical values and virtues and is rather loosely articulated. Many religious and philosophical doctrines aspire to be both general and comprehensive.

3. The third feature of a political conception of justice is that its content is expressed in terms of certain fundamental ideas seen as implicit in the public political culture of a democratic society. This public culture comprises the political institutions of a constitutional regime and the public traditions of their interpre-

---

14. See "Basic Structure as Subject," p. 260f.

tation (including those of the judiciary), as well as historic texts and documents that are common knowledge. Comprehensive doctrines of all kinds—religious, philosophical, and moral—belong to what we may call the "background culture" of civil society. This is the culture of the social, not of the political. It is the culture of daily life, of its many associations: churches and universities, learned and scientific societies, and clubs and teams, to mention a few. In a democratic society there is a tradition of democratic thought, the content of which is at least familiar and intelligible to the educated common sense of citizens generally. Society's main institutions, and their accepted forms of interpretation, are seen as a fund of implicitly shared ideas and principles.

Thus, justice as fairness starts from within a certain political tradition and takes as its fundamental idea[15] that of society as a fair system of cooperation over time, from one generation to the next (§3). This central organizing idea is developed together with two companion fundamental ideas: one is the idea of citizens (those engaged in cooperation) as free and equal persons (§§3.3 and 5); the other is the idea of a well-ordered society as a society effectively regulated by a political conception of justice (§6).[16]

---

15. I comment that I use "ideas" as the more general term and as covering both concepts and conceptions. This pair is distinguished as they were in *Theory*, pp. 5f. Roughly, the concept is the meaning of a term, while a particular conception includes as well the principles required to apply it. To illustrate: the concept of justice, applied to an institution, means, say, that the institution makes no arbitrary distinctions between persons in assigning basic rights and duties, and that its rules establish a proper balance between competing claims. Whereas a conception includes, besides this, principles and criteria for deciding which distinctions are arbitrary and when a balance between competing claims is proper. People can agree on the meaning of the concept of justice and still be at odds, since they affirm different principles and standards for deciding those matters. To develop a concept of justice into a conception of it is to elaborate these requisite principles and standards. Thus, to give another example, in §3.3 I consider the concept of the person in law and in political philosophy, while in §5 I set out the further necessary elements of a conception of the person as a democratic citizen. This distinction between concept and conception I took from H. L. A. Hart's, *The Concept of Law* (Oxford: Clarendon Press, 1961), pp. 155–59.

16. Two other fundamental ideas are those of the basic structure, discussed in §2.1;

We suppose also that these ideas can be elaborated into a political conception of justice that can gain the support of an overlapping consensus (IV). Such a consensus consists of all the reasonable opposing religious, philosophical, and moral doctrines likely to persist over generations and to gain a sizable body of adherents in a more or less just constitutional regime, a regime in which the criterion of justice is that political conception itself.[17] Whether justice as fairness (or some similar view) can gain the support of an overlapping consensus so defined is a speculative question. One can reach an educated conjecture only by working it out and exhibiting the way it might be supported.

§ 3. The Idea of Society as a Fair System of Cooperation

1. As I have indicated, the fundamental organizing idea of justice as fairness, within which the other basic ideas are systematically connected, is that of society as a fair system of cooperation over time, from one generation to the next. We start the exposition with this idea, which we take to be implicit in the public culture of a democratic society. In their political thought, and in the discussion of political questions, citizens do not view the social order as a fixed natural order, or as an institutional hierarchy justified by religious or aristocratic values.

Here it is important to stress that from other points of view, for example, from the point of view of personal morality, or from the point of view of members of an association, or of one's religious or philosophical doctrine, various aspects of the world and one's relation to it may be regarded in a different way. These other points of view are not, in general, to be introduced into

---

and of the original position, discussed in §4. These are not seen as ideas familiar to educated common sense but rather as ideas introduced for the purpose of presenting justice as fairness in a unified and prespicuous way.

17. The idea of an overlapping consensus, or perhaps better the term, was introduced in *Theory*, pp. 387f., as a way to weaken the conditions for the reasonableness of civil disobedience in a nearly just democratic society. Here and later in these lectures I use it in a different sense and in a far wider context.

political discussion of constitutional essentials and basic questions of justice.

2. We can make the idea of social cooperation more specific by noting three of its elements:

a. Cooperation is distinct from merely socially coordinated activity, for example, from activity coordinated by orders issued by some central authority. Cooperation is guided by publicly recognized rules and procedures that those cooperating accept and regard as properly regulating their conduct.

b. Cooperation involves the idea of fair terms of cooperation: these are terms that each participant may reasonably accept, provided that everyone else likewise accepts them. Fair terms of cooperation specify an idea of reciprocity: all who are engaged in cooperation and who do their part as the rules and procedure require, are to benefit in an appropriate way as assessed by a suitable benchmark of comparison. A conception of political justice characterizes the fair terms of cooperation. Since the primary subject of justice is the basic structure of society, these fair terms are expressed by principles that specify basic rights and duties within its main institutions and regulate the arrangements of background justice over time, so that the benefits produced by everyone's efforts are fairly distributed and shared from one generation to the next.

c. The idea of social cooperation requires an idea of each participant's rational advantage, or good. This idea of good specifies what those who are engaged in cooperation, whether individuals, families, or associations, or even the governments of peoples, are trying to achieve, when the scheme is viewed from their own standpoint.

Several points about the idea of reciprocity introduced in (b) above call for comment. One is that the idea of reciprocity lies between the idea of impartiality, which is altruistic (being moved by the general good), and the idea of mutual advantage understood as everyone's being advantaged with respect to each person's present or expected future situation as things are.[18] As understood in justice as fairness, reciprocity is a relation between citizens expressed by principles of justice that regulate a social world in which everyone benefits judged with respect to an appropriate benchmark of equality defined with respect to that world. This brings out the further point that reciprocity is a relation between citizens in a well-ordered society (§6) expressed by its public political conception of justice. Hence the two principles of justice with the difference principle (§1.1), with its implicit reference to equal division as a benchmark, formulate an idea of reciprocity between citizens.

Finally, it is clear from these observations that the idea of reciprocity is not the idea of mutual advantage. Suppose that we transpose people from a society in which property, in good part as a result of fortune and luck, is very unequal into a well-ordered society regulated by the two principles of justice. There is no guarantee that all will gain by the change if they judge matters by their previous attitudes. Those owning large properties may have lost greatly and historically they have resisted such changes. No reasonable conception of justice could pass the test of mutual advantage thus interpreted. This is not, however, to the point. The aim is to specify an idea of reciprocity between free and equal citizens in a well-ordered society. The so-called strains of commitment are strains that arise in such a society between its requirements of justice and citizens' legitimate interests its just institutions allow. Important among these strains are those between the political conception of justice and permissible comprehensive doctrines. These strains do not arise from a desire to preserve the benefits of previous injustice. Strains such as these belong to the process of transition but questions connected

18. This thought is expressed by Allan Gibbard in his review of Brian Barry's *Theories of Justice* (Berkely: University of California Press, 1989). Barry thinks justice as fairness hovers uneasily between impartiality and mutual advantage, where Gibbard thinks it perches between on reciprocity. I think Gibbard is right about this. See his "Constructing Justice," *Philosophy and Public Affairs* 20 (Summer 1991):266f.

with this are covered by nonideal theory and not by the principles of justice for a well-ordered society.[19]

3. Now consider the fundamental idea of the person.[20] There are, of course, many aspects of human nature that can be singled out as especially significant, depending on our point of view. This is witnessed by such expressions as "homo politicus" and "homo oeconomicus," "homo ludens" and "homo faber." Since our account of justice as fairness begins with the idea that society is to be conceived as a fair system of cooperation over time between generations, we adopt a conception of the person to go with this idea. Beginning with the ancient world, the concept of the person has been understood, in both philosophy and law, as the concept of someone who can take part in, or who can play a role in, social life, and hence exercise and respect its various rights and duties. Thus, we say that a person is someone who can be a citizen, that is, a normal and fully cooperating member of society over a complete life. We add the phrase "over a complete life" because society is viewed not only as closed (§2.1) but as a more or less complete and self-sufficient scheme of cooperation, making room within itself for all the necessities and activities of life, from birth until death. A society is also conceived as existing in perpetuity: it produces and reproduces itself and its institutions and culture over generations and there is no time at which it is expected to wind up its affairs.

Since we start within the tradition of democratic thought, we

19. Allen Buchanan has an instructive discussion of these points in his *Marx and Justice* (Totowa, N.J.: Rowman and Littlefield, 1982), pp. 145–49.

20. It should be emphasized that a conception of the person, as I understand it here, is a normative conception, whether legal, political, or moral, or indeed also philosophical or religious, depending on the overall view to which it belongs. In the present case the conception of the person is a moral conception, one that begins from our everyday conception of persons as the basic units of thought, deliberation, and responsibility, and adapted to a political conception of justice and not to a comprehensive doctrine. It is in effect a political conception of the person, and given the aims of justice as fairness, a conception suitable for the basis of democratic citizenship. As a normative conception, it is to be distinguished from an account of human nature given by natural science and social theory and it has a different role in justice as fairness. On this last, see II:8.

also think of citizens as free and equal persons. The basic idea is that in virtue of their two moral powers (a capacity for a sense of justice and for a conception of the good) and the powers of reason (of judgment, thought, and inference connected with these powers), persons are free. Their having these powers to the requisite minimum degree to be fully cooperating members of society makes persons equal.[21]

To elaborate: since persons can be full participants in a fair system of social cooperation, we ascribe to them the two moral powers connected with the elements in the idea of social cooperation noted above: namely, a capacity for a sense of justice and a capacity for a conception of the good. A sense of justice is the capacity to understand, to apply, and to act from the public conception of justice which characterizes the fair terms of social cooperation. Given the nature of the political conception as specifying a public basis of justification, a sense of justice also expresses a willingness, if not the desire, to act in relation to others on terms that they also can publicly endorse (II:1). The capacity for a conception of the good is the capacity to form, to revise, and rationally to pursue a conception of one's rational advantage or good.

In addition to having these two moral powers, persons also have at any given time a determinate conception of the good that they try to achieve. Such a conception must not be understood narrowly but rather as including a conception of what is valuable in human life. Thus, a conception of the good normally consists of a more or less determinate scheme of final ends, that is, ends we want to realize for their own sake, as well as attachments to other persons and loyalties to various groups and associations. These attachments and loyalties give rise to devotions and affections, and so the flourishing of the persons and associations who are the objects of these sentiments is also part of our conception of the good. We also connect with such a conception a view of our relation to the world—religious, philosophical, and moral—

21. See *Theory*, §77, where this basis of equality is discussed.

by reference to which the value and significance of our ends and attachments are understood. Finally, persons' conceptions of the good are not fixed but form and develop as they mature, and may change more or less radically over the course of life.

4. Since we begin from the idea of society as a fair system of cooperation, we assume that persons as citizens have all the capacities that enable them to be cooperating members of society. This is done to achieve a clear and uncluttered view of what, for us, is the fundamental question of political justice: namely, what is the most appropriate conception of justice for specifying the terms of social cooperation between citizens regarded as free and equal, and as normal and fully cooperating members of society over a complete life?

By taking this as the fundamental question we do not mean to say, of course, that no one ever suffers from illness and accident; such misfortunes are to be expected in the ordinary course of life, and provision for these contingencies must be made. But given our aim, I put aside for the time being these temporary disabilities and also permanent disabilities or mental disorders so severe as to prevent people from being cooperating members of society in the usual sense. Thus, while we begin with an idea of the person implicit in the public political culture, we idealize and simplify this idea in various ways in order to focus first on the main question.

Other questions we can discuss later, and how we answer them may require us to revise answers already reached. This back-and-forth procedure is to be expected. We may think of these other questions as problems of extension. Thus, there is the problem of extending justice as fairness to cover our duties to future generations, under which falls the problem of just savings.[22]

---

22. The account in *Theory,* §44, is defective. A better approach is one based on an idea given to me by Thomas Nagel and Derek Parfit, I believe in February of 1972. The same idea was proposed independently later by Jane English in her "Justice Between Generations," *Philosophical Studies* 31 (1977):98. This better account is indicated in "The Basic Structure as Subject," included in this volume. See VII:6 and

Another problem is how to extend justice as fairness to cover the law of peoples, that is, the concepts and principles that apply to international law and the relations between political societies.[23] Moreover, since we have assumed (as noted above) that persons are normal and fully cooperating members of society over a complete life, and so have the requisite capacities for assuming that role, there is the question of what is owed to those who fail to meet this condition, either temporarily (from illness and accident) or permanently, all of which covers a variety of cases.[24] Finally, there is the problem of what is owed to animals and the rest of nature.

While we would like eventually to answer all these questions, I very much doubt whether that is possible within the scope of justice as fairness as a political conception. I think it yields reasonable answers to the first two problems of extension: to future generations and to the law of peoples, and to part of the third, to the problem of providing for what we may call normal health care. With regard to the problems on which justice as fairness may fail, there are several possibilities. One is that the idea of political justice does not cover everything, nor should we expect it to. Or the problem may indeed be one of political justice but justice as fairness is not correct in this case, however well it may do for other cases. How deep a fault this is must wait until the case itself can be examined. Perhaps we simply lack the ingenuity to see how the extension may proceed. In any case, we should not expect justice as fairness, or any account of justice, to cover all cases of right and wrong. Political justice needs always to be complemented by other virtues.

In these lectures I leave aside these problems of extension and focus on what above I called the fundamental question of political justice. I do this because the fault of *Theory* these lectures

---

n. 12. I simply missed this better solution, which leaves the motivation assumption unchanged.

23. See *Theory*, §58.

24. See V:3.5 and the writings of Norman Daniels there referred to.

address (as explained in the introduction) lies in its answer to that fundamental question. And that this question is indeed fundamental is shown by the fact that it has been the focus of the liberal critique of aristocracy in the seventeenth and eighteenth centuries, of the socialist critique of liberal constitutional democracy in the nineteenth and twentieth centuries, and of the conflict between liberalism and conservatism at the present time over the claims of private property and the legitimacy (as opposed to the effectiveness) of the social policies associated with what has come to be called the "welfare state." It is this question that fixes the initial boundaries of our discussion.

§ 4. The Idea of the Original Position

1. I now take up the idea of the original position.[25] This idea is introduced in order to work out which traditional conception of justice, or which variant of one of those conceptions, specifies the most appropriate principles for realizing liberty and equality once society is viewed as a fair system of cooperation between free and equal citizens. Assuming we want to know which conception of justice does that, why introduce the idea of the original position and how does it help to answer this question?

Consider again the idea of social cooperation. How are the fair terms of cooperation to be determined? Are they simply laid down by some outside authority distinct from the persons cooperating? Are they, for example, laid down by God's law? Or are these terms to be recognized by these persons as fair by reference to their knowledge of an independent moral order? For example, are they recognized as required by natural law, or by a realm of values known by rational intuition? Or are these terms established by an undertaking among those persons themselves in the light of what they regard as their reciprocal advantage? Depending on which answer we give, we get a different conception of social cooperation.

25. See *Theory*, §§3–4 and chap. 3, as well as the index.

Justice as fairness recasts the doctrine of the social contract and adopts a form of the last answer: the fair terms of social cooperation are conceived as agreed to by those engaged in it, that is, by free and equal citizens who are born into the society in which they lead their lives. But their agreement, like any other valid agreement, must be entered into under the appropriate conditions. In particular, these conditions must situate free and equal persons fairly and must not allow some persons greater bargaining advantages than others. Further, such things as threats of force and coercion, deception and fraud must be excluded.

2. So far so good. The foregoing considerations are familiar from everyday life. But agreements in everyday life are made in some more or less clearly specified situation embedded within the background institutions of the basic structure. Our task, however, is to extend the idea of agreement to this background framework itself. Here we face a difficulty for any political conception of justice that uses the idea of contract, whether social or otherwise. The difficulty is this: we must find some point of view, removed from and not distorted by the particular features and circumstances of the all-encompassing background framework, from which a fair agreement between persons regarded as free and equal can be reached.

The original position, with the features I have called "the veil of ignorance," is this point of view.[26] The reason the original position must abstract from and not be affected by the contingencies of the social world is that the conditions for a fair agreement on the principles of political justice between free and equal persons must eliminate the bargaining advantages that inevitably arise within the background institutions of any society from cumulative social, historical, and natural tendencies. These contingent advantages and accidental influences from the past should not affect an agreement on the principles that are to regulate the institutions of the basic structure itself from the present into the future.

---

26. For the veil of ignorance, ibid., §§4 and 24 and the index.

3. Here we face a second difficulty, which is, however, only apparent. To explain: from what we have said it is clear that the original position is to be seen as a device of representation and hence any agreement reached by the parties must be regarded as both hypothetical and nonhistorical. But if so, since hypothetical agreements cannot bind, what is the significance of the original position? The answer is implicit in what has already been said: it is given by the role of the various features of the original position as a device of representation.

That the parties are symmetrically situated is required if they are to be seen as representatives of free and equal citizens who are to reach an agreement under conditions that are fair. Moreover, one of our considered convictions, I assume, is this: the fact that we occupy a particular social position is not a good reason for us to propose, or to expect others to accept, a conception of justice that favors those in this position. Similarly, the fact that we affirm a particular religious, philosophical, or moral comprehensive doctrine with its associated conception of the good is not a reason for us to propose, or to expect others to accept, a conception of justice that favors those of that persuasion. To model this conviction in the original position, the parties are not allowed to know the social position of those they represent, or the particular comprehensive doctrine of the person each represents.[27] The same idea is extended to information about

___

27. Not allowing the parties to know people's comprehensive doctrines is one way in which the veil of ignorance is thick rather than thin. (This contrast is discussed in "Kantian Constructivism" [1980], pp. 549f.) Many have thought a thick veil of ignorance without justification and have queried its grounds, especially given the great significance of comprehensive doctrines. Since we should justify, or at least explain, features of the original position when we can, consider the following. Recall our problem stated at the beginning. We seek a political conception of justice for a democratic society viewed as a system of fair cooperation between free and equal citizens who, as politically autonomous (II:6), willingly accept the publicly recognized principles of justice specifing the fair terms of cooperation. However, the society in question is one in which there is diversity of comprehensive doctrines, all perfectly reasonable. This is the fact of reasonable pluralism, as opposed to the fact of pluralism as such (§6.2 and II:3). Now if all citizens are freely to endorse the political conception of justice, that conception must be able to gain the support of citizens

people's race and ethnic group, sex and gender, and their various native endowments such as strength and intelligence, all within the normal range. We express these limits on information figuratively by saying the parties are behind a veil of ignorance. Thus, the original position is simply a device of representation: it describes the parties, each of whom is responsible for the essential interests of a free and equal citizen, as fairly situated and as reaching an agreement subject to conditions that appropriately limit what they can put forward as good reasons.[28]

4. Both of the above mentioned difficulties, then, are overcome by viewing the original position as a device of representation: it models what we regard—here and now—as fair conditions under which the representatives of free and equal citizens are to specify the terms of social cooperation in the case of the

---

who affirm different and opposing though reasonable comprehensive doctrines, in which case we have an overlapping consensus of reasonable doctrines. This suggests that we leave aside how people's comprehensive doctrines connect with the content of the political conception of justice and regard that content as arising from the various fundamental ideas drawn from the public political culture of a democratic society. We model this by putting people's comprehensive doctrines behind the veil of ignorance. This enable us to find a political conception of justice that can be the focus of an overlapping consensus and thereby serve as a public basis of justification in a society marked by the fact of reasonable pluralism. None of this puts in question the description of a political conception of justice as a free-standing view (§§1.4 and 2.2) but it does mean that to give the rationale of the thick veil of ignorance, we invoke the fact of reasonable pluralism and the idea of an overlapping consensus of reasonable comprehensive doctrines. I am grateful to Wilfried Hinsch for seeing the need to discuss this question explicitly. Above I have followed the general idea of his valuable unpublished paper on this topic, "The Veil of Ignorance and the Idea of an Overlapping Consensus," Bad Homburg, July 1992.

28. The original position models a basic feature of both Kant's moral constructivism and of political constructivism, namely, the distinction between the reasonable and the rational, with the reasonable prior to the rational. The relevance of the distinction here is that *Theory* more or less consistently speaks not of the rational but of the reasonable (or sometimes the fitting or appropriate) conditions as constraints on arguments for principles of justice (pp. 18f., 20f., 120f., 130f., 138, 446, 516f., 578, 584f.). These constraints are modeled in the original position and thereby imposed on the parties: their deliberations are subject—and subject absolutely—to the reasonable conditions the modeling of which makes the original position fair. As we shall see later, that the reasonable is prior to the rational gives the priority of right (V).

25

basic structure of society; and since it also models what, for this case, we regard as acceptable restrictions on reasons available to the parties for favoring one political conception of justice over another, the conception of justice the parties would adopt identifies the conception of justice that we regard—here and now—as fair and supported by the best reasons.

The idea is to use the original position to model both freedom and equality and restrictions on reasons in such a way that it becomes perfectly evident which agreement would be made by the parties as citizens' representatives. Even should there be, as surely there will be, reasons for and against each conception of justice available, there may still be an overall balance of reasons plainly favoring one conception over the rest. As a device of representation the idea of the original position serves as a means of public reflection and self-clarification. It helps us work out what we now think, once we are able to take a clear and uncluttered view of what justice requires when society is conceived as a scheme of cooperation between free and equal citizens from one generation to the next. The original position serves as a mediating idea by which all our considered convictions, whatever their level of generality—whether they concern fair conditions for situating the parties or reasonable constraints on reasons, or first principles and precepts, or judgments about particular institutions and actions—can be brought to bear on one another. This enables us to establish greater coherence among all our judgments; and with this deeper self-understanding we can attain wider agreement among one another.

5. We introduce an idea like that of the original position because there seems no better way to elaborate a political conception of justice for the basic structure from the fundamental idea of society as an ongoing and fair system of cooperation between citizens regarded as free and equal. This seems particularly evident once we think of society as extending over generations and as inheriting its public culture and existing political and social institutions (along with its real capital and stock of natural resources) from those who have gone before. There are, how-

ever, certain dangers in using this idea. As a device of representation its abstractness invites misunderstanding. In particular, the description of the parties may seem to presuppose a particular metaphysical conception of the person; for example, that the essential nature of persons is independent of and prior to their contingent attributes, including their final ends and attachments, and indeed their conception of the good and character as a whole.[29]

I believe this to be an illusion caused by not seeing the original position as a device of representation. The veil of ignorance, to mention one prominent feature of that position, has no specific metaphysical implications concerning the nature of the self; it does not imply that the self is ontologically prior to the facts about persons that the parties are excluded from knowing. We can, as it were, enter this position at any time simply by reasoning for principles of justice in accordance with the enumerated restrictions on information. When, in this way, we simulate being in the original position, our reasoning no more commits us to a particular metaphysical doctrine about the nature of the self than our acting a part in a play, say of Macbeth or Lady Macbeth, commits us to thinking that we are really a king or a queen engaged in a desperate struggle for political power. Much the same holds for role playing generally. We must keep in mind that we are trying to show how the idea of society as a fair system of social cooperation can be unfolded so as to find principles specifying the basic rights and liberties and the forms of equality most appropriate to those cooperating, once they are regarded as citizens, as free and equal persons.

6. Having surveyed the idea of the original position, I add the

---

29. See the important work of Michael Sandel, *Liberalism and the Limits of Justice* (Cambridge: Cambridge University Press, 1982). This metaphysical conception of the person is attributed to *Theory* in the introduction and criticized from various standpoints in much of the book. I believe the reply found in chap. 4 of Will Kymlicka's *Liberalism, Community, and Culture* (Oxford: Clarendon Press, 1989) is on the whole satisfactory, modulo adjustments that may need to be made to fit it within political liberalism as opposed to liberalism as a comprehensive doctrine.

following to avoid misunderstanding. It is important to distinguish three points of view: that of the parties in the original position, that of citizens in a well-ordered society, and finally, that of ourselves—of you and me who are elaborating justice as fairness and examining it as a political conception of justice.

The first two points of view belong to the conception of justice as fairness and are specified by reference to its fundamental ideas. But whereas the conceptions of a well-ordered society and of citizens as free and equal might conceivably be realized in our social world, the parties as rational representatives who specify the fair terms of social cooperation by agreeing to principles of justice are simply parts of the original position. This position is set up by you and me in working out justice as fairness, and so the nature of the parties is up to us: they are merely the artificial creatures inhabiting our device of representation. Justice as fairness is badly misunderstood if the deliberations of the parties, and the motives we attribute to them, are mistaken for an account of the moral psychology, either of actual persons or of citizens in a well-ordered society.[30] Rational autonomy (II:5) must not be confused with full autonomy (II:6). The latter is a political ideal and part of the more complete ideal of a well-ordered society. Rational autonomy is not, as such, an ideal at all, but a way to model the idea of the rational (versus the reasonable) in the original position.

The third point of view—that of you and me—is that from which justice as fairness, and indeed any other political conception, is to be assessed. Here the test is that of reflective equilibrium: how well the view as a whole articulates our more firm considered convictions of political justice, at all levels of generality, after due examination, once all adjustments and revisions that seem compelling have been made. A conception of justice that meets this criterion is the conception that, so far as we can now ascertain, is the one most reasonable for us.

30. Many have made this error. I tried to identify it more clearly and set it to rest in "Fairness to Goodness," *Philosophical Review* 84 (October 1975):542f.

§ 5. The Political Conception of the Person

1. I remarked earlier that the idea of the original position and the description of the parties may tempt us to think that a metaphysical doctrine of the person is presupposed. While I said that this interpretation is mistaken, it is not enough simply to disavow reliance on metaphysical doctrines, for despite one's intent they may still be involved. To rebut claims of this nature requires discussing them in detail and showing that they have no foothold. I cannot do that here.[31]

I can, however, sketch an account of a political conception of the person drawn on in setting up the original position(§3.3). To understand what is meant by describing a conception of the person as political, consider how citizens are represented in that position as free persons. The representation of their freedom seems to be one source of the idea that a metaphysical doctrine is presupposed. Now citizens are conceived as thinking of themselves as free in three respects, so I survey each of these and indicate the way in which the conception of the person is political.

---

31. Part of the difficulty is that there is no accepted understanding of what a metaphysical doctrine is. One might say, as Paul Hoffman has suggested to me, that to develop a political conception of justice without presupposing, or explicitly using, a particular metaphysical doctrine, for example, some particular metaphysical conception of the person, is already to presuppose a metaphysical thesis: namely, that no metaphysical doctrine is required for this purpose. One might also say that our ordinary conception of persons as the basic units of deliberation and responsibility presupposes, or in some way involves, certain metaphysical theses about the nature of persons as moral or political agents. Following the precept of avoidance, I should not want to deny these claims. What should be said is the following. If we look at the presentation of justice as fairness and note how it is set up, and note the ideas and conceptions it uses, no particular metaphysical doctrine about the nature of persons, distinctive and opposed to other metaphysical doctrines, appears among its premises, or seems required by its argument. If metaphysical presuppositions are involved, perhaps they are so general that they would not distinguish between the metaphysical views—Cartesian, Leibnizian, or Kantian; realist, idealist, or materialist—with which philosophy has traditionally been concerned. In this case they would not appear to be relevant for the structure and content of a political conception of justice one way or the other. I am grateful to Daniel Brudney and Paul Hoffman for discussion of these matters.

2. First, citizens are free in that they conceive of themselves and of one another as having the moral power to have a conception of the good. This is not to say that, as part of their political conception, they view themselves as inevitably tied to the pursuit of the particular conception of the good that they affirm at any given time. Rather, as citizens, they are seen as capable of revising and changing this conception on reasonable and rational grounds, and they may do this if they so desire. As free persons, citizens claim the right to view their persons as independent from and not identified with any particular such conception with its scheme of final ends. Given their moral power to form, revise, and rationally pursue a conception of the good, their public identity as free persons is not affected by changes over time in their determinate conception of it.

For example, when citizens convert from one religion to another, or no longer affirm an established religious faith, they do not cease to be, for questions of political justice, the same persons they were before. There is no loss of what we may call their public, or institutional, identity, or their identity as a matter of basic law. In general, they still have the same basic rights and duties, they own the same property and can make the same claims as before, except insofar as these claims were connected with their previous religious affiliation. We can imagine a society (history offers many examples) in which basic rights and recognized claims depend on religious affiliation and social class. Such a society has a different political conception of the person. It lacks a conception of equal citizenship, for this conception goes with that of a democratic society of free and equal citizens.

There is a second sense of identity specified by reference to citizens' deeper aims and commitments. Let's call it their noninstitutional or moral identity.[32] Citizens usually have both political and nonpolitical aims and commitments. They affirm the values of political justice and want to see them embodied in

---

32. I am indebted to Erin Kelly for the distinction between the two kinds of aims that characterize peoples' moral identity as described in this and the next paragraph.

political institutions and social policies. They also work for the other values in nonpublic life and for the ends of the associations to which they belong. These two aspects of their moral identity citizens must adjust and reconcile. It can happen that in their personal affairs, or in the internal life of associations, citizens may regard their final ends and attachments very differently from the way the political conception supposes. They may have, and often do have at any given time, affections, devotions, and loyalties that they believe they would not, indeed could and should not, stand apart from and evaluate objectively. They may regard it as simply unthinkable to view themselves apart from certain religious, philosophical, and moral convictions, or from certain enduring attachments and loyalties.

These two kinds of commitments and attachments—political and nonpolitical—specify moral identity and give shape to a person's way of life, what one sees oneself as doing and trying to accomplish in the social world. If we suddenly lost them, we would be disoriented and unable to carry on. In fact, there would be, we might think, no point in carrying on.[33] But our conceptions of the good may and often do change over time, usually slowly but sometimes rather suddenly. When these changes are sudden, we are likely to say that we are no longer the same person. We know what this means: we refer to a profound and pervasive shift, or reversal, in our final ends and commitments; we refer to our different moral (which includes our religious) identity. On the road to Damascus Saul of Tarsus becomes Paul the Apostle. Yet such a conversion implies no change in our public or institutional identity, nor in our personal identity as this concept is understood by some writers in the philosophy of mind.[34] Moreover, in a well-ordered society supported by an

---

33. This role of commitments is often emphasized by Bernard Williams, for example, in "Persons, Character and Morality," in *Moral Luck* (Cambridge: Cambridge University Press, 1981), pp. 10–14.

34. Though I have used the term *identity* in the text, it would, I think, cause less misunderstanding to use the phrase "our conception of ourselves," or "the kind of person we want to be." Doing so would distinguish the question with important

overlapping consensus, citizens' (more general) political values and commitments, as part of their noninstitutional or moral identity, are roughly the same.

3. A second respect in which citizens view themselves as free is that they regard themselves as self-authenticating sources of valid claims. That is, they regard themselves as being entitled to make claims on their institutions so as to advance their conceptions of the good (provided these conceptions fall within the range permitted by the public conception of justice). These claims citizens regard as having weight of their own apart from being derived from duties and obligations specified by a political conception of justice, for example, from duties and obligations owed to society. Claims that citizens regard as founded on duties and obligations based on their conception of the good and the moral doctrine they affirm in their own life are also, for our purposes here, to be counted as self-authenticating. Doing this is reason-

---

moral elements from the question of the sameness, or identity, of a substance, continuant, or thing, through different changes in time and space. In saying this I assume that an answer to the problem of personal identity tries to specify the various criteria (for example, psychological criteria of memories and physical continuity of body, or some part thereof) in accordance with which two different psychological states or actions, say, which occur at two different times may be said to be states or actions of the same person who endures over time; and it also tries to specify how this enduring person is to be conceived, whether as a Cartesian or a Leibnizian substance, or a Kantian transcendental ego, or as a continuant of some kind, for example, bodily or physical. See the collection of essays edited by John Perry, *Personal Identity* (Berkeley: University of California Press, 1975), especially Perry's introduction, pp. 1–30; and Sydney Shoemaker's essay in *Personal Identity* (Oxford: Basil Blackwell, 1984), both of which consider a number of views. Sometimes in discussions of this problem, continuity of fundamental aims is largely ignored, for example in views like H. P. Grice's (in Perry's collection), which emphasizes continuity of memory. However, once the continuity of these aims is counted as also basic, as in Derek Parfit's *Reasons and Persons* (Oxford: Clarendon Press, 1984), pt. III, there is no sharp distinction between the problem of a person's nonpublic or moral identity and the problem of their personal identity. The latter problem raises profound questions on which past and current philosophical views widely differ and surely will continue to differ. For this reason it is important to try to develop a political conception of justice that avoids this problem as far as possible. Even so, to refer to the example in the text, all agree, I assume, that for the purposes of public life, Saul of Tarsus and St. Paul the Apostle are the same person. Conversion is irrelevant to our public, or institutional, identity.

32

able in a political conception of justice for a constitutional democracy, for provided the conceptions of the good and the moral doctrines citizens affirm are compatible with the public conception of justice, these duties and obligations are self-authenticating from a political point of view.

When we describe the way in which citizens regard themselves as free, we describe how citizens think of themselves in a democratic society when questions of political justice arise. That this aspect belongs to a particular political conception is clear from the contrast with a different political conception in which people are not viewed as self-authenticating sources of valid claims. Rather, their claims have no weight except insofar as they can be derived from the duties and obligations owed to society, or from their ascribed roles in a social hierarchy justified by religious or aristocratic values.

To take an extreme case, slaves are human beings who are not counted as sources of claims, not even claims based on social duties or obligations, for slaves are not counted as capable of having duties or obligations. Laws that prohibit the maltreatment of slaves are not based on claims made by slaves, but on claims originating from slaveholders, or from the general interests of society (which do not include the interests of slaves). Slaves are, so to speak, socially dead: they are not recognized as persons at all.[35] This contrast with slavery makes clear why conceiving of citizens as free persons in virtue of their moral powers and their having a conception of the good goes with a particular political conception of justice.

4. The third respect in which citizens are viewed as free is that they are viewed as capable of taking responsibility for their ends and this affects how their various claims are assessed.[36] Very roughly, given just background institutions and given for each person a fair index of primary goods (as required by the princi-

35. For the idea of social death, see Orlando Patterson's *Slavery and Social Death* (Cambridge, Mass.: Harvard University Press, 1982), esp. pp. 5–9, 38–45, 337.
36. See further V:3–4, esp. 3.6.

ples of justice), citizens are thought to be capable of adjusting their aims and aspirations in the light of what they can reasonably expect to provide for. Moreover, they are viewed as capable of restricting their claims in matters of justice to the kinds of things the principles of justice allow.

Citizens are to recognize, then, that the weight of their claims is not given by the strength and psychological intensity of their wants and desires (as opposed to their needs as citizens), even when their wants and desires are rational from their point of view. The procedure is as before: we start with the basic idea of society as a fair system of cooperation. When this idea is developed into a conception of political justice, it implies that, viewing citizens as persons who can engage in social cooperation over a complete life, they can also take responsibility for their ends: that is, they can adjust their ends so that those ends can be pursued by the means they can reasonably expect to acquire in return for what they can reasonably expect to contribute. The idea of responsibility for ends is implicit in the public political culture and discernible in its practices. A political conception of the person articulates this idea and fits it into the idea of society as a fair system of cooperation.

5. To sum up, I recapitulate three main points of this and the preceding two sections:

First, in §3 persons were regarded as free and equal persons in virtue of their possessing to the requisite degree the two powers of moral personality, namely, the capacity for a sense of justice and the capacity for a conception of the good. These powers we associated with the two main elements of the idea of cooperation, the idea of the fair terms of cooperation, and the idea of each participant's rational advantage, or good.

Second, in this section (§5), we surveyed three respects in which persons are regarded as free, and have noted that in the public political culture of a constitutional democratic regime citizens conceive of themselves as free in these ways.

Third, since the question of which conception of political justice is most appropriate for realizing in basic institutions the values of liberty and equality has long been deeply controversial within the very tradition in which citizens are regarded as free and equal, the aim of justice as fairness is to resolve this question by starting from the idea of society as a fair system of cooperation in which the fair terms of cooperation are agreed upon by citizens so conceived. In §4, we saw why this approach, once the basic structure of society is taken as the primary subject of justice, leads to the idea of the original position as a device of representation.

§ 6. The Idea of a Well-Ordered Society

1. I have said that in justice as fairness the fundamental idea of society as a fair system of cooperation over generations is developed in conjunction with two companion ideas: the idea of citizens as free and equal persons, and the idea of a well-ordered society as a society effectively regulated by a public political conception of justice. Having discussed the first companion idea, I now discuss the second.

To say that a society is well-ordered conveys three things: first (and implied by the idea of a publicly recognized conception of justice), it is a society in which everyone accepts, and knows that everyone else accepts, the very same principles of justice; and second (implied by the idea of the effective regulation of such a conception), its basic structure—that is, its main political and social institutions and how they fit together as one system of cooperation—is publicly known, or with good reason believed, to satisfy these principles. And third, its citizens have a normally effective sense of justice and so they generally comply with society's basic institutions, which they regard as just. In such a society the publicly recognized conception of justice establishes a shared point of view from which citizens' claims on society can be adjudicated.

This is a highly idealized concept. Yet any conception of justice that cannot well order a constitutional democracy is inadequate as a democratic conception. This might happen because

35

of the familiar reason that its content renders it self-defeating when it is publicly recognized. It might also happen because, adopting a distinction from Cohen, a democratic society is marked by the fact of reasonable pluralism.[37] Thus, a conception of justice may fail because it cannot gain the support of reasonable citizens who affirm reasonable comprehensive doctrines; or as I shall often say, it cannot gain the support of a reasonable overlapping consensus. Being able to do this is necessary for an adequate political conception of justice.

2. The reason for this is that the political culture of a democratic society is characterized (I assume) by three general facts understood as follows.

The first is that the diversity of reasonable comprehensive religious, philosophical, and moral doctrines found in modern democratic societies is not a mere historical condition that may soon pass away; it is a permanent feature of the public culture of democracy. Under the political and social conditions secured by the basic rights and liberties of free institutions, a diversity of conflicting and irreconcilable—and what's more, reasonable—comprehensive doctrines will come about and persist if such diversity does not already obtain.

This fact of reasonable pluralism must be distinguished from the fact of pluralism as such. It is the fact that free institutions tend to generate not simply a variety of doctrines and views, as one might expect from peoples' various interests and their tendency to focus on narrow points of view. Rather, it is the fact that among the views that develop are a diversity of reasonable comprehensive doctrines. These are the doctrines that reasonable citizens affirm and that political liberalism must address.

37. I am grateful to Joshua Cohen for instructive discussion on this point; and also for insisting on the importance of the distinction between reasonable pluralism and pluralism as such, as specified in the paragraphs immediately below in §6.2, and later in II:3. These matters he discusses in illuminating detail in "Moral Pluralism and Political Consensus," in *The Idea of Democracy,* edited by David Copp, Jean Hampton, and John Roemer (Cambridge: Cambridge University Press, 1993).

They are not simply the upshot of self- and class interests, or of peoples' understandable tendency to view the political world from a limited standpoint. Instead, they are in part the work of free practical reason within the framework of free institutions. Thus, although historical doctrines are not, of course, the work of free reason alone, the fact of reasonable pluralism is not an unfortunate condition of human life. In framing the political conception so that it can, at the second stage, gain the support of reasonable comprehensive doctrines, we are not so much adjusting that conception to brute forces of the world but to the inevitable outcome of free human reason.[38]

A second and related general fact is that a continuing shared understanding on one comprehensive religious, philosophical, or moral doctrine can be maintained only by the oppressive use of state power. If we think of political society as a community united in affirming one and the same comprehensive doctrine, then the oppressive use of state power is necessary for political community. In the society of the Middle Ages, more or less united in affirming the Catholic faith, the Inquisition was not an accident; its suppression of heresy was needed to preserve that shared religious belief. The same holds, I believe, for any reasonable comprehensive philosophical and moral doctrine, whether religious or nonreligious. A society united on a reasonable form of utilitarianism, or on the reasonable liberalisms of Kant or Mill, would likewise require the sanctions of state power to remain so.[39] Call this "the fact of oppression."[40]

38. In II:2–3 there is an account of the burdens of judgment and a discussion of a reasonable comprehensive doctrine that gives rather minimal necessary conditions for such a doctrine, though conditions suitable for the purposes of political liberalism. It is not suggested that all reasonable doctrines so defined are equally reasonable for other purposes or from other points of view. Plainly citizens will have different opinions about these further matters.

39. This statement may seem paradoxical. If one objects that, consistent with Kant's or Mill's doctrine, the sanctions of state power cannot be used, I quite agree. But this does not contradict the text, which says that a society in which every one affirms a reasonable liberal doctrine if by hypothesis it should exist, cannot long

Finally, a third general fact is that an enduring and secure democratic regime, one not divided into contending doctrinal confessions and hostile social classes, must be willingly and freely supported by at least a substantial majority of its politically active citizens. Together with the first general fact, this means that to serve as a public basis of justification for a constitutional regime a political conception of justice must be one that can be endorsed by widely different and opposing though reasonable comprehensive doctrines.[41]

3. Since there is no reasonable religious, philosophical, or moral doctrine affirmed by all citizens, the conception of justice affirmed in a well-ordered democratic society must be a conception limited to what I shall call "the domain of the political" and its values. The idea of a well-ordered democratic society must be framed accordingly. I assume, then, that citizens' overall views have two parts: one part can be seen to be, or to coincide with, the publicly recognized political conception of justice; the other part is a (fully or partially) comprehensive doctrine to which the political conception is in some manner related. How it may be related I note later in IV:8. The point to stress here is that, as I have said, citizens individually decide for themselves in what way the public political conception all affirm is related to their own more comprehensive views.

With this understood, I note briefly how a well-ordered democratic society meets a necessary (but certainly not sufficient) condition of realism and stability. Such a society can be well-

---

endure. With unreasonable doctrines, and with religions that emphasize the idea of institutional authority, we may think the text correct; and we may mistakenly think there are exceptions for other comprehensive views. The point of the text is: there are no exceptions. I owe this observation to comments of Cass Sanstein.

40. I borrow this name from Sanford Shieh.

41. For completeness I add as a fourth general fact a fact we have used all along in speaking of the public culture. This is the fact that the political culture of a democratic society, which has worked reasonably well over a considerable period of time, normally contains, at least implicitly, certain fundamental intuitive ideas from which it is possible to work up a political conception of justice suitable for a constitutional regime. This fact is important when we specify the general features of a political conception of justice and elaborate justice as fairness as such a view.

ordered by a political conception of justice so long as, first, citizens who affirm reasonable but opposing comprehensive doctrines belong to an overlapping consensus: that is, they generally endorse that conception of justice as giving the content of their political judgments on basic institutions; and second, unreasonable comprehensive doctrines (these, we assume, always exist) do not gain enough currency to undermine society's essential justice. These conditions do not impose the unrealistic—indeed, the utopian—requirement that all citizens affirm the same comprehensive doctrine, but only, as in political liberalism, the same public conception of justice.

4. The idea of an overlapping consensus is easily misunderstood given the idea of consensus used in everyday politics. Its meaning for us arises thus: we suppose a constitutional democratic regime to be reasonably just and workable, and worth defending. Yet given the fact of reasonable pluralism, how can we frame our defense of it so that it can win sufficiently wide support to achieve stability?

To this end, we do not look to the comprehensive doctrines that in fact exist and then draw up a political conception that strikes some kind of balance of forces between them. To illustrate: in specifying a list of primary goods,[42] say, we can proceed in two ways. One is to look at the various comprehensive doctrines actually found in society and specify an index of such goods so as to be near to those doctrines' center of gravity, so to speak; that is, so as to find a kind of average of what those who affirmed those views would need by way of institutional claims and protections and all-purpose means. Doing this might seem the best way to insure that the index provides the basic elements necessary to advance the conceptions of the good associated with existing doctrines and thus improve the likelihood of securing an overlapping consensus.

This is not how justice as fairness proceeds; to do so would

42. The idea of primary goods is introduced in II:5.3 and discussed in some detail in V:3–4.

make it political in the wrong way. Rather, it elaborates a political conception as a freestanding view (§1.4) working from the fundamental idea of society as a fair system of cooperation and its companion ideas. The hope is that this idea, with its index of primary goods arrived at from within, can be the focus of a reasonable overlapping consensus. We leave aside comprehensive doctrines that now exist, or that have existed, or that might exist. The thought is not that primary goods are fair to comprehensive conceptions of the good associated with such doctrines, by striking a fair balance among them, but rather fair to free and equal citizens as those persons who have those conceptions.

The problem, then, is how to frame a conception of justice for a constitutional regime such that those who support, or who might be brought to support, that kind of regime might also endorse the political conception provided it did not conflict too sharply with their comprehensive views. This leads to the idea of a political conception of justice as a freestanding view starting from the fundamental ideas of a democratic society and presupposing no particular wider doctrine. We put no doctrinal obstacles to its winning allegiance to itself, so that it can be supported by a reasonable and enduring overlapping consensus.

§ 7. Neither a Community nor an Association

1. A well-ordered democratic society is neither a community nor, more generally, an association.[43] There are two differences between a democratic society and an association. The first is that we have assumed that a democratic society, like any political society, is to be viewed as a complete and closed social system. It is complete in that it is self-sufficient and has a place for all the main purposes of human life. It is also closed, as I have said (§2.1), in that entry into it is only by birth and exit from it is only

43. By definition, let's think of a community as a special kind of association, one united by a comprehensive doctrine, for example, a church. The members of other associations often have shared ends but these do not make up a comprehensive doctrine and may even be purely intrumental.

40

by death. We have no prior identity before being in society: it is not as if we came from somewhere but rather we find ourselves growing up in this society in this social position, with its attendant advantages and disadvantages, as our good or ill fortune would have it. For the moment we leave aside entirely relations with other societies and postpone all questions of justice between peoples until a conception of justice for a well-ordered society is on hand. Thus, we are not seen as joining society at the age of reason, as we might join an association, but as being born into society where we will lead a complete life.

Think, then, of the principles of justice as designed to form the social world in which our character and our conception of ourselves as persons, as well as our comprehensive views and their conceptions of the good, are first acquired, and in which our moral powers must be realized, if they are to be realized at all. These principles must give priority to those basic freedoms and opportunities in background institutions of civil society that enable us to become free and equal citizens in the first place, and to understand our role as persons with that status.

2. A second basic difference between a well-ordered democratic society and an association is that such a society has no final ends and aims in the way that persons or associations do. Here by ends and aims I mean those that have a special place in comprehensive doctrines. By contrast, the constitutionally specified ends of society, such as those given in the preamble to a constitution—a more perfect justice, the blessings of liberty, the common defense—must fall under a political conception of justice and its public reason. This means that citizens do not think there are antecedent social ends that justify them in viewing some people as having more or less worth to society than others and assigning them different basic rights and privileges accordingly. Many past societies have thought otherwise: they pursued as final ends religion and empire, dominion and glory; and the rights and status of individuals and classes have depended on their role in gaining those ends. In this respect they have seen themselves as an association.

41

By contrast, a democratic society with its political conception does not see itself as an association at all. It is not entitled, as associations within society generally are, to offer different terms to its members (in this case those born into it) depending on the worth of their potential contribution to society as a whole, or to the ends of those already members of it. When doing this is permissible in the case of associations, it is because in their case the prospective or continuing members are already guaranteed the status of free and equal citizens, and the institutions of background justice in society assure that other alternatives are open to them.[44]

3. While a well-ordered democratic society is not an association, it is not a community either, if we mean by a community a society governed by a shared comprehensive religious, philosophical, or moral doctrine. This fact is crucial for a well-ordered society's idea of public reason. To think of a democracy as a community (so defined) overlooks the limited scope of its public reason founded on a political conception of justice. It mistakes the kind of unity a constitutional regime is capable of without violating the most basic democratic principles. A zeal for the

44. The distinction made in this section between society and an association is in many ways similar to the distinction made by Michael Oakeshott in the central essay of *On Human Conduct* ((Oxford: Clarendon Press, 1975) between a practical association and a purposive association. Terry Vardin, who explains and uses this distinction to instructive effect in his *Law, Morality and the Relations of States* (Princeton: Princeton University Press, 1983), might not agree. He thinks that *Theory* views society as a purposive association, since it describes society as a scheme of cooperation (pp. 262–67). Yet this is not, I think, decisive. Rather, what is decisive is what persons are cooperating as and what their cooperation achieves. As the text says, what characterizes a democratic society is that people are cooperating as free and equal citizens and what their cooperation achieves (in the ideal case) is a just basic structure with background institutions realizing principles of justice and providing citizens with the all-purpose means to meet their needs as citizens. Their cooperation is to assure one another political justice. Whereas in an association people cooperate as members of the association to achieve whatever it is that moved them to join the association, which will vary from one association to another. As citizens they cooperate to achieve their common shared end of justice; as members of associations they cooperate to realize ends falling under their different comprehensive conceptions of the good.

whole truth tempts us to a broader and deeper unity that cannot be justified by public reason.

But it is also mistaken to think of a democratic society as an association and to suppose its public reason includes nonpolitical aims and values. Doing this overlooks the prior and fundamental role of its basic institutions in establishing a social world within which alone we can develop with care, nurture, and education, and no little good fortune, into free and equal citizens. The just background of that social world is given by the content of the political conception so that by public reason all citizens can understand its role and share its political values in the same way.

§ 8. On the Use of Abstract Conceptions

1. In order to state what I have called political liberalism, I have started with a number of familiar and basic ideas implicit in the public political culture of a democratic society. These have been worked up into a family of conceptions in terms of which political liberalism can be formulated and understood. First among these is the conception of political justice itself (§2); and next the three fundamental ideas: the conception of society as a fair system of social cooperation over time (§3), and its two companion ideas: the political conception of the person as free and equal (§5), and the conception of a well-ordered society (§6). We also have the two ideas used to present justice as fairness: the conceptions of the basic structure (§2) and of the original position (§4). Finally, to these ideas we add, so as to present a well-ordered society as a possible social world, the ideas of an overlapping consensus and of a reasonable comprehensive doctrine (§6). Reasonable pluralism is specified by reference to this last. The nature of social unity is given by a stable overlapping consensus of reasonable comprehensive doctrines (IV:1). In later lectures other basic ideas are introduced to fill out the content of political liberalism, such as the ideas of the domain of the political (IV) and of public reason (VI).

With these conceptions and their connections understood, I

recall the combined question[45] that political liberalism addresses and say: three conditions seem to be sufficient for society to be a fair and stable system of cooperation between free and equal citizens who are deeply divided by the reasonable comprehensive doctrines they affirm. First, the basic structure of society is regulated by a political conception of justice; second, this political conception is the focus of an overlapping consensus of reasonable comprehensive doctrines; and third, public discussion, when constitutional essentials and questions of basic justice are at stake, is conducted in terms of the political conception of justice. This brief summation characterizes political liberalism and how it understands the ideal of constitutional democracy.[46]

2. Some may protest the use of so many abstract conceptions. It may be helpful to see why we are led to conceptions of this kind. In political philosophy the work of abstraction is set in motion by deep political conflicts.[47] Only ideologues and visionaries fail to experience deep conflicts of political values and conflicts between these and nonpolitical values. Profound and long-lasting controversies set the stage for the idea of reasonable justification as a practical and not as an epistemological or metaphysical problem (§1). We turn to political philosophy when our shared political understandings, as Walzer might say, break down, and equally when we are torn within ourselves. We recognize

45. This question was stated in the brief introduction before §1.

46. The three conditions stated in the text are to be understood as sufficient and not necessary conditions. Whether they can be weakened, for example, to a family of workable but quite general principles, or even to a family of rules, such as the rules of an established constitution, rather than to a political conception of justice, is discussed in IV:3.5. There I consider what I refer to as the depth, breadth, and specificity of an overlapping consensus and note that the three conditions express an ideal case.

47. Here I am indebted to Joshua Cohen's review of Michael Walzer's *Spheres of Justice* (New York: Basic Books, 1983) in the *Journal of Philosophy* 83 (1986):457–68. See especially his discussion of what he calls Walzer's "simple communitarian dilemma," pp. 463–67, and pp. 467f., where he argues that Walzer's view about how political philosophy should begin does not differ essentially from Plato, Kant, and Sidgwick. The difference is where Walzer argues it must end up, namely, with our shared understandings.

this if we imagine Alexander Stephens rejecting Lincoln's appeal to the abstractions of natural right and replying to him by saying: the North must respect the South's shared political understandings on the slavery question.[48] Surely the reply to this will lead into political philosophy.

Political philosophy does not, as some have thought, withdraw from society and the world. Nor does it claim to discover what is true by its own distinctive methods of reason apart from any tradition of political thought and practice. No political conception of justice could have weight with us unless it helped to put in order our considered convictions of justice at all levels of generality, from the most general to the most particular. To help us do this is one role of the original position.

Political philosophy cannot coerce our considered convictions any more than the principles of logic can. If we feel coerced, it may be because, when we reflect on the matter at hand, values, principles, and standards are so formulated and arranged that they are freely recognized as ones we do, or should, accept. We can use the original position to further this recognition. Our feeling coerced is perhaps our being surprised at the consequences of those principles and standards, at the implications of our free recognition. Still, we may reaffirm our more particular judgments and decide instead to modify the proposed conception of justice with its principles and ideals until judgments at all levels of generality are at last in line on due reflection. It is a mistake to think of abstract conceptions and general principles as always overriding our more particular judgments. These two sides of our practical thought (not to mention intermediate levels of generality in between) are complementary, and to be adjusted to one another so as to fit into a coherent view.

The work of abstraction, then, is not gratuitous: not abstrac-

48. For Lincoln's side of the correspondence of November-December 1860, see *Collected Works*, vol. IV, pp. 146, 160f. Their correspondence is reprinted and discussed by Nicolay and Hay, *Abraham Lincoln* (New York: Century Co., 1917) (1st ed. 1886, 1890), vol. 3, pp. 270–75; and Allan Nevins, *The Emergence of Lincoln* (New York: Charles Scribner's, 1950), vol. II, pp. 466f.

tion for abstraction's sake. Rather, it is a way of continuing public discussion when shared understandings of lesser generality have broken down. We should be prepared to find that the deeper the conflict, the higher the level of abstraction to which we must ascend to get a clear and uncluttered view of its roots.[49] Since the conflicts in the democratic tradition about the nature of toleration and the basis of cooperation for a footing of equality have been persistent, we may suppose they are deep. Therefore, to connect these conflicts with the familiar and basic, we look to the fundamental ideas implicit in the public political culture and seek to uncover how citizens themselves might, on due reflection, want to conceive of their society as a fair system of cooperation over time. Seen in this context, formulating idealized, which is to say abstract, conceptions of society and person connected with those fundamental ideas is essential to finding a reasonable political conception of justice.

49. This idea is implicit in T. M. Scanlon's review of Stuart Hampshire's *Morality and Conflict* (Cambridge, Mass.: Harvard University Press, 1983) and of Michael Walzer's *Spheres of Justice* in the *London Review of Books,* September 5, 1985, pp. 17f. This idea was more fully stated in the manuscript of the review before it was abridged for reasons of space.

Powers of Citizens and Their Representation

In the first lecture I began by saying that political liberalism addresses two fundamental questions. The first question is: what is the most appropriate conception of justice for specifying the fair terms of social cooperation between citizens regarded as free and equal? The second question is: what are the grounds of toleration understood in a general way, given the fact of reasonable pluralism as the inevitable result of the powers of human reason at work within enduring free institutions? Combining these two questions into one we have: how is it possible for there to exist over time a just and stable society of free and equal citizens who still remain profoundly divided by reasonable religious, philosophical, and moral doctrines?

These lectures fill out the details of the answer as follows: the basic structure of such a society is effectively regulated by a political conception of justice that is the focus of an overlapping consensus of at least the reasonable comprehensive doctrines affirmed by its citizens. This enables that shared political conception to serve as the basis of public reason in debates about political questions when constitutional essentials and matters of basic justice are at stake (I:8.1).

The ideas of the reasonable and the rational, and of a reasonable comprehensive doctrine, so important for an overlapping consensus, play a central role in this answer. So far I have used those ideas without much explanation. I must now remedy this lack since they are difficult ideas, and the idea of the reasonable especially, whether applied to persons, institutions, or doctrines, easily becomes vague and obscure. I try to mitigate this by fixing on two basic aspects of the reasonable as a virtue of persons engaged in social cooperation among equals. I then develop from those two aspects the content of the reasonable. I examine next how doing this provides a basis for toleration in a society marked by reasonable pluralism. With these things done (§§1–3), I discuss the way in which citizens' moral powers of the reasonable and the rational are modeled in the original position as a device of representation.

§ 1. The Reasonable and the Rational

1. What is it that distinguishes the reasonable from the rational? In everyday speech we are aware of a difference and common examples readily bring it out. We say: "Their proposal was perfectly rational given their strong bargaining position, but it was nevertheless highly unreasonable, even outrageous." Rather than define the reasonable directly, I specify two of its basic aspects as virtues of persons.[1]

---

1. The distinction between the reasonable and the rational goes back, I believe, to Kant: it is expressed in his distinction between the categorical and the hypothetical

Persons are reasonable in one basic aspect when, among equals say, they are ready to propose principles and standards as fair terms of cooperation and to abide by them willingly, given the assurance that others will likewise do so. Those norms they view as reasonable for everyone to accept and therefore as justifiable to them; and they are ready to discuss the fair terms that others propose.[2] The reasonable is an element of the idea of society as

---

imperative in the *Foundations* and his other writings. The first represents pure practical reason, the second represents empirical practical reason. For the purposes of a political conception of justice, I give the reasonable a more restricted sense and associate it, first, with the willingness to propose and honor fair terms of cooperation, and second, with the willingness to recognize the burdens of judgment and to accept their consequences. The distinction between the reasonable and the rational was instructively discussed in a general way some time ago by W. M. Sibley in "The Rational Versus the Reasonable," *Philosophical Review* 62 (October 1953):554–60. My discussion accords with his basic distinction as summarized on p. 560: knowing that people are rational we do not know the ends they will pursue, only that they will pursue them intelligently. Knowing that people are reasonable where others are concerned, we know that they are willing to govern their conduct by a principle from which they and others can reason in common; and reasonable people take into account the consequences of their actions on others' well-being. The disposition to be reasonable is neither derived from nor opposed to the rational but it is incompatible with egoism, as it is related to the disposition to act morally. Sibley's account of the reasonable is broader but consistent with that expressed by the two basic aspects of being reasonable used in the text.

2. I think both aspects of the reasonable (discussed in this and the next two sections) are closely connected with T. M. Scanlon's principle of moral motivation. This principle is one of the three basic principles of his contractualism, as stated in "Contractualism and Utilitarianism," in *Utilitarianism and Beyond,* edited by Amartya Sen and Bernard Williams (Cambridge: Cambridge University Press, 1982). I do not attempt to show the connection here but simply remark that Scanlon's principle is more than a psychological principle of motivation (though it is that) since it concerns the fundamental question why anyone should care about morality at all. The principle answers this by saying that we have a basic desire to be able to justify our actions to others on grounds they could not reasonably reject—reasonably, that is, given the desire to find principles that others similarly motivated could not reasonably reject. See pp. 104f., 115f. The two aspects of the reasonable as a virtue of persons one may see as two related expressions of this desire. To accept the connection between the two aspects of the reasonable and Scanlon's principle is to include this form of motivation in the conception of reasonable persons from which justice as fairness starts. Doing this does not explain this motivation, or say how it comes about. For the limited purpose of giving an account of stability, the moral psychology discussed later in §7 may serve. See also *Theory,* p. 478, where its analog appears at the end of

a system of fair cooperation and that its fair terms be reasonable for all to accept is part of its idea of reciprocity. As I have said (I:3.2) the idea of reciprocity lies between the idea of impartiality, which is altruistic (as moved by the general good), and the idea of mutual advantage understood as everyone's being advantaged with respect to one's present or expected situation as things are.

Reasonable persons, we say, are not moved by the general good as such but desire for its own sake a social world in which they, as free and equal, can cooperate with others on terms all can accept. They insist that reciprocity should hold within that world so that each benefits along with others.

By contrast, people are unreasonable in the same basic aspect when they plan to engage in cooperative schemes but are unwilling to honor, or even to propose, except as a necessary public pretense, any general principles or standards for specifying fair terms of cooperation. They are ready to violate such terms as suits their interests when circumstances allow.

2. Reasonable and rational agents are normally the units of responsibility in political and social life and may be charged with violations of reasonable principles and standards. The rational is, however, a distinct idea from the reasonable and applies to a single, unified agent (either an individual or corporate person) with the powers of judgment and deliberation in seeking ends and interests peculiarly its own. The rational applies to how these ends and interests are adopted and affirmed, as well as to how they are given priority. It also applies to the choice of means, in which case it is guided by such familiar principles as: to adopt the most effective means to ends, or to select the more probable alternative, other things equal.

Yet rational agents are not limited to means-ends reasoning,

---

moral development of the morality of principles. The point is, though, that in setting out justice as fairness we rely on the kind of motivation Scanlon takes as basic. In §7 below the basic desire to be able to justify our actions to others on grounds they could not reasonably reject I characterize as a conception-dependent desire.

as they may balance final ends by their significance for their plan of life as a whole, and by how well these ends cohere with and complement one another. Nor are rational agents as such solely self-interested: that is, their interests are not always interests in benefits to themselves. Every interest is an interest of a self (agent), but not every interest is in benefits to the self that has it. Indeed, rational agents may have all kinds of affections for persons and attachments to communities and places, including love of country and of nature; and they may select and order their ends in various ways.

What rational agents lack is the particular form of moral sensibility that underlies the desire to engage in fair cooperation as such, and to do so on terms that others as equals might reasonably be expected to endorse. I do not assume the reasonable is the whole of moral sensibility; but it includes the part that connects with the idea of fair social cooperation.[3] Rational agents approach being psychopathic when their interests are solely in benefits to themselves.

3. In justice as fairness the reasonable and the rational are taken as two distinct and independent basic ideas. They are distinct in that there is no thought of deriving one from the other; in particular, there is no thought of deriving the reasonable from the rational. In the history of moral thought some have tried to do this. They think the rational is more basic, for who does not endorse the (or an) idea of rationality (for there are several) as specified by such familiar principles as those above? They think that if the reasonable can be derived from the rational, that is, if some definite principles of justice can be derived from the preferences, or decisions, or agreements of merely

---

3. Rational people lack what Kant calls in the *Religion*, Ak, VI:26, "the predisposition to moral personality"; or in the present case, the particular form of moral sensibility that underlies the capacity to be reasonable. Kant's merely rational agent has only the predispositions to humanity and animality (to use his terms); this agent understands the meaning of the moral law, its conceptual content, but is unmoved by it: to such an agent it is simply a curious idea.

rational agents in suitably specified circumstances, then the reasonable is at last put on a firm basis. The moral skeptic has been answered.[4]

Justice as fairness rejects this idea. It does not try to derive the reasonable from the rational. Indeed, the attempt to do so may suggest that the reasonable is not basic and needs a basis in a way the rational does not. Rather, within the idea of fair cooperation the reasonable and the rational are complementary ideas. Each is an element in this fundamental idea and each connects with its distinctive moral power, respectively, with the capacity for a sense of justice and the capacity for a conception of the good. They work in tandem to specify the idea of fair terms of cooperation, taking into account the kind of social cooperation in question, the nature of the parties and their standing with respect to one another.[5]

As complementary ideas, neither the reasonable nor the rational can stand without the other. Merely reasonable agents would have no ends of their own they wanted to advance by fair cooperation; merely rational agents lack a sense of justice and fail to recognize the independent validity of the claims of others.[6] Only as a result of philosophy, or a subject in which the rational has a large place (as in economics or social decision theory), would anyone think it necessary to derive the reasonable from the rational, moved by the thought that only the latter was intelligible. It seems likely that any plausible derivation must situate rational agents in circumstances in which they are subject to certain appropriate conditions and these conditions will express the reasonable. As we saw in I:4, in the fundamental case of social cooperation within the basic structure of society, the representatives of citizens as reasonable and rational agents must be situated reasonably, that is, fairly or symmetrically, with no

4. David Gauthier's *Morals by Agreement* (Oxford: Clarendon Press, 1986) is an example of this idea.

5. How they work in tandem can be seen from the set up of the original position.

6. This is not to deny that given special loyalties or attachments, they would recognize others' claims, but not as having validity independent of those bonds.

52

one having superior bargaining advantages over the rest. This last is done by the veil of ignorance. To see justice as fairness as trying to derive the reasonable from the rational misinterprets the original position.[7]

It may not be possible to prove that the reasonable cannot be derived from the rational. A negative statement of this kind is simply a conjecture. The best one may be able to do is to show that the serious attempts (Gauthier's is an example) to derive the reasonable from the rational do not succeed, and so far as they appear to succeed, they rely at some point on conditions expressing the reasonable itself. If sound, these remarks suggest that in philosophy questions at the most fundamental level are not usually settled by conclusive argument. What is obvious to some persons and accepted as a basic idea is unintelligible to others. The way to resolve the matter is to consider after due reflection which view, when fully worked out, offers the most coherent and convincing account. About this, of course, judgments may differ.

4. A further basic difference between the reasonable and the rational is that the reasonable is public in a way the rational is not.[8] This means that it is by the reasonable that we enter as equals the public world of others and stand ready to propose, or to accept, as the case may be, fair terms of cooperation with them. These terms, set out as principles, specify the reasons we are to share and publicly recognize before one another as grounding our social relations. Insofar as we are reasonable, we are ready to work out the framework for the public social world,

7. Here I correct a remark in *Theory*, p. 16, where it is said that the theory of justice is a part of the theory of rational decision. From what we have just said, this is simply incorrect. What should have been said is that the account of the parties, and of their reasoning, uses the theory of rational decision, though only in an intuitive way. This theory is itself part of a political conception of justice, one that tries to give an account of reasonable principles of justice. There is no thought of deriving those principles from the concept of rationality as the sole normative concept. I believe that the text of *Theory* as a whole supports this interpretation.

8. Samuel Freeman emphasizes this point in his instructive discussion, "Reason and Agreement in Social Contract Views," *Philosophy and Public Affairs* 19 (Spring 1990):141–47.

a framework it is reasonable to expect everyone to endorse and act on, provided others can be relied on to do the same. If we cannot rely on them, then it may be irrational or self-sacrificial to act from those principles. Without an established public world, the reasonable may be suspended and we may be left largely with the rational, although the reasonable always binds *in foro interno,* to use Hobbes's phrase.

Finally, as we have seen, the reasonable (with its idea of reciprocity) is not the altruistic (the impartial acting solely for the interests of others) nor is it the concern for self (and moved by its ends and affections alone). In a reasonable society, most simply illustrated in a society of equals in basic matters, all have their own rational ends they hope to advance, and all stand ready to propose fair terms that others may reasonably be expected to accept, so that all may benefit and improve on what every one can do on their own. This reasonable society is neither a society of saints nor a society of the self-centered. It is very much a part of our ordinary human world, not a world we think of much virtue, until we find ourselves without it. Yet the moral power that underlies the capacity to propose, or to endorse, and then to be moved to act from fair terms of cooperation for their own sake is an essential social virtue all the same.

§ 2. The Burdens of Judgment

1. The first basic aspect of the reasonable, then, is the willingness to propose fair terms of cooperation and to abide by them provided others do. The second basic aspect, as I review now, is the willingness to recognize the burdens of judgment and to accept their consequences for the use of public reason in directing the legitimate exercise of political power in a constitutional regime.

Recall that in the first lecture (I:6) we noted two general facts about the public culture of a constitutional regime: the fact of reasonable pluralism and the fact that this diversity can be overcome only by the oppressive use of state power. These facts call for explanation. For why should free institutions lead to reasonable pluralism, and why should state power be required to suppress it? Why does not our conscientious attempt to reason with one another lead to reasonable agreement? It seems to do so in natural science, at least in the long run.

There are, of course, various explanations. We might suppose, say, that most people hold views that advance their own more narrow interests; and since their interests are different, so are their views. Or perhaps people are often irrational and not very bright, and this mixed with logical errors leads to conflicting opinions. But while such explanations explain much, they are too easy and not the kind we want. We want to know how reasonable disagreement is possible, for we always work at first within ideal theory. Thus we ask: how might reasonable disagreement come about?

2. One explanation is this. Let's say that reasonable disagreement is disagreement between reasonable persons: that is, between persons who have realized their two moral powers to a degree sufficient to be free and equal citizens in a constitutional regime, and who have an enduring desire to honor fair terms of cooperation and to be fully cooperating members of society. Given their moral powers, they share a common human reason, similar powers of thought and judgment: they can draw inferences, weigh evidence, and balance competing considerations.

The idea of reasonable disagreement involves an account of the sources, or causes, of disagreement between reasonable persons so defined. These sources I refer to as the burdens of judgment.[9] The account of these burdens must be such that it is fully compatible with, and so does not impugn, the reasonableness of those who disagree. What, then, goes wrong? An explanation of the right kind is that the sources of reasonable disagreement—the burdens of judgment—among reasonable persons are

---

9. The idea of the burdens of judgment should not be confused with the idea of the burden of proof in legal cases, whether, say, the burden of proof falls on the plaintiff or the defendant.

the many hazards involved in the correct (and conscientious) exercise of our powers of reason and judgment in the ordinary course of political life.

As reasonable and rational we have to make different kinds of judgments. As rational we have to balance our various ends and estimate their appropriate place in our way of life; and doing this confronts us with grave difficulties in making correct judgments of rationality. On the other hand, as reasonable we must assess the strength of peoples' claims, not only against our claims, but against one another, or on our common practices and institutions, all this giving rise to difficulties in our making sound reasonable judgments. In addition, there is the reasonable as it applies to our beliefs and schemes of thought, or the reasonable as appraising our use of our theoretical (and not our moral and practical) powers, and here too we meet the corresponding kinds of difficulties. We need to keep in mind these three kinds of judgments with their characteristic burdens.

3. Except for the last two sources below, the ones I mention are not peculiar to the reasonable and the rational in their moral and practical use; items (a) to (d) apply mainly to the theoretical uses of our reason. Also, the list I give is not complete. It covers only the more obvious sources.

a. The evidence—empirical and scientific—bearing on the case is conflicting and complex, and thus hard to assess and evaluate.

b. Even where we agree fully about the kinds of considerations that are relevant, we may disagree about their weight, and so arrive at different judgments.

c. To some extent all our concepts, and not only moral and political concepts, are vague and subject to hard cases; and this indeterminacy means that we must rely on judgment and interpretation (and on judgments about interpretations) within some range (not sharply specifiable) where reasonable persons may differ.

d. To some extent (how great we cannot tell) the way we

assess evidence and weigh moral and political values is shaped by our total experience, our whole course of life up to now; and our total experiences must always differ. Thus, in a modern society with its numerous offices and positions, its various divisions of labor, its many social groups and their ethnic variety, citizens' total experiences are disparate enough for their judgments to diverge, at least to some degree, on many if not most cases of any significant complexity.

e. Often there are different kinds of normative considerations of different force on both sides of an issue and it is difficult to make an overall assessment.[10]

f. Finally, as we note in referring to Berlin's view (V:6.2), any system of social institutions is limited in the values it can admit so that some selection must be made from the full range of moral and political values that might be realized. This is because any system of institutions has, as it were, a limited social space. In being forced to select among cherished values, or when we hold to several and must restrict each in view of the requirements of the others, we face great difficulties in setting priorities and making adjustments. Many hard decisions may seem to have no clear answer.

10. This source could, of course, be described from within a comprehensive moral doctrine, as when Nagel says that there are basic conflicts of value in which there seem to be decisive and sufficient (normative) reasons for two or more incompatible courses of action; and yet some decision must be made. Moreover, these reasons, he says, are not evenly balanced, and so it matters greatly what course is adopted; the lack of even balance holds because in such cases the values are incomparable: they are each specified by one of the several irreducibly different perspectives within which values arise; in particular, the perspectives that specify obligations, rights, utility, perfectionist ends, and personal commitments. Put another way, these values have different bases and this fact is reflected in their different formal features. These basic conflicts reveal what Nagel views as the fragmentation of value. See the essay with this name in *Mortal Questions* (Cambridge: Cambridge University Press, 1979), pp. 128–41. Nagel's discussion is not implausible, but a political conception tries to avoid, so far as possible, disputed philosophical theses and to give an account of the burdens of reason that rests on plain facts open to all. It suffices for our purposes simply to assert (e).

4. So much for some sources of the difficulties in arriving at agreement in judgment, sources that are compatible with those judging being fully reasonable. In noting these six sources—these burdens of judgment—we do not, of course, deny that prejudice and bias, self- and group interest, blindness and willfulness, play their all too familiar part in political life. But these sources of unreasonable disagreement stand in marked contrast to those compatible with everyone's being fully reasonable.

Religious and philosophical doctrines express views of the world and of our life with one another, severally and collectively, as a whole. Our individual and associative points of view, intellectual affinities, and affective attachments, are too diverse, especially in a free society, to enable those doctrines to serve as the basis of lasting and reasoned political agreement. Different conceptions of the world can reasonably be elaborated from different standpoints and diversity arises in part from our distinct perspectives. It is unrealistic—or worse, it arouses mutual suspicion and hostility—to suppose that all our differences are rooted solely in ignorance and perversity, or else in the rivalries for power, status, or economic gain.

These remarks lead to a fifth general fact[11] stated thus: that many of our most important judgments are made under conditions where it is not to be expected that conscientious persons with full powers of reason, even after free discussion, will all arrive at the same conclusion. Some conflicting reasonable judgments (especially important are those belonging under peoples' comprehensive doctrines) may be true, others false; conceivably, all may be false. These burdens of judgment are of first significance for a democratic idea of toleration.

§ 3. Reasonable Comprehensive Doctrines

1. The second basic aspect of our being reasonable is, I have said, our recognizing and being willing to bear the consequences

11. The first four general facts are given in I:6.

58

of the burdens of judgment. I shall now try to show how this aspect limits the scope of what reasonable persons think can be justified to others, and how this leads to a form of toleration and supports the idea of public reason (VI).

Assume first that reasonable persons affirm only reasonable comprehensive doctrines.[12] Now we need a definition of such doctrines. They have three main features. One is that a reasonable doctrine is an exercise of theoretical reason: it covers the major religious, philosophical, and moral aspects of human life in a more or less consistent and coherent manner. It organizes and characterizes recognized values so that they are compatible with one another and express an intelligible view of the world. Each doctrine will do this in ways that distinguish it from other doctrines, for example, by giving certain values a particular primacy and weight. In singling out which values to count as especially significant and how to balance them when they conflict, a reasonable comprehensive doctrine is also an exercise of practical reason. Both theoretical and practical reason (including as appropriate the rational) are used together in its formulation. Finally, a third feature is that while a reasonable comprehensive view is not necessarily fixed and unchanging, it normally belongs to, or draws upon, a tradition of thought and doctrine. Although stable over time, and not subject to sudden and unexplained changes, it tends to evolve slowly in the light of what, from its point of view, it sees as good and sufficient reasons.

This account of reasonable comprehensive doctrines is deliberately loose. We avoid excluding doctrines as unreasonable without strong grounds based on clear aspects of the reasonable itself. Otherwise our account runs the danger of being arbitrary and exclusive. Political liberalism counts many familiar and traditional doctrines—religious, philosophical, and moral—as reasonable even though we could not seriously entertain them for

---

12. As stated in the introduction, that political liberalism must use in its formulation an idea of a reasonable comprehensive doctrine, I owe to Wilfried Hinsch. See his account in §III of his introduction to a translation of my *Gesammelte Aufsätze, 1978–1989* (Frankfurt am Main: Suhrkamp, 1992).

ourselves, as we think they give excessive weight to some values and fail to allow for the significance of others. A tighter criterion is not, however, needed for the purposes of political liberalism.[13]

2. The evident consequence of the burdens of judgment is that reasonable persons do not all affirm the same comprehensive doctrine. Moreover, they also recognize that all persons alike, including themselves, are subject to those burdens, and so many reasonable comprehensive doctrines are affirmed, not all of which can be true (indeed none of them may be true). The doctrine any reasonable person affirms is but one reasonable doctrine among others. In affirming it, a person, of course, believes it to be true, or else reasonable, as the case may be.

Thus, it is not in general unreasonable to affirm any one of a number of reasonable comprehensive doctrines.[14] We recognize that our own doctrine has, and can have, for people generally, no special claims on them beyond their own view of its merits. Others who affirm doctrines different from ours are, we grant, reasonable also, and certainly not unreasonable. Since there are many reasonable doctrines, the idea of the reasonable does not require us, or others, to believe any specific reasonable doctrine, though we may do so. When we take the step beyond recognizing the reasonableness of a doctrine and affirm our belief in it, we are not being unreasonable.

3. Beyond this, reasonable persons will think it unreasonable to use political power, should they possess it, to repress comprehensive views that are not unreasonable, though different from their own. This is because, given the fact of reasonable pluralism,

13. Certainly, comprehensive doctrines will themselves, as they present their case in the background culture, urge far tighter standards of reasonableness and truth. Within that culture we may regard many doctrines as plainly unreasonable, or untrue, that we think it correct to count as reasonable by the criterion in the text. That criterion we should see as giving rather minimal conditions appropriate for the aims of political liberalism. I am indebted to Erin Kelly for this point.

14. In a particular case someone may, of course, affirm a reasonable doctrine in an unreasonable way, for example, blindly or capriciously. That does not make the doctrine as such unreasonable. A reasonable doctrine is one that can be affirmed in a reasonable way.

a public and shared basis of justification that applies to comprehensive doctrines is lacking in the public culture of a democratic society. But such a basis is needed to mark the difference, in ways acceptable to a reasonable public, between comprehensive beliefs as such and true comprehensive beliefs.[15]

Since many doctrines are seen to be reasonable, those who insist, when fundamental political questions are at stake, on what they take as true but others do not, seem to others simply to insist on their own beliefs when they have the political power to do so. Of course, those who do insist on their beliefs also insist that their beliefs alone are true: they impose their beliefs because, they say, their beliefs are true and not because they are their beliefs.[16] But this is a claim that all equally could make; it is also a claim that cannot be made good by anyone to citizens generally. So, when we make such claims others, who are themselves reasonable, must count us unreasonable. And indeed we are, as we want to use state power, the collective power of equal citizens, to prevent the rest from affirming their not unreasonable views.

To conclude: reasonable persons see that the burdens of judgment set limits on what can be reasonably justified to others, and so they endorse some form of liberty of conscience and freedom of thought. It is unreasonable for us to use political power, should we possess it, or share it with others, to repress comprehensive views that are not unreasonable.

4. To confirm this conclusion, let us look at the case from another point of view and say: citizens as free and equal have an equal share in the corporate political and coercive power of

15. I am much indebted here to Thomas Nagel, "Moral Conflict and Political Legitimacy," *Philosophy and Public Affairs* 17 (Summer 1987):227–37, where these points are made with greater elaboration; and with some revision, in his book *Partiality and Equality* (Oxford: Oxford University Press, 1991), chap. 14. I am also much indebted to Joshua Cohen, "Moral Pluralism and Political Consensus."

16. In the hardcover edition I quoted Bossuet as saying: "I have the right to persecute you, because I am right and you are wrong." I have learned, however, that this was only an interpretation of Bossuet's thought by Preserved Smith in his *History of Modern Culture* (New York: Henry Holt, 1932–34), p. 556 of Vol. II. I thank Alyssa Bernstein for finding my error.

society, and all are equally subject to the burdens of judgment. There is no reason, then, why any citizen, or association of citizens, should have the right to use the state's police power to decide constitutional essentials or basic questions of justice as that person's, or that association's, comprehensive doctrine directs. This can be expressed by saying that when equally represented in the original position, no citizen's representative could grant to any other person, or association of persons, the political authority to do that. Such authority is without grounds in public reason. What would be proposed instead is a form of toleration and freedom of thought consistent with the preceding reasoning.

Observe that here being reasonable is not an epistemological idea (though it has epistemological elements). Rather, it is part of a political ideal of democratic citizenship that includes the idea of public reason. The content of this ideal includes what free and equal citizens as reasonable can require of each other with respect to their reasonable comprehensive views. In this case they cannot require anything contrary to what the parties as their representatives in the original position could grant. So, for example, they could not grant that everyone must affirm a particular comprehensive view. As I note later (VI:4.4), this means that the guidelines and procedures of public reason are seen as selected in the original position and belong to the political conception of justice. As I remarked earlier (§1.4), the reasonable, in contrast with the rational, addresses the public world of others.[17] The original position as a device of representation helps to show how it does so.

5. I add two further comments. The first is about the skepticism that may seem to be suggested by the account of the burdens of judgment. Since skepticism must be avoided if an overlapping consensus of reasonable doctrines is to be possible, the

---

17. When understood as proposed by the parties in the original position, the guidelines of public reason can be seen as falling under the first aspect of the reasonable: they are principles proposed as fair terms of social cooperation in conducting public reason that we are ready to abide by provided others do.

account of those burdens must not proceed as a skeptical argument. Such arguments offer a philosophical analysis of the conditions of knowledge, say of the external world of objects. After examining our ordinary ways of inquiry, they come to the conclusion that we cannot know those objects because one or more of the necessary conditions of knowledge can never be satisfied. Descartes and Hume said this in their different ways.[18]

The account of the burdens of judgment does none of these things. It simply lists some of the circumstances that make political agreement in judgment, especially in judgments about comprehensive doctrines, far more difficult. This difficulty is borne out by historical experience, by centuries of conflict about religious, philosophical, and moral beliefs. Political liberalism does not question that many political and moral judgments of certain specified kinds are correct and it views many of them as reasonable. Nor does it question the possible truth of affirmations of faith. Above all, it does not argue that we should be hesitant and uncertain, much less skeptical, about our own beliefs. Rather, we are to recognize the practical impossibility of reaching reasonable and workable political agreement in judgment on the truth of comprehensive doctrines, especially an agreement that might serve the political purpose, say, of achieving peace and concord in a society characterized by religious and philosophical differences. The limited scope of this conclusion is of special importance. A constitutional regime does not require an agreement on a comprehensive doctrine: the basis of its social unity lies elsewhere.

6. A second comment involves the important distinction, first mentioned in I:6.2, between the fact of pluralism as such and the fact of reasonable pluralism. That a democracy is marked by the

18. See Barry Stroud, *The Significance of Philosophical Skepticism* (Oxford: Clarendon Press, 1984) for a careful examination of philosophical skepticism and the bearing of its arguments. Descartes's view is discussed in chap. 1 and off and on throughout the book. A brief comparison with Hume, showing his similarity with Descartes, is found on pp. 105–11 in a discussion of G. E. Moore.

fact of pluralism as such is not surprising, for there are always many unreasonable views.[19] But that there are also many reasonable comprehensive doctrines affirmed by reasonable people may seem surprising, as we like to see reason as leading to the truth and to think of the truth as one.

The question now arises whether this distinction between the fact of pluralism as such and the fact of reasonable pluralism affects the exposition of justice as fairness. The first consideration is this: we need to keep in mind the two stages of the exposition. In the first stage we set out justice as fairness as a freestanding view, an account of a political conception of justice that applies in the first instance to the basic structure and articulates two kinds of political values, those of political justice and of public reason (VI:4.1). Since the idea of an overlapping consensus is not introduced until the second stage, when the problem of stability is discussed, our question at the first stage is whether the distinction between the two forms of pluralism is relevant. Does it matter whether the parties assume that pluralism as such obtains or that reasonable pluralism obtains?

The answer is crucial: the same principles of justice are selected in both cases. The parties must always guarantee the basic rights and liberties of those for whom they are trustees. If they suppose reasonable pluralism obtains (I:6.2), they know that most of these liberties may already be secure as things are, but even if they could rely on that, they would for reasons of publicity select the two principles of justice, or similar principles. Besides, they must express in their selection of principles the political conception they find most congenial to the fundamental interests of the citizens they represent. On the other hand, if they assume pluralism as such to obtain, and hence that there may be comprehensive doctrines that would suppress, if they could, liberty of conscience and freedom of thought, the preced-

19. That there are doctrines that reject one or more democratic freedoms is itself a permanent fact of life, or seems so. This gives us the practical task of containing them—like war and disease—so that they do not overturn political justice.

ing considerations become all the more the urgent. At the first stage, then, the contrast between the two pluralisms does not affect the content of justice as fairness.

We can assume either fact as appropriate. To say that justice as fairness has broad scope, the parties suppose that pluralism as such obtains. To say that the content of justice as fairness is not influenced by the existence of unreason, that is, by the existence of unreasonable comprehensive doctrines, the parties suppose that reasonable pluralism obtains. Having the same content in each case shows both that justice as fairness is broad in scope and that its principles are not determined by unreason.

7. How about the second stage? The idea of an overlapping consensus is not introduced until this stage because the question of stability does not arise until the principles of justice are already provisionally selected. Then we have to check whether, when realized, just institutions as specified by those principles can gain sufficient support. Now, as we saw in I:6, the problem of stability for a democratic society requires that its political conception can be the focus of an overlapping consensus of reasonable doctrines that can support a constitutional regime. We need to show how an overlapping consensus on a political conception of justice, or parts thereof, such as a principle of toleration, can first arise.

How this might happen I discuss in IV:6–7. And when it does, then by the definition of such a consensus, the political conception is supported by a plurality of reasonable comprehensive doctrines that persist over time and maintain a sizable body of adherents. Views that would suppress altogether the basic rights and liberties affirmed in the political conception, or suppress them in part, say its liberty of conscience, may indeed exist, as there will always be such views. But they may not be strong enough to undermine the substantive justice of the regime. That is the hope; there can be no guarantee.

What if it turns out that the principles of justice as fairness cannot gain the support of reasonable doctrines, so that the case for stability fails? Justice as fairness as we have stated it is then in difficulty. We should have to see whether acceptable changes in the principles of justice would achieve stability; or indeed whether stability could obtain for any democratic conception. I do not pursue this inquiry but assume, on the basis of a number of plausible considerations, that the case for the stability of justice as fairness, or some similar conception, goes through.

§ 4. The Publicity Condition: Its Three Levels

1. A well-ordered society, as defined in I:6, is regulated by an effective public conception of justice. Since we want the idea of such a society to be suitably realistic, we assume it to exist under circumstances of justice. These circumstances are of two kinds: first, there are the objective circumstances of moderate scarcity, and second, the subjective circumstances of justice. These latter circumstances are, in general, the fact of pluralism as such; although in a well-ordered society of justice as fairness, they include the fact of reasonable pluralism. This last fact and its possibility we must try to understand.

Now the idea of publicity as understood in justice as fairness has three levels, which may be described as follows:

The first has already been mentioned in I:6. This level is achieved when society is effectively regulated by public principles of justice: citizens accept and know that others likewise accept those principles, and this knowledge in turn is publicly recognized. Further, the institutions of the basic structure of society are just (as defined by those principles) and everyone with reason recognizes this. They do so on the basis of commonly shared beliefs confirmed by methods of inquiry and ways of reasoning generally accepted as appropriate for questions of political justice.

The second level of publicity concerns the general beliefs in the light of which first principles of justice themselves can be accepted, that is, the general beliefs about human nature and the way political and social institutions generally work, and indeed all such beliefs relevant to political justice. Citizens in a well-ordered society roughly agree on these beliefs because they can be supported (as at the first level) by publicly shared methods of inquiry and forms of reasoning. As discussed in VI:4, I assume these methods to be familiar from common sense and to include the procedures and conclusions of science and social thought, when these are well established and not controversial. It is precisely these general beliefs, reflecting the current public views in a well-ordered society, that we—that is, you and I who are setting up justice as fairness (I:4.6)—ascribe to the parties in the original position.

The third and last level of publicity has to do with the full justification of the public conception of justice as it would be presented in its own terms. This justification includes everything that we would say—you and I—when we set up justice as fairness and reflect why we proceed in one way rather than another. At this level I suppose this full justification also to be publicly known, or better, at least to be publicly available. This weaker condition (that full justification be available) allows for the possibility that some will not want to carry philosophical reflection about political life so far, and certainly no one is required to. But if citizens wish to, the full justification is present in the public culture, reflected in its system of law and political institutions, and in the main historical traditions of their interpretation.

2. Let us stipulate that a well-ordered society satisfies all three levels of publicity so that what we may call "the full publicity condition" is satisfied. (I reserve the adjective "full" for the aspects of the conception of justice of a well-ordered society.) This full condition may seem much too strong. It is adopted, though, because it is appropriate for a political conception of justice for reasonable and rational citizens who are free and equal. The condition may be less compelling for comprehensive doctrines generally; but whether and how far it applies to them is left open as a separate question.

Here it is relevant that political society is distinctive in two ways. As I discuss in IV:1.2, one is that it specifies a relationship between persons within the basic structure of society, a society we have assumed is closed: it is self-contained and has no relations to other societies (I:2.1 and 7.1). We enter it only by birth and exit only by death. The other distinctive aspect of the political is that, while political power is always coercive power, in a constitutional regime it is the power of the public, that is, the power of free and equal citizens as a collective body. In addition, the institutions of the basic structure have deep and long-term social effects and in fundamental ways shape citizens' character and aims, the kinds of persons they are and aspire to be.

It is fitting, then, that the fair terms of social cooperation between citizens as free and equal should meet the requirements of full publicity. For if the basic structure relies on coercive sanctions, however rarely and scrupulously applied, the grounds of its institutions should stand up to public scrutiny. When a political conception of justice satisfies this condition, and basic social arrangements and individual actions are fully justifiable, citizens can give reasons for their beliefs and conduct before one another confident that this avowed reckoning itself will strengthen and not weaken public understanding.[20] The political order does not, it seems, depend on historically accidental or established delusions, or other mistaken beliefs resting on the deceptive appearances of institutions that mislead us as to how they work. Of course, there can be no certainty about this. But publicity ensures, so far as practical measures allow, that citizens are in a position to know and to accept the pervasive influences of the basic structure that shape their conception of themselves, their character and ends. As we shall see, that citizens should be in this position is a condition of their realizing their freedom as fully autonomous, politically speaking. It means that in their public political life nothing need be hidden.[21]

---

20. See *Theory*, pp. 478, 582.

21. The text does not say that nothing is hidden but only that nothing need be hidden. We cannot guarantee that nothing is hidden, for there is always much we do not and perhaps cannot know, and many ways in which we can be misled by institutional appearances. But perhaps we can make sure that nothing need be hidden; in a free society that all correctly recognize as just there is no need for the illusions and

3. Now observe that the first level of the publicity condition is easily modeled in the original position: we simply require the parties as representatives to assess conceptions of justice bearing in mind that the principles they agree to must serve as a public political conception of justice. Principles are to be rejected that might work quite well provided they were not publicly acknowledged, or provided the general facts upon which they are founded are not commonly known or believed.

For example, consider the doctrine of pure penal law as discussed by later scholastic writers.[22] This doctrine distinguishes between natural law and the law of the sovereign as based on the sovereign's legitimate authority. It is a moral fault to violate natural law, but depending on the intentions of the lawgiver and the kind of law in question, it is not a fault not to do what the sovereign's law requires. While there is no law without some obligation, in this case the obligation consists only in not resisting the sovereign's penalty should one be apprehended. Plainly, in a country where the doctrine of penal law is publicly accepted as applying to tax laws, it may be difficult to have a fair system of, say, income taxation. People will see no wrong in concealing their income and not paying taxes; this burdens the government's penal power and undermines a public sense of fairness. This kind of case illustrates how the parties must weigh the consequences of the public knowledge of proposed principles and the principles of justice they adopt will depend on these assessments.

---

delusions of ideology for society to work properly and for citizens to accept it willingly. In this sense a well-ordered society may lack ideological, or false, consciousness.

22. This is a late scholastic doctrine much debated in the works of the Spanish theologians from Vitoria (1530) to Suarez (1612). The deeper philosophical importance of the doctrine is that it reflects a divide between those who make God's intellect primary in determining law and those who make God's will primary. See Thomas E. Davitt, SJ, *The Nature of Law* (St. Louis: Herder, 1951). The idea of pure penal law seems to have been widespread among the poorer people in Spain as a way to justify resistance to the sales and wood taxes imposed by the Crown as it sought to recoup its losses following the expulsion of the Moors. See William Daniel, SJ, *The Purely Penal Law Theory* (Rome: Gregorian University Press, 1968), chap. 4. For these references I am indebted to Paul Weithman and Seana Shiffrin.

The modeling of the second level of full publicity is also straightforward: it is, in effect, modeled by the veil of ignorance. This level is simply that the general beliefs that are used by the parties in weighing conceptions of justice must also be publicly known. Since the parties' reasoning is a representation of the grounds for the public conception of justice, citizens in a well-ordered society know what general beliefs are held to support the recognized principles of justice and belong to their complete public justification. This presupposes that, when the original position is set up, we stipulate that the parties must reason only from general beliefs shared by citizens generally, as part of their public knowledge. These beliefs are the general facts on which their selection of the principles of justice is based and, as we saw (I:4.4), the veil of ignorance allows these beliefs as reasons.[23]

As for the point of view of you and me—the point of view of the full justification of justice as fairness in its own terms—this point of view we model by our description of the thought and judgment of fully autonomous citizens in the well-ordered society of justice as fairness. For they can do anything we can do, for they are an ideal description of what a democratic society would be like should we fully honor our political conception.

4. Two last comments. First, in discussing previously how the second level of publicity is modeled by the veil of ignorance, I said that the parties must reason only from general beliefs shared by citizens as part of public knowledge. Here the question arises:

23. This stipulation was discussed in "Kantian Constructivism in Moral Theory," *Journal of Philosophy* 77 (September 1990):565f. It raises the question whether the principles of justice might change over time as the theory of human nature and knowledge of social institutions changed. I answered that the possibility of such a change is just that, a mere possibility mentioned to explain the nature of justice as fairness. I went on to say that "changes in the theory of human nature or social theory generally which do not affect the feasibility of the ideals of the person and of a well-ordered society do not affect the agreement of the parties in the original position. It is hard to imagine realistically any new knowledge that should convince us that these ideals are not feasible, given what we know about the general nature of the world, as opposed to our particular social and historical circumstances. . . . Such advances in human knowledge as may take place do not affect our moral conception." Here "our moral conception" means our public conception of justice.

what is the reason for limiting the parties in this way and not allowing them to take into account all true beliefs? Some comprehensive religious, philosophical, or moral doctrines must be true, even if they only deny false or incoherent doctrines. Why isn't the most reasonable political conception of justice that which is founded on the whole truth and not simply on a part of it, much less on commonly based beliefs that happen to be publicly accepted at any given time? This is a leading objection to the idea of public reason and I shall discuss it in VI.

A second comment is that the idea of publicity belongs to the wide rather than the narrow role of a political conception of justice.[24] The narrow role is restricted to achieving the more or less minimum conditions of effective social cooperation, for example, to specifying standards to settle competing claims and to setting up rules for coordinating and stabilizing social arrangements. Public norms are regarded as inhibiting self- or group-centered tendencies, and aimed at encouraging less limited sympathies. Any political conception or moral doctrine endorses these requirements in some form.

Yet such requirements do not involve the publicity condition. Once this condition is imposed, a political conception assumes a wide role as part of public culture. Not only are its first principles embodied in political and social institutions and in public traditions of their interpretation, but the derivation of citizens' rights, liberties, and opportunities also contains a conception of citizens as free and equal. In this way citizens are made aware of and educated to this conception. They are presented with a way of regarding themselves that otherwise they would most likely never be able to entertain. To realize the full publicity condition is to realize a social world within which the ideal of citizenship can be learned and may elicit an effective desire to be that kind of person. This political conception as educator characterizes the wide role.

---

24. The terms *narrow* and *wide* are suggested by a similar distinction drawn by J. L. Mackie, *Ethics* (New York: Penguin, 1977), pp. 106f., 134ff.

§ 5. Rational Autonomy: Artificial not Political

1. I now turn to the distinction between citizens' rational and full autonomy and to how these conceptions are modeled in the original position. Our task is to explain how the conditions, imposed on the parties in the original position along with the description of their deliberations, model these conceptions and how citizens think of themselves as free and equal.

As we saw in I:5, citizens think of themselves as free in three respects: first, as having the moral power to form, to revise, and rationally to pursue a conception of the good; second, as being self-authenticating sources of valid claims; and third, as capable of taking responsibility for their ends. Being free in these respects enables citizens to be both rationally and fully autonomous. Rational autonomy, which I take up first, rests on persons' intellectual and moral powers. It is shown in their exercising their capacity to form, to revise, and to pursue a conception of the good, and to deliberate in accordance with it. It is shown also in their capacity to enter into an agreement with others (when subject to reasonable constraints).

Thus, rational autonomy is modeled by making the original position a case of pure procedural justice. That is, whatever principles the parties select from the list of alternatives presented to them are accepted as just. Put another way, following the idea that citizens themselves (via their representatives) are to specify the fair terms of their cooperation (and putting aside for the present the criterion of reflective equilibrium), the outcome of the original position yields, we conjecture, the appropriate principles of justice for free and equal citizens.

This contrasts with perfect procedural justice, where there is an independent and already given criterion of what is just (or fair), and the procedure can be designed to insure an outcome satisfying that criterion. This is illustrated by the familiar example of dividing a cake: if equal division is accepted as fair, then we simply require the person who cuts the cake to have the last piece. (I forego the assumptions necessary to make the illustration rigorous.) The essential feature of pure procedural justice, as opposed to perfect procedural justice, is that what is just is specified by the outcome of the procedure, whatever it may be. There is no prior and already given criterion against which the outcome is to be checked.[25]

2. Taking the original position as a case of pure procedural justice, we describe the parties' deliberations so that they model citizens' rational autonomy. To see this, we say there are the two ways in which the parties are rationally autonomous. The first way is that the appropriate principles of justice for specifying fair terms of social cooperation are those that would be selected as the outcome of a process of rational deliberation, a process visualized as being carried out by the parties. The appropriate weight of reasons for and against the various principles available is given by their weight for the parties, and the weight of all reasons on balance determines the principles that would be agreed to. Pure procedural justice means that in their rational deliberations the parties do not view themselves as required to apply, or as bound by, any antecedently given principles of right and justice. Put another way, they recognize no standpoint external to their own point of view as rational representatives from which they are constrained by prior and independent principles of justice. This models the idea that when citizens are fairly situated with respect to one another, it is up to them to specify the fair terms of social cooperation in light of what they each regard as to their advantage, or good. Recall (from I:4) that those terms are not laid down by some outside authority, say by God's law; nor are they recognized as fair by reference to a prior and independent order of values known by rational intuition.

The second way in which the parties are rationally autonomous is in the nature of the interests that guide their delibera-

25. In the case of imperfect procedural justice there is again an independent criterion of the just outcome, but we cannot design a procedure sure to achieve it in all, but only, we hope, in most cases. A criminal trial is an example: only true offenders are to be found guilty but miscarriages of justice are bound to occur. For a further discussion of these contrasts, see *Theory,* pp. 85f.

tions as citizens' representatives. Since citizens are regarded as having the two moral powers, we ascribe to them two corresponding higher-order interests in developing and exercising these powers. To say that these interests are "higher-order" interests means that, as the fundamental idea of the person is specified, these interests are viewed as basic and hence as normally regulative and effective. Someone who has not developed and cannot exercise the moral powers to the minimum requisite degree cannot be a normal and fully cooperating member of society over a complete life. From this it follows that as citizens' representatives the parties adopt principles that guarantee conditions securing for those powers their adequate development and full exercise.[26]

In addition, we suppose that the parties represent citizens regarded as having at any given time a determinate conception of the good, that is, a conception specified by certain definite final ends, attachments, and loyalties to particular persons and institutions, and interpreted in the light of some comprehensive religious, philosophical, or moral doctrine. To be sure, the parties do not know the content of these determinate conceptions, or the doctrines used to interpret them. But they still have a third higher-order interest to guide them, for they must try to adopt principles of justice that enable the persons represented to protect and advance some determinate (but unspecified) conceptions of the good over a complete life, allowing for possible changes of mind and conversions from one comprehensive conception to another.

To sum up, just as citizens are rationally autonomous in two ways—they are free within the limits of political justice to pursue their (permissible) conceptions of the good; and they are motivated to secure their higher-order interests associated with their moral powers—so the parties are rationally autonomous in two ways: they are free within the constraints of the original position

26. These grounds of the basic rights and liberties are discussed in "The Basic Liberties and Their Priority," pp. 310–24, 333–40.

to agree to whatever principles of justice they think most to the advantage of those they represent; and in estimating this advantage they consider those persons' higher-order interests. In both ways, therefore, the description of the parties models citizens' rational autonomy.

Observe that rational autonomy is but an aspect of freedom, and differs from full autonomy. As merely rationally autonomous the parties are but artificial persons we fashion to inhabit the original position as a device of representation. Thus the tag to the title of this section: "Artificial not Political." Here "artificial" is understood in the older sense of characterizing something as an artifice of reason, for such is the original position.

3. Before we discuss full autonomy, however, we must mention here (and later resolve) a problem raised by the veil of ignorance. It is this: from what we have said so far, the restrictions on information imposed by that constraint mean that the parties have only the three higher-order interests to guide their deliberations. These interests are purely formal: for example, the sense of justice is the highest-order interest in developing and exercising the capacity to understand, to apply, and to act from whatever principles of justice are rationally adopted by the parties. This capacity assures the parties that once their undertaking is made, it can be complied with and hence is not in vain; but that assurance does not by itself favor any particular principles of justice. Similar considerations hold for the other two higher-order interests. How, then, can the parties make a rational agreement on specific principles that are better designed than the other available alternatives to protect the determinate interests (conceptions of the good) of those they represent?

Here we introduce the idea of primary goods. We stipulate that the parties evaluate the available principles by estimating how well they secure the primary goods essential to realize the higher-order interests of the person for whom each acts as a trustee. In this way we endow the parties with sufficiently specific aims so that their rational deliberations reach a definite result. To identify the primary goods we look to social background conditions and general all-purpose means normally needed for developing and exercising the two moral powers and for effectively pursuing conceptions of the good with widely different contents.

In V:3–4 primary goods are specified to include such things as the basic rights and liberties covered by the first principle of justice, freedom of movement, and free choice of occupation protected by fair equality of opportunity of the first part of the second principle, and income and wealth and the social bases of self-respect. It is rational, then, for the parties to use the primary goods to assess principles of justice.

4. To conclude the account of how parties' deliberations model citizens' rational autonomy: this autonomy depends, we said, upon the interests that the parties are concerned to protect and not solely on their not being bound by any prior and independent principles of right and justice. Were the parties moved to protect only the material and physical desires of those they represent, say their desires for money and wealth, for food and drink, we might think that the original position modeled citizens' heteronomy rather than their rational autonomy. But at the basis of the parties' reliance on primary goods is their recognition that these goods are essential all-purpose means to realize the higher-order interests connected with citizens' moral powers and their determinate conceptions of the good (so far as the restrictions on information permit the parties to know this). The parties are trying to guarantee the political and social conditions for citizens to pursue their good and to exercise the moral powers that characterize them as free and equal.

If we suppose that citizens give the parties instructions as to how they want their interests represented, and if these instructions are followed in how we have said the parties deliberate under the constraints of the original position, then citizens' motivation in giving those instructions is not heteronomous or self-centered. In a democratic culture we expect, and indeed want, citizens to care about their basic liberties and opportunities in order to develop and exercise their moral powers and to pursue

76

their conceptions of the good. We think they show a lack of self-respect and weakness of character in not doing so.

Thus, the aim of the parties is to agree on principles of justice that enable the citizens they represent to become full persons, that is, adequately to develop and exercise fully their moral powers and to pursue the determinate conceptions of the good they come to form. The principles of justice must lead to a scheme of basic institutions—a social world—congenial to this end.

§ 6. Full Autonomy: Political not Ethical

1. We have just seen that citizens' rational autonomy is modeled in the original position by the way the parties deliberate as their representatives. By contrast, citizens' full autonomy is modeled by the structural aspects of the original position, that is, by how the parties are situated with respect to one another and by the limits on information to which their deliberations are subject. To see how this modeling is done, consider the idea of full autonomy.

Note that it is not the parties but citizens of a well-ordered society in their public life who are fully autonomous. This means that in their conduct citizens not only comply with the principles of justice, but they also act from these principles as just. Moreover, they recognize these principles as those that would be adopted in the original position. It is in their public recognition and informed application of the principles of justice in their political life, and as their effective sense of justice directs, that citizens achieve full autonomy. Thus, full autonomy is realized by citizens when they act from principles of justice that specify the fair terms of cooperation they would give to themselves when fairly represented as free and equal persons.

Here I stress that full autonomy is achieved by citizens: it is a political and not an ethical value. By that I mean that it is realized in public life by affirming the political principles of justice and enjoying the protections of the basic rights and liberties; it is also realized by participating in society's public affairs and sharing in its collective self-determination over time. This full autonomy of political life must be distinguished from the ethical values of autonomy and individuality, which may apply to the whole of life, both social and individual, as expressed by the comprehensive liberalisms of Kant and Mill. Justice as fairness emphasizes this contrast: it affirms political autonomy for all but leaves the weight of ethical autonomy to be decided by citizens severally in light of their comprehensive doctrines.

2. Clearly the satisfaction of the full publicity condition (described in §4 above) is necessary for the achievement of full autonomy for citizens generally. Only if the full explanation and justification of justice as fairness is publicly available can citizens come to understand its principles in accordance with the idea of society as a fair system of cooperation. All this presupposes that the fundamental ideas of justice as fairness are present in the public culture, or at least implicit in the history of its main institutions and the traditions of their interpretation.

Now, as remarked above, the basic elements of full autonomy are modeled in the original position in its structural aspects. From the preceding lecture (I:4) we know that these aspects model what we regard—here and now—as fair conditions under which the representatives of free and equal persons are to specify the terms of social cooperation in the case of the basic structure. They also model what, for the special case of that structure, we regard as appropriate restrictions on what the parties are to count as good reasons. Beyond this, the original position also requires the parties to select (if possible) principles that may be stable, given the fact of reasonable pluralism; and hence to select principles that can be the focus of an overlapping consensus of reasonable doctrines.

Since citizens' full autonomy is expressed by acting from the public principles of justice understood as specifying the fair terms of cooperation they would give to themselves when they are fairly situated, their full autonomy is modeled by how the original position is set up. Full autonomy is modeled by the reasonable conditions imposed on the parties as rationally autonomous. Citizens realize that autonomy by acting from the political conception of justice guided by its public reason, and in their pursuit of the good in public and nonpublic life.

3. We have yet to say why the original position is regarded as fair. Here we appeal to the fundamental idea of equality as found in the public political culture of a democratic society just as we did with the three ways in which citizens regard themselves as free persons (I:5). We noted this idea in saying that citizens are equal in virtue of possessing, to the requisite minimum degree, the two moral powers and the other capacities that enable us to be normal and fully cooperating members of society. All who meet this condition have the same basic rights, liberties, and opportunities, and the same protections of the principles of justice.

To model this equality in the original position we say that the parties, as representatives of those who meet this condition, are symmetrically situated. This requirement is fair because in establishing the fair terms of social cooperation (in the case of the basic structure) the only relevant feature of persons is their possessing the moral powers (to the sufficient minimum degree) and having the normal capacities to be a cooperating member of society over a complete life. Features relating to social position, native endowment, and historical accident, as well as to the content of persons' determinate conceptions of the good, are irrelevant, politically speaking, and hence placed behind the veil of ignorance (I:4.2–3). Of course, some of those features may be relevant as decided by the principles of justice for our claim to hold this or that public office, or to qualify for this or that more highly rewarded position; and those features may also be relevant for our membership in this or that association or social group within society. However, they are not relevant for the status of equal citizenship shared by all members of society.

Therefore, accepting the highly general considered conviction expressed by the precept that equals in all relevant respects are to be represented equally, it follows that it is fair that citizens, viewed as free and equal persons, when represented equally in the original position, are represented fairly.

4. As noted above, this idea of equality recognizes that some persons have special traits and abilities that qualify them for offices of greater responsibility with their attendant rewards.[27] For example, judges are expected to have a deeper understanding of society's conception of political justice than others, and a greater facility in applying its principles and in reaching reasonable decisions, especially in the more difficult cases. The judicial virtues depend on acquired wisdom and require special training. Although such special abilities and knowledge make those who possess them better qualified than others for positions of judicial responsibility (the fulfillment of which entitles them to the rewards of office); nevertheless, given every one's actual role and status in a well-ordered society, including the status of equal citizenship, all citizens' sense of justice is equally sufficient relative to what is expected of them. Everyone is, therefore, represented equally in the original position. And that being so, all receive the same protections of the public principles of justice.

Observe further the following: all citizens in a well-ordered society conform to its public requirements and hence all are (more or less) above reproach from the standpoint of political justice.[28] This follows from the stipulation that everyone has an equally effective sense of political justice. The usual differences in individuals in these matters do not exist. Since we suppose that in a well-ordered society there are many social and economic inequalities, they cannot be accounted for by how closely indi-

---

27. These are variations "above the line" as described in V:3.5. What is said there amplifies the text above.

28. It is essential here to add that they are above reproach, politically and legally speaking, and not above reproach, morally speaking, or all things considered. It would be an error to say, for example, that the more fortunate or those lucky in life, and who affirm and honor the principles of justice, may consider themselves above reproach, just like that. After all, perhaps they can honor the requirements of public justice more easily. Some would say we ought never to consider ourselves above reproach, once we look at our life as whole from a religious, philosophical, or moral point of view.

viduals respect the requirements of public justice. The political conception of justice regulating these inequalities, whatever it is, cannot be the precept: to persons according to their political virtue.[29]

§ 7. The Basis of Moral Motivation in the Person

1. I begin by listing in summary fashion the basic elements of the conceptions of citizens as reasonable and rational. Some of these are familiar, others are still to be discussed.

First, the familiar: these are a) the two moral powers, the capacity for a sense of justice and the capacity for a conception of the good. As necessary for the exercise of the moral powers we add b) the intellectual powers of judgment, thought, and inference. Citizens are also assumed c) to have at any given time a determinate conception of the good interpreted in the light of a (reasonable) comprehensive view. Finally, we suppose d) that citizens have the requisite capacities and abilities to be normal and cooperating members of society over a complete life. These elements are set out in I:3–5, and we assume them to be realized. In having these powers to the essential minimum degree, citizens are equal (§6.3).

Besides these elements, citizens have four special features which I take as aspects of their being reasonable and having this form of moral sensibility. As discussed in §1, there is a) their readiness to propose fair terms of cooperation it is reasonable to expect others to endorse, as well as their willingness to abide by these terms provided others can be relied on to do likewise. Then as we considered in §2, they b) recognize the burdens of judgment as limiting what can be justified to others and affirm only reasonable comprehensive doctrines.

Beyond this and still familiar, we suppose c) that not only are they normal and fully cooperating members of society, but they further want to be, and to be recognized as, such members. This

---

29. See *Theory*, §48.

supports their self-respect as citizens. So does counting certain primary goods, such as the equal basic rights and liberties, the fair value of the political liberties and fair equality of opportunity, as social bases of self-respect.[30] Finally, we say d) that citizens have what I shall call "a reasonable moral psychology" sketched below.

2. To elaborate points (a) and (b) above concerning the moral sensibility of the reasonable, I distinguish three kinds of desires as follows:

First, object-dependent desires: here the object of desire, or the state of affairs that fulfills it, can be described without the use of any moral conceptions, or reasonable or rational principles. This definition presupposes some way of distinguishing moral from nonmoral conceptions and principles; but let us assume we have some mutually agreed way of doing this; or else that our judgments usually agree.

Indefinitely many kinds of desires are object-dependent: they include such bodily desires as those for food and drink and sleep; desires to engage in pleasurable activities of innumerable kinds as well as desires that depend on social life: desires for status, power and glory, and for property and wealth. Add to these attachments and affections, loyalties and devotions of many kinds, and desires to pursue certain vocations and to prepare oneself for them. But, as many vocations include a moral description, the corresponding desire falls in one of the categories discussed below.

3. Next, there are principle-dependent desires. What distinguishes these desires is that the object or aim of the desire, or the activity in which we desire to engage, cannot be described without using the principles, rational or reasonable as the case may be, that enter into specifying that activity. Only a rational or reasonable being who can understand and apply these principles, or who has a reasonable hope of doing so, can have these desires.[31]

---

30. See V:3.

31. It is important to stress that the force, or weight, of principle-dependent desires is given entirely by the principle to which the desire is attached, and not by the

Principle-dependent desires are of two kinds, turning on whether the principle in question is rational or reasonable.

First, rational principles we have mentioned in §1.2: such principles as a) to adopt the most effective means to our ends; and b) to select the more probable alternative, other things equal. To these add: c) to prefer the greater good (which helps to account for scheduling and adjusting ends to be mutually supporting); and d) to order our objectives (by priorities) when they conflict.

Let us view these principles as given by enumeration and not derived from a definition of practical rationality, as there is no agreement on the best way of defining this conception. For the present we have to allow that there are different conceptions of rationality, at least in certain kinds of cases such as decisions under great uncertainty. As we saw in §1, the general idea is that these principles guide a single agent in rational deliberation, whether that agent be an individual or association, or a community or government.

The second kind of principle-dependent desires are tied to reasonable principles: those that regulate how a plurality of agents (or a community or society of agents), whether of individual persons or groups, are to conduct themselves in their relations with one another. Principles of fairness and justice that define the fair terms of cooperation are canonical examples. So are principles associated with the moral virtues recognized by common sense such as truthfulness and fidelity.

4. Finally, there are also conception-dependent desires. For us

---

psychological strength of the desire itself. This strength I assume to exist and it may enter into explanations of how people in fact behave but it can never enter into how they should behave, or should have behaved, morally speaking. A person with a good will, to use Kant's term, is someone whose principle-dependent desires have strengths in complete accordance with the force, or priority, of the principles to which they are attached. This explanatory remark holds also of conception-dependent desires, mentioned later in the text. In this case the many desires attached to the conception will form a hierarchy given by the ordering of the various principles associated with the conception in question. I am indebted to Christine Korsgaard for valuable discussion on this and other points in this and the following section.

these are the most important, for reasons that will become clear. These desires can be described by saying that the principles we desire to act from are seen as belonging to, and as helping to articulate, a certain rational or reasonable conception, or a political ideal.

For example, we may desire to conduct ourselves in a manner appropriate to someone who is rational, whose conduct is guided by practical reasoning. Desiring to be this kind of person involves having and acting from these principle-dependent desires, and not only from object-dependent desires governed by custom and habit. However, the principles specifying principle-dependent desires must be suitably related to the conception in question. Our reasoning about our future presupposes, let us say, a conception of ourselves as enduring over time, from the past into the future. To speak of our having conception-dependent desires we must be able to form the corresponding conception and to see how the principles belong to and help to articulate it.[32]

Plainly, for us the main case is the ideal of citizenship as characterized in justice as fairness. The structure and content of this conception of justice lay out how, by the use of the original position, the principles and standards of justice for society's basic institutions belong to and help to articulate the conception of reasonable and rational citizens as free and equal. Thus we have an ideal of citizens as such persons. When we say, as we said above in c), that not only are citizens normal and fully cooperating members of society, but further they want to be, and to be recognized as, such members, we are saying that they want to realize in their person, and have it recognized that they realize, that ideal of citizens.

Note here the obvious non-Humean character of this account of motivation and how it runs counter to attempts to limit the

32. On this topic, see the instructive account by Thomas Nagel, *The Possibility of Altruism* (Oxford: Clarendon Press, 1970), pt. II, pp. 27–76, on which I rely here. See also his *The View From Nowhere* (New York: Oxford University Press, 1986), pp. 132ff.

84

kinds of motives people may have. Once we grant—what seems plainly true—that there exist principle-dependent and conception-dependent desires, along with desires to realize various political and moral ideals, then the class of possible motives is wide open. Capable of reason and judgment, we can understand complex religious and philosophical, moral and political doctrines of right and justice, as well as doctrines of the good. We may find ourselves drawn to the conceptions and ideals that both the right and the good express. How is one to fix limits on what people might be moved by in thought and deliberation and hence may act from?[33]

Thus, the account of justice as fairness connects the desire to realize a political ideal of citizenship with citizens' two moral powers and their normal capacities, as these are educated to that ideal by the public culture and its historical traditions of interpre-

---

33. To illustrate: suppose that in some fashion the conception-dependent desire that Scanlon proposes (the basic desire to act in ways that can be justified to others) or the conception-dependent desire to act in ways worthy of a reasonable and equal citizen, becomes one of the desires by which we are moved. Then to ascertain what answers to that desire, what it means to act in ways that can be justified to others, or in ways worthy of a reasonable and equal citizen, will call upon reasoning of many kinds. A line of thought and reasoning is needed to spell out what the conception-dependent desire requires. This means, then, that once conception-dependent desires are admitted as elements of what Williams calls "a person's motivational set"—I believe he would allow for this possibility—then the line between his allegedly Humean view of motivation and Kant's view, or ones related to it, begins to dissolve. To see this we have only to suppose that Kant's idea of the categorical imperative is coherent and say that a person with a good will is some one effectively moved by the conception-dependent desire to act as that imperative requires. Of course, the view of the historical Hume was different. His official doctrine seems to lack a view of practical reasoning altogether, or at best to allow for only instrumental reasoning. But leaving this aside, if it is asked how principle- and conception-dependent desires become elements in people's motivational sets in the first place, then the superficial answer, proposed in the text, is that they are learned from the public political culture. This is part of the idea of publicity. How these conceptions and ideals enter into the public culture itself and often stay there, that is a long and different story. In these remarks I am indebted to Christine Korsgaard's "Skepticism about Practical Reason," *Journal of Philosophy* 83 (January 1986): 19–25, in which she criticizes Bernard Williams's broadly Humean account of motivation in his paper "Internal and External Reasons," in *Moral Luck* (Cambridge: Cambridge University Press, 1981), pp. 101–13.

tation. This illustrates the wide role of a political conception as educator (§4.4).

5. This brings us to d): that citizens have a reasonable moral psychology.[34] The features we have attributed to citizens—their readiness to propose and to abide by fair terms of cooperation, their recognizing the burdens of judgment and affirming only reasonable comprehensive doctrines, and their wanting to be full citizens—provide a basis for ascribing to them a reasonable moral psychology, several aspects of which are consequences of these features.

Thus very briefly: i) besides a capacity for a conception of the good, citizens have a capacity to acquire conceptions of justice and fairness and a desire to act as these conceptions require; ii) when they believe that institutions or social practices are just, or fair (as these conceptions specify), they are ready and willing to do their part in those arrangements provided they have reasonable assurance that others will also do their part; iii) if other persons with evident intention[35] strive to do their part in just or fair arrangements, citizens tend to develop trust and confidence in them; iv) this trust and confidence becomes stronger and more complete as the success of cooperative arrangements is sustained over a longer time; and v) the same is true as the basic institutions framed to secure our fundamental interests (the basic rights and liberties) are more firmly and willingly recognized.

§ 8. Moral Psychology: Philosophical not Psychological

1. This completes our sketch of the moral psychology of the person. I stress that it is a moral psychology drawn from the political conception of justice as fairness. It is not a psychology originating in the science of human nature but rather a scheme

---

34. This psychology is relied on in IV:6–7 in explaining why an overlapping consensus is not utopian.

35. This phrase is from Rousseau's *Emile*, as explained in *Theory*, p. 463*n*. Observe how the points stated here connect with the two basic aspects of being reasonable as discussed in II:1, 3.

of concepts and principles for expressing a certain political conception of the person and an ideal of citizenship. Whether it is correct for our purposes depends on whether we can learn and understand it, on whether we can apply and affirm its principles and ideals in political life, and on whether we find the political conception of justice to which it belongs acceptable on due reflection. Human nature and its natural psychology are permissive: they may limit the viable conceptions of persons and ideals of citizenship, and the moral psychologies that may support them, but do not dictate the ones we must adopt.

That is the answer to the objection that our account is unscientific. We cannot say anything we want, since the account has to meet the practical needs of political life and reasoned thought about it. Like any other political conception, for it to be practicable, its requirements and ideal of citizenship must be ones that people can understand and apply, and be sufficiently motivated to honor. Those are stringent enough conditions in forming a viable conception of justice and its political ideal, though different conditions than those of human psychology as a natural science.

2. Of course, it would seem that an ideal presupposes a view of human nature and social theory; and given the aims of a political conception of justice, we might say that it tries to specify the most reasonable conception of the person that the general facts about human nature and society seem to allow. The difficulty is that beyond the lessons of historical experience and such bits of wisdom as not relying too much on scarce motives and abilities (say, altruism and high intelligence), there is not much to go on. History is full of surprises. We have to formulate an ideal of constitutional government to see whether it has force for us and can be put into practice successfully in the history of society.

Within these limits the political philosophy of a constitutional regime is autonomous in two ways. One is that its political conception of justice is a normative scheme of thought. Its family of fundamental ideas is not analyzable in terms of some natural basis, say the family of psychological and biological concepts, or even in terms of the family of social and economic concepts. If we can learn this normative scheme and use it to express ourselves in it in our moral and political thought and action, that suffices.

The other way political philosophy is autonomous is that we need not explain its role and content scientifically, in terms of natural selection, for instance.[36] If in its environment it is not destructive of itself but flourishing and nature permits it, that again suffices. We strive for the best we can attain within the scope the world allows.[37]

36. Allan Gibbard, in his *Wise Choices, Apt Feelings* (Cambridge, Mass.: Harvard University Press, 1990), surmises that the broad features of morality and its content can be explained in this way.
37. I am indebted to Joshua Cohen for discussion on this point.

Political
Constructivism

In this lecture I discuss political constructivism in contrast with Kant's moral constructivism on the one hand and with rational intuitionism as a form of moral realism on the other. Of the three parts, §§1–4 take up the meaning of constructivism and provide a general account of its procedure of construction; §§5–7 consider the way in which both kinds of constructivism are objective; and §8 examines why, as part of political liberalism, political constructivism is limited to the political. Thus we shall see that political constructivism provides political liberalism with an appropriate conception of objectivity.

Political constructivism is a view about the structure and content of a political conception. It says that once, if ever, reflective equilibrium is attained, the principles of political justice (content) may be represented as the outcome of a certain procedure of construction (structure). In this procedure, as modeled by the original position (I:4), rational agents, as representatives of citizens and subject to reasonable conditions, select the public principles of justice to regulate the basic structure of society. This procedure, we conjecture, embodies all the relevant requirements of practical reason and shows how the principles of justice follow from the principles of practical reason in union with conceptions of society and person, themselves ideas of practical reason.

The full significance of a constructivist political conception lies in its connection with the fact of reasonable pluralism and the need for a democratic society to secure the possibility of an overlapping consensus on its fundamental political values. The reason such a conception may be the focus of an overlapping consensus of comprehensive doctrines is that it develops the principles of justice from public and shared ideas of society as a fair system of cooperation and of citizens as free and equal by using the principles of their common practical reason. In honoring those principles of justice citizens show themselves autonomous, politically speaking, and thus in a way compatible with their reasonable comprehensive doctrines.

§ 1. The Idea of a Constructivist Conception

1. We are here concerned with a constructivist conception of political justice and not with a comprehensive moral doctrine.[1]

---

1. This essay develops further some of the ideas in the third lecture entitled "Construction and Objectivity" in the *Journal of Philosophy* 77 (September 1980). The title of the three lectures was "Kantian Constructivism in Moral Theory." As stated at the end of the introduction, this final version has been revised after correspondence with Tyler Burge, especially in §§1, 2, and 5, with some modifications elsewhere to make the whole consistent. Here I distinguish, as I should have done in the original of 1980, between moral and political constructivism; and I try to give what I hope is a clearer statement of the features of a constructivist conception and to remain throughout within the limits of a political conception of justice. I am indebted also to Thomas Nagel and T. M. Scanlon for numerous instructive conversations on the topic of constructivism. The idea of constructivism has not been much

To fix ideas I first examine moral realism in the form illustrated by rational intuitionism as found in the English tradition in Clarke and Price, and Sidgwick and Ross, among others. In §2 I contrast Kant's moral constructivism with the political constructivism of justice as fairness.

Rational intuitionism may be characterized by four basic features that distinguish it from political constructivism. I state these four features and then describe political constructivism by setting out four corresponding though contrasting features.[2]

The first feature of rational intuitionism says that moral first principles and judgments, when correct, are true statements about an independent order of moral values; moreover, this order does not depend on, nor is it to be explained by, the activity of any actual (human) minds, including the activity of reason.

The second feature says that moral first principles are known by theoretical reason. This feature is suggested by the idea that

discussed outside of the philosophy of mathematics, but I should mention the following: Scanlon's "Contractualism and Utilitarianism"; see, for example, pp. 117f. opposing intuitionism, although the terms "intuitionism" and "constructivism" are not used. To this add: Ronald Dworkin, "Justice and Rights" (1973) in *Taking Rights Seriously* (Cambridge, Mass.: Harvard University Press, 1977), pp. 159–68, which was the first to suggest that justice as fairness is constructivist, but he understood it differently than I do here; Onora O'Neill, *Constructions of Reason* (Cambridge: Cambridge University Press, 1989), especially chap. 11; and Brian Barry, *Theories of Justice,* vol. I, especially pp. 264–82, 348–53. See David Brink, *Moral Realism and the Foundations of Ethics* (Cambridge: Cambridge University Press, 1989) for a criticism of constructivism, especially appendix 4. Of these writers only Scanlon and Barry understand constructivism as I do, although their constructivisms are different. Finally, see the essay by Thomas Hill, "Kantian Constructivism in Ethics," in his *Dignity and Practical Reason in Kent's Moral Theory* (Ithaca: Cornell University Press, 1992); and the account of constructivism in Stephen Darwall, Allan Gibbard, and Peter Railton, "Toward *Fin de Siecle* Ethics: Some Trends," *Philosophical Review* 101 (January 1992):137–44.

2. These four features are found in Samuel Clarke's *Boyle Lectures* of 1704–5 and in Richard Price's *Review,* 3d ed. 1787. See the selections in J. B. Schneewind's *Moral Philosophy from Montaigne to Kant,* 2 vols. (Cambridge: Cambridge University Press, 1990). For Clarke, vol. I, pp. 295–306; for Price, vol. II, pp. 588–603; or in D. D. Raphael, *British Moralists, 1650–1800,* 2 vols. (Oxford: Clarendon Press, 1969), now republished by Hackett. For Clarke, vol. I, §§224—61; for Price, vol. II, §§655–762. I use these writers as a standard example for purposes of contrast, not of criticism.

moral knowledge is gained in part by a kind of perception and intuition, as well as organized by first principles found acceptable on due reflection. It is strengthened by the comparison intuitionists make between moral knowledge and knowledge of mathematics in arithmetic and geometry. The order of moral values is said to lie in God's reason and to direct the divine will.[3]

The third feature concerns the sparse conception of the person. Although not explicitly stated, this feature may be gathered from the fact that rational intuitionism does not require a fuller conception of the person and needs little more than the idea of the self as knower. This is because the content of first principles is given by the order of moral values available to perception and intuition as organized and expressed by principles acceptable on due reflection. The main requirement, then, is that we be able to know the first principles expressing those values and to be moved by that knowledge.[4] Here a basic assumption is that recognizing first principles as true gives rise, in a being capable of knowing them, to a desire to act from them for their own sake. Moral motivation is defined by reference to desires that have a special kind of origin: an intuitive knowledge of first principles.

Rational intuitionism is not, to be sure, forced to use this sparse conception of the person. It simply has no need for more complex conceptions of person and society; whereas in constructivism such conceptions are required to provide the form and structure of its constructivist procedure.

Finally, we add a fourth feature: rational intuitionism conceives of truth in a traditional way by viewing moral judgments as true when they are both about and accurate to the independent order of moral values. Otherwise they are false.

---

3. For perception and intuition: Clarke, pp. 296f., §227; Price, pp. 589, 596f., §§672–74, 704; for comparison with mathematics: Clarke, pp. 295f., §§226–27; Price, pp. 592, §684; for the order of values in God's reason: Clarke, pp. 299, §230; Price, pp. 598f., §§709–12. Although intuitionists at times speak of moral judgments as self-evident, I do not emphasize this. It is not essential.

4. Clarke, pp. 299, §231; Price, pp. 593, 600–3; §§688, 757–61.

2. The four corresponding though different features of political constructivism are these.

The first feature, as already noted, is that the principles of political justice (content) may be represented as the outcome of a procedure of construction (structure). In this procedure rational agents, as representatives of citizens and subject to reasonable conditions, select the principles to regulate the basic structure of society.

The second feature is that the procedure of construction is based essentially on practical reason and not on theoretical reason. Following Kant's way of making the distinction, we say: practical reason is concerned with the production of objects according to a conception of those objects—for example, the conception of a just constitutional regime taken as the aim of political endeavor—while theoretical reason is concerned with the knowledge of given objects.[5] Note that to say that the procedure of construction is based essentially on practical reason is not to deny that theoretical reason has a role. It shapes the beliefs and knowledge of the rational persons who have a part in the construction; and these persons also use their general capacities of reasoning, inference, and judgment in selecting the principles of justice.

The third feature of political constructivism is that it uses a rather complex conception of person and society to give form and structure to its construction. As we have seen, political constructivism views the person as belonging to political society understood as a fair system of social cooperation from one generation to the next. Persons are said to possess the two moral powers paired with this idea of social cooperation—a capacity for a sense of justice and for a conception of the good. All these stipulations and more are needed to work out the idea that the principles of justice issue from a suitable procedure of construc-

---

5. For Kant's distinction, see *Critique of Practical Reason,* for example Ak:V:15f., 65f., 89f.

tion. Intuitionism's sparse conception of the person would not be adequate to this purpose.

As before, we again add a fourth feature: political constructivism specifies an idea of the reasonable and applies this idea to various subjects: conceptions and principles, judgments and grounds, persons and institutions. In each case, it must, of course, also specify criteria to judge whether the subject in question is reasonable. It does not, however, as rational intuitionism does, use (or deny) the concept of truth; nor does it question that concept, nor could it say that the concept of truth and its idea of the reasonable are the same. Rather, within itself the political conception does without the concept of truth, in part for reasons considered later in §8. One thought is that the idea of the reasonable makes an overlapping consensus of reasonable doctrines possible in ways the concept of truth may not. Yet, in any case, it is up to each comprehensive doctrine to say how its idea of the reasonable connects with its concept of truth, should it have one.

If we ask how the reasonable is understood, we say: for our purposes here, the content of the reasonable is specified by the content of a reasonable political conception. The idea of the reasonable itself is given in part, again for our purposes, by the two aspects of persons' being reasonable (II:1, 3): their willingness to propose and abide by fair terms of social cooperation among equals and their recognition of and willingness to accept the consequences of the burdens of judgment. Add to this the principles of practical reason and the conceptions of society and person on which the political conception is based.[6] We come to understand this idea by understanding the two aspects of the reasonableness of persons and how these enter into the procedure of construction and why. We decide whether the whole conception is acceptable by seeing whether we can endorse it upon due reflection.

3. These four corresponding features give a broad contrast

---

6. The concept of a reasonable judgment as opposed to a true judgment is discussed further in §8.

between political constructivism and rational intuitionism as a form of moral realism. I add a few remarks to clarify the relations between the two views.

First, it is crucial for political liberalism that its constructivist conception does not contradict rational intuitionism, since constructivism tries to avoid opposing any comprehensive doctrine. To explain how this is possible in this case, let us suppose that the argument from the original position, as indicated in I:4, is correct: it shows that rational persons under reasonable, or fair, conditions would select certain principles of justice. To be consistent with rational intuitionism, we do not say that the procedure of construction makes, or produces, the order of moral values. For the intuitionist says this order is independent and constitutes itself, as it were. Political constructivism neither denies nor asserts this. Rather, it claims only that its procedure represents an order of political values proceeding from the values expressed by the principles of practical reason, in union with conceptions of society and person, to the values expressed by certain principles of political justice.

Political liberalism adds: this represented order is the most appropriate one for a democratic society marked by the fact of reasonable pluralism. This is because it provides the most reasonable conception of justice as the focus of an overlapping consensus.

Rational intuitionists can also accept the argument from the original position and say that it displays the correct order of values. On these matters, they can agree with political constructivism: from within their own comprehensive view, they can affirm the political conception and join an overlapping consensus. Justice as fairness does not deny what they want to assert: namely, that the order of values displayed by constructivism is backed by an independent order of values that constitutes itself (as stated above as the first feature of intuitionism).

4. A further point of clarification: both constructivism and rational intuitionism rely on the idea of reflective equilibrium. Otherwise intuitionism could not bring its perceptions and intui-

tions to bear on each other and check its account of the order of moral values against our considered judgments on due reflection. Similarly, constructivism could not check the formulation of its procedure by seeing whether the conclusions reached match those judgments.

The difference in the views shows up in how they interpret conclusions that are unacceptable and must be revised. The intuitionist regards a procedure as correct because following it correctly usually gives the correct independently given judgment, whereas the political constructivist regards a judgment as correct because it issues from the reasonable and rational procedure of construction when correctly formulated and correctly followed (assuming, as always, that the judgment relies on true information).[7] So if the judgment is not acceptable, intuitionism says that its procedure reflects a mistaken account of the independent order of values. The constructivist says the fault must lie in how the procedure models the principles of practical reason in union with the conceptions of society and person. For the constructivist's conjecture is that the correct model of practical reason as a whole will give the correct principles of justice on due reflection.[8]

Once reflective equilibrium is reached, the intuitionists will say that their considered judgments are now true, or very likely so, of an independent order of moral values. The constructivist will say that the procedure of construction now correctly models the principles of practical reason in union with the appropriate conceptions of society and person. In so doing it represents the order of values most suited to a democratic regime. As to how we find the correct procedure, the constructivist says: by reflection, using our powers of reason. But since we are using our

7. This way of putting it I owe to Thomas Nagel.
8. Of course, the repeated failure to formulate the procedure so that it yields acceptable conclusions may lead us to abandon political constructivism. It must eventually add up or be rejected. I am indebted to Anthony Laden for instructive discussion about this and on related points to David Estlund and Gregory Kavka.

reason to describe itself and reason is not transparent to itself, we can misdescribe our reason as we can anything else. The struggle for reflective equilibrium continues indefinitely, in this case as in all others.

5. It may already be clear why a political conception that sees the public principles of justice as founded on the principles and conceptions of practical reason is of great significance for a constitutional regime. Still, let us pull the threads together.

Consider again the idea of social cooperation. How are fair terms of cooperation to be determined? Are they to be simply laid down by some outside authority distinct from the persons cooperating, say by God's law? Or are these terms to be accepted by these persons as fair in view of their knowledge of an independent moral order? Or should these terms be established by an undertaking among those persons themselves in view of what they regard as their reciprocal advantage?

Justice as fairness, we said, adopts a form of the last answer (I:4.1). This is because, given the fact of reasonable pluralism, citizens cannot agree on any moral authority, whether a sacred text, or institution. Nor do they agree about the order of moral values, or the dictates of what some regard as natural law. We adopt, then, a constructivist view to specify the fair terms of social cooperation as given by the principles of justice agreed to by the representatives of free and equal citizens when fairly situated. The bases of this view lie in fundamental ideas of the public political culture as well as in citizens' shared principles and conceptions of practical reason. Thus, if the procedure can be correctly formulated, citizens should be able to accept its principles and conceptions along with their reasonable comprehensive doctrine. The political conception of justice can then serve as the focus of an overlapping consensus.

Thus, it is only by affirming a constructivist conception—one which is political and not metaphysical—that citizens generally can expect to find principles that all can accept. This they can do without denying the deeper aspects of their reasonable comprehensive doctrines. Given their differences, citizens cannot fulfill in any other way their conception-dependent desire[9] to have a shared political life on terms acceptable to others as free and equal. This idea of a shared political life does not invoke Kant's idea of autonomy, or Mill's idea of individuality, as moral values belonging to a comprehensive doctrine. The appeal is rather to the political value of a public life conducted on terms that all reasonable citizens can accept as fair. This leads to the ideal of democratic citizens settling their fundamental differences in accordance with an idea of public reason (VI:2).

6. To these observations, political liberalism adds that the order represented in the argument from the original position is the most appropriate way to see the political values as ordered. Doing this enables us to state the meaning of an autonomous political doctrine as one that represents, or displays, the political principles of justice—the fair terms of social cooperation—as reached by using the principles of practical reason in union with the appropriate conceptions of persons as free and equal and of society as a fair system of cooperation over time. The argument from the original position exhibits this line of thought. Autonomy is a matter of how the view presents the political values as ordered. Think of this as doctrinal autonomy.

A view is autonomous, then, because in its represented order, the political values of justice and public reason (expressed by their principles) are not simply presented as moral requirements externally imposed. Nor are they required of us by other citizens whose comprehensive doctrines we do not accept. Rather, citizens can understand those values as based on their practical reason in union with the political conceptions of citizens as free and equal and of society as a system of fair cooperation. In affirming the political doctrine as a whole we, as citizens, are ourselves autonomous, politically speaking. An autonomous political conception provides, then, an appropriate basis and order-

9. Conception-dependent desires are defined and explained in II:7.4

ing of political values for a constitutional regime characterized by reasonable pluralism.

§ 2. Kant's Moral Constructivism

1. Let us now note four differences between Kant's moral constructivism and the political constructivism of justice as fairness.

The first difference is that Kant's doctrine is a comprehensive moral view in which the ideal of autonomy has a regulative role for all of life. This makes it incompatible with the political liberalism of justice as fairness. A comprehensive liberalism based on the ideal of autonomy may, of course, belong to a reasonable overlapping consensus that endorses a political conception, justice as fairness among them; but as such it is not suitable to provide a public basis of justification.

A second difference is clear once we introduce a second meaning of autonomy. As we have just seen, for political liberalism whether a political view is autonomous depends on how it represents political values as ordered. A political view, we said, is autonomous if it represents, or displays, the order of political values as based on principles of practical reason in union with the appropriate political conceptions of society and person. This, we said earlier, is doctrinal autonomy. Otherwise a view is doctrinally heteronomous.

Another and deeper meaning of autonomy says that the order of moral and political values must be made, or itself constituted, by the principles and conceptions of practical reason. Let us refer to this as constitutive autonomy. In contrast with rational intuitionism, constitutive autonomy says that the so-called independent order of values does not constitute itself but is constituted by the activity, actual or ideal, of practical (human) reason itself. I believe this, or something like it, is Kant's view. His constructivism is deeper and goes to the very existence and constitution of the order of values. This is part of his transcendental idealism.

The intuitionist's independently given order of values is part of the transcendental realism Kant takes his transcendental idealism to oppose.

Political liberalism must, of course, reject Kant's constitutive autonomy; yet his moral constructivism can endorse political constructivism as far as it goes.[10] And certainly political constructivism accepts his view that the principles of practical reason originate, if we insist on saying they originate anywhere, in our moral consciousness as informed by practical reason. They derive from nowhere else. Kant is the historical source of the idea that reason, both theoretical and practical, is self-originating and self-authenticating. Still, accepting this, it is a separate question whether the principles of practical reason constitute the order of values.

2. The third difference is that the basic conceptions of person and society in Kant's view have, let us assume, a foundation in his transcendental idealism. I pass over what this foundation might be, except to say that certainly there are many ways in which it has been understood; and one of them we might accept as true within our comprehensive view. Recall that I suppose we all have a comprehensive view extending well beyond the domain of the political, though it may be partial, and often fragmentary and incomplete. But that is irrelevant here. What is essential is that justice as fairness uses as basic organizing ideas certain fundamental ideas that are political. Transcendental idealism and other such metaphysical doctrines play no role in their organization and exposition.

These differences connect with a fourth difference: the distinct aims of the two views. Justice as fairness aims at uncovering a public basis of justification on questions of political justice given the fact of reasonable pluralism. Since justification is addressed to others, it proceeds from what is, or can be, held in common; and so we begin from shared fundamental ideas implicit in the public political culture in the hope of developing

10. This is as important for political liberalism as is the endorsement of the rational intuitionist.

100

from them a political conception that can gain free and reasoned agreement in judgment, this agreement being stable in virtue of its gaining the support of an overlapping consensus of reasonable comprehensive doctrines. These conditions suffice for a reasonable political conception of justice.

Kant's aims are difficult to describe briefly. But I believe he views the role of philosophy as apologia: the defense of reasonable faith. This is not the older theological problem of showing the compatibility of faith and reason, but that of showing the coherence and unity of reason, both theoretical and practical, with itself; and of how we are to view reason as the final court of appeal, as alone competent to settle all questions about the scope and limits of its own authority.[11] Kant tries in the first two *Critiques* to defend both our knowledge of nature and our knowledge of our freedom through the moral law; he also wants to find a way of conceiving of natural law and moral freedom so that they are not incompatible. His view of philosophy as defense rejects any doctrine that undermines the unity and coherence of theoretical and practical reason; it opposes rationalism, empiricism, and skepticism so far as they tend to that result. Kant shifts the burden of proof: the affirmation of reason is rooted in the thought and practice of ordinary (sound) human reason from which philosophical reflection must begin. Until that thought and practice appears to be at odds with itself, it needs no defense.

Any one of these differences is far-reaching enough to distinguish justice as fairness from Kant's moral constructivism. Yet the differences are connected: the fourth, the difference of aim, together with the fact of reasonable pluralism, leads to the first three. Justice as fairness would, however, accept Kant's view of philosophy as defense this far: given reasonably favorable conditions, it understands itself as the defense of the possibility of a just constitutional democratic regime.

11. I am indebted to Susan Neiman for this reading.

§ 3. Justice as Fairness as a Constructivist View

1. Before turning to the constructivist aspects of justice as fairness, a preliminary remark. While constructivist views have a legitimate place within moral and political philosophy, they also have some affinity with constructivist ideas in the philosophy of mathematics. Kant's account of the synthetic a priori nature of arithmetic and geometry is, of course, one of the historical origins of those views.[12]

One similarity is instructive: in both cases the idea is to formulate a procedural representation in which, so far as possible, all the relevant criteria of correct reasoning—mathematical, moral, or political—are incorporated and open to view.[13] Judgments are reasonable and sound if they result in following the correct procedure correctly and rely only on true premises. In Kant's account of moral reasoning, the procedural representation is given by the categorical imperative that expresses the requirements that pure practical reason imposes on our rational maxims. In arithmetic the procedure expresses how the natural numbers are generated from the basic concept of a unit, each number from the preceding. Different numbers are distinguished by their place in the series thus generated. The procedure shows the basic properties that constitute facts about numbers, so that proposi-

12. Especially valuable are Charles Parsons, "Kant's Philosophy of Arithmetic," (1969) reprinted in *Mathematics and Philosophy* (Ithaca: Cornell University Press, 1983) and his article "Mathematics, Foundations of," in Paul Edwards, ed., *The Encyclopedia of Philosophy*, 8 vols. (New York: Academic Press, 1977); and Michael Friedman, *Kant and the Exact Sciences* (Cambridge, Mass.: Harvard University Press, 1992), chaps. 1 and 2.

13. Because the procedure is viewed as embedding, so far as possible, all the relevant criteria, it is said to specify an ideal, say of the ideal mathematician, or the ideal of a rational and reasonable person who understands and applies the categorical imperative procedure correctly; or the ideal of a realm of ends, a community of such ideal persons. Above we must say: "as far as possible all the relevant criteria," because no specification of these criteria can be declared to be and treated as final; any rendering of them is always open to be checked by critical reflection. This is so, even if for the present, we are fully confident of our formulations of principles and cannot see how they can be in serious error.

tions about numbers that are correctly derived from it are correct.

2. To explain political constructivism we need to ask three questions.

First, in this form of constructivism, what is it that is constructed? Answer: the content of a political conception of justice. In justice as fairness this content is the principles of justice selected by the parties in the original position as they try to advance the interests of those they represent.

A second question is this: as a procedural device of representation, is the original position itself constructed? No: it is simply laid out. We start with the fundamental idea of a well-ordered society as a fair system of cooperation between reasonable and rational citizens regarded as free and equal. We then lay out a procedure that exhibits reasonable conditions to impose on the parties, who as rational representatives are to select public principles of justice for the basic structure of such a society. Our aim in doing this is to express in that procedure all the relevant criteria of reasonableness and rationality that apply to principles and standards of political justice. If we do this properly, we conjecture that the correct working through of the argument from the original position should yield the most appropriate principles of justice to govern the political relations between citizens. In this way the political conception of citizens as cooperating in a well-ordered society shapes the content of political right and justice.

3. This leads to the third question: what does it mean to say that the conceptions of citizen and of a well-ordered society are embedded in, or modeled by, the constructivist procedure? It means that the form of the procedure, and its more particular features, are drawn from those conceptions taken as its basis.

To illustrate: elsewhere we have said that citizens have two moral powers. The first is a capacity for a sense of justice that enables them to understand, apply, and to act from the reasonable principles of justice that specify fair terms of social cooperation. The second moral power is a capacity for a conception of the good: a conception of the ends and purposes worthy of our devoted pursuit, together with an ordering of those elements to guide us over a complete life. Citizens' capacity for a conception of their good in a manner suited for political justice is modeled within the procedure by the rationality of the parties. By contrast, citizens' capacity for a sense of justice is modeled within the procedure itself by such features as the reasonable condition of symmetry (or equality) in which their representatives are situated as well as by the limits on information expressed by the veil of ignorance.

Moreover, the capacity for a sense of justice, which is exhibited in the reasoning of citizens in the political life of a well-ordered society, is also modeled by the procedure as a whole. As such citizens, we are both reasonable and rational, in contrast to the parties in the original position, who—it is important to emphasize—as artificial persons inhabiting a device of representation, are merely rational. In addition, part of the idea of a well-ordered society is that its political conception is public. This is modeled by the feature that in selecting principles of justice the parties must, for example, take into account the consequences of those principles being mutually recognized and how this affects citizens' conceptions of themselves and their motivation to act from those principles.

To conclude: not everything, then, is constructed; we must have some material, as it were, from which to begin. In a more literal sense, only the substantive principles specifying content of political right and justice are constructed. The procedure itself is simply laid out using as starting points the basic conceptions of society and person, the principles of practical reason, and the public role of a political conception of justice.

4. I said (two paragraphs earlier) that the capacity for a sense of justice, which characterizes citizens' reasoning in a well-ordered society, is modeled by the procedure as a whole. To show the importance of this fact, I consider an objection that parallels a criticism Schopenhauer made to Kant's doctrine of the categor-

ical imperative.[14] Schopenhauer maintained that, in arguing for the duty of mutual aid in situations of distress (the fourth example in *Grundlegung*), Kant appeals to what rational agents, as finite beings with needs, can consistently will to be universal law. In view of our need for love and sympathy, on at least some occasions, we cannot will a social world in which others are always indifferent to our pleas in such cases. From this Schopenhauer claimed that Kant's view is at bottom egoistic, from which it follows that it is but a disguised form of heteronomy after all.

Here I am not concerned with defending Kant against this criticism but in pointing out why the parallel objection to justice as fairness is incorrect. To this end, observe that there are offhand two things that prompt Schopenhauer's objection. First, he believes that, when maxims are made universal laws, Kant asks us to test them in the light of their general consequences for our natural inclinations and needs, with inclinations and needs viewed egoistically. Second, the rules that define the procedure for testing maxims Schopenhauer interprets as external constraints and not as derived from the essential features of persons as reasonable. These constraints are imposed, so to speak, from the outside by the limitations of our situation, limitations we would like to overcome. These two considerations lead Schopenhauer to say that the categorical imperative is a principle of reciprocity that egoism cunningly accepts as a compromise. As such a principle, it may be appropriate for a confederation of nation-states but not as a moral principle.

5. Now consider the parallel objection to justice as fairness in regard to these two points. Concerning the first, the parties in the original position have no direct interests except an interest

14. See *On the Basis of Ethics* (1840), part II, §7, translated by E. F. J. Payne (New York: Liberal Arts Press, 1965), pp. 89–92. I am indebted to Joshua Cohen for pointing out to me that my previous reply to this criticism misses the force of Schopenhauer's objection. See *Theory,* pp. 147f., and "Kantian Constructivism," p. 530*n*. Thanks to him, I believe the reply in the text much improved and connects with the revised account of primary goods. I am indebted also to Stephen Darwall's "A Defense of the Kantian Interpretation," *Ethics* 86 (January 1976).

in the person each of them represents and they assess principles of justice in terms of primary goods. In addition, they are concerned with securing for the person they represent the higher-order interests we have in developing and exercising our two moral powers and in securing the conditions under which we can further our determinate conception of the good, whatever it is. The list of primary goods and the index of these goods is to be explained so far as possible by reference to those interests, assuming always that those represented have to the minimum requisite degree the capacities fitting them to be normal cooperating members of society over a complete life. Since those interests are taken to specify people's needs as reasonable and rational, the parties' aims are not egoistic but entirely fitting and proper. They are doing what trustees are expected to do for the person they represent. Moreover, it accords with the conception of free persons that citizens should instruct their representatives to secure the conditions for realizing and exercising their moral powers and for furthering their conception of the good, as well as the social bases and the means of their self-respect (II:5.4). This contrasts with Schopenhauer's belief that in Kant's doctrine maxims are tested by how likely they are to meet the agent's natural needs and inclinations seen as egoistic.

Turning to the second point, the constraints imposed on the parties in the original position are indeed external to them as rational agents of construction, mere artificial personages inhabiting our device of representation. Nevertheless, those constraints express the reasonable and so the formal conditions implicit in the moral powers of the members of a well-ordered society whom the parties represent. As we have seen, these powers are modeled by the symmetrical situation of the parties in the original position and by their being subject to the restrictions on valid reasons for affirming principles of justice expressed by the veil of ignorance (I:4). This contrasts with Schopenhauer's second presumption that the constraints of the categorical imperative derive from the limits of our finite nature which, prompted by our natural inclinations, we should like to overcome. In justice as fairness, however, to develop and exercise our moral power (corresponding to the reasonable) is one of our higher-order interests; and this interest goes with the political conception of the person as free and equal. Once this is understood, the constraints of the original position are no longer seen as external. Again the parallel to Schopenhauer's objection does not apply, and shows, as we considered in II:6, how the original position models citizens' full (as opposed to their rational) autonomy, with full autonomy understood as a political and not as an ethical value for all or much of life.

§ 4. Role of Conceptions of Society and Person

1. I have said all along that political constructivism proceeds from the union of practical reason with appropriate conceptions of society and person and the public role of principles of justice. Constructivism does not proceed from practical reason alone but requires a procedure that models conceptions of society and person. But what conceptions are appropriate and how do they arise?

The general answer is this: the principles of practical reason—both reasonable principles and rational principles—and the conceptions of society and person are complementary. Just as the principles of logic, inference, and judgment would not be used were there no persons who could think, infer, and judge, the principles of practical reason are expressed in the thought and judgment of reasonable and rational persons and applied by them in their social and political practice. Those principles do not apply themselves, but are used by us in forming our intentions and actions, and plans and decisions, in our relations with other persons. This being so, we may call the conceptions of society and person "conceptions of practical reason": they characterize the agents who reason and they specify the context for the problems and questions to which principles of practical reason apply. Thus, practical reason has two aspects: principles of practical reason and judgment, on the one hand, and persons, natural or corporate, whose conduct is informed by those principles, on the other. Without conceptions of society and person, the principles of practical reason would have no point, use, or application.

Although conceptions of society and person characterize the agents who reason and specify the context of practical questions, those conceptions have the general form they do because they are used with principles of practical reason. We ask: what must persons be like to engage in practical reason? To answer we say that persons have the two moral powers as well as a determinate conception of the good. Their being reasonable and rational means that they can understand, apply, and act from the two kinds of practical principles. This means in turn that they have a capacity for a sense of justice and for a conception of the good; and since this last capacity is normally developed and put to work, persons' conceptions of the good are assumed, at any given time, to be determinate: that is, they express a scheme of final ends and attachments together with a comprehensive doctrine in light of which those elements are interpreted.

The conceptions of society and person as ideas of reason are not, certainly, constructed any more than the principles of practical reason are constructed. But we can think of them as assembled and connected. As we have just done, we can reflect on how these ideas appear in our practical thought and try to set out an order in which they can be related, from the general and simpler to the more specific and complex. Thus the basic idea of society is one whose members engage, not merely in activities coordinated by orders from a central authority, but in activities guided by publicly recognized rules and procedures that those cooperating accept and regard as properly regulating their conduct. We get an idea of political society by adding that the cooperative activities suffice for all the main purposes of life and its members inhabit a certain well-defined territory over generations (I:3.2– 3). This idea belongs to practical reason and involves the idea of proper, appropriate, or right conduct.

2. What is missing in this sketch of the basic idea of society is

a conception of the right and the good on the basis of which its members accept the rules and procedures that guide their activities. In justice as fairness this missing conception is constructed using the principles of practical reason in union with political conceptions of society and person. This is a special case in which the members of society are citizens regarded as free and equal in virtue of their possessing the two moral powers to the requisite degree. This is the basis of equality. The moral agent here is the free and equal citizen as a member of society, not the moral agent in general.

Other societies take a different view founded on certain religious or philosophical doctrines. Their conceptions of justice are most unlikely to be constructivist, as we have used that term, and they will probably be comprehensive and not political. I need not here mention examples, but whatever these religious and philosophical doctrines may be, I assume they all contain a conception of the right and the good that includes a conception of justice that can be understood as in some way advancing the common good. It must be possible to understand this conception so that when it is followed, society takes into account the good of all its members and of society as a whole. Rules and procedures, joined with shared religious, philosophical, and other public beliefs, do not exclude this possibility. This idea of justice may seem weak. Still, some such idea is necessary if we are to have a society with a legal system imposing what are correctly believed to be genuine obligations, rather than a society that merely coerces its subjects who are unable to resist.[15] Definite

15. I have in mind here that in order to be viable a legal system must have a certain content, for example, H. L. A. Hart's minimum content of natural law discussed in his *The Concept of Law,* pp. 189–95. Or stronger than this, one might argue, as Philip Soper does, that a legal system must honor certain rights if it is to give rise to morally binding obligations and not merely to coerce: for example, a minimum right to the security of life, liberty, and property; a right to justice understood to support at least formal equality, and a reciprocal relation between ruler and ruled allowing for mutual respect; all this in turn requires a right of discourse and a good faith official claim to administer justice. See Soper's *A Theory of Law* (Cambridge, Mass.: Harvard University Press, 1984), pp. 125–47. I assume a society has a conception of justice that

conceptions of society and person are essential elements of any conception of justice and the good.

Let us say, then, that the conceptions of society and person, and the public role of principles of justice, are ideas of practical reason. Not only do they assume a form that practical reason requires for its application, but they provide the context within which practical questions and problems arise: what is the nature of social cooperation? Are those cooperating free and equal, or are their roles different and unequal as settled by religion and culture? Without the ideas of society and person, conceptions of the right and the good have no place. They are as basic as the ideas of judgment and inference, and the principles of practical reason.

§ 5. Three Conceptions of Objectivity

1. Rational intuitionism, Kant's moral constructivism, and the political constructivism of justice as fairness each have a conception of objectivity, although they understand objectivity in a different way. Each may think the others' conceptions are based on incorrect assumptions; we shall see, however, that both intuitionism and Kant's view could grant that political constructivism provides an appropriate basis of objectivity for its limited political purposes. To explain these matters, I survey in this section how each view allows for five essential elements of a conception of objectivity.[16]

The first essential is that a conception of objectivity must establish a public framework of thought sufficient for the concept of judgment to apply and for conclusions to be reached on the basis of reasons and evidence after discussion and due reflection. Indeed, this is required for all kinds of inquiry, whether moral, political, or scientific, or matters of common sense. So if the idea

---

meets conditions of this kind cohering with an idea of advancing the common good. Otherwise we may not have a society but something else.

16. These essentials are widely recognized. There is nothing new in my rendering of them here.

of reasoning and judgment applies to our moral and political statements, as opposed simply to our voicing our psychological state, we must be able to make judgments and draw inferences on the basis of mutually recognized criteria and evidence; and in that way, and not in some other way, say by mere rhetoric or persuasion, reach agreement by the free exercise of our powers of judgment.

As a corollary of this first essential, the second is this. It is definitive of judgment (moral or otherwise) that it aims at being reasonable, or true, as the case may be. Thus, a conception of objectivity must specify a concept of a correct judgment made from its point of view, and hence subject to its norms. It may conceive of correct judgments in the familiar way as true of an independent order of values, as in rational intuitionism; or, as in political constructivism, it may see correct judgments as reasonable: that is, as supported by the preponderance of reasons specified by the principles of right and justice issuing from a procedure that correctly formulates the principles of practical reason in union with appropriate conceptions of society and person.

2. As a third essential, a conception of objectivity must specify an order of reasons as given by its principles and criteria, and it must assign these reasons to agents, whether individual or corporate, as reasons they are to weigh and be guided by in certain circumstances. They are to act from these reasons, whether moved by them or not; and so these assigned reasons may override the reasons agents have, or think they have, from their own point of view.

Again as a corollary, we have a fourth essential: namely, a conception of objectivity must distinguish the objective point of view—as given, say, by the point of view of certain appropriately defined reasonable and rational agents—from the point of view of any particular agent, individual or corporate, or of any particular group of agents, at any particular time. It is part of understanding the concept of objectivity that we never suppose that our thinking something is just or reasonable, or a group's thinking it so, makes it so.

111

The fifth essential is that a conception of objectivity has an account of agreement in judgment among reasonable agents. It may say, as in intuitionism, that reasonable agents have the intellectual and moral powers that enable them to know the independent order of values and to examine, adjust, and coordinate their judgments concerning it by discussion and reflection. Or alternatively, it may, as in political constructivism, see reasonable persons as able to learn and master the concepts and principles of practical reason as well as the principles of right and justice that issue from the procedure of construction.[17] With those things learned and mastered, reasonable persons can apply those principles and standards correctly, and assuming they rely on the same (true) information, they reach the same (or a similar) conclusion.

To sum up: a moral and political conception is objective only if it establishes a framework of thought, reasoning, and judgment that answers to these five essentials. From the way a conception's order of reasons is presented it is clear that the judgment of any agent, individual or corporate, may be mistaken. A distinction is made between reasoning and judgment, however sincere and seemingly correct, and what is true, or reasonable (depending on the view in question). Let's add that it is definitive of reasonable agents that they recognize these essentials, and that their recognition helps to secure the background necessary for agreement in judgment. A sixth essential, discussed in the next section, requires that we be able to explain disagreements in a certain way (§7.2).

3. To say that the three views we have discussed have different conceptions of objectivity is to say they do not explain these essential elements of objectivity in the same way. Consider rational intuitionism: as to the second essential, it views a correct moral judgment as one that is true of an independent order of moral values. Neither Kant's moral constructivism nor political

17. This does not imply that we have a knowledge of this procedure; but rather we can use the principles that issue from it.

constructivism regards moral judgments as objective in that way, since neither asserts an independent order of values (although political constructivism does not deny it). Certain kinds of rational intuitionism are also heteronomous in the first and doctrinal sense (§1.6); and this distinguishes them not only from Kant's constructivism but also from the political constructivism of justice as fairness. Yet for political constructivism, heteronomy in this doctrinal sense is not a feature of rational intuitionism as such, but only a feature of how certain variants of it see, or display, the order of values.

But how does rational intuitionism meet the fourth essential for objectivity, that is, how does it distinguish the agent's point of view from the objective point of view and explain how the agent may be mistaken? Here intuitionism may rely on an account of first principles and conceptions of practical reason acceptable on due reflection (§1.4). The agent's point of view is then distinguished from that. Rational intuitionism can agree with political constructivism that there is no way of having well-grounded knowledge of, or forming reasonable beliefs about, the order of values without reasoned discussion, though intuitionism appeals to ideas of moral perception and intuition in ways constructivism does not.

4. From this it follows that a variant of rational intuitionism and political constructivism—we suppose for the moment that both are considering political values—could agree on the very same principles of practical reason and conceptions of society and person. Both could also accept the constructivist argument from the original position that yields the principles of political justice. They would each be using the same framework to distinguish between an agent's point of view and the objective point of view. The difference is that rational intuitionism would add that a reasonable judgment is true, or probably true (depending on the strength of the reasons), of an independent order of values. Political constructivism would neither assert nor deny that. For its aims, as we see later, the concept of the reasonable suffices.

Thus rational intuitionism may grant that political constructivism has a kind of objectivity, one that is appropriate to its political and practical purposes. Its objection is that constructivism lacks a proper conception of the truth of moral judgments, one that views moral principles as being true or false of an independent order of values. Political constructivism doesn't use this idea of truth, adding that to assert or to deny a doctrine of this kind goes beyond the bounds of a political conception of justice framed so far as possible to be acceptable to all reasonable comprehensive doctrines. A rational intuitionist who agreed with the content of justice as fairness (or a similar constructivist view), and who affirmed a connection between its reasonable judgments and true ones, could also consider those reasonable judgments as true. There would be no conflict (§8).[18]

As for Kant's moral constructivism (§2), a correct moral judgment is one that meets all the relevant criteria of reasonableness and rationality incorporated into the categorical imperative procedure for testing maxims. A judgment properly supported by principles and precepts that pass that test are acknowledged as correct by any fully reasonable and rational (and informed) person. This is what Kant means when he says that these judgments are universally communicable: as reasonable and rational we recognize, apply, and can explain to others, the same procedure for validating them. All the essential elements of objectivity are provided for.

5. What is the role of the essentials of the objective point of view and what do they do? Recall from II:1.4 that the reasonable is public in ways the rational is not: it is by the reasonable that we enter the public world of others and stand ready to propose, or accept, as the case may be, reasonable principles to specify fair terms of cooperation. These principles issue from a procedure of construction that expresses the principles of practical reason in union with appropriate conceptions of society and person, and as such, they may be used to support our judgments

18. This parallels "Kantian Constructivism in Moral Theory," pp. 507f.

114

as reasonable. Together they yield a political conception of justice for judging basic institutions and specify the political values in terms of which those institutions can be appraised. The essentials of objectivity are, then, the features required of a framework of thought and judgment if it is to be an open and public basis of justification for citizens as free and equal. When citizens share a reasonable political conception of justice, they share common ground on which public discussion of fundamental questions can proceed.

We can see this by checking the essentials in turn. The first essential covers roughly what we have just said: it states that a conception of objectivity must establish a public framework sufficient for the concept of judgment to apply and conclusions to be reached on the basis of mutually recognizable reasons and evidence. The second essential adds that, in the case of constructivism, it is definitive of judgment that we aim at making a reasonable judgment, one supported by the preponderance of reasons as given by an appropriate procedure.

The third essential requires that the order of reasons given by its principles be assigned to agents as reasons to which they are to give due priority and to distinguish from the reasons they have from their own point of view. Were this not required, a shared basis of public justification would be lacking. Finally, as a corollary, the fourth essential reinforces the third by stressing the distinction between the objective point of view and that of any particular person. In general, thought and judgment is always needed to bring our point of view in line with the objective point of view. Again, this is necessary for a shared public basis of justification.

Observe that in constructivism the objective point of view is always understood as that of certain reasonable and rational persons suitably specified. In Kant's doctrine, it is the point of view of such persons as members of a realm of ends. This shared point of view is possible since it is given by the categorical imperative which represents the principles and criteria implicit in their common human reason. Similarly, in justice as fairness it is the point of view of free and equal citizens as properly represented. Thus, in contrast to what Nagel calls "the impersonal point of view,"[19] constructivism both moral and political says that the objective point of view must always be from somewhere. This is because, as calling upon practical reason, it must express the point of view of persons, individual[20] or corporate, suitably characterized as reasonable and rational. There is no such thing as the point of view of practical reason as such. This connects with what I said in §4 about the role of conceptions of person and society.

A last remark. I said above that the essentials of objectivity (including the sixth in §7.2) are necessary for a shared public basis of justification. To this add that they are also sufficient. With this, political liberalism has an account of objectivity that suffices for the purposes of a political conception of justice. As we have said, it need not go beyond its conception of a reasonable judgment and may leave the concept of a true moral judgment to comprehensive doctrines.

§ 6. Objectivity Independent of the Causal View of Knowledge

1. Constructivism holds that the objectivity of practical reason is independent of the causal theory of knowledge. To clarify this point and the preceding remarks I consider an objection. Some writers might say that none of the three conceptions reviewed is a conception of objectivity at all. They hold that the objectivity of judgments and beliefs depends on their having a suitable explanation within a causal view of knowledge. They think a judgment (or belief) is objective just in case the content of our judgment is (in part) the outcome of an appropriate kind of causal process affecting our sense experience, say, on which the judgment is based.

---

19. See Thomas Nagel, *The View from Nowhere* (New York: Oxford University Press, 1986), pp. 138–43 and elsewhere.

20. Hume's judicious spectator in *The Treatise*, III:3.i, is an example of such an individual.

For example, our perceptual judgment that the cat is on the mat is the result (in part) of an appropriate causal process affecting our perceptual experience of the cat's being on the mat. The view is that there is a familiar common sense explanation of such perceptual experiences on which perceptual judgments about medium-sized physical objects are based. Eventually cognitive psychology should be able to fill in the story even for our more theoretical, higher-order beliefs. The beliefs of theoretical physicists will in due course be explained in some such fashion. Even those beliefs are objective because they have an explanation showing that physicists' affirming them is the result (in part) of an appropriate causal process related to the world's being the way physicists think it is.[21]

2. This objection raises profound questions about the idea of objectivity. These I cannot discuss but simply state an opinion as follows. Political constructivism accepts Kant's view this far: it holds that there are different conceptions of objectivity appropriate for theoretical and practical reason. Perhaps this is because, as we have seen, he thinks the former concerns the knowledge of given objects, whereas the latter concerns the production of objects in accordance with a conception of those objects. As reasonable and rational we must, as it were, suitably construct the principles of right and justice that specify the conception of the objects we are to produce and in this way guide our public conduct by practical reason. A plausible conception of objectivity for logic and mathematics poses special difficulties which I shall not consider.[22] Nevertheless, as we have seen, the compar-

21. This conception of objectivity was applied to moral judgments by Gilbert Harman in his *The Nature of Morality* (New York: Oxford University Press, 1977), chaps. 1–2 to argue that they are not objective. Warren Quinn's essay "Truth and Explanation in Ethics," *Ethics* 96 (April 1986), contains an extensive criticism of Harman's view. Much the same conception is used by Bernard Williams in *Ethics and the Limits of Philosophy* (Cambridge, Mass.: Harvard University Press, 1985). For a critical review, see Quinn's "Reflections on the Loss of Moral Knowledge and Williams on Objectivity," *Philosophy and Public Affairs* (Spring 1987). I am indebted to both of Quinn's essays.

22. For these difficulties see Paul Benacerraf, "Mathematical Truth," *Journal of*

ison between practical reasoning and mathematical thought is instructive. To meet the objection halfway, let us grant that its causal requirement is part of an appropriate conception of objectivity for judgments of theoretical reason, or at least in much of natural science, and likewise for perceptual judgments.[23]

Nevertheless, that requirement is not essential for all conceptions of objectivity, and not for a conception suitable for moral and political reasoning. This is shown by the fact that we do not require of a moral or political judgment that the reasons for it show it to be related to an appropriate causal process, or require an explanation of it within cognitive psychology. Rather, it is enough that the reasons offered be sufficiently strong. We explain our judgment, so far as we do, simply by going over the grounds for it: the explanation lies in the reasons we sincerely affirm. What more is there to say except to question our sincerity and reasonableness?

Of course, given the many obstacles to agreement in political judgment even among reasonable persons, we will not reach agreement all the time, or perhaps even much of the time. But we should be able at least to narrow our differences and so come closer to agreement, and this in the light of what we view as shared principles and criteria of practical reasoning.

Philosophy 70 (November 1973). Here I should add that I assume that common sense knowledge (for example, our perceptual judgments), natural science and social theory (as in economics and history), and mathematics are (or can be) objective, perhaps each in their own appropriate way. The problem is to elucidate how they are, and to give a suitably systematic account. Any argument against the objectivity of moral and political reasoning that would, by parallel reasoning applied against common sense, or natural science, or mathematics, show them not to be objective, must be incorrect. The objectivity of practical reasoning is an ill-chosen battleground to contest the question of objectivity in general.

23. Quinn, in his essay "Reflections on the Loss of Moral Knowledge" (n. 20 above), argues against granting even this much; and thinks it does not hold for physics, or for science in general. I think he may be right about this but I don't need to consider the point here.

§ 7. When Do Objective Reasons Exist, Politically Speaking?

1. So far we have surveyed three different conceptions of objectivity reviewing what these conceptions mean and how they allow us to speak of there being reasons in an objective order of reasons. But, of course, none of this shows that such an order of reasons exists, any more than a clear concept of unicorn shows that unicorns exist. When can we say, then, that a political conception of justice yields objective reasons, politically speaking?

Let us say the following. Political convictions (which are also, of course, moral convictions) are objective—actually founded on an order of reasons—if reasonable and rational persons, who are sufficiently intelligent and conscientious in exercising their powers of practical reason, and whose reasoning exhibits none of the familiar defects of reasoning, would eventually endorse those convictions, or significantly narrow their differences about them, provided that these persons know the relevant facts and have sufficiently surveyed the grounds that bear on the matter under conditions favorable to due reflection.[24] (Here I assume that the practical conceptions people affirm satisfy the five essentials for objectivity already discussed [§5].) To say that a political conviction is objective is to say that there are reasons, specified by a reasonable and mutually recognizable political conception (satisfying those essentials), sufficient to convince all reasonable persons that it is reasonable. Whether such an order of reasons actually obtains, and whether such claims are in general reasonable, can only be shown by the overall success over time of the shared practice of practical reasoning by those who are reasonable and rational, and allow for the burdens of judgment. Granted this success, there is no defect in reasons of right and justice that needs to be made good by connecting them with a causal process.

2. I do not say that there being an objective order of political reasons consists in various activities of sound reasoning, or in the

24. I view this conception of objectivity for practical reasoning as essentially Kantian. A similar statement is found in Quinn's "Reflections," p. 199.

shared practice thereof, or in its success. Rather, the success of the shared practice among those reasonable and rational is what warrants our saying that there is an order of reasons. The idea is that if we can learn to use and apply the concepts of judgment and inference, and ground and evidence, as well as the principles and standards that single out the kind of facts to count as reasons of political justice; and if we find that by reasoning in the light of these mutually recognized criteria we can reach agreement in judgment; or if not agreement, that we can in any case narrow our differences sufficiently to secure what strikes us as just or fair, honorable or decent, relations between us; then all this supports the conviction that there are objective reasons. Those are the kind of grounds that support such a conviction.

Thus, given a background of successful practice over time, this considered agreement in judgment, or narrowing of differences, normally suffices for objectivity. As we have seen, the explanation of our convictions is often trivial: we assert a judgment and think it correct because we suppose we have correctly applied the relevant principles and criteria of practical reasoning. This parallels the reply of mathematicians who, when asked why they believe there are an infinity of primes, say: any mathematician knows the proof. The proof lays out the reasoning on which their belief is based. The absence of an explanation in cognitive psychology is not to the point: being able to give the proof, or to state sufficient reasons for judgment, is already the best possible explanation of the beliefs of those who are reasonable and rational.[25] At least for political purposes, there is no need to go beyond it to a better one, or behind it to a deeper one.[26]

25. Here the parallel with mathematics is instructive: for in this case we have objectivity without even knowing how to make sense of a wanted tie with a causal process.

26. This Kantian point is made by Nagel, who says: "The explanation of our conviction can be given by the content and validity of the argument"; *The View from Nowhere,* p. 145. It is the Kantian point we noted earlier (at the end of §2) in saying that he wanted to show the coherence and unity of reason, both theoretical and practical, with itself; and that reason is the final court of appeal and alone competent to settle the scope and limits of its own authority; and to specify its own principles

To be sure, when we cannot reach agreement, or narrow our disagreement, psychological considerations may become relevant. For this reason a sixth essential for objectivity is that we should be able to explain the failure of our judgments to converge by such things as the burdens of judgment: the difficulties of surveying and assessing all the evidence, or else the delicate balance of competing reasons on opposite sides of the issue, either of which leads us to expect that reasonable persons may differ (II:2). Thus, much important disagreement is consistent with objectivity, as the burdens of judgment allow. Yet disagreement may also arise from a lack of reasonableness, or rationality, or conscientiousness of one or more of the persons involved. But if we say this, we must be careful that the evidence for these failings is not simply the fact of disagreement itself. We must have independent grounds identifiable in the particular circumstances for thinking such causes of disagreement are at work. These grounds must also be in principle recognizable by those who disagree with us.[27] At this point psychology may enter in.

3. Finally, to prevent misunderstanding, I add a further point about constructivism. No constructive views, including Scanlon's, say that the facts that are relevant in practical reasoning and judgment are constructed, any more than they say that the conceptions of person and society are constructed.[28] To explain: we can distinguish two kinds of facts relevant for political reasoning. One kind is cited in giving reasons why an action or institution is, say, right or wrong, or just or unjust. These facts are the so-called right-and-wrong-making characteristics. The other kind is about the content of justice, or the nature of the virtues, or the political conception itself. They are given by the nature of

---

and canons of validity. We cannot ground these principles and canons on something outside reason. Its concepts of judgment and inference, and the rest, are irreducible. With these concepts explanations come to an end; one of philosophy's tasks is to quiet our distress at this thought.

27. Nagel makes this point in "Moral Conflict and Political Legitmacy," p. 231.

28. Here I revise considerably how I expressed this point in the third lecture of 1980. I am indebted to instructive criticism and comment by David Sachs and T. M. Scanlon.

the constructivist procedure. To illustrate the first kind of fact, to argue that slavery is unjust we appeal to the fact that it allows some persons to own others as their property and thus to control and own the product of their labor. To illustrate the second kind of fact, we may appeal straightaway to the fact that the nature of justice condemns slavery as unjust; or to the fact that the principles of justice condemn slavery as unjust. Basic to the political conception of justice as fairness is the fact that among the political virtues are toleration and mutual respect, and a sense of fairness and civility.[29]

With regard to the first kind of relevant facts, a constructivist procedure is framed to yield the principles and criteria that specify which facts about actions, institutions, persons, and the social world generally, are relevant in political deliberation. In claiming that slavery is unjust the relevant fact about it is not when it arose historically, or even whether it is economically efficient, but that it allows some persons to own others as their property. That is a fact about slavery, already there, so to speak, and independent of the principles of justice. The idea of constructing facts seems incoherent. In contrast, the idea of a constructivist procedure yielding principles and precepts to identify which facts are to count as reasons is quite clear. Recall how Kant's categorical imperative procedure accepts some maxims and rejects others; or how the original position selects principles of justice. Apart from a reasonable moral or political conception, facts are simply facts. What is wanted is a framework of reasoning within which to identify the facts that are relevant from the appropriate point of view and to determine their weight as reasons.[30] So understood, a constructivist political conception is not at odds with our commonsense ideas of truth and matters of fact.

---

29. On this point, see V:5.4.

30. I believe the above considerations hold of Scanlon's contractualism. To see this, consider what he says in "Contractualism and Utilitarianism," p. 118: namely, that while there are morally relevant properties in the world, as it were, these properties do not constitute instances of what John Mackie, in *Ethics: Inventing Right*

With regard to the second kind of relevant facts—those about the political conception itself—we say that these are not constructed but are facts about the possibilities of construction.[31] When we work out a political conception for a constitutional regime starting from the fundamental ideas of a well-ordered society as a fair system of cooperation between citizens, then it is a possibility of construction, implicit in the family of conceptions and principles of practical reasoning that are the basis of the construction, that slavery is unjust, and that the virtues of toleration and mutual respect, and a sense of fairness and civility, are great political virtues that such a regime may encourage. We may think of these possibilities as analogous to the way in which an infinity of primes is viewed (in constructivist arithmetic) as a possibility of construction.[32] This analogy does not commit us to a constructivist view of mathematics, which we want to avoid. We use it merely to clarify the idea of political constructivism. For this it suffices to understand the analogy; the truth of constructivism in mathematics is a separate matter.

4. Some may ask: why look for something to ground the fact that slavery is unjust? What is wrong with the trivial answer:

---

and Wrong (London: Penguin, 1977), chap. 1, refers to as intrinsically action-guiding. Rather, their moral force in justification, as well as their link with motivation, is to be explained by the contractualist idea of agreement, that is, in terms of principles that no one could reasonably reject. Without these principles those morally relevant properties lack, in Scanlon's view, any connection with either justification or motivation. Those principles are needed to identify the facts to count as reasons. Note en passant the way in which this feature of constructivism enables it to avoid the obscurity of the concept of intrinsic action-guidingness as sometimes stated.

31. The possibilities referred to here are those characterizing the moral or political conception that meets the tests of objectivity discussed earlier in this section. It is such a conception that concerns us.

32. For the idea of possibilities of construction, see Parsons's account of constructivism in "Mathematics, Foundations of," pp. 204f. (n. 12 above). He says: "Constructivist mathematics would proceed as if the last arbiter of mathematical existence and mathematical truth were the possibilities of construction," where the possibilities in question are those of an appropriately idealized procedure. The remark in the text about the infinity of primes rests on the fact that a constructivist proof of their infinity can be given.

slavery is unjust because slavery is unjust? Can't we stop with that? Why talk about possibilities of construction?[33]

Political constructivism does not look for something for the reasonableness of the statement that slavery is unjust to consist in, as if the reasonableness of it needed some kind of grounding. We may accept provisionally, though with confidence, certain considered judgments as fixed points, as what we take as basic facts, such as slavery is unjust. But we have a fully philosophical political conception only when such facts are coherently connected together by concepts and principles acceptable to us on due reflection. These basic facts do not lie around here and there like so many isolated bits. For there is: tyranny is unjust, exploitation is unjust, religious persecution is unjust, and on and on. We try to organize these indefinitely many facts into a conception of justice by the principles that issue from a reasonable procedure of construction.

Further, constructivism thinks it illuminating to say about slavery that it violates principles that would be agreed to in the original position by the representatives of persons as free and equal; or to put it in Scanlon's way, that it violates principles that cannot be reasonably rejected by persons who are motivated to find a free and informed basis of willing agreement in political life. The point here is that a basic form of moral motivation is the desire, expressed by the two aspects of being reasonable (II:1, 3), to arrange our common political life on terms that others cannot reasonably reject. Some such general characterization as this links together the many facts such as: slavery is unjust, tyranny is unjust, exploitation is unjust, and the rest. This is what is meant in saying that the basic facts are not disconnected. They can be joined by principles issuing from a procedure incorporating the requirements of practical reason, or so political constructivism claims (always limiting ourselves to the political). That the basic facts can be connected is not a fact

33. I am indebted to Rogers Albritton for illuminating discussion about these questions.

behind all the separate facts; it is simply the fact of those connections now open to view and expressed by the principles free and equal persons would accept when suitably represented.

5. Finally, some may object to the idea of possibilities of construction. Yet given the practice of arithmetic, they do not presumably object to the idea of the possibilities of counting, say, of counting from 1 to 100, or of counting the prime numbers from 1 to 1,000. Similarly, given that we can understand, use, and apply a constructivist procedure, then surely there are possibilities of construction associated with it. Without a clear idea of such a procedure, without being able to understand and apply it, the idea of the possibilities of construction is obscure. But granted those things, these possibilities seem straightforward. They are not offered as an explanation of there being the constructivist procedure, or for our being able to understand and apply it. The answer to these questions, so far as there is one, lies in the ideas of practical reason and how we understand them.

Why introduce the idea of a possibility of construction at all? It goes with the conception of justice we use to connect together the various facts about justice. There are facts about justice that may be discovered, as there are possibilities before anyone goes through a construction, say the possibilities that certain principles would be agreed to in the original position. Similarly, there are no possibilities in other cases; for example, there is no possibility that a principle allowing slavery would be agreed to. That is a fact related to the injustice of slavery.

§ 8: The Scope of Political Constructivism

1. From the beginning the scope of political constructivism has been limited to the political values that characterize the domain of the political; it is not proposed as an account of moral values generally. It does not say, as I assume Kant did, that not only is the order of all values presented by a constructivist argument but also that the moral order itself is constituted or made by the principles of practical reason.

The political values of a constitutional democracy are, however, seen as distinctive in the sense that they can be worked out
using the fundamental idea of society as a fair system of cooperation between free and equal citizens as reasonable and rational.
Granting all this, it does not follow, although it might be so, that
other kinds of values can also be appropriately constructed. Political constructivism neither asserts nor denies this. Otherwise a
constructivist conception could not be the focus of an overlapping consensus of reasonable comprehensive doctrines, since on
this question citizens will hold conflicting positions.

Political constructivism also holds that if a conception of justice is correctly founded on correctly stated principles and conceptions of practical reason, then that conception of justice is
reasonable for a constitutional regime (§1.5). Further, if that
conception can be the focus of an overlapping consensus of
reasonable doctrines, then, for political purposes, this suffices to
establish a public basis of justification. As we discuss in IV:3.3–
5, such a consensus is not a mere modus vivendi but is moral
in both its object and its content. An overlapping consensus
of reasonable doctrines may not be possible under many historical conditions, as the efforts to achieve it may be overwhelmed by unreasonable and even irrational (and sometimes
mad) comprehensive doctrines.

2. Many if not most citizens may want to give the political
conception a metaphysical foundation as part of their own comprehensive doctrine; and this doctrine (I assume) includes a conception of the truth of moral judgments. Let us say, then, that
when we speak of the moral truth of a political conception, we
assess it from the point of view of our comprehensive doctrine.[34]

34. I do not assume, however, that all comprehensive doctrines use the traditional
conception of a true moral judgment, or a modern variant thereof based on the
concepts of reference and satisfaction. They may use instead another concept of
correctness, say a concept of reasonableness that belongs to a comprehensive view in
that the concept of reasonableness is extended to cover a range of subjects beyond
the political, even if it is not fully universal. Thus, a form of contractualism can be a
comprehensive doctrine that uses a conception of reasonableness as its final criterion
of correctness.

Even when we think political constructivism gives a sufficient public basis of justification for political questions, we may not think, when we see things as individuals, or as members of religious or other associations, that it gives the full story about the truth of its principles and judgments. These further claims political constructivism neither asserts nor denies. As I have said, here it does not speak. It says only that for a reasonable and workable political conception, no more is needed than a public basis in the principles of practical reason in union with conceptions of society and person.

Political constructivism does not criticize, then, religious, philosophical, or metaphysical accounts of the truth of moral judgments and of their validity. Reasonableness is its standard of correctness, and given its political aims, it need not go beyond that. To see this, let us pick up again our discussion from II:3 about the reasonable, and suppose that there is an overlapping consensus of all the reasonable comprehensive doctrines (all agreeing on the political conception) and that there are no other doctrines in society. Then, as stated by Cohen, the following conditions hold:[35]

a. In appealing to reasons based on the political conception, citizens are appealing not only to what is publicly seen to be reasonable, but also to what all see as the correct moral reasons from within their own comprehensive view.

b. In accepting the political conception as the basis of public reason on fundamental political questions, and so appealing to only a part of the truth—that part expressed in the political conception—citizens are not simply acknowledging the political power of others. They are also recognizing that one another's comprehensive views are reasonable, even when they think them mistaken.

c. In recognizing others' views as reasonable, citizens also recognize that to insist on their own comprehensive view

35. These points are found in Joshua Cohen, "Moral Pluralism and Political Consensus," pp. 283f. I have simply rephrased them here.

must be seen by the rest as their simply insisting on their own beliefs (II:3.3). This is because, while people can recognize everyone else's comprehensive views as reasonable, they cannot recognize them all as true, and there is no shared public basis to distinguish the true beliefs from the false.

3. Observe, however, this further important fact: if any of those reasonable comprehensive doctrines supports only true moral judgments, the political conception itself is correct, or close thereto, since it is endorsed by a true doctrine. Thus, the truth of any one doctrine in the consensus guarantees that all the reasonable doctrines yield the right conception of political justice, even though they do not do so for the right reasons as specified by the one true doctrine. When citizens differ, not all can be fully correct, for some are correct for the wrong reasons; yet if one of their doctrines should be true, all citizens are correct, politically speaking: that is, they all appeal to a sound political conception of justice. Besides, we always think our own view is not only reasonable but also morally speaking true, or reasonable, as the case may be. Thus, everyone in a reasonable overlapping consensus finds the political conception acceptable, whatever each person's final criterion of correctness may be.

Should we think that any of the reasonable doctrines present in society are true, or approximately so, even in the long run? The political conception itself does not speak to this question. It aims to work out a political conception of justice that citizens as reasonable and rational can endorse on due reflection, and thus reach free and informed agreement on questions of constitutional essentials and basic matters of justice. With that done, the political conception is a reasonable basis of public reason, and that suffices.

From within our own comprehensive view, however, we can ask ourselves whether the support of an overlapping consensus of reasonable doctrines, especially when this support is sustained and increasingly strong over time, tends to confirm the political conception as in line with the correct account of the truth of moral judgments. We are to answer this question for ourselves individually, or as members of associations, keeping in mind always that reasonable pluralism—as opposed to pluralism as such—is the long-run outcome of the work of human reason under enduring free institutions. Whatever our specific view of the truth, or the reasonableness, of moral judgments may be, must we not suppose that at least the way to truth, or reasonableness, is to be found in one of the reasonable doctrines (or some mix thereof) arising under those conditions? And must not we add that this will be the more likely the more enduring and firm the consensus? To be sure, within a political conception of justice, we cannot define truth as given by the beliefs that would stand up even in an idealized consensus, however far extended. But in our comprehensive view is there no connection?

The advantage of staying within the reasonable is that there can be but one true comprehensive doctrine, though as we have seen, many reasonable ones. Once we accept the fact that reasonable pluralism is a permanent condition of public culture under free institutions, the idea of the reasonable is more suitable as part of the basis of public justification for a constitutional regime than the idea of moral truth. Holding a political conception as true, and for that reason alone the one suitable basis of public reason, is exclusive, even sectarian, and so likely to foster political division.

PART TWO

Political Liberalism: Three Main Ideas

The Idea of an Overlapping Consensus

We saw at the outset that political liberalism tries to answer the question: how is it possible that there can be a stable and just society whose free and equal citizens are deeply divided by conflicting and even incommensurable religious, philosophical, and moral doctrines? The first three lectures set out the first stage of the exposition of justice as fairness as a freestanding view addressed to this question. This first stage gives the principles of justice that specify the fair terms of cooperation among citizens and specify when a society's basic institutions are just.

The second stage of the exposition—to which we now turn—considers how the well-ordered democratic society of justice as fairness may establish and preserve unity and stability given the reasonable pluralism characteristic of it. In such a society, a reasonable comprehensive doctrine cannot secure the basis of social unity, nor can it provide the content of public reason on fundamental political questions. Thus, to see how a well-ordered society can be unified and stable, we introduce another basic idea of political liberalism to go with the idea of a political conception of justice, namely, the idea of an overlapping consensus of reasonable comprehensive doctrines. In such a consensus, the reasonable doctrines endorse the political conception, each from its own point of view. Social unity is based on a consensus on the political conception; and stability is possible when the doctrines making up the consensus are affirmed by society's politically active citizens and the requirements of justice are not too much in conflict with citizens' essential interests as formed and encouraged by their social arrangements.

After considering how political liberalism itself is possible and explaining the question of stability, I distinguish an overlapping consensus from a modus vivendi. Then I take up several objections to the idea of social unity based on a consensus of that kind. These objections need to be answered, as they stand in the way of what I believe is the most reasonable basis of social unity available to us.

§ 1. How Is Political Liberalism Possible?

1. One of the deepest distinctions between conceptions of justice is between those that allow for a plurality of reasonable though opposing comprehensive doctrines each with its own conception of the good, and those that hold that there is but one such conception to be recognized by all citizens who are fully reasonable and rational. Conceptions of justice that fall on opposite sides of this divide are distinct in many fundamental ways. Plato and Aristotle, and the Christian tradition as represented by Augustine and Aquinas, fall on the side of the one reasonable and rational good. Such views hold that institutions are justifiable to the extent that they effectively promote that good. Indeed,

134

beginning with Greek thought the dominant tradition seems to have been that there is but one reasonable and rational conception of the good. The aim of political philosophy—always viewed as part of moral philosophy, together with theology and metaphysics—is then to determine its nature and content. The classical utilitarianism of Bentham, Edgeworth, and Sidgwick belongs to this dominant tradition.[1]

By contrast, we have seen that political liberalism supposes that there are many conflicting reasonable comprehensive doctrines with their conceptions of the good, each compatible with the full rationality of human persons, so far as that can be ascertained with the resources of a political conception of justice.[2] As noted before (I:6.2), this reasonable plurality of conflicting and incommensurable doctrines is seen as the characteristic work of practical reason over time under enduring free institutions. So the question the dominant tradition has tried to answer has no answer: no comprehensive doctrine is appropriate as a political conception for a constitutional regime.[3]

2. Before asking how political liberalism is possible let us note that the political relationship in a constitutional regime has these two special features:

First, it is a relationship of persons within the basic structure of society, a structure of basic institutions we enter only by birth

1. So likewise do the recent forms of ethical liberalism as expressed by Joseph Raz in *The Morality of Freedom* (Oxford: Clarendon Press, 1986) and Ronald Dworkin, "The Foundations of Liberalism," in *The Tanner Lectures on Human Values* (Salt Lake City: University of Utah Press, 1991), vol. XI.

2. The point here is that while some would want to claim that given the full resources of philosophical reason, there is but one reasonable conception of the good, that cannot be shown by the resources of a reasonable political conception of justice.

3. This conclusion does not mean that the liberalisms of Kant and Mill are not reasonable and appropriate doctrines which lead one to support democratic institutions. But they are two such doctrines among others, and so but two of the philosophical views likely to persist and to gain adherents in a reasonably just democratic regime. Indeed, their liberalisms have a certain historical preeminence as being among the first and most important doctrines to affirm modern constitutional democracy and to develop ideas that have been significant in its justification and defense.

and exit only by death (or so we may appropriately assume). To us it seems that we have simply materialized, as it were, from nowhere at this position in this social world with all its advantages and disadvantages, according to our good or bad fortune. I say from nowhere because we have no prior public or nonpublic identity: we have not come from somewhere else into this social world. Political society is closed: we come to be within it and we do not, and indeed cannot, enter or leave it voluntarily.[4]

Second, political power is always coercive power backed by the government's use of sanctions, for government alone has the authority to use force in upholding its laws. In a constitutional regime the special feature of the political relation is that political power is ultimately the power of the public, that is, the power of free and equal citizens as a collective body. This power is regularly imposed on citizens as individuals and as members of associations, some of whom may not accept the reasons widely said to justify the general structure of political authority—the constitution—or when they do accept that structure, they may not regard as justified many of the statutes enacted by the legislature to which they are subject.

3. This raises the question of the legitimacy of the general structure of authority with which the idea of public reason (VI) is intimately connected. The background of this question is that, as always, we view citizens as reasonable and rational, as well as free and equal, and we also view the diversity of reasonable religious, philosophical, and moral doctrines found in democratic societies as a permanent feature of their public culture. Granting

---

4. The appropriateness of this assumption rests in part on a fact I shall only mention here: namely, that the right of emigration does not make the acceptance of political authority voluntary in the way that freedom of thought and liberty of conscience make the acceptance of ecclesiastical authority voluntary (VI:3.2). This brings out a further feature of the domain of the political, one that distinguishes it from the associational. Immigration is also a common fact but we can abstract from it to get an uncluttered view of the fundamental question of political philosophy (I:3.3). Of course, immigration is an important question and must be discussed at some stage. I surmise this is best done in discussing the appropriate relations between peoples, or the law of peoples, which I don't consider in these lectures.

this, and seeing political power as the power of citizens as a collective body, we ask: when is that power appropriately exercised? That is, in the light of what principles and ideals must we, as free and equal citizens, be able to view ourselves as exercising that power if our exercise of it is to be justifiable to other citizens and to respect their being reasonable and rational?

To this political liberalism says: our exercise of political power is fully proper only when it is exercised in accordance with a constitution the essentials of which all citizens as free and equal may reasonably be expected to endorse in the light of principles and ideals acceptable to their common human reason. This is the liberal principle of legitimacy. To this it adds that all questions arising in the legislature that concern or border on constitutional essentials, or basic questions of justice, should also be settled, so far as possible, by principles and ideals that can be similarly endorsed. Only a political conception of justice that all citizens might be reasonably expected to endorse can serve as a basis of public reason and justification.[5]

Let us say, then, that in a constitutional regime there is a special domain of the political identified by the two features above described, among others. The political is distinct from the associational, which is voluntary in ways that the political is not; it is also distinct from the personal and the familial, which are affectional, again in ways the political is not. (The associational, the personal, and the familial are simply three examples of the nonpolitical; there are others.)

4. Given the existence of a reasonably well-ordered constitutional regime, two points are central to political liberalism. First, questions about constitutional essentials and matters of basic

5. This paragraph can be stated more rigorously if we wish. One way to do this is to look at the question of legitimacy from the point of view of the original position. We suppose the parties to know the facts of reasonable pluralism and of oppression along with other relevant general information. We then try to show that the principles of justice they would adopt would in effect incorporate this principle of legitimacy and would justify only institutions it would count legitimate. See, further, VI:4.4.

justice are so far as possible to be settled by appeal to political values alone. Second, again with respect to those same fundamental questions, the political values expressed by its principles and ideals normally have sufficient weight to override all other values that may come in conflict with them.

Now in holding these convictions we clearly imply some relation between political and nonpolitical values. If it is said that outside the church there is no salvation, and therefore a constitutional regime cannot be accepted unless it is unavoidable, we must make some reply. In view of II:2–3 we say that such a doctrine is unreasonable: it proposes to use the public's political power—a power in which citizens have an equal share—to enforce a view bearing on constitutional essentials about which citizens as reasonable persons are bound to differ uncompromisingly. When there is a plurality of reasonable doctrines, it is unreasonable or worse to want to use the sanctions of state power to correct, or to punish, those who disagree with us.

Here it is important to stress that this reply does not say, for example, that the doctrine *extra ecclesiam nulla salus* is not true. Rather, it says that those who want to use the public's political power to enforce it are being unreasonable (II:3). That does not mean that what they believe is false. A reply from within a comprehensive view—the kind of reply we should like to avoid in political discussion—would say that the doctrine in question is a misapprehension of the divine nature, and hence not true. However, as we see below in §4, there may be no way to avoid entirely implying its lack of truth, even when considering constitutional essentials.

A basic point, however, is that in saying it is unreasonable to enforce a doctrine, while we may reject that doctrine as incorrect, we do not necessarily do so. Quite the contrary: it is vital to the idea of political liberalism that we may with perfect consistency hold that it would be unreasonable to use political power to enforce our own comprehensive view, which we must, of course, affirm as either reasonable or true.

5. Finally, we come to the question of how, as I have charac-

138

terized it, political liberalism is possible. That is, how can the values of the special domain of the political—the values of a subdomain of the realm of all values—normally outweigh whatever values may conflict with them? Put another way, how can we affirm our comprehensive doctrine and yet hold that it would not be reasonable to use state power to gain everyone's allegiance to it?

The answer to this question, the various aspects of which we shall discuss from now on, has two complementary parts. The first part says that values of the political are very great values and hence not easily overridden: these values govern the basic framework of social life—the very groundwork of our existence[6]—and specify the fundamental terms of political and social cooperation. In justice as fairness some of these great values—the values of justice—are expressed by the principles of justice for the basic structure: among them, the values of equal political and civil liberty; fair equality of opportunity; the values of economic reciprocity; the social bases of mutual respect between citizens.

Other great political values—the values of public reason—are expressed in the guidelines for public inquiry and in the steps taken to make such inquiry free and public, as well as informed and reasonable. We saw in II:4.1 that an agreement on a political conception of justice is to no effect without a companion agreement on guidelines of public inquiry and rules for assessing evidence. The values of public reason not only include the appropriate use of the fundamental concepts of judgment, inference, and evidence, but also the virtues of reasonableness and fairmindedness as shown in abiding by the criteria and procedures of commonsense knowledge and accepting the methods and conclusions of science when not controversial. We also owe respect to the precepts governing reasonable political discussion.

Together these values express to the liberal political ideal that since political power is the coercive power of free and equal citizens as a corporate body, this power should be exercised,

---

6. The phrase is from J. S. Mill, *Utilitarianism,* chap. 5, par. 25.

when constitutional essentials and basic questions of justice are at stake, only in ways that all citizens can reasonably be expected to endorse in the light of their common human reason.

6. Political liberalism tries, then, to present an account of these values as those of a special domain—the political—and hence as a freestanding view. It is left to citizens individually—as part of liberty of conscience—to settle how they think the values of the political domain are related to other values in their comprehensive doctrine. For we always assume that citizens have two views, a comprehensive and a political view; and that their overall view can be divided into two parts, suitably related. We hope that by doing this we can in working political practice ground the constitutional essentials and basic institutions of justice solely in those political values, with these values understood as the basis of public reason and justification.

But for this to hold, we need the second, and complementary, part of the answer as to how political liberalism is possible. This part says that the history of religion and philosophy shows that there are many reasonable ways in which the wider realm of values can be understood so as to be either congruent with, or supportive of, or else not in conflict with, the values appropriate to the special domain of the political as specified by a political conception of justice. History tells of a plurality of not unreasonable comprehensive doctrines. This makes an overlapping consensus possible, thus reducing the conflict between political and other values.

§ 2. The Question of Stability

1. Justice as fairness is best presented in two stages (I:3.6).[7] In the first stage it is worked out as a freestanding political (but of

---

7. These two stages correspond to the two parts of the argument from the original position for the two principles of justice in *Theory*. In the first part the parties select principles without taking into account the effects of the special psychologies while in the second part they ask whether a society well ordered by the principles selected in the first part would be stable: that is, generate in its members a sufficiently strong

course moral) conception for the basic structure of society. Only with this done and its content—its principles of justice and ideals—provisionally on hand do we take up, in the second stage, the problem whether justice as fairness is sufficiently stable. Unless it is so, it is not a satisfactory political conception of justice and it must be in some way revised.

Stability involves two questions: the first is whether people who grow up under just institutions (as the political conception defines them) acquire a normally sufficient sense of justice so that they generally comply with those institutions. The second question is whether in view of the general facts that characterize a democracy's public political culture, and in particular the fact of reasonable pluralism, the political conception can be the focus of an overlapping consensus. I assume this consensus to consist of reasonable comprehensive doctrines likely to persist and gain adherents over time within a just basic structure (as the political conception defines it).

Each question of stability has a separate answer. The first is answered by setting out the moral psychology (II:7) in accordance with which citizens in a well-ordered society acquire a normally sufficient sense of justice so that they comply with its just arrangements. The second is answered by the idea of an overlapping consensus and meeting the various difficulties arising in connection with it (§§4–7).

While the problem of stability has been on our minds from the outset, the explicit discussion of it begins only at the second stage since the principles of justice for the basic structure are not on hand until then. Their content is not affected in any way by the particular comprehensive doctrines that may exist in society. This is because, at the first stage, justice as fairness abstracts from the knowledge of citizens' determinate conceptions of the good and proceeds from shared political conceptions of society and

---

sense of justice to counteract tendencies to injustice. See chaps. VIII–IX. The argument for the principles of justice is not complete until the principles selected in the first part are shown in the second part to be sufficiently stable; and doing this extends to the next to last section, §86. For these two parts, cf. pp. 144, 530f.

person that are required in applying the ideals and principles of practical reason. So while a political conception of justice addresses the fact of reasonable pluralism, it is not political in the wrong way: that is, its form and content are not affected by the existing balance of political power between comprehensive doctrines. Nor do its principles strike a compromise between the more dominant ones.

2. To clarify the idea of stability, let us distinguish two ways in which a political conception may be concerned with it.[8] In one way we view stability as a purely practical matter: if a conception fails to be stable, it is futile to try to realize it. Perhaps we think there are two separate tasks: one is to work out a political conception that seems sound, or reasonable, at least to us; the other is to find ways to bring others who reject it also to share it; or failing that, to act in accordance with it, if need be prompted by penalties enforced by state power. As long as the means of persuasion or enforcement can be found, the conception is viewed as stable.

But, as a liberal conception, justice as fairness is concerned with stability in a different way. Finding a stable conception is not simply a matter of avoiding futility. Rather, what counts is the kind of stability, the nature of the forces that secure it. To answer the first question of stability noted above, we try to show that, given certain assumptions specifying a reasonable human psychology and the normal conditions of human life, those who grow up under just basic institutions acquire a sense of justice and a reasoned allegiance to those institutions sufficient to render them stable. Expressed another way, citizens' sense of justice, given their traits of character and interests as formed by living under a just basic structure, is strong enough to resist the normal tendencies to injustice. Citizens act willingly so as to give one another justice over time. Stability is secured by sufficient

8. In this and the next several paragraphs I am indebted to helpful discussion with Scanlon.

142

motivation of the appropriate kind acquired under just institutions.[9]

To answer the second question as to whether, given the fact of reasonable pluralism, justice as fairness can be the focus of an overlapping consensus, we have to discuss not only the idea of such a consensus and the difficulties it raises, but also to show how, with the same reasonable moral psychology used in answering the first question, justice as fairness can indeed assume that role.

3. The kind of stability required of justice as fairness is based, then, on its being a liberal political view, one that aims at being acceptable to citizens as reasonable and rational, as well as free and equal, and so as addressed to their public reason. Earlier, in §1.2, we saw how this feature of liberalism connects with the feature of political power in a constitutional regime: namely, that it is the power of equal citizens as a collective body. If justice as fairness were not expressly designed to gain the reasoned support of citizens who affirm reasonable although conflicting comprehensive doctrines—the existence of such conflicting doctrines being a feature of the kind of public culture that liberal conception itself encourages—it would not be liberal.

The point, then, is that the problem of stability is not that of bringing others who reject a conception to share it, or to act in accordance with it, by workable sanctions, if necessary, as if the task were to find ways to impose that conception once we are convinced it is sound. Rather, justice as fairness is not reasonable in the first place unless in a suitable way it can win its support by addressing each citizen's reason, as explained within its own framework.[10] Only so is it an account of the legitimacy of political authority as opposed to an account of how those who hold

9. How this happens I have discussed in *Theory,* esp. chap. VIII. I hope that account suffices, for our purposes here, to convey the main idea.

10. The force of the phrase "within its own framework" as used in the text is expressed by the two parts of the argument from the original position as stated in n. 7 above. Both parts are carried out within the same framework and subject to the same conditions embedded in the original position as a device of representation.

political power can satisfy themselves, and not citizens generally, that they are acting properly.[11] A conception of political legitimacy aims for a public basis of justification and appeals to public reason, and hence to free and equal citizens viewed as reasonable and rational.

§ 3. Three Features of an Overlapping Consensus

1. Before beginning, I recall two main points about the idea of an overlapping consensus. The first is that we look for a consensus of reasonable (as opposed to unreasonable or irrational) comprehensive doctrines. The crucial fact is not the fact of pluralism as such, but of reasonable pluralism (I:6.2). This diversity political liberalism sees, as I have said, as the long-run result of the powers of human reason within an enduring background of free institutions. The fact of reasonable pluralism is not an unfortunate condition of human life, as we might say of pluralism as such, allowing for doctrines that are not only irrational but mad and aggressive. In framing a political conception of justice so it can gain an overlapping consensus, we are not bending it to existing unreason, but to the fact of reasonable pluralism, itself the outcome of the free exercise of free human reason under conditions of liberty.

For the second point about an overlapping consensus, recall that, at the end of I:1.3–4, I said that in a constitutional democracy the public conception of justice should be, so far as possible, presented as independent of comprehensive religious, philosophical, and moral doctrines. This meant that justice as fairness is to be understood at the first stage of its exposition as a freestanding view that expresses a political conception of justice. It does not provide a specific religious, metaphysical, or epistemological doctrine beyond what is implied by the political conception itself. As remarked in I:2.2, the political conception is a

---

11. For this distinction, see Thomas Nagel's *Equality and Partiality* (New York: Oxford University Press, 1991), chap. 3, p. 23.

module, an essential constituent part, that in different ways fits into and can be supported by various reasonable comprehensive doctrines that endure in the society regulated by it.

2. There are at least four objections likely to be raised against the idea of social unity founded on an overlapping consensus on a political conception of justice. I begin with perhaps the most obvious of these, namely, that an overlapping consensus is a mere modus vivendi.

To fix ideas I shall use a model case of an overlapping consensus to indicate what is meant; and I shall return to this example from time to time. It contains three views: one affirms the political conception because its religious doctrine and account of free faith[12] lead to a principle of toleration and underwrite the fundamental liberties of a constitutional regime; while the second view affirms the political conception on the basis of a comprehensive liberal moral doctrine such as those of Kant or Mill. The third, however, is not systematically unified: besides the political values formulated by a freestanding political conception of justice, it includes a large family of nonpolitical values. It is a pluralist view, let us say, since each subpart of this family has its own account based on ideas drawn from within it, leaving all values to be balanced against one another, either in groups or singly, in particular kinds of cases.

In this model case the religious doctrine and the liberalisms of Kant and Mill are taken to be general and comprehensive. The third view is only partially comprehensive but holds, with politi-

---

12. This idea is illustrated by various of Locke's statements in *A Letter Concerning Toleration* (1690). He says such things as: 1) God has given no man authority over another (p. 129); 2) no man can abandon the care of his own salvation to the care of another (pp. 129, 139, 154); 3) the understanding cannot be compelled by force to belief (p. 129); 4) the care of men's souls is not given to the magistrate as that would determine faith by where we were born (p. 130); 5) a church is a voluntary society, and no man is bound to any particular church and he may leave it as freely as he entered (p. 131); 6) excommunication does not affect civil relationships (p. 134); 7) only faith and inward sincerity gain our salvation and acceptance with God (p. 143). (Page references are to the edition of J. W. Gough, *Two Treatises of Government with A Letter on Toleration* (Oxford: Basil Blackwell, 1956). Other writers on toleration would have served as well.)

145

cal liberalism, that under reasonably favorable conditions that make democracy possible, political values normally outweigh whatever nonpolitical values conflict with them. The previous views agree with the last in this respect and so all views lead to roughly the same political judgments and thus overlap on the political conception.

3. To begin with the objection: some will think that even if an overlapping consensus were sufficiently stable, the idea of political unity founded on an overlapping consensus must still be rejected, since it abandons the hope of political community and settles instead for a public understanding that is at bottom a mere modus vivendi. To this objection, we say that the hope of political community must indeed be abandoned, if by such a community we mean a political society united in affirming the same comprehensive doctrine. This possibility is excluded by the fact of reasonable pluralism together with the rejection of the oppressive use of the state power to overcome it.[13] The substantive question concerns the significant features of such a consensus and how these features affect social concord and the moral qual-

13. Note that what is impracticable is not all values of community (recall that a community is understood as an association or society whose unity rests on a comprehensive conception of the good) but only political community and its values. Justice as fairness assumes, as other liberal political views do also, that the values of community are not only essential but realizable, first in the various associations that carry on their life within the framework of the basic structure, and second in those associations that extend across the boundaries of political societies, such as churches and scientific societies. Liberalism rejects political society as a community because, among other things, it leads to the systematic denial of basic liberties and may allow the oppressive use of the government's monopoly of (legal) force. Of course, in the well-ordered society of justice as fairness citizens share a common aim, and one that has high priority: namely, the aim of insuring that political and social institutions are just, and of giving justice to persons generally, as what citizens need for themselves and want for one another. It is not true, then, that in a liberal view citizens have no fundamental common aims (V:7). Nor is it true that the aim of political justice is not an important part of their noninstitutional, or moral, identity (as discussed in I:5.2). But this common aim of political justice must not be mistaken for (what I have called) "a conception of the good." For a discussion of this last point, see Amy Gutmann, "Communitarian Critics of Liberalism," *Philosophy and Public Affairs* 14 (Summer 1985):311, footnote.

ity of public life. I turn to why an overlapping consensus is not a mere modus vivendi.

A typical use of the phrase "modus vivendi" is to characterize a treaty between two states whose national aims and interests put them at odds. In negotiating a treaty each state would be wise and prudent to make sure that the agreement proposed represents an equilibrium point: that is, that the terms and conditions of the treaty are drawn up in such a way that it is public knowledge that it is not advantageous for either state to violate it. The treaty will then be adhered to because doing so is regarded by each as in its national interest, including its interest in its reputation as a state that honors treaties. But in general both states are ready to pursue their goals at the expense of the other, and should conditions change they may do so. This background highlights the way in which such a treaty is a mere modus vivendi. A similar background is present when we think of social consensus founded on self- or group interests, or on the outcome of political bargaining: social unity is only apparent, as its stability is contingent on circumstances remaining such as not to upset the fortunate convergence of interests.

4. That an overlapping consensus is quite different from a modus vivendi is clear from our model case. In that example, note two aspects: first, the object of consensus, the political conception of justice, is itself a moral conception. And second, it is affirmed on moral grounds, that is, it includes conceptions of society and of citizens as persons, as well as principles of justice, and an account of the political virtues through which those principles are embodied in human character and expressed in public life. An overlapping consensus, therefore, is not merely a consensus on accepting certain authorities, or on complying with certain institutional arrangements, founded on a convergence of self- or group interests. All those who affirm the political conception start from within their own comprehensive view and draw on the religious, philosophical, and moral grounds it provides. The fact that people affirm the same political conception on those grounds does not make their affirming it any less religious,

philosophical, or moral, as the case may be, since the grounds sincerely held determine the nature of their affirmation.

The preceding two aspects of an overlapping consensus— moral object and moral grounds—connect with a third aspect, that of stability. This means that those who affirm the various views supporting the political conception will not withdraw their support of it should the relative strength of their view in society increase and eventually become dominant. So long as the three views are affirmed and not revised, the political conception will still be supported regardless of shifts in the distribution of political power. Each view supports the political conception for its own sake, or on its own merits. The test for this is whether the consensus is stable with respect to changes in the distribution of power among views. This feature of stability highlights a basic contrast between an overlapping consensus and a modus vivendi, the stability of which does depend on happenstance and a balance of relative forces.

This becomes clear once we change our example and include the views of Catholics and Protestants in the sixteenth century. At that time there was not an overlapping consensus on the principle of toleration. Both faiths held that it was the duty of the ruler to uphold the true religion and to repress the spread of heresy and false doctrine.[14] In such a case the acceptance of the principle of toleration would indeed be a mere modus vivendi, because if either faith becomes dominant, the principle of toleration would no longer be followed. Stability with respect to the distribution of power is lacking. So long as such views as those of Catholic and Protestant in the sixteenth century are very much in the minority, and are likely to remain so, they do not significantly affect the moral quality of public life and the basis of social concord. For the vast majority in society are confident that the distribution of power will range over and be widely shared by views in the consensus that affirm the political conception of

14. See J. W. Allen, *A History of Political Thought in the Sixteenth Century* (London: Methuen, 1941), pt. I, chap. 5, pt. II, chap. 9, pt. III, Chaps. 4, 6, 8; and Quentin Skinner, *The Foundations of Modern Political Thought* (Cambridge: Cambridge University Press, 1978), vol. II, esp. pt. III.

justice for its own sake. But should this situation change, the moral quality of political life will also change in ways that are obvious and require no comment.

5. In conclusion I comment briefly on what we may call "the depth and breadth of an overlapping consensus" and the specificity of its focus; that is, how deep does the consensus go into citizens' comprehensive doctrines? How broad are the institutions to which it applies? And how specific is the conception agreed to?

The preceding account says that the consensus goes down to the fundamental ideas within which justice as fairness is worked out. It supposes agreement deep enough to reach such ideas as those of society as a fair system of cooperation and of citizens as reasonable and rational, and free and equal. As for its breadth, it covers the principles and values of a political conception (in this case those of justice as fairness) and it applies to the basic structure as a whole. This degree of depth and breadth and specificity helps to fix ideas and keeps before us the main question: consistent with plausibly realistic assumptions, what is the deepest and widest feasible conception of political justice?

There are, of course, other possibilities. I have not supposed that an overlapping consensus on a political conception is necessary for certain kinds of social unity and stability. Rather I have said that, with two other conditions, it is sufficient for the most reasonable basis of social unity available to us (I:8.1). Yet as Baier has suggested, a less deep consensus on the principles and rules of a workable political constitution may be sufficient for less demanding purposes and far easier to obtain. He thinks that in fact in the United States we have actually achieved something like that. So rather than supposing that the consensus reaches down to a political conception covering principles for the whole of the basic structure, a consensus may cover only certain fundamental procedural political principles for the constitution.[15] I

15. These points are made by Kurt Baier in a valuable discussion, "Justice and the Aims of Political Philosophy," *Ethics* 99 (July 1989):771–90. His idea of a consensus on constitutional principles (which he thinks we largely have), rather than on a conception of justice, is found at pp. 775f.

return to these matters in §§6–7 when we discuss the steps from "constitutional consensus," as I shall call it, to overlapping consensus.

§ 4. An Overlapping Consensus not Indifferent or Skeptical

1. I turn to a second objection to the idea of an overlapping consensus on a political conception of justice: namely, that the avoidance of general and comprehensive doctrines implies indifference or skepticism as to whether a political conception of justice can be true, as opposed to reasonable in the constructivist sense. This avoidance may appear to suggest that such a conception might be the most reasonable one for us even when it is known not to be true, as if truth were simply beside the point. In reply, it would be fatal to the idea of a political conception to see it as skeptical about, or indifferent to, truth, much less as in conflict with it. Such skepticism or indifference would put political philosophy in opposition to numerous comprehensive doctrines, and thus defeat from the outset its aim of achieving an overlapping consensus.

We try, so far as we can, neither to assert nor to deny any particular comprehensive religious, philosophical, or moral view, or its associated theory of truth and the status of values. Since we assume each citizen to affirm some such view, we hope to make it possible for all to accept the political conception as true or reasonable from the standpoint of their own comprehensive view, whatever it may be. Properly understood, then, a political conception of justice need be no more indifferent, say, to truth in philosophy and morals than the principle of toleration, suitably understood, need be indifferent to truth in religion. Since we seek an agreed basis of public justification in matters of justice, and since no political agreement on those disputed questions can reasonably be expected, we turn instead to the fundamental ideas we seem to share through the public political culture. From these ideas we try to work out a political conception of justice congruent with our considered convictions on due reflection. Once this is done, citizens may within their comprehensive doctrines regard the political conception of justice as true, or as reasonable, whatever their view allows.

2. Some may not be satisfied with this; they may reply that, despite these protests, a political conception of justice must express indifference or skepticism. Otherwise it could not lay aside fundamental religious, philosophical, and moral questions because they are politically difficult to settle, or may prove intractable. Certain truths, it may be said, concern things so important that differences about them have to be fought out, even should this mean civil war. To this we say first that questions are not removed from the political agenda, so to speak, solely because they are a source of conflict. We appeal instead to a political conception of justice to distinguish between those questions that can be reasonably removed from the political agenda and those that cannot. Some questions still on the agenda will be controversial, at least to some degree; this is normal with political issues.

To illustrate: from within a political conception of justice let us suppose we can account both for equal liberty of conscience, which takes the truths of religion off the political agenda, and the equal political and civil liberties, which by ruling out serfdom and slavery take the possibility of those institutions off the agenda.[16] But controversial issues inevitably remain: for ex-

16. To explain: when certain matters are taken off the political agenda, they are no longer regarded as appropriate subjects for political decision by majority or other plurality voting. For example, in regard to equal liberty of conscience and the rejection of slavery and serfdom, this means that the equal basic liberties in the constitution that cover these matters are reasonably taken as fixed, as correctly settled once and for all. They are part of the public charter of a constitutional regime and not a suitable topic for ongoing public debate and legislation, as if they can be changed, one way or the other by the requisite majorities. Moreover, the more established political parties likewise acknowledge these matters as settled. See Stephen Holmes, "Gag Rules or the Politics of Omission," in *Constitutional Democracy,* edited by J. Elster and R. Slagstad (Cambridge: Cambridge University Press, 1987).

Of course, that certain matters are reasonably taken off the political agenda does not mean that a political conception of justice should not provide the grounds and

ample, how more exactly to draw the boundaries of the basic liberties when they conflict (where to set "the wall between church and state"); how to interpret the requirements of distributive justice even when there is considerable agreement on general principles for the basic structure; and finally, questions of policy such as the use of nuclear weapons. These cannot be removed from politics. But by avoiding comprehensive doctrines we try to bypass religion and philosophy's profoundest controversies so as to have some hope of uncovering a basis of a stable overlapping consensus.

3. Nevertheless, in affirming a political conception of justice we may eventually have to assert at least certain aspects of our own comprehensive religious or philosophical doctrine (by no means necessarily fully comprehensive).[17] This will happen whenever someone insists, for example, that certain questions are so fundamental that to insure their being rightly settled justifies civil strife. The religious salvation of those holding a particular religion, or indeed the salvation of a whole people, may be said to depend on it. At this point we may have no alternative but to deny this, or to imply its denial and hence to maintain the kind of thing we had hoped to avoid.

To consider this, imagine rationalist believers who contend

---

reasons why this should be done. Indeed, as I note above, a political conception should do precisely this. But normally the fuller discussions of these questions between various political doctrines and their roots in comprehensive doctrines is part of the background culture (I:2.3).

Finally, in saying that certain matters are taken off the political agenda once and for all, some may object that we can be mistaken, as we have been in the past about toleration and slavery. Certainly we have been mistaken, but does anyone doubt for that reason that the principle of toleration may be mistaken or that it is wrong to have abolished slavery? Who seriously thinks so? Is there any real chance of a mistake? And surely we don't want to say: we take certain matters off the agenda for the time being. Or until the next election. Or the next generation. Why isn't "once and for all" the best way to put it? By using that phrase citizens express to one another a firm commitment about their common status. They express a certain ideal of democratic citizenship.

17. As I said in I:2, a doctrine is fully comprehensive if it covers all recognized values and virtues within one rather precisely articulated system; whereas a doctrine is only partially comprehensive when it comprises a number of nonpolitical values and virtues and is rather loosely articulated. This limited scope and looseness turns out to be important with regard to stability in §6 below.

that these beliefs are open to and can be fully established by reason (uncommon though this view may be).[18] In this case the believers simply deny what we have called "the fact of reasonable pluralism." So we say of the rationalist believers that they are mistaken in denying that fact; but we need not say that their religious beliefs are not true, since to deny that religious beliefs can be publicly and fully established by reason is not to say that they are not true. Of course, we do not believe the doctrine believers here assert, and this is shown in what we do. Even if we do not, say, hold some form of the doctrine of free religious faith that supports equal liberty of conscience, our actions nevertheless imply that we believe the concern for salvation does not require anything incompatible with that liberty. Still, we do not put forward more of our comprehensive view than we think needed or useful for the political aim of consensus.

4. The reason for this restraint is to respect, as best we can, the limits of public reason (discussed in VI). Let us suppose that by respecting these limits we succeed in reaching an overlapping consensus on a conception of political justice. It will then be, for the moment at least, reasonable. Some might insist that reaching this reflective agreement is itself sufficient grounds for regarding that conception as true, or at any rate highly probable. But we refrain from this further step: it is unnecessary and may interfere with the practical aim of finding an agreed public basis of justification. For many the true, or the religiously and the metaphysically well-grounded, goes beyond the reasonable. The idea of an overlapping consensus leaves this step to be taken by citizens individually in line with their own comprehensive views.[19]

---

18. The idea of rationalist believers is adapted from Joshua Cohen's discussion, "Moral Pluralism and Political Consensus." My reply is similar to his, as I understand it. Cohen also discusses the case of nonrationalist believers who do not claim that reason supports their faith but who do claim that since their beliefs are true, state power is properly used to enforce it. This claim is replied to in II:3.3.

19. Recall here the further important fact from III:8.3: namely, that if any of the reasonable comprehensive doctrines in the existing overlapping consensus is true, then the political conception itself is true, or close thereto in the sense of being endorsed by a true doctrine. The truth of any one doctrine guarantees that all doctrines yield the right conception of political justice, even though all are not right

Were justice as fairness to make an overlapping consensus possible it would complete and extend the movement of thought that began three centuries ago with the gradual acceptance of the principle of toleration and led to the nonconfessional state and equal liberty of conscience. This extension is required for an agreement on a political conception of justice given the historical and social circumstances of a democratic society. To apply the principles of toleration to philosophy itself is to leave to citizens themselves to settle the questions of religion, philosophy, and morals in accordance with views they freely affirm.

§ 5. A Political Conception Need not be Comprehensive

1. A third objection is the following: even if we grant that an overlapping consensus is not a modus vivendi, as I have defined it, some may say that a workable political conception must be general and comprehensive. Without such a doctrine on hand, there is no way to order the many conflicts of justice that arise in public life. The deeper the conceptual and philosophical bases of those conflicts, the objection continues, the more general and comprehensive the level of philosophical reflection must be if their roots are to be laid bare and an appropriate ordering found. It is useless, the objection concludes, to try to work out a political conception of justice expressly for the basic structure apart from any comprehensive doctrine. As we have just seen, we may be forced to refer, at least in some way, to such a view.[20]

---

for the right reasons as given by the one true doctrine. So, as we have said, when citizens differ, not all can be fully correct; yet if one of their doctrines should be true, all citizens are correct, politically speaking.

20. There is a distinction between general and comprehensive views and views that are abstract. When justice as fairness begins from the fundamental idea of society as a fair system of cooperation and proceeds to elaborate that idea, the resulting conception of political justice may be said to be abstract. It is abstract in the same way that the conception of a perfectly competitive market, or of general economic equilibrium, is abstract: that is, it singles out certain aspects of society as especially significant from the standpoint of political justice and leaves others aside. But whether the conception that results itself is general and comprehensive, as I have used those

This objection is perfectly natural, as we are tempted to ask: how else could these conflicting claims be adjudicated? Yet part of the answer is found in the third view of our model case. This view is pluralist, we said, and not systematically unified: besides the political values formulated by a freestanding political conception of justice, it includes a large family of nonpolitical values. Each subpart of this family has its own account based on ideas drawn from within it, leaving all values to be balanced against one another (§3.2). Thus the political conception can be seen as part of a comprehensive doctrine but it is not a consequence of that doctrine's nonpolitical values. Nevertheless, its political values normally outweigh whatever other values oppose them, at least under the reasonably favorable conditions that make a constitutional democracy possible.

Those who hold this conception recognize values and virtues belonging to other parts of life. They differ from citizens holding the first two views in our model case in having no fully (as opposed to partially)[21] comprehensive doctrine within which they see all values and virtues as being more or less systematically ordered. They do not say such a doctrine is impossible, but rather, practically speaking, unnecessary. Their conviction is that, within the scope allowed by the basic liberties and the other provisions of a just constitutional regime, all citizens can pursue their way of life on fair terms and properly respect its (nonpolitical) values. With those constitutional guarantees secure, they think no conflict of values is likely to arise that justifies their opposing the political conception as a whole, or on such fundamental matters as liberty of conscience, or equal political liberties, or basic civil rights.

2. This partially comprehensive view might be explained as

---

terms, is a separate question. I believe the conflicts implicit in the fact of reasonable pluralism force political philosophy to present conceptions of justice that are abstract, if it is to achieve its aims (I:8.2); but the same conflicts prevent those conceptions from being general and comprehensive.

21. For the distinction between a doctrine's being fully vs. partially comprehensive, see I:2.2.

follows. We do best not to assume that there exist generally acceptable answers for all or even for many questions of political justice. Rather, we must be prepared to accept the fact that only a few questions we are moved to ask can be satisfactorily resolved. Political wisdom consists in identifying those few, and among them the most urgent.

That done, we must frame the institutions of the basic structure so that intractable conflicts are unlikely to arise; we must also accept the need for clear and simple principles, the general form and content of which we hope can be publicly understood. A political conception is at best but a guiding framework of deliberation and reflection which helps us reach political agreement on at least the constitutional essentials and the basic questions of justice. If it seems to have cleared our view and made our considered convictions more coherent; if it has narrowed the gap between the conscientious convictions of those who accept the basic ideas of a constitutional regime, then it has served its practical political purpose.[22]

This remains true even if we cannot fully explain our agreement: we know only that citizens who affirm the political conception, and who have been raised in and are familiar with the fundamental ideas of the public political culture, find that, when they adopt its framework of deliberation, their judgments converge sufficiently so that political cooperation on the basis of mutual respect can be maintained. They view the political conception as itself normally sufficient and may not expect, or think they need, greater political understanding than that.

3. Here we are bound to ask: how can a political conception of justice express values that, under the reasonably favorable conditions that make democracy possible, normally outweigh whatever other values are likely to conflict with them? One reason is this. As I have said, the most reasonable political conception of justice for a democratic regime will be, broadly speaking, liberal. This means that it protects the familiar basic rights

22. See *Theory,* pp. 44f., 89f., 303, 364.

and assigns them a special priority; it also includes measures to insure that all citizens have sufficient material means to make effective use of those basic rights. Faced with the fact of reasonable pluralism, a liberal view removes from the political agenda the most divisive issues, serious contention about which must undermine the bases of social cooperation.

The virtues of political cooperation that make a constitutional regime possible are, then, very great virtues. I mean, for example, the virtues of tolerance and being ready to meet others halfway, and the virtue of reasonableness and the sense of fairness. When these virtues are widespread in society and sustain its political conception of justice, they constitute a very great public good, part of society's political capital.[23] Thus, the values that conflict with the political conception of justice and its sustaining virtues may be normally outweighed because they come into conflict with the very conditions that make fair social cooperation possible on a footing of mutual respect.

4. The other reason political values normally win out is that severe conflicts with other values are much reduced. This is because when an overlapping consensus supports the political conception, this conception is not viewed as incompatible with basic religious, philosophical, and moral values. We need not consider the claims of political justice against the claims of this or that comprehensive view; nor need we say that political values are intrinsically more important than other values and that is why the latter are overridden. Having to say that is just what we hope to avoid, and achieving an overlapping consensus enables us to do so.

To conclude: given the fact of reasonable pluralism, what the work of reconciliation by public reason does, thus enabling us to

---

23. The term *capital* is appropriate in this connection because these virtues are built up slowly over time and depend not only on existing political and social institutions (themselves slowly built up), but also on citizens' experience as a whole and their knowledge of the past. Again, like capital, these virtues depreciate, as it were, and must be constantly renewed by being reaffirmed and acted from in the present.

157

avoid reliance on general and comprehensive doctrines, is two things: first, it identifies the fundamental role of political values in expressing the terms of fair social cooperation consistent with mutual respect between citizens regarded as free and equal; and second, it uncovers a sufficiently inclusive concordant fit among political and other values seen in a reasonable overlapping consensus. We discuss this further below.

§ 6. Steps to Constitutional Consensus

1. The last difficulty I consider is that an overlapping consensus is utopian: that is, there are not sufficient political, social, or psychological forces either to bring about an overlapping consensus (when one does not exist), or to render one stable (should one exist). I can only touch on this question and merely outline one way in which it seems such a consensus might come about and its stability secured.

The outline is in two stages. The first stage ends with a constitutional consensus,[24] the second with an overlapping consensus. The constitution at the first stage satisfies certain liberal principles of political justice. As a constitutional consensus, these principles are accepted simply as principles and not as grounded in certain ideas of society and person of a political conception, much less in a shared public conception. And so the consensus is not deep.

In constitutional consensus, a constitution satisfying certain basic principles establishes democratic electoral procedures for moderating political rivalry within society. This rivalry includes not only that between classes and interests but also between those favoring certain liberal principles over others, for whatever

24. For the idea of constitutional consensus I am indebted to Kurt Baier's views cited in n. 15 above. I am indebted also to David Peritz for valuable correspondence and for instructive comments on the text. But for them I would not have made this revision in my original account as given in VI–VII of "The Idea of an Overlapping Consensus," *Oxford Journal of Legal Studies* 7 (February 1987).

reasons. While there is agreement on certain basic political rights and liberties—on the right to vote and freedom of political speech and association, and whatever else is required for the electoral and legislative procedures of democracy—there is disagreement among those holding liberal principles as to the more exact content and boundaries of these rights and liberties, as well as on what further rights and liberties are to be counted as basic and so merit legal if not constitutional protection. The constitutional consensus is not deep and it is also not wide: it is narrow in scope, not including the basic structure but only the political procedures of democratic government.

2. How might a constitutional consensus come about? Suppose that at a certain time, because of various historical events and contingencies, certain liberal principles of justice are accepted as a mere modus vivendi, and are incorporated into existing political institutions. This acceptance has come about, let us say, in much the same way as the acceptance of the principle of toleration came about as a modus vivendi following the Reformation: at first reluctantly, but nevertheless as providing the only workable alternative to endless and destructive civil strife. Our question, then, is this: how might it happen that over time the initial acquiescence in a constitution satisfying these liberal principles of justice develops into a constitutional consensus in which those principles themselves are affirmed?

At this point, a certain looseness in our comprehensive views, as well as their not being fully comprehensive, may be particularly significant. To see this, let us return to our model case (§3.2). One way in which that example may be atypical is that two of the three doctrines were described as fully general and comprehensive: a religious doctrine of free faith and the comprehensive liberalism of Kant or Mill. In these cases the acceptance of the political conception was said to be derived from and to depend solely on the comprehensive doctrine. But how far in practice does the allegiance to a principle of political justice actually depend on the knowledge of or the belief in its derivation from a comprehensive view rather than on seeming reasonable in itself or as being viewed as part of a pluralist view, which is the third doctrine in our model case?

There are several possibilities. Distinguish three cases: in the first the political principles are derived from a comprehensive doctrine; in the second they are not derived from but are compatible with that doctrine; and in the third, they are incompatible with it. In everyday life we have not usually decided, or even thought much about, which of these cases hold. To decide among them would raise highly complicated questions; and it is not clear that we need to decide among them. Most people's religious, philosophical, and moral doctrines are not seen by them as fully general and comprehensive, and these aspects admit of variations of degree. There is lots of slippage, so to speak, many ways for liberal principles of justice to cohere loosely with those (partially) comprehensive views, and many ways within the limits of political principles of justice to allow for the pursuit of different (partially) comprehensive doctrines.

This suggests that many if not most citizens come to affirm the principles of justice incorporated into their constitution and political practice without seeing any particular connection, one way or the other, between those principles and their other views. It is possible for citizens first to appreciate the good those principles accomplish both for themselves and those they care for, as well as for society at large, and then to affirm them on this basis. Should an incompatibility later be recognized between the principles of justice and their wider doctrines, then they might very well adjust or revise these doctrines rather than reject those principles.[25]

3. At this point we ask: in virtue of what political values might

25. Note that here we distinguish between the initial allegiance to, or appreciation of, the political conception and the later adjustment or revision of comprehensive doctrines to which that allegiance or appreciation leads when inconsistencies arise. These adjustments or revisions we may suppose to take place slowly over time as the political conception shapes comprehensive views to cohere with it. For the main idea of this approach I am indebted to Samuel Scheffler.

liberal principles of justice gain allegiance to themselves? An allegiance to institutions and to the principles that regulate them may, of course, be based in part on long-term self- and group interests, custom and traditional attitudes, or simply on the desire to conform to what is expected and normally done. Widespread allegiance may also be encouraged by institutions that secure for all citizens the political values included under what Hart calls "the minimum content of natural law." But here we are concerned with the further bases of allegiance generated by liberal principles of justice.[26]

When liberal principles effectively regulate basic political institutions, they achieve three requirements of a stable constitutional consensus. First, given the fact of reasonable pluralism—the fact that leads to constitutional government as a modus vivendi in the first place—liberal principles meet the urgent political requirement to fix, once and for all, the content of certain political basic rights and liberties, and to assign them special priority. Doing this takes those guarantees off the political agenda and puts them beyond the calculus of social interests, thereby establishing clearly and firmly the rules of political contest. To regard that calculus as relevant in these matters leaves the status and content of those rights and liberties still unsettled; it subjects them to the shifting circumstances of time and place, and by greatly raising the stakes of political controversy, dangerously increases the insecurity and hostility of public life. The refusal to take these matters off the agenda perpetuates the deep divisions latent in society; it betrays a readiness to revive those antagonisms in the hope of gaining a more favorable position should later circumstances prove propitious.

4. The second requirement of a stable constitutional consensus is connected with the kind of public reason that applying

---

26. See the *The Concept of Law* (Oxford: Clarendon Press, 961), pp. 189–95, for what Hart calls "the minimum content of natural law." I assume that a liberal conception (as do many other familiar conceptions) includes this minimum content; and so in the text I focus on the bases of allegiance such a conception generates in virtue of the distinctive content of its principles.

liberal principles of justice involves. Given the content of these principles, their reference solely to institutional facts about political procedures and their basic rights and liberties, and to the availability of opportunities and all-purpose means, liberal principles can be applied following the usual guidelines of public inquiry and rules for assessing evidence.[27] Moreover, in view of the fact of reasonable pluralism, those guidelines and rules must be specified by reference to forms of reasoning and argument available to citizens generally, and so in terms of common sense, and by the procedures and conclusions of science when not controversial. This helps to insure that public reasoning can publicly be seen to be—as it should be—correct and reasonably reliable in its own terms.

Hence applying liberal principles has a certain simplicity. To illustrate: even if general and comprehensive teleological principles were adopted as political principles of justice, the form of public reasoning they specify tends to be politically unworkable. For if the elaborate theoretical calculations involved in applying their principles are publicly admitted in questions of political justice, the highly speculative nature and enormous complexity of these calculations are bound to make citizens with opposing views and interests highly suspicious of one another's arguments. (Consider what is involved in applying the principle of utility to constitutional procedures and general matters of social policy, not to mention the basic structure.) The information they presuppose is difficult if not impossible to obtain, and often there are insuperable problems in reaching an objective and agreed assessment. Even though we think our arguments sincere and not self-serving, we must consider what it is reasonable to expect others to think who stand to lose when our reasoning prevails.[28]

27. These guidelines are discussed in VI:4 and enter into the idea of primary goods considered in V:3–4. However, it should be noted that since we are here dealing with constitutional and not overlapping consensus, the values of public reason are more restricted than they are in the latter case. This observation I owe to David Peritz.

28. One might say: arguments and evidence supporting political judgments should, if possible, not only be sound but such that they can be publicly seen to be sound. The maxim that justice must not only be done, but also be seen to be done, holds good not only in law but in public reason.

5. Whether the third requirement of stable constitutional consensus is met by liberal principles depends on the success of the preceding two. The basic political institutions incorporating these principles and the form of public reason shown in applying them—when working effectively and successfully for a sustained period of time (as I am here assuming)—tend to encourage the cooperative virtues of political life: the virtue of reasonableness and a sense of fairness, a spirit of compromise and a readiness to meet others halfway, all of which are connected with the willingness to cooperate with others on political terms that everyone can publicly accept.

The explanation for this lies in applying the moral psychology sketched in II:7. Recall that we said that a) besides a capacity for a conception of the good, citizens have a capacity to accept reasonable political principles of justice and a desire to act on these principles; b) when citizens believe that political institutions and procedures are just (as these principles specify), they are ready to do their part in those arrangements when assured others will do theirs; c) if other persons with evident intention do their part, people tend to develop trust in them; and d) this trust and confidence becomes stronger as success of the arrangements is sustained; and e) trust also increases as the basic institutions framed to secure our fundamental interests are more firmly and willingly recognized. I stress the significance of the role of public reason in this explanation. For it is through citizens using and following this reason that they can see that their political institutions and democratic procedures are willingly recognized. It is on that recognition—on that evident intention—that so much depends.

To conclude: at the first stage of constitutional consensus the liberal principles of justice, initially accepted reluctantly as a modus vivendi and adopted into a constitution, tend to shift citizens' comprehensive doctrines so that they at least accept the principles of a liberal constitution. These principles guarantee certain basic political rights and liberties and establish democratic procedures for moderating the political rivalry, and for determining issues of social policy. To this extent citizens' comprehensive views are reasonable if they were not so before: simple pluralism moves toward reasonable pluralism and constitutional consensus is achieved.

§ 7. Steps to Overlapping Consensus

1. Our next task is to describe the steps whereby a constitutional consensus on certain principles of basic political rights and liberties and on democratic procedures becomes an overlapping consensus as earlier defined (§3). Recall that we distinguished between the depth and breadth of an overlapping consensus, and how specific its content is. The depth of an overlapping consensus requires that its political principles and ideals be founded on a political conception of justice that uses fundamental ideas of society and person as illustrated by justice as fairness. Its breadth goes beyond political principles instituting democratic procedures to include principles covering the basic structure as a whole; hence its principles also establish certain substantive rights such as liberty of conscience and freedom of thought, as well as fair equal opportunity and principles covering certain essential needs.

Finally, as to how far an overlapping consensus is specific, I have for simplicity assumed all along that its focus is a specific political conception of justice, with justice as fairness as the standard example. There is, however, another possibility that is more realistic and more likely to be realized. In this case the focus of an overlapping consensus is a class of liberal conceptions that vary within a certain more or less narrow range. The more restricted the range, the more specific the consensus. In a political society with a consensus of this kind, several conceptions of justice will be political rivals and no doubt favored by different interests and political strata. When overlapping consensus is characterized this way, the role of justice as fairness will have a special place within conceptions defining the focus of the consensus. This special place I define below (§7.4).

2. What are the forces that push a constitutional consensus

toward an overlapping consensus, even supposing a full overlapping consensus is never achieved but at best only approximated? I mention some of these forces as they relate to depth, breadth, and how specific, or how narrow, the class of conceptions in the focus.

As for depth, once a constitutional consensus is in place, political groups must enter the public forum of political discussion and appeal to other groups who do not share their comprehensive doctrine. This fact makes it rational for them to move out of the narrower circle of their own views and to develop political conceptions in terms of which they can explain and justify their preferred policies to a wider public so as to put together a majority. As they do this, they are led to formulate political conceptions of justice (as defined in I:2). These conceptions provide the common currency of discussion and a deeper basis for explaining the meaning and implications of the principles and policies each group endorses.

Again, new and fundamental constitutional problems inevitably arise, even if only occasionally. Consider, for example, the Reconstruction amendments following the crisis of the Civil War. Debate over those and other fundamental amendments forced competing groups to work out political conceptions that contained fundamental ideas in the light of which the constitution as so far understood could be changed. A constitutional consensus at the level of principles viewed apart from any underlying conception of society and citizen—each group having its own reasons—is a consensus taken literally. It lacks the conceptual resources to guide how the constitution should be amended and interpreted.

A last reason relates to depth. In a constitutional system with judicial review, or review conducted by some other body, it will be necessary for judges, or the officers in question, to develop a political conception of justice in the light of which the constitution, in their view, is to be interpreted and important cases decided. Only so can the enactments of the legislature be declared constitutional or unconstitutional; and only so have they a reasonable basis for their interpretation of the values and standards the constitution ostensibly incorporates. Plainly these conceptions will have an important role in the politics of constitutional debates.

3. Let us next look at considerations relating to breadth. The main one is that a purely political and procedural constitutional consensus will prove too narrow. For unless a democratic people is sufficiently unified and cohesive, it will not enact the legislation necessary to cover the remaining constitutional essentials and basic matters of justice, and conflict will arise about these. There must be fundamental legislation that guarantees liberty of conscience and freedom of thought generally and not merely of political speech and thought. Equally there must be legislation assuring freedom of association and freedom of movement; and beyond this, measures are required to assure that the basic needs of all citizens can be met so that they can take part in political and social life.[29]

About this last point, the idea is not that of satisfying needs as opposed to mere desires and wants; nor is it that of redistribution in favor of greater equality. The constitutional essential here is rather that below a certain level of material and social well-being, and of training and education, people simply cannot take part in society as citizens, much less as equal citizens. What determines the level of well-being and education below which this happens is not for a political conception to say. One must look to the society in question. But that does not mean that the constitutional essential itself is not perfectly clear: it is what is required to give due weight to the idea of society as a fair system of cooperation between free and equal citizens, and not to regard it, in practice if not in speech, as so much rhetoric.

The main point under breadth, then, is that the rights and liberties and procedures included in a constitutional consensus cover but a limited part of the fundamental political questions that will be debated. There are forces tending to amend the

29. On this last see Frank Michelman, "Welfare Rights in a Constitutional Democracy," *Washington University Law Quarterly* (Summer 1979), esp. pp. 680–85.

constitution in certain ways to cover further constitutional essentials, or else to enact the necessary legislation with much the same effect. In either case, groups will tend to develop broad political conceptions covering the basic structure as a whole in order to explain their point of view in a politically consistent and coherent way.

4. Finally, how specific is the consensus, or how wide is the range of the liberal conceptions defining it? Here there are two considerations. One concerns the range of views that can plausibly be elaborated from the fundamental ideas of society and person found in the public culture of a constitutional regime. Justice as fairness works from the fundamental ideas of society as a fair system of cooperation together with the conception of the person as free and equal. These ideas are taken as central to the democratic ideal. Are there other ideas equally central, and if there are, would they give rise to ideals and principles markedly different from those of justice as fairness? We might conjecture that, other things equal, a political conception elaborated from such central ideas would certainly be typical of the focal class of an overlapping consensus, should such a consensus ever be reached.

The second consideration is that different social and economic interests may be assumed to support different liberal conceptions. The differences between conceptions expresses, in part, a conflict between these interests. Let us define the relevant interests for each conception as those that it would encourage and be supported by in a stable basic structure regulated by it. The width of the range of liberal conceptions will be determined by the degree of opposition among these interests.

There is not time to examine these highly speculative matters. I simply conjecture that the narrower the differences between the liberal conceptions when correctly based on fundamental political ideas in a democratic public culture, and the more compatible the underlying interests that support them in a stable basic structure regulated by them, the narrower the range of liberal conceptions defining the focus of the consensus. In order for justice as fairness to specify the center of the focal class, it would seem the following two conditions must hold:

   a. it is correctly based on more central fundamental ideas; and
   b. it is stable in view of the interests that support it and are encouraged by it.

Thus, if the liberal conceptions correctly framed from fundamental ideas of a democratic public culture are supported by and encourage deeply conflicting political and economic interests, and if there be no way of designing a constitutional regime so as to overcome that, a full overlapping consensus cannot, it seems, be achieved.

I have outlined in this and the previous section how an initial acquiescence in a liberal conception of justice as a mere modus vivendi could change over time first into a constitutional consensus and then into an overlapping consensus. In this process I have supposed that the comprehensive doctrines of most people are not fully comprehensive, and this allows scope for the development of an independent allegiance to the political conception that helps to bring about a consensus. This independent allegiance in turn leads people to act with evident intention in accordance with constitutional arrangements, since they have reasonable assurance (based on past experience) that others will also comply. Gradually, as the success of political cooperation continues, citizens gain increasing trust and confidence in one another. This is all we need say in reply to the objection that the idea of overlapping consensus is utopian.

§ 8. Conception and Doctrines: How Related?

1. We have distinguished an overlapping consensus from a modus vivendi and noted that in the former the political conception is affirmed as a moral conception and citizens are ready to act from it on moral grounds. We have also stated the two grounds that underwrite the thesis of political liberalism: first,

168

that the values of the political are very great values and not easily overridden; and second, that there are many reasonable comprehensive doctrines that understand the wider realm of values to be congruent with, or supportive of, or else not in conflict with, political values as these are specified by a political conception of justice for a democratic regime. These two grounds secure the basis of public reason, for they imply that fundamental political questions can be settled by the appeal to political values expressed by the political conception endorsed by the overlapping consensus.

In these circumstances a balance of reasons as seen within each citizen's comprehensive doctrine, and not a compromise compelled by circumstances, is the basis of citizens' respect for the limits of public reason. Any realistic idea of a well-ordered society may seem to imply that some such compromise is involved. Indeed, the term "overlapping consensus" may suggest that. We must show, then, that this is not the case. To see that there need be no compromise, let us illustrate the different ways in which a political conception can be related to comprehensive doctrines by returning to the model case of an overlapping consensus similar to the one introduced in §3.2, except that for Mill's view we substitute the utilitarianism of Bentham and Sidgwick. This consensus consisted of four views. I put the religious doctrine with its account of free faith aside for a bit and consider the other three.

2. After the religious view the first was of Kant's moral philosophy with its ideal of autonomy. From within his view, or within a view sufficiently similar to it, the political conception with its principles of justice and their appropriate priority, can, let us say, be derived. The reasons for taking the basic structure of society as the primary subject of justice are likewise derivable. Here the relation is deductive, even though the argument can hardly be set out very rigorously. The point is that someone who affirms Kant's doctrine, or one similar to it, regards that view as the deductive basis of the political conception and in that way continuous with it.

The next view is the utilitarianism of Bentham and Sidgwick, the strict classical doctrine. While it might be more plausible revised as average utilitarianism, I ignore this here. Suppose the relation in this case between the comprehensive view and the political conception is one of approximation. This utilitarianism supports the political conception for such reasons as our limited knowledge of social institutions generally and on our knowledge about ongoing circumstances. It stresses further the bounds on complexity of legal and institutional rules as well as the simplicity necessary in guidelines for public reason (§6.4). These and other reasons may lead the utilitarian to think a political conception of justice liberal in content a satisfactory, perhaps even the best, workable approximation to what the principle of utility, all things tallied up, would require.

The third view was a pluralist account of the realms of values that included the political conception as the part covering political values. What is characteristic of this view is that different domains of value—of which the political is but one—are unified (so far as they are unified) largely by ideas and concepts drawn from their own domain. Each domain of value has, then, its own free-standing account. In this comprehensive pluralist view the political conception is affirmed by balancing judgments that support the great values of the political against whatever values normally conflict with them in a well-ordered democratic regime.

There are many other possible comprehensive views but the three mentioned will suffice to illustrate some of the possible relations between comprehensive views and a political conception. Add to them religious doctrines with an account of free faith. Here I shall suppose—perhaps too optimistically—that, except for certain kinds of fundamentalism, all the main historical religions admit of such an account and thus may be seen as reasonable comprehensive doctrines.

3. Now to state the main point: in the overlapping consensus consisting in the views just described, the acceptance of the political conception is not a compromise between those holding

different views, but rests on the totality of reasons specified within the comprehensive doctrine affirmed by each citizen.

True, each comprehensive view is related to the political conception in a different way. While they all endorse it, the first does so as deductively supported and so continuous from within; the second as a satisfactory and possibly the best workable approximation given normal social conditions; and the last as resting on considered judgments balancing competing values, all things tallied up. No one accepts the political conception driven by political compromise. Of course, acceptance depends on certain conditions. Utilitarianism refers to limits on information and upper bounds on the complexity of legal rules; political liberalism looks to such general facts as the facts of reasonable pluralism; even in Kant's doctrine, as it applies to human beings, the content of particular categorical imperatives is adjusted to the laws of nature, as any suitable rendering of the procedure for applying the categorical imperative would show.

However a doctrine's adjusting its requirements to conditions such as these is not political compromise, or giving in to brute force or unreason on the world. It's simply adjusting to the general conditions of any normal and human social world, as any political view must do.

4. To conclude: in this lecture I have discussed four objections to political liberalism and its view of social unity. Two of those objections are particularly important: one is the charge of skepticism and indifference; the other is that political liberalism cannot gain sufficient support to assure compliance with its principles of justice. Both of these objections are answered by finding a reasonable liberal conception that can be supported by an overlapping consensus of reasonable doctrines. For such a consensus achieves compliance by a concordant fit between the political conception and the comprehensive views together with the public recognition of the great values of the political virtues. To succeed in finding such a consensus political philosophy must be, so far as possible, suitably independent of other parts of philoso-

phy, especially from philosophy's long-standing problems and controversies. Doing this gives rise to the objection that political liberalism is skeptical of religious, philosophical, and moral truth, or indifferent to their values. Once we connect the role of a political conception to the fact of reasonable pluralism and to what is essential for a shared basis of public reason, this objection is seen to be mistaken.

These matters connect with the larger question of how political liberalism is possible. One step in showing how it is possible is to exhibit the possibility of an overlapping consensus in a society with a democratic tradition characterized by the fact of reasonable pluralism. In trying to do these things political philosophy assumes the role Kant gave to philosophy generally: the defense of reasonable faith (III:2.2). As I said then, in our case this becomes the defense of reasonable faith in the possibility of a just constitutional regime.

The Priority
of Right
and Ideas
of the Good

The idea of the priority of right is an
essential element in what I have called
"political liberalism" and it has a central role in justice as fairness as a
form of that view. This priority may
give rise to misunderstandings: it may
be thought, for example, to imply that
a liberal political conception of justice cannot use any ideas of the good
at all, except perhaps those that are
purely instrumental; or else those that
are a matter of preference or of individual choice. This must be incorrect, since the right and the good are
complementary: no conception of
justice can draw entirely upon one or
the other, but must combine both in
a definite way. The priority of right
does not deny this. I try to remove

these and other misunderstandings by surveying five ideas of the good used in justice as fairness.

Here questions arise. How can justice as fairness even use ideas of the good without making claims about the truth of this or that comprehensive doctrine in ways incompatible with political liberalism? A further question may be explained as follows. In justice as fairness the priority of right means that the principles of political justice impose limits on permissible ways of life; and hence the claims citizens make to pursue ends that transgress those limits have no weight. But surely just institutions and the political virtues expected of citizens would not be institutions and virtues of a just and good society unless those institutions and virtues not only permitted but also sustained ways of life fully worthy of citizens' devoted allegiance. A political conception of justice must contain within itself sufficient space, as it were, for such ways of life. Thus, while justice draws the limit, and the good shows the point, justice cannot draw the limit too narrowly. How is it possible, though, within the bounds of political liberalism, to specify those worthy ways of life, or identify what is sufficient space? Justice as fairness itself cannot invoke the standpoint of some wider view to say that it draws the limit at the right place and so the comprehensive doctrines it allows are worthy of allegiance. After a survey of five ideas of the good used in justice as fairness and of how their use accords with the priority of right, I return to these questions in (§8).[1]

§ 1. How a Political Conception Limits Conceptions of the Good

1. I begin by recalling briefly the distinction (I:2) that is basic for my discussion: namely, the distinction between a political conception of justice and a comprehensive religious, philosophical, or moral doctrine. I said there that the features of a political

---

1. I am indebted to discussion with Erin Kelly in formulating these questions and in seeing the apparent difficulty they pose for political liberalism.

conception of justice are, first, that it is a moral conception worked out for a specific subject, namely, the basic structure of a constitutional democratic regime; second, that accepting the political conception does not presuppose accepting any particular comprehensive religious, philosophical, or moral doctrine; rather, the political conception presents itself as a reasonable conception for the basic structure alone; and third, that it is not formulated in terms of any comprehensive doctrine but in terms of certain fundamental ideas viewed as latent in the public political culture of a democratic society.

Thus, as we said in I:2.2, the distinction between political conceptions of justice and other moral conceptions is a matter of scope: that is, the range of subjects to which a conception applies, and the wider content a wider range requires. A conception is said to be general when it applies to a wide range of subjects (in the limit to all subjects); it is comprehensive when it includes conceptions of what is of value in human life, as well as ideals of personal virtue and character, that are to inform much of our nonpolitical conduct (in the limit our life as a whole). There is a tendency for religious and philosophical conceptions to be general and fully comprehensive; indeed, their being so is sometimes regarded as an ideal to be realized. A doctrine is fully comprehensive when it covers all recognized values and virtues within one rather precisely articulated scheme of thought; whereas a doctrine is only partially comprehensive when it comprises certain (but not all) nonpolitical values and virtues and is rather loosely articulated. Note that, by definition, for a conception to be even partially comprehensive, it must extend beyond the political and include nonpolitical values and virtues.

2. Political liberalism presents, then, a political conception of justice for the main institutions of political and social life, not for the whole of life. Of course, it must have the kind of content we associate with liberalism historically: for example, it must affirm certain basic rights and liberties, assign them a certain priority, and more. As I have said, the right and the good are complementary: a political conception must draw upon various ideas of the

good. The question is: subject to what restriction may political liberalism do so?

The main restriction would seem to be this: the ideas of the good included must be political ideas; that is, they must belong to a reasonable political conception of justice so that we may assume:

  a. that they are, or can be, shared by citizens regarded as free and equal; and

  b. that they do not presuppose any particular fully (or partially) comprehensive doctrine.

In justice as fairness this restriction is expressed by the priority of right. In its general form, then, this priority means that admissible ideas of the good must respect the limits of, and serve a role within, the political conception of justice.[2]

§ 2. Goodness as Rationality

1. To spell out the meaning of the priority of right stated in this general form, I consider how five ideas of the good found in justice as fairness meet these conditions. In the order discussed, these ideas are: a) the idea of goodness as rationality; b) the idea of primary goods; c) the idea of permissible comprehensive conceptions of the good (those associated with comprehensive doctrines); d) the idea of the political virtues; and e) the idea of the good of a well-ordered (political) society.

The first idea—that of goodness as rationality[3]—is, in some

2. The particular meaning of the priority of right is that comprehensive conceptions of the good are admissible, or can be pursued in society, only if their pursuit conforms to the political conception of justice (does not violate its principles of justice), as discussed in §6 below.

3. This idea is discussed most fully in *Theory*, chap. 7. I do not want to take up its details in this lecture and only state in the text the most basic points relevant for the present discussion. However, I might mention here that there are several ways in which I would now revise the presentation of goodness as rationality. Perhaps the most important would be to make sure that it is understood as part of a political conception of justice as a form of political liberalism, and not as part of a comprehen-

variant, taken for granted by almost any political conception of justice. This idea supposes that the members of a democratic society have, at least in an intuitive way, a rational plan of life in the light of which they schedule their more important endeavors and allocate their various resources (including those of mind and body, time and energy) so as to pursue their conceptions of the good over a complete life, if not in the most rational, then at least in a sensible (or satisfactory), way. In drawing up these plans people are assumed, of course, to take into account their reasonable expectations concerning their needs and requirements in their future circumstances in all stages of life, so far as they can ascertain them from their present position in society and the normal conditions of human life.

2. Given these suppositions, any workable political conception of justice that is to serve as a public basis of justification that citizens may reasonably be expected to acknowledge must count human life and the fulfillment of basic human needs and purposes as in general good, and endorse rationality as a basic principle of political and social organization. A political doctrine for a democratic society may safely assume, then, that all participants in political discussion of questions of right and justice accept these values, when understood in a suitably general way. Indeed, if the members of society did not do so, the problems of political justice, in the form with which we are familiar with them, would not arise.

It should be emphasized that these basic values do not, of course, suffice by themselves to specify any particular political view. As used in *A Theory of Justice,* goodness as rationality is a

sive moral doctrine. As such a doctrine both it and the full theory are inadequate, but this does not make them unsuitable for their role in a political conception. The distinction between a comprehensive doctrine and a political conception is unfortunately absent from *Theory* and while I believe nearly all the structure and substantive content of justice as fairness (including goodness as rationality) goes over unchanged into that conception as a political one, the understanding of the view as a whole is significantly shifted. Charles Larmore in his *Patterns of Moral Complexity* (Cambridge: Cambridge University Press, 1987), pp.118–30, is quite correct in vigorously criticizing the ambiguity of *Theory* on this fundamental matter.

basic idea from which, in conjunction with other ideas (for example, the political idea of the person), to elaborate in sequence other ideas of the good when these are needed. As what I referred to in that work as the thin theory of the good, goodness as rationality provides part of a framework serving two main roles: first, it helps us to identify a workable list of primary goods;[4] and second, relying on an index of these goods, it enables us both to specify the aims (or motivation) of the parties in the original position and to explain why those aims (or motivation) are rational. The second role I discussed in II:5 and so I now take up the first.

§ 3. Primary Goods and Interpersonal Comparisons

1. As I have just said, one aim of the idea of goodness as rationality is to provide part of a framework for an account of primary goods. But to complete this framework that idea must be combined with a political conception of citizens as free and equal. With this done, we then work out what citizens need and require when they are regarded as such persons and as normal and fully cooperating members of society over a complete life.

It is crucial here that the conception of citizens as persons be seen as a political conception and not as one belonging to a comprehensive doctrine. It is this political conception of persons, with its account of their moral powers and higher-order interests,[5] together with the framework of goodness as rationality and the basic facts of social life and the conditions of human growth and nurture, that provides the requisite background for specifying citizens' needs and requirements. All this enables us to arrive at a workable list of primary goods, as we saw in II:5.3.

---

4. *Theory*, p. 396, says of the thin theory of the good that "its purpose is to secure the premises about primary goods required to arrive at the principles of justice. Once this theory is worked out and the primary goods accounted for, we are free to use the principles of justice in the further development of . . . the full theory of the good."

5. See the discussion in I:3, 5; II:1–2, 8.

2. The role of the idea of primary goods is as follows.[6] A basic feature of a well-ordered political society is that there is a public understanding not only about the kinds of claims it is appropriate for citizens to make when questions of political justice arise, but also a public understanding about how such claims are to be supported. A political conception of justice provides a basis for such an understanding and thereby enables citizens to reach agreement in assessing their various claims and in determining their relative weight. This basis, as I comment below in §4, turns out to be a conception of citizens' needs—that is, of persons' needs as citizens—and this allows justice as fairness to hold that the fulfillment of claims appropriately related to these needs is to be publicly accepted as advantageous, and thus counted as improving the circumstances of citizens for the purposes of political justice. An effective political conception of justice includes, then, a political understanding of what is to be publicly recognized as citizens' needs and hence as advantageous for all.

In political liberalism the problem of interpersonal comparisons arises as follows: given the conflicting comprehensive conceptions of the good, how is it possible to reach such a political understanding of what are to count as appropriate claims? The difficulty is that the government can no more act to maximize the fulfillment of citizens' rational preferences, or wants (as in utilitarianism),[7] or to advance human excellence, or the values of

6. The account of primary goods stated here and in the next section draws on my essay "Social Unity and Primary Goods," in *Utilitarianism and Beyond*. However, in adjusting to Sen's important criticisms, referred to in n. 12 below, I have made a number of changes both from that account and also from the one that appeared in an article with the same title as this lecture in *Philosophy and Public Affairs* 17 (Summer 1988). I hope that now our views are in accord on the topics that concern us here, though his view has much broader aims than mine, as I note later.

7. In the case of a utilitarianism such as that of Henry Sidgwick in *Methods of Ethics,* or of R. B. Brandt in *The Good and the Right* (Oxford: Clarendon Press, 1979), which aims to be an account of the good of individuals as they must understand it, when they are rational, and in which the good is characterized hedonistically, or in terms of satisfaction of desire or interests, the claim in the text is, I think, correct. But as T. M. Scanlon has maintained, the point of another idea of utility often found in welfare economics is quite different: it is not to give an account of individuals' good as they

perfection (as in perfectionism), than it can act to advance Catholicism or Protestantism, or any other religion. None of these views of the meaning, value, and purpose of human life, as specified by the corresponding comprehensive religious or philosophical doctrines, is affirmed by citizens generally, and so the pursuit of any one of them through basic institutions gives political society a sectarian character. To find a shared idea of citizens' good appropriate for political purposes, political liberalism looks for an idea of rational advantage within a political conception that is independent of any particular comprehensive doctrine and hence may be the focus an overlapping consensus.

3. The conception of primary goods addresses this practical political problem. The answer proposed rests on identifying a partial similarity in the structure of citizens' permissible conceptions of the good. Here permissible conceptions are comprehensive doctrines the pursuit of which is not excluded by the principles of political justice. Even though citizens do not affirm the same (permissible) conception, complete with all its final ends and loyalties, two things suffice for a shared idea of rational advantage: first, that citizens affirm the same political conception of themselves as free and equal persons; and second, that their (permissible) conceptions of the good, however distinct their content and their related religious and philosophical doctrines, require for their advancement roughly the same primary goods, that is, the same basic rights, liberties, and opportunities, and the same all-purpose means such as income and wealth, with all of these supported by the same social bases of self-respect. These goods, we say, are things citizens need as free and equal persons, and claims to these goods are counted as appropriate claims.[8]

---

should understand it from a purely personal point of view. Rather, it is to find a general characterization of individuals' good that abstracts from how they more specifically understand it and is appropriately impartial between persons and hence may be used in moral argument and in normative economic theory in considering questions of public policy. See Scanlon's "The Moral Basis of Interpersonal Comparisons," in *Interpersonal Comparisons of Well-Being,* edited by J. Elster and J. Roemer (Cambridge: Cambridge University Press, 1991), pp. 22–30. The view stated in the text may need to be restated to deal with this use of the idea of utility.

8. Expressed in terms of goodness as rationality, we suppose that all citizens have a

The basic list of primary goods (to which we may add should it prove necessary) has five headings as follows:

  a. basic rights and liberties, also given by a list;
  b. freedom of movement and free choice of occupation against a background of diverse opportunities;
  c. powers and prerogatives of offices and positions of responsibility in the political and economic institutions of the basic structure;
  d. income and wealth; and finally,
  e. the social bases of self-respect.

This list includes mainly features of institutions, that is, basic rights and liberties, institutional opportunities, and prerogatives of office and position, along with income and wealth. The social bases of self-respect are explained by the structure and content of just institutions together with features of the public political culture, such as the public recognition and acceptance of the principles of justice.

4. The thought behind the introduction of primary goods is to find a practicable public basis of interpersonal comparisons based on objective features of citizens' social circumstances open to view, all this given the background of reasonable pluralism. Provided due precautions are taken, we can, if need be, expand the list to include other goods, for example, leisure time,[9] and even

---

rational plan of life that requires for its fulfillment roughly the same kind of primary goods. (As indicated in §2, in saying this we rely on various common sense psychological facts about human needs, their phases of development, and so on. See *Theory,* chap. 7, pp. 433f., 447.) This assumption is of great importance for it enormously simplifies the problem of finding a workable index of primary goods. Without restrictive assumptions of this kind, the index problem is known to be insoluble. Sen has an instructive discussion of these matters in his "On Indexing Primary Goods and Capabilities," July 1991 (unpublished). At the same time, these restrictive assumptions bring out that, unless otherwise stated, we address what I take as the fundamental question of political justice: what are fair terms of cooperation between free and equal citizens as fully cooperating and normal members of society over a complete life (I:3.4)?

9. The question of how to handle leisure time was raised by R. A. Musgrave in "Maximin, Uncertainty, and the Leisure Trade-off," *Quarterly Journal of Economics* 88 (November 1974). I shall only comment here that twenty-four hours less a standard

certain mental states such as freedom from physical pain.[10] These matters I shall not pursue here. What is crucial is always to recognize the limits of the political and the practicable:

first, we must stay within the limits of justice as fairness as a political conception of justice that can serve as the focus of an overlapping consensus; and

second, we must respect the constraints of simplicity and availability of information to which any practicable political conception (as opposed to a comprehensive moral doctrine)[11] is subject.

Several urgent practicable concerns have been raised by Arrow and Sen.[12] They note the many significant variations among persons in their capacities—moral, intellectual, and physical— and in their determinate conceptions of the good, as well as in their preferences and tastes. They point out that these variations are sometimes so great that it is hardly fair to secure everyone the same index of primary goods to cover their needs as citizens

---

working day might be included in the index as leisure. Those who were unwilling to work under conditions where there is much work that needs to be done (I assume that positions and jobs are not scarce or rationed) would have extra leisure stipulated as equal to the index of the least advantaged. So those who surf all day off Malibu must find a way to support themselves and would not be entitled to public funds. Plainly, this brief remark is not intended as endorsing any particular social policy at all. To do that would require a careful study of the circumstances. The point is simply to indicate, as do the comments in the text, that if necessary the list of primary goods can in principle be expanded.

10. Here I adopt a suggestion of T. M. Scanlon in his "Moral Basis of Interpersonal Comparisons," p. 41.

11. See Richard Arneson's "Equality and Equal Opportunity for Welfare," *Philosophical Studies* 54 (1988):79–95, as an example. I believe this idea runs afoul of the constraints in the text. In political life citizens cannot sensibly apply or follow it. See Daniels's comments in "Equality of What: Welfare, Resources, or Capabilities?," *Philosophy and Phenomenological Research* I (supplement) (Fall 1990):20f.

12. See K. J. Arrow, "Some Ordinalist Notes on Rawls' Theory of Justice,'" *Journal of Philosophy* (1973), esp. pp. 253f.; and Amartya Sen, "Equality of What?" (1979) reprinted in *Choice, Welfare and Measurement* (Cambridge, Mass.: MIT Press, 1982), esp. pp. 364–69; "Well-Being, Agency and Freedom," *Journal of Philosophy* 82 (April 1985), esp. pp. 195–202; and most recently "Justice: Means versus Freedoms," *Philosophy and Public Affairs* 19 (Spring 1990):111–21.

and let matters go at that. Arrow mentioned variations in people's needs for medical care and in how expensive it is for them to satisfy their tastes and preferences. Sen has stressed the importance of variations among people in their basic capabilities and therefore in their ability to use primary goods to attain their aims. Arrow and Sen are surely right that in some of these cases the same index for everyone would be unfair.

Before I reply, I should say, however, that I do not try to convey here the full depth of Sen's understanding of basic capabilties. For him they refer to the overall freedoms to choose between combinations of functionings (strictly n-tuples of functionings) and they constitute the basis of his view of the different forms of freedom, well-being freedom and agency freedom. Beyond this they lay the ground for importantly different kinds of value judgments.[13] I believe that for my limited purposes I need not go into these deeper questions.

So, by way of reply, the following: I have assumed throughout, and shall continue to assume, that while citizens do not have equal capacities, they do have, at least to the essential minimum degree, the moral, intellectual, and physical capacities that enable them to be fully cooperating members of society over a complete life. Recall that for us the fundamental question of political philosophy is how to specify the fair terms of cooperation among persons so conceived (I:3.4). I agree with Sen that basic capabilities are of first importance and that the use of primary goods is always to be assessed in the light of assumptions about those capabilities (II:5.2–3).

5. There is still the question: how to deal with these variations? Space does not allow an adequate discussion but a few remarks are needed. Let us distinguish four main kinds of variations and then ask whether a variation places people above or below the line: that is, whether it leaves them with more or less than the minimum essential capacities required to be a normal cooperating member of society.

---

13. For these matters, see Sen's "Well-Being, Agency, and Freedom."

Four main kinds of variations are a) variations in moral and intellectual capacities and skills; b) variations in physical capacities and skills, including the effects of illness and accident on natural abilities; c) variations in citizens' conceptions of the good (the fact of reasonable pluralism); as well as d) variations in tastes and preferences, though the latter are less deep.

Given our assumption throughout that everyone has the capacity to be a normal cooperating member of society, we say that when the principles of justice (with their index of primary goods) are satisfied, none of these variations among citizens are unfair and give rise to injustice. Indeed, this is one of the main claims of justice as fairness.

To see this proceed by cases. In case (a), the only variations in moral, intellectual, and physical capacities are above the line. As we saw in II:6.3–4, these variations are handled by the social practices of qualifying for positions and free competition against the background of fair equality of opportunity, including fair equality of opportunity in education, together with the regulation of inequalities in income and wealth by the difference principle. In case (b), the variations that put some citizens below the line as a result of illness and accident (once we allow for these) can be dealt with, I believe, at the legislative stage when the prevalence and kinds of these misfortunes are known and the costs of treating them can be ascertained and balanced along with total government expenditure. The aim is to restore people by health care so that once again they are fully cooperating members of society.[14]

As for case (c), variations in conceptions of the good raise larger questions and some of these are discussed in §6 below. There I hold that justice as fairness is fair to conceptions of the good, or rather to the persons who have these conceptions of the

14. See the brief remarks in "Social Unity and Primary Goods," p. 168. Here I should follow the general idea of the much further worked out view of Norman Daniels in his "Health Care Needs and Distributive Justice," *Philosophy and Public Affairs* 10 (Spring 1981), and more completely developed in his *Just Health Care* (Cambridge: Cambridge University Press, 1985), chaps. 1–3.

good, even though some conceptions are judged not permissible and all conceptions do not have the same chance to flourish. Finally, turning to case (d), variations in preferences and tastes are seen as our own responsibility. As we saw in I:5.4, that we can take responsibility for our ends is part of what free citizens may expect of one another. Taking responsibility for our tastes and preferences, whether or not they have arisen from our actual choices, is a special case of that responsibility. As citizens with realized moral powers, this is something we must learn to deal with. This still allows us to view as a special problem preferences and tastes that are incapacitating and render someone unable to cooperate normally in society. The situation is then a medical or psychiatric one and to be treated accordingly.[15]

Thus, once we distinguish the four main kinds of variations and variations when between people fall above or below the line, the account of primary goods seems adequate for all cases, except possibly for case (b), which covers instances of illness and accident placing citizens below the line. For this case, Sen forcefully raises the question whether an index of primary goods can be sufficiently flexible to be just or fair. I cannot pursue the matter here and simply state the conjecture that by taking advantage of the information that becomes available at the legislative stage, a sufficiently flexible index can be devised in that it gives judgments as just or fair as those of any political conception we can work out. Keep in mind that, as Sen urges, any such index will

15. In viewing preferences and tastes when they become incapacitating as calling for psychiatric treatment, I have followed Norman Daniels's "Equality of What: Welfare, Resources, or Capabilities?," pp. 288–92 in his discussion of the views of Arneson (see n. 10 above) and G. A. Cohen, "On the Currency of Egalitarian Justice," *Ethics* 99 (July 1989). To take Arrow's example: suppose we have been accustomed to a diet including plover's eggs and pre-phylloxera clarets (having been brought up in a wealthy family) and after some misfortune we become despondent and claim a need to financial aid in order to purchase them. Daniels proposes that such a case be seen as one in which our normal capacity as cooperating members of society to take responsibility for our ends is out of order. Its malfunctioning calls for treatment. We don't say that because the preferences arose from upbringing and not from choice that society owes us compensation. Rather, it is a normal part of being human to cope with the preferences our upbringing leaves us with.

consider basic capabilities, and its aim will be to restore citizens to their proper role as normal cooperating members of society.

6. To conclude: The use of primary goods assumes that by virtue of their moral powers citizens have some part in forming and cultivating their final ends and preferences. Hence it is not by itself an objection to the use of primary goods that an index does not accommodate those with unusual or expensive tastes. One must argue in addition that it is unreasonable, if not unjust, to hold such persons responsible for their preferences and to require them to make out as best they can. But given their capacity to assume responsibility for their ends, we do not view citizens as passive carriers of desires. That capacity is part of the moral power to form, to revise, and rationally to pursue a conception of the good; and it is public knowledge conveyed by the political conception that citizens are to be held responsible. It is supposed that they have adjusted their likes and dislikes, whatever they are, over the course of their lives to the income and wealth and station in life they could reasonably expect. It is regarded as unfair that they should now have less in order to spare others from the consequences of their lack of foresight or self-discipline.

Still, the idea of holding citizens responsible for their ends is reasonable only on certain assumptions. First, we must assume that citizens can regulate and revise their ends and preferences in the light of their expectations of primary goods. This assumption is, as I have said, implicit in the moral powers attributed to them. But by itself this assumption does not suffice. We must also find workable criteria for interpersonal comparisons that can be publicly and, if possible, easily applied. Thus we try to show, second, how primary goods are connected with the higher-order interests associated with the moral powers so that the primary goods are indeed feasible public criteria for questions of political justice. Finally, the effective use of primary goods assumes also that the conception of the person which lies at the basis of these two assumptions is at least implicitly accepted as an ideal underlying the public conception of justice. Otherwise citizens would be less willing to accept responsibility in the sense required.[16]

§ 4. Primary Goods as Citizens' Needs

1. With this account of primary goods, we have answered our main question (posed at the start of the second paragraph of §3.2): namely, how, given the fact of reasonable pluralism, a public understanding is possible concerning what is to be counted as advantageous in matters of political justice. In showing how such an understanding is possible, we have stressed the practical nature of primary goods. By this I mean that we can actually present a scheme of equal basic liberties and fair opportunities, which, when guaranteed by the basic structure, ensures for all citizens the adequate development and full exercise of their two moral powers and a fair share of the all-purpose means essential for advancing their determinate (permissible) conceptions of the good. Of course, it is neither possible nor just to allow all conceptions of the good to be pursued (some involve the violation of basic rights and liberties). Yet we can say that when basic institutions satisfy a political conception of justice mutually acknowledged by citizens affirming comprehensive doctrines in a reasonable overlapping consensus, this fact confirms that those institutions allow sufficient space for ways of life worthy of citizens' devoted support. This they must do if they are to be the institutions of a just and good society.[17]

Looking back at what we said in §3 above, observe first that fair shares of primary goods are clearly not intended as a measure

16. The text of the last two paragraphs revises my earliest account of responsibility for ends and primary goods in "Kantian Equality," *Cambridge Review* (February 1975) and in doing so I am much indebted to Scanlon and to Samuel Scheffler. I believe my account now accords with Scanlon's "Preference and Urgency," *Journal of Philosophy* 82 (November 1975):655–69.

17. This is not to say, as considered below in §6, that they can achieve a social world without loss.

of citizens' expected overall psychological well-being, or of their utility, as economists might say. Justice as fairness rejects the idea of comparing and maximizing overall well-being in matters of political justice. Nor does it try to estimate the extent to which individuals succeed in advancing their way of life or to judge the intrinsic worth (or the perfectionist value) of their ends. When seen as rights, liberties, and opportunities, and as general all-purpose means, primary goods are clearly not anyone's idea of the basic values of human life and must not be so understood, however essential their possession.

2. We say instead that, given the political conception of citizens, primary goods specify what their needs are—part of what their good is as citizens—when questions of justice arise. It is this political conception (supplemented by the framework of goodness as rationality) that enables us to work out what primary goods are needed. While an index of these goods may be made more specific at the constitutional and legislative stages, and interpreted even more specifically at the judicial stage,[18] the index is not intended to approximate an idea of rational advantage, or good, specified by a nonpolitical (comprehensive) conception. Rather, a more specific index defines for more concrete cases what are to count as citizens' needs, allowing as necessary for the variations (surveyed in §3.5).

Alternatively, the specification of these needs is a construct worked out from within a political conception and not from within a comprehensive doctrine. The thought is that this construct provides, given the fact of reasonable pluralism, the best available standard of justification of competing claims that is mutually acceptable to citizens generally.[19] Even if in most cases

18. For these stages, see *Theory*, §32.

19. This idea of citizens' needs as a construct parallels in many ways what Scanlon calls the "conventionalist" interpretation of his concept of urgency. In the next to last paragraph of "Preference and Urgency," p. 668, Scanlon distinguishes between two interpretations of urgency, a naturalist and a conventionalist. An index of primary goods is close to Scanlon's description of a conventionalist interpretation of urgency as "a construct put together for the purposes of moral [I would say political] argu-

the index does not approximate very accurately what many people most want and value as judged by their comprehensive views, primary goods will surely be regarded by all, or nearly all, as highly valuable in pursuing those views. Thus, they can endorse the political conception and hold that what is really important in questions of justice is the fulfillment of citizens' needs by the institutions of the basic structure in ways the principles of justice, acknowledged by an overlapping consensus, specify as fair.[20]

3. The preceding account of primary goods includes what we may call "a social division of responsibility": society, citizens as a collective body, accepts responsibility for maintaining the equal basic liberties and fair equality of opportunity, and for providing a fair share of the primary goods for all within this framework; while citizens as individuals and associations accept responsibility for revising and adjusting their ends and aspirations in view of the all-purpose means they can expect, given their present and foreseeable situation. This division of responsibility relies on the capacity of persons to assume responsibility for their ends and to moderate the claims they make on their social institutions accordingly.

We arrive, then, at the idea that citizens as free and equal are to be at liberty to take charge of their lives and each is expected by others to adapt their conception of the good to their expected

---

ment . . . its usefulness . . . stems from the fact that it represents, under the circumstances [e.g., of reasonable pluralism], the best available standard of justification that is mutually acceptable to persons whose preferences diverge."

20. I might add here that the idea of need used in the text views needs as relative to a political conception of the person, and to their role and status. The requirements, or needs, of citizens as free and equal persons are different from the needs of patients or of students, say. And needs are different from desires, wishes, and likings. Citizens' needs are objective in a way that desires are not: that is, they express requirements of persons with certain higher-order interests who have a certain role or status. If these requirements are not met, they cannot maintain their role and status, or achieve their essential aims. A citizen's claim that something is a need can be denied when it is not a requirement. In effect, the political conception of the person and the idea of primary goods specify a special kind of need for a political conception of justice. Needs in any other sense, along with desires and aspirations, play no role. See "Social Unity and Primary Goods," p. 172f.

fair share of primary goods. The only restriction on plans of life is their being compatible with the public principles of justice, and claims may be advanced only for certain kinds of things (primary goods) and in ways specified by those principles. This implies that strong feelings and zealous aspirations for certain goals do not, as such, give people a claim to social resources, or a claim to design public institutions to achieve these goals. Desires and wants, however intense, are not by themselves reasons in matters of constitutional essentials and basic justice.[21] The fact that we have a compelling desire in such cases does not argue for the propriety of its satisfaction any more than the strength of a conviction argues for its truth. Combined with an index of primary goods the principles of justice detach reasons of justice not only from the ebb and flow of fluctuating wants and desires but even from sentiments and commitments. The significance of this is illustrated by religious toleration, which gives no weight to the strength of conviction by which we may oppose the religious beliefs and practices of others.

§ 5. Permissible Conceptions of the Good and Political Virtues

1. Historically one common theme of liberal thought is that the state must not favor any comprehensive doctrines and their associated conception of the good. But it is equally a common theme of critics of liberalism that it fails to do this and is, in fact, arbitrarily biased in favor of one or another form of individualism. As I noted at the outset, the assertion of the priority of right may seem to leave justice as fairness (as a form of political liberalism) open to a similar objection.

Thus, in discussing the next two ideas—those of permissible conceptions of the good (those permitted by the principles of

---

21. This does not deny that they may be, depending on the comprehensive view, perfectly good reasons in other kinds of cases.

justice) and of the political virtues—I shall use the familiar idea of neutrality as a way of introducing the main problems. I believe, however, that the term *neutrality* is unfortunate; some of its connotations are highly misleading, others suggest altogether impracticable principles. For this reason I have not used it before in these lectures. But with due precautions taken, and using it only as a stage piece, as it were, we may clarify how the priority of right connects with the above two ideas of the good.

2. Neutrality can be defined in quite different ways.[22] One way is procedural, for example, by reference to a procedure that can be legitimated, or justified, without appealing to any moral values at all. Or if this seems impossible, since showing something justified appears to involve an appeal to some values, a neutral procedure may be said to be one justified by an appeal to neutral values, that is, to values such as impartiality, consistency in application of general principles to all reasonably related cases (compare to: cases similar in relevant respects are to be treated similarly),[23] and equal opportunity for the contending parties to present their claims.

These are values that regulate fair procedures for adjudicating, or arbitrating, between parties whose claims are in conflict. The specification of a neutral procedure may also draw on values that underlie the principles of free rational discussion between rea-

22. A number of these I discuss in the text. One I don't take up is William Galston's view that some forms of liberalism are neutral in the sense that they use no ideas of the good at all except ones that are purely instrumental (neutral means, as it were). See his "Defending Liberalism," in *American Political Science Review* 72 (September 1982):622. Contrary to his suggestion, justice as fairness is not neutral in this way, as will become clear, if it is not clear already.

23. Thus Herbert Wechsler, in his well-known discussion of principled judicial decisions (he is concerned mainly with decisions of the Supreme Court), thinks of neutral principles as those general principles that we are persuaded apply not only to the present case but to all reasonably foreseeable related cases likely to arise given the constitution and the existing political structure. Neutral principles transcend the case at hand and must be defensible as widely applicable. Wechsler says little about the derivation of such principles from the constitution itself or from precedent. See "Towards Neutral Principles of Constitutional Law," in *Principles, Politics, and Fundamental Law* (Cambridge, Mass.: Harvard University Press, 1961).

sonable persons fully capable of thought and judgment, and concerned to find the truth or to reach reasonable agreement based on the best available information.[24]

3. Justice as fairness is not procedurally neutral. Clearly its principles of justice are substantive and express far more than procedural values, and so do its political conceptions of society and person, which are represented in the original position (II:4–6). As a political conception it aims to be the focus of an overlapping consensus. That is, the view as a whole hopes to articulate a public basis of justification for the basic structure of a constitutional regime working from fundamental intuitive ideas implicit in the public political culture and abstracting from comprehensive religious, philosophical, and moral doctrines. It seeks common ground—or if one prefers, neutral ground—given the fact of pluralism. This common ground is the political conception itself as the focus of an overlapping consensus. But common ground, so defined, is not procedurally neutral ground.

A very different way of defining neutrality is in terms of the aims of basic institutions and public policy with respect to comprehensive doctrines and their associated conceptions of the good. Here neutrality of aim as opposed to neutrality of procedure means that those institutions and policies are neutral in the sense that they can be endorsed by citizens generally as within the scope of a public political conception. Thus, neutrality might mean for example:

a. that the state is to ensure for all citizens equal opportunity to advance any conception of the good they freely affirm;

24. For this kind of view, see the instructive discussion of Charles Larmore, *Patterns of Moral Complexity,* pp. 53–59. He speaks of the "neutral justification of political neutrality as one based on a universal norm of rational dialogue" (p. 53), and he draws on (while modifying) the important ideas of Jürgen Habermas. See the latter's *Legitimation Crisis,* translated by Thomas McCarthy (Boston: Beacon Press, 1976), pt. III; and "Discursethik—Notizen zu einem Begründungsprogramm," in *Moralbewusstsein und kommunikatives Handeln* (Frankfurt: Suhrkamp, 1983), pp. 53–125.

b. that the state is not to do anything intended to favor or promote any particular comprehensive doctrine rather than another, or to give greater assistance to those who pursue it;[25]

c. that the state is not to do anything that makes it more likely that individuals accept any particular conception rather than another unless steps are taken to cancel, or to compensate for, the effects of policies that do this.[26]

The priority of right excludes the first meaning of neutrality of aim, for it allows that only permissible conceptions (those that respect the principles of justice) can be pursued. The first meaning can be amended to allow for this; and as so amended, the state is to secure equal opportunity to advance any permissible conception. In this case, depending on the meaning of equal opportunity, justice as fairness may be neutral in aim. As for the second meaning, it is satisfied in virtue of the features of a political conception expressing the priority of right: so long as the basic structure is regulated by such a view, its institutions are not intended to favor any comprehensive doctrine. In regard to the third meaning, however (as we consider further in §6 below), it is surely impossible for the basic structure of a just constitutional regime not to have important effects and influences as to which comprehensive doctrines endure and gain adherents over time; and it is futile to try to counteract these effects and influences, or even to ascertain for political purposes how deep and pervasive they are. We must accept the facts of commonsense political sociology.

To summarize: we may distinguish procedural neutrality from neutrality of aim; but the latter is not to be confused with neutrality of effect or influence. As a political conception for the basic structure justice as fairness as a whole tries to provide

25. This is the meaning of neutrality in Ronald Dworkin's essay "Liberalism." See *A Matter of Principle* (Cambridge, Mass.: Harvard University Press, 1985) pp. 191ff.
26. This statement of the three versions of neutrality draws on Joseph Raz's formulations in his *Morality of Freedom* (Oxford: Clarendon Press, 1986) pp. 114f.

common ground as the focus of an overlapping consensus. It also hopes to satisfy neutrality of aim in the sense that basic institutions and public policy are not to be designed to favor any particular comprehensive doctrine.[27] Neutrality of effect or influence political liberalism abandons as impracticable, and since this idea is strongly suggested by the term itself, this is a reason for avoiding it.[28]

4. Even though political liberalism seeks common ground and is neutral in aim, it is important to emphasize that it may still affirm the superiority of certain forms of moral character and encourage certain moral virtues. Thus, justice as fairness includes an account of certain political virtues—the virtues of fair social cooperation such as the virtues of civility and tolerance, of reasonableness and the sense of fairness (IV:5–7). The crucial point is that admitting these virtues into a political conception does not lead to the perfectionist state of a comprehensive doctrine.

We can see this once we are clear about the idea of a political conception of justice. As I have said (in §1), ideas of the good may be freely introduced as needed to complement the political conception of justice, so long as they are political ideas, that is, so long as they belong to a reasonable political conception of justice for a constitutional regime. This allows us to assume that they are shared by citizens and do not depend on any particular comprehensive doctrine. Since the ideals connected with the political virtues are tied to the principles of political justice and to the forms of judgment and conduct essential to sustain fair social cooperation over time, those ideals and virtues are compatible with political liberalism. They characterize the ideal of a

27. This distinction between neutrality of procedure and neutrality of outcome is adapted from Larmore, *Patterns of Moral Complexity,* pp. 42–47.

28. Some may feel that abandoning neutrality of effect or influence as impractical may lead to an excessively secular public life and background culture. How far this is a worry should be considered in the light of what is said in the next section, especially in §6:3–4 about religious sects that oppose the culture of the modern world and about trying to answer the question of requirements on children's education within the limits of the political conception. I am indebted to Dennis Thompson for the need to call attention to this connection.

good citizen of a democratic state—a role specified by its political institutions. In this way the political virtues must be distinguished from the virtues that characterize ways of life belonging to comprehensive religious and philosophical doctrines, as well as from the virtues falling under various associational ideals (the ideals of churches and universities, occupations and vocations, clubs and teams) and of those appropriate to roles in family life and to the relations between individuals.

Thus, if a constitutional regime takes certain steps to strengthen the virtues of toleration and mutual trust, say by discouraging various kinds of religious and racial discrimination (in ways consistent with liberty of conscience and freedom of speech), it does not thereby become a perfectionist state of the kind found in Plato or Aristotle, nor does it establish a particular religion as in the Catholic and Protestant states of the early modern period. Rather, it is taking reasonable measures to strengthen the forms of thought and feeling that sustain fair social cooperation between its citizens regarded as free and equal. This is very different from the state's advancing a particular comprehensive doctrine in its own name.[29]

§ 6. Is Justice as Fairness Fair to Conceptions of the Good?

1. The principles of any reasonable political conception must impose restrictions on permissible comprehensive views, and the basic institutions those principles require inevitably encourage some ways of life and discourage others, or even exclude them altogether. Thus, the question arises over how the basic structure (realized by a political conception) encourages and discourages certain comprehensive doctrines and ways of life associated with

---

29. Keep in mind here that the political virtues are identified and justified by the need for certain qualities of character in the citizens of a just and stable constitutional regime. This is not to deny that these same characteristics, or similar ones, might not also be nonpolitical virtues insofar as they are valued for other reasons within various particular comprehensive views.

them and whether how it does this is just. Considering this question will explain the sense in which the state, at least as concerns constitutional essentials, is not to do anything intended to favor any particular comprehensive view.[30] At this point the contrast between political and comprehensive liberalism becomes clear and fundamental.[31]

The encouraging or discouraging of comprehensive doctrines comes about for at least two reasons: their associated ways of life may be in direct conflict with the principles of justice; or else they may be admissible but fail to gain adherents under the political and social conditions of a just constitutional regime. The first case is illustrated by a conception of the good requiring the repression or degradation of certain persons on, say, racial, or ethnic, or perfectionist grounds, for example, slavery in ancient Athens, or in the antebellum South. Examples of the second case may be certain forms of religion. Suppose that a particular religion, and the conception of the good belonging to it, can survive only if it controls the machinery of state and is able to practice

---

30. This was the second meaning of neutrality of aim noted in the previous section; it is satisfied by a political conception.

31. The next several paragraphs are adapted from my reply in "Fairness to Goodness," *Philosophical Review* 82 (April 1975):548–51, to an objection raised by Thomas Nagel in his review, same journal, 82 (April 1973):226–29. In an instructive discussion that I shan't attempt to summarize here, Nagel argues that the set up of the original position in *Theory,* although it is ostensibly neutral between different conceptions of the good, is not actually so. He thinks this is because the suppression of knowledge (by the veil of ignorance) required to bring about unanimity is not equally fair to all parties. The reason is that primary goods, on which the parties base their selection of principles of justice, are not equally valuable in pursuit of all conceptions of the good. Moreover, he says that the well-ordered society of justice as fairness has a strong individualistic bias, and one that is arbitrary because objectivity between conceptions of the good is not established. The reply in the text above supplements that in "Fairness to Goodness" in two ways. It makes clear first, that the conception of the person used in arriving at a workable list of primary goods is a political conception; and second, that justice as fairness itself is a political conception of justice. Once we understand justice as fairness and the conceptions that belong to it in this way, we can make a more forceful reply to Nagel's objection, provided of course it is accepted that neutrality of influence is impracticable.

effective intolerance. This religion will cease to exist in the well-ordered society of political liberalism. Let us assume there are such cases; and that some other comprehensive doctrines may endure but always among relatively small segments of society.

2. The question is this: if some conceptions will die out and others survive only barely in a just constitutional regime, does this by itself imply that its political conception of justice is not fair to them? Is the political conception arbitrarily biased against these views, or better, is it just or unjust to the persons whose conceptions they are, or might be? Without further explanation, it would not appear to be unfair to them, for social influences favoring some doctrines over others cannot be avoided by any view of political justice. No society can include within itself all forms of life. We may indeed lament the limited space, as it were, of social worlds, and of ours in particular; and we may regret some of the inevitable effects of our culture and social structure. As Berlin has long maintained (it is one of his fundamental themes), there is no social world without loss: that is, no social world that does not exclude some ways of life that realize in special ways certain fundamental values. The nature of its culture and institutions proves too uncongenial.[32] But these social necessities are not to be taken for arbitrary bias or injustice.

---

32. For a clear presentation of Berlin's view, see his essay "The Pursuit of the Ideal," in *The Crooked Timber of Humanity* (New York: Knopf, 1991), esp. pp. 11–19. Thus, he says on p. 13: "Some among the Great Goods cannot live together. That is a conceptual truth. We are doomed to choose, and every choice may entail an irreparable loss." See also "Two Concepts of Liberty" (1958), reprinted in *Four Essays on Liberty* (New York: Oxford University Press, 1969), pp. 167ff. For Berlin the realm of values is objective, but values clash and the full range of values is too extensive to fit into any one social world; not only are they incompatible with one another, imposing conflicting requirements on institutions; but there exists no family of workable institutions that can allow sufficient space for them all. That there is no social world without loss is rooted in the nature of values and the world, and much human tragedy reflects that. A just liberal society may have far more space than other social worlds but it can never be without loss. The basic error is to think that because values are objective and hence truly values, they must be compatible. In the realm of values, as opposed to the world of fact, not all truths can fit into one social world.

The objection must go further and hold that the well-ordered society of political liberalism fails to establish, in ways that existing circumstances allow—circumstances that include the fact of reasonable pluralism—a just basic structure within which permissible forms of life have a fair opportunity to maintain themselves and to gain adherents over generations. But if a comprehensive conception of the good is unable to endure in a society securing the familiar equal basic liberties and mutual toleration, there is no way to preserve it consistent with democratic values as expressed by the idea of society as a fair system of cooperation among citizens viewed as free and equal. This raises, but does not of course settle, the question of whether the corresponding way of life is viable under other historical conditions, and whether its passing is to be regretted.[33]

Historical experience shows that many ways of life pass the test of enduring and gaining adherents over time in a democratic society; and if numbers are not the measure of success—and why should they be?—many pass that test with equal success: different groups with distinctive traditions and ways of life find different comprehensive views fully worthy of their allegiance. Thus, whether political liberalism is arbitrarily biased against certain

---

33. In the passage from "Fairness to Goodness," which Galston criticizes at p. 627, I should have mentioned and endorsed Berlin's view as indicated in the text. Indeed we may often want to say that the passing of certain forms of life is to be lamented. What is said in that passage is not, I think, inconsistent with political liberalism, but it is seriously lacking by not also emphasizing Berlin's view. It should have gone on explicitly to reject the idea, which Galston rightly rejects, that only unworthy forms of life lose out in a just constitutional regime. That optimistic view is mistaken. It may still be objected by those who affirm the conceptions that cannot flourish that political liberalism does not allow sufficient space for them. But there is no criterion for what counts as sufficient space except that of a reasonable and defensible political conception of justice itself. The idea of sufficient space is metaphorical and has no meaning beyond that shown in the range of comprehensive doctrines which the principles of such a conception permit and which citizens can affirm as worthy of their full allegiance. The objection might still be that the political conception fails to identify the right space, but this is simply the question of which is the most reasonable political conception.

conceptions and in favor of others turns on whether, given the fact of reasonable pluralism and the other historical conditions of the modern world, realizing its principles in institutions specifies fair background conditions for different and even antagonistic conceptions of the good to be affirmed and pursued. Political liberalism is unjustly biased against certain comprehensive conceptions only if, say, individualistic ones alone can endure in a liberal society, or they so predominate that associations affirming values of religion or community cannot flourish, and moreover the conditions leading to this outcome are themselves unjust, in view of present and foreseeable circumstances.

3. An example may clarify this point: various religious sects oppose the culture of the modern world and wish to lead their common life apart from its unwanted influences. A problem now arises about their children's education and the requirements the state can impose. The liberalisms of Kant and Mill may lead to requirements designed to foster the values of autonomy and individuality as ideals to govern much if not all of life. But political liberalism has a different aim and requires far less. It will ask that children's education include such things as knowledge of their constitutional and civic rights so that, for example, they know that liberty of conscience exists in their society and that apostasy is not a legal crime, all this to insure that their continued membership when they come of age is not based simply on ignorance of their basic rights or fear of punishment for offenses that do not exist. Moreover, their education should also prepare them to be fully cooperating members of society and enable them to be self-supporting; it should also encourage the political virtues so that they want to honor the fair terms of social cooperation in their relations with the rest of society.

Here it may be objected that requiring children to understand the political conception in these ways is in effect, though not in intention, to educate them to a comprehensive liberal conception. Doing the one may lead to the other, if only because once we know the one, we may of our own accord go on to the other.

It must be granted that this may indeed happen in the case of some. And certainly there is some resemblance between the values of political liberalism and the values of the comprehensive liberalisms of Kant and Mill.[34] But the only way this objection can be answered is to set out carefully the great differences in both scope and generality between political and comprehensive liberalism (as specified in §1.1). The unavoidable consequences of reasonable requirements for children's education may have to be accepted, often with regret. I would hope the exposition of political liberalism in these lectures provides a sufficient reply to the objection.

4. Beyond the requirements already described, justice as fairness does not seek to cultivate the distinctive virtues and values of the liberalisms of autonomy and individuality, or indeed of any other comprehensive doctrine. For in that case it ceases to be a form of political liberalism. Justice as fairness honors, as far as it can, the claims of those who wish to withdraw from the modern world in accordance with the injunctions of their religion, provided only that they acknowledge the principles of the political conception of justice and appreciate its political ideals of person and society.

Observe here that we try to answer the question of children's education entirely within the political conception. Society's concern with their education lies in their role as future citizens, and so in such essential things as their acquiring the capacity to understand the public culture and to participate in its institutions, in their being economically independent and self-supporting members of society over a complete life, and in their developing the political virtues, all this from within a political point of view.

34. And that of Raz in his *The Morality of Freedom,* esp. chaps. 14 and 15, to mention a contemporary example.

§ 7. The Good of Political Society

1. A fifth idea of the good in justice as fairness is that of the good of political society: more specifically, the good that citizens realize both as persons and as a corporate body in maintaining a just constitutional regime and in conducting its affairs. As before, we try to explain this good entirely within the political conception.

Let us begin by considering the objection that by not basing itself on a comprehensive religious, philosophical, or moral doctrine, justice as fairness abandons the ideal of a political community and views society as so many distinct individuals, or distinct associations, cooperating solely to pursue their own personal, or associational, advantage without having any final ends in common. (Here a final end is understood as an end valued or wanted for its own sake and not solely as a means to something else.) As a form of political liberalism, justice as fairness is said to regard political institutions as purely instrumental to individual or associational ends, as the institutions of what we may call a "private society." As such, political society itself is not a good at all, but at best a means to individual or associational good.

In reply, justice as fairness does indeed abandon the ideal of political community if by that ideal is meant a political society united on one (partially or fully) comprehensive religious, philosophical, or moral doctrine. That conception of social unity is excluded by the fact of reasonable pluralism; it is no longer a political possibility for those who accept the constraints of liberty and toleration of democratic institutions. As we have seen, political liberalism conceives of social unity in a different way: namely, as deriving from an overlapping consensus on a political conception of justice suitable for a constitutional regime.

2. Recall (from I:6.1) that to say a society is well-ordered by a conception of justice means three things: a) that it is a society in which everyone accepts, and knows that everyone else accepts and publicly endorses, the very same principles of justice; b) that its basic structure—its main political and social institutions and

how they hang together as one system of cooperation—is publicly known, or with good reason believed, to satisfy those principles; and c) that citizens have a normally effective sense of justice, that is, one that enables them to understand and to apply the principles of justice, and for the most part to act from them as their circumstances require. I believe that social unity so understood is the most desirable conception of unity available to us; it is the limit of the practical best.

A well-ordered society, as thus specified, is not, then, a private society; for in the well-ordered society of justice as fairness citizens do have final ends in common. While it is true that they do not affirm the same comprehensive doctrine, they do affirm the same political conception of justice; and this means that they share one very basic political end, and one that has high priority: namely, the end of supporting just institutions and of giving one another justice accordingly, not to mention many other ends they must also share and realize through their political arrangements. Besides, the end of political justice may be among citizens' most basic aims by reference to which they express the kind of person they very much want to be.

3. Together with other assumptions made, these shared final ends provide the basis for the good of a well-ordered society. We have seen that citizens are regarded as having the two moral powers, and the basic rights and liberties of a constitutional regime are to assure that everyone can adequately develop these powers and exercise them fully over the course of a complete life as they so decide. Such a society also provides its citizens with adequate all-purpose means (the primary goods, say, of income and wealth) to do this. Under normal circumstances, then, we may suppose those moral powers to be developed and exercised within institutions of political freedom and liberty of conscience, and their exercise to be supported and sustained by the social bases of mutual and self-respect.

These matters assumed, the well-ordered society of justice as fairness is a good in two ways. The first way is as a good for persons individually, and this for two reasons. One is that the exercise of the two moral powers is experienced as good. This is a consequence of the moral psychology used in justice as fairness.[35] And that their exercise may be an important good, and will be one for many people, is clear from the central role of these powers in the political conception of citizens as persons. We view citizens, for the purposes of political justice, as normal and fully cooperating members of society over a complete life, and thus as having the moral powers that enable them to assume this role. In this context we might say: part of the essential nature of citizens (within the political conception) is their having the two moral powers which root their capacity to participate in fair social cooperation.

A second reason political society is a good for citizens is that it secures for them the good of justice and the social bases of their mutual self-respect. Thus, in securing the equal basic rights and liberties, fair equality of opportunity, and the like, political society guarantees the essentials of persons' public recognition as free and equal citizens. In securing these things political society secures their fundamental needs.

Now the good involved in the exercise of the moral powers and in the public recognition of persons' status as citizens belongs to the political good of a well-ordered society and not that of a comprehensive religious, philosophical, or moral doctrine. Repeatedly we must insist on this distinction, even though a comprehensive doctrine may endorse this good from within its own point of view. Otherwise we lose sight of the path justice as fairness must follow if it is to gain the support of an overlapping consensus. As I have emphasized throughout, the priority of right does not mean that ideas of the good must be avoided; that is impossible. Rather, it means that the ideas used must be political ideas: they must be tailored to meet the restrictions imposed by the political conception of justice and fit into the space it allows.

35. In *Theory*, §65, this psychology uses the so-called Aristotelian principle; other views might adopt different principles to reach much the same conclusion.

4. A well-ordered political society is also a good in a second way. For whenever there is a shared final end, an end that requires the cooperation of many to achieve, the good realized is social: it is realized through citizens' joint activity in mutual dependence on the appropriate actions being taken by others. Thus, establishing and successfully conducting reasonably just (though of course always imperfect) democratic institutions over a long period of time, perhaps gradually reforming them over generations, though not, to be sure, without lapses, is a great social good and appreciated as such. This is shown by the fact that a people refer to it as one of the significant achievements of their history.

That there should be such a political and social good is no more mysterious than that members of an orchestra, or players on a team, or even both teams in a game, should take pleasure and a certain (proper) pride in a good performance, or in a good play of the game, one that they will want to remember. No doubt the requisite conditions become more difficult to satisfy as societies become larger and the social distance between citizens becomes greater, but these differences, as great and inhibiting as they may be, do not affect the psychological principle involved in realizing the good of justice in a well-ordered political society. Moreover, this good can be significant even when the conditions for realizing it are quite imperfect; and the sense of its loss can also be significant. This is made clear when a democratic people distinguish different periods in their history, as well as their pride in distinguishing themselves from nondemocratic peoples. But these reflections I shall not pursue. We need to establish only that the good of a well-ordered society is a significant good within a political conception of justice, and this we have done. So our account of the five ideas of the good is complete.[36]

36. It may be asked, however, how far the good of political society is strictly speaking a political good: it is granted that political institutions encourage the development of and provide scope for the exercise of the two moral powers and that this is a good. But these powers are also exercised in many other parts of life for many purposes and surely this wider exercise is not just a political good; rather political institutions protect and secure this good. In reply, the point is that in political good

5. By contrast, a few remarks about classical republicanism and civic humanism will clarify these explanations about the good of political society. Classical republicanism I take to be the view that if the citizens of a democratic society are to preserve their basic rights and liberties, including the civil liberties which secure the freedoms of private life, they must also have to a sufficient degree the "political virtues" (as I have called them) and be willing to take part in public life.[37] The idea is that without a widespread participation in democratic politics by a vigorous and informed citizen body, and certainly with a general retreat into private life, even the most well-designed political institutions will fall into the hands of those who seek to dominate and impose their will through the state apparatus either for the sake of power and military glory, or for reasons of class and economic interest, not to mention expansionist religious fervor and nationalist fanaticism. The safety of democratic liberties requires the active participation of citizens who possess the political virtues needed to maintain a constitutional regime.

With classical republicanism so understood, justice as fairness as a form of political liberalism has no fundamental opposition. At most there can be certain differences on matters of institutional design and the political sociology of democratic regimes. These differences, if there be such, are not by any means trivial; they can be extremely important. But there is no fundamental opposition because classical republicanism does not presuppose a comprehensive religious, philosophical, or moral doctrine. Nothing in classical republicanism, as characterized above, is incompatible with political liberalism as I have described it.

---

strictly speaking we suppose that the moral powers are exercised in political life and in basic institutions as citizens endeavor to maintain these institutions and to use them to conduct public business. Of course, it is true that the moral powers are also exercised far more generally, and one hopes that the political and the nonpolitical sides of life are mutually supporting. This can be granted without denying that as defined political good exists.

37. Machiavelli in *The Discourses* is sometimes taken as illustrating classical republicanism. See Quentin Skinner, *Machiavelli* (New York: Hill and Wang, 1981), esp. chap. 3. A more appropriate example from our standpoint here would be Tocqueville's *Democracy in America*.

But with civic humanism, as I understand it, there is indeed fundamental opposition. For as a form of Aristotelianism, it is sometimes stated as the view that man is a social, even a political, animal whose essential nature is most fully realized in a democratic society in which there is widespread and vigorous participation in political life. Participation is not encouraged as necessary for the protection of the basic liberties of democratic citizenship, and as in itself one form of good among others, however important for many persons. Rather, taking part in democratic politics is seen as the privileged locus of the good life.[38] It is a return to giving a central place to what Constant called the "liberties of the ancients" and has all the defects of that.

From the standpoint of political liberalism, the objection to this comprehensive doctrine is the same as to all other such doctrines, so I need not elaborate. It remains to say only that justice as fairness does not of course deny that some will find their most important good in political life, and therefore that political life is central to their comprehensive good. Indeed, in a well-framed polity it is generally to the good of society as a whole that this be so, in the same way as it is generally beneficial that people develop their different and complementary talents and skills, and engage in mutually advantageous cooperation. This leads to a further idea of the good: namely, that of a well-ordered society as a social union of social unions. This idea is too involved to sketch here and it is not needed for our purposes in these lectures.[39]

38. This interpretation of civic humanism I borrow from Charles Taylor, *Philosophical Papers* (Cambridge: Cambridge University Press, 1985), vol. 2, pp. 334f. Taylor is discussing Kant and attributes this view to Rousseau, but notes that Kant does not accept it. So understood, a form of civic humanism is powerfully if pessimistically expressed by Hannah Arendt (and, she thinks, the ancient Greeks), who holds that freedom and worldliness, best realized in politics, are the only values that redeem human life from the endless round of nature and make it worth living. See her *The Human Condition* (Chicago: University of Chicago Press, 1958). I follow the perceptive study of Arendt's view of the primacy of politics found in George Kateb, *Hannah Arendt: Politics, Conscience, Evil* (Towanda: Rowman and Allanheld, 1984), chap. 1.

39. See *Theory*, §79, where the idea of a well-ordered society as a social union of

§ 8. That Justice as Fairness is Complete

1. I conclude by surveying several ways in which justice as fairness is complete as a political conception. The first way is that the ideas of the good it uses are political ideas and they are generated and have their role within it. As to their generation, observe that those ideas are built up in a sequence starting with goodness as rationality.[40] The exposition started with this idea. It is used to explain primary goods as things citizens need, granted the conception of citizens as persons with higher-order interests who have, we suppose, rational plans of life. Once the primary goods are on hand, the argument from the original position can proceed, so we arrive next at the two principles of justice. Then we use these principles both to specify permissible (comprehensive) conceptions of the good and to characterize the political virtues of citizens required to support a just basic structure. Finally, by drawing on the Aristotelian principle and other elements in justice as fairness, we spell out the ways in which the well-ordered political society of justice as fairness is intrinsically good.

This last step is particularly significant, for it means that the political conception expresses ways in which a political society itself can be an intrinsic good—specified within that conception—for citizens both as individuals and as a corporate body. (Recall the contrast with what we referred to as private society [§7.1].) With the ideas of good used (including the intrinsic good of political society), justice as fairness is complete in this way: it

---

social unions is discussed. In sec. VI of "The Basic Liberties and Their Priority," *The Tanner Lectures on Human Values* (Salt Lake City: University of Utah Press, 1982), vol. III, I took up the idea again and sketched an argument to show that the two principles of justice as fairness are especially suitable to society viewed as a social union of social unions. I am not entirely satisfied with that argument but I think it not without some force. See VIII:6, pp. 315–24.

40. This construction, so to speak, of a sequence of ideas of the good, beginning with the good as rationality, has a parallel in the way Kant can be seen to construct six ideas of the good in his moral view. I have tried to explain how Kant's construction goes in §2 of "Themes in Kant's Moral Philosophy," in *Kant's Transcendental Deductions,* edited by Eckhart Förster (Stanford: Stanford University Press, 1989).

generates from within itself the requisite ideas so that all perform their complementary roles with its framework.

2. A corollary of this completeness is that it brings out, in a way we could not express before, why an overlapping consensus is not a mere modus vivendi. In a society well ordered by the principles mutually recognized in an overlapping consensus, citizens have many final ends in common and among them is giving one another mutual political justice. Drawing on all five ideas of the good, we may speak of the mutual good of mutual justice. For goodness as rationality allows us to say that things are good (within the political conception) if they have the properties it is rational for us to want as free and equal citizens, given our rational plan of life. From the point of view of the parties in the original position, who represent our fundamental interests, mutual justice meets this condition. As citizens in society we normally want justice from everybody else. Much the same holds for the political virtues.[41] This deepens the idea that a political conception supported by an overlapping consensus is a moral conception affirmed on moral grounds (IV:3.4).

A second corollary of completeness is that it strengthens the account of how a modus vivendi with the content of a liberal conception of justice might gradually develop over time into an overlapping consensus (IV:6–7). There much depended on the fact that most people's political conceptions are normally only partially comprehensive. Usually we do not have anything like a fully comprehensive religious, philosophical, or moral view, much less have we attempted to study the other views that do exist in society, or to work one out for ourselves. Hence that there are significant intrinsic goods internal to political life means that the political conception can win our initial allegiance more deeply independently of our comprehensive views and prior to conflicts with them. When conflicts do arise, the political conception has

---

41. Of course, to show all this convincingly requires a long story. I have tried to sketch some of it in *Theory*, §66, drawing on the full theory of the good.

a better chance of sustaining itself and shaping those views to fit within its limits.

Earlier we said that political liberalism holds that under reasonably favorable conditions that make a constitutional democracy possible, political institutions satisfying the principles of a liberal conception of justice realize political values and ideals that normally outweigh whatever other values oppose them. The preceding corollaries of completeness strengthen its stability: allegiance based on those political values is stronger, and so the likelihood that they will be outweighed by opposing values is that much less.

3. I now turn to another way in which justice as fairness is complete by taking up the first question stated at the outset: namely, how can political liberalism use ideas of the good at all without making claims about the truth of this or that comprehensive doctrine in ways not allowed by political liberalism itself? This question we can now answer by reviewing what we have said.

First, the priority of right means (in its general meaning) that the ideas of the good used must be political ideas (§1.2), so that we need not rely on comprehensive conceptions of the good but only on ideas tailored to fit within the political conception. Second, the priority of right means (in its particular meaning) that the principles of justice set limits to permissible ways of life (§1.2): the claims that citizens make to pursue ends transgressing those limits have no weight. The priority of right gives the principles of justice a strict precedence in citizens' deliberations and limits their freedom to advance certain ways of life. It characterizes the structure and content of justice as fairness and what it regards as good reasons in deliberation.

4. Next, consider the second question stated at the outset. We said that just institutions and the political virtues expected of citizens would not be those of a just and good society, unless they not only permitted but also sustained ways of life fully worthy of citizens' devoted allegiance. A conception of political

justice must contain within itself sufficient space, as it were, for such ways of life. Here the question is: unless we appeal to some view beyond the political, how are we to say when ways of life are worthy of our full allegiance, or to tell when a society contains sufficient space? As we said, justice as fairness itself cannot say, from the standpoint of some larger view, that the various comprehensive doctrines it allows are worthy of full allegiance. How, then, are we to proceed?

At this point we invoke the idea of an overlapping consensus and say: if a political conception of justice is mutually recognized by reasonable and rational citizens who affirm the reasonable comprehensive doctrines in an overlapping consensus (as these ideas are explained in II:1–3), this fact itself confirms that its free basic institutions allow sufficient space for ways of life worthy of citizens' devoted allegiance. I assume, of course, that the political conception of justice endorsed by the reasonable consensus meets, so far as we can see, all the reasonable criteria of critical reflection. Citizens' due reflection as expressed in the consensus confirms that. This is the most reasonable assurance political liberalism allows—and the most we can reasonably have—that our political institutions contain sufficient space for worthy ways of life, and that in this sense our political society is just and good.

A final point: although justice as fairness cannot answer the preceding questions from the standpoint of some wider view, this does not prevent it from imposing constraints—as any reasonable political view must—on comprehensive doctrines; for example, the constraint of their being reasonable, as we have done in II:3. This constraint is not peculiar to the political conception and applies to all doctrines that we may reasonably expect to include in an overlapping consensus. What is crucial about these constraints is that they are either the general ones of theoretical or practical reason, or else they are part of justice as fairness as a political conception. They invoke the ideas of reasonableness and rationality as applied to citizens and shown in the exercise of their moral powers. The constraints do not refer to, although they limit, the substantive content of comprehensive conceptions of the good.[42]

42. A contrast will bring out what is meant here: consider Ronald Dworkin's view as given in "Foundations of Liberal Equality," in *Tanner Lectures on Human Values* (Salt Lake City: University of Utah Press, 1990), vol. 11. His aim is to show how the principles of liberal justice (in his formulation) can be given an ethical foundation. This means that those principles can be derived as the political principles for the basic structure of society that best provide the conditions for people to live well, to lead ethically good lives. To this end, he develops an account of the ethical value of living well by presenting the challenge model of value as the correct account. This model is said to be formal and not to rule out substantive conceptions of the good, as most though not all such conceptions can be interpreted to fall under that model. With the model of challenge on hand, he argues that in an original position, let us say, where every one is a fully informed ethical liberal and hence accepts the challenge model, the principles of liberal justice will be adopted. In this way, a general account of what it means to live well—an account that belongs to philosophical ethics—provides the wanted philosophical foundation for the political principles of liberalism. The point of the contrast is this: the constraints Dworkin imposes on substantive conceptions of the good issue from an ethical conception of value (the challenge model). Whereas in justice as fairness, the constraints imposed on reasonable comprehensive doctrines are either the general ones of theoretical or practical reason or issue from the conceptions (e.g., of citizens as free and equal persons with the two moral powers) that belong to the account of political justice. I raise no objection to Dworkin's view: like the comprehensive liberalisms of Kant and Mill it has a proper place in the background culture and serves there in a supporting role for political liberalism.

The Idea
of Public
Reason[1]

A political society, and indeed every
reasonable and rational agent, whether
it be an individual, or a family or an
association, or even a confederation
of political societies, has a way of formulating its plans, of putting its ends
in an order of priority and of making
its decisions accordingly. The way a
political society does this is its reason; its ability to do these things is
also its reason, though in a different

1. Two lectures on this topic were first given
at the University of California at Irvine in late
February and early March of 1990 to inaugurate
the Melden Lectures, named in honor after A. I.
Melden. While much revised, this lecture greatly
benefits from discussion then with Sharon Lloyd,
Gerasimos Santas, Lawrence Solum, Gary Watson, and Paul Weithman. I have gained much
since from many conversations with Samuel
Freeman, Peter de Marneffe, and David Estlund.

sense: it is an intellectual and moral power, rooted in the capacities of its human members.

Not all reasons are public reasons, as there are the nonpublic reasons of churches and universities and of many other associations in civil society. In aristocratic and autocratic regimes, when the good of society is considered, this is done not by the public, if it exists at all, but by the rulers, whoever they may be. Public reason is characteristic of a democratic people: it is the reason of its citizens, of those sharing the status of equal citizenship. The subject of their reason is the good of the public: what the political conception of justice requires of society's basic structure of institutions, and of the purposes and ends they are to serve. Public reason, then, is public in three ways: as the reason of citizens as such, it is the reason of the public; its subject is the good of the public and matters of fundamental justice; and its nature and content is public, being given by the ideals and principles expressed by society's conception of political justice, and conducted open to view on that basis.

That public reason should be so understood and honored by citizens is not, of course, a matter of law. As an ideal conception of citizenship for a constitutional democratic regime, it presents how things might be, taking people as a just and well-ordered society would encourage them to be. It describes what is possible and can be, yet may never be, though no less fundamental for that.

§ 1. The Questions and Forums of Public Reason

1. The idea of public reason has been often discussed and has a long history, and in some form it is widely accepted.[2] My aim

2. The title is suggested by Kant's distinction between public and private reason in "What is Enlightenment?" (1784), although his distinction is different from the one used here. There are other relevant discussions in Kant's works, for example, *Critique of Pure Reason*, B767–97. For a valuable account, see Onora O'Neill, *Constructions of Reason*, (Cambridge: Cambridge University Press, 1989), chap. 2, "The Public Use of Reason." See also her recent essay, "Vindicating Reason," in *The Cambridge*

here is to try to express it in an acceptable way as part of a political conception of justice that is broadly speaking liberal.[3]

To begin: in a democratic society public reason is the reason of equal citizens who, as a collective body, exercise final political and coercive power over one another in enacting laws and in amending their constitution. The first point is that the limits imposed by public reason do not apply to all political questions but only to those involving what we may call "constitutional essentials" and questions of basic justice. (These are specified in §5.) This means that political values alone are to settle such fundamental questions as: who has the right to vote, or what religions are to be tolerated, or who is to be assured fair equality of opportunity, or to hold property. These and similar questions are the special subject of public reason.

Many if not most political questions do not concern those fundamental matters, for example, much tax legislation and many laws regulating property; statutes protecting the environment and controlling pollution; establishing national parks and preserving wilderness areas and animal and plant species; and laying aside funds for museums and the arts. Of course, sometimes these do involve fundamental matters. A full account of public

---

Companion to Kant, edited by Paul Guyer (Cambridge: Cambridge University Press, 1992).

3. For some recent views that are roughly speaking liberal though importantly different, see David Lyons, *Ethics and the Rule of Law* (Cambridge: Cambridge University Press, 1984), with a clear statement, p. 190f.; Ronald Dworkin, "The Forum of Principle," in *A Matter of Principle,* pp. 33–71; Charles Larmore, *Patterns of Moral Complexity* and "Political Liberalism," *Political Theory* 18 (August 1990); Thomas Nagel, *Equality and Partiality* (New York: Oxford University Press, 1991), chap. 14. For a valuable discussion of the idea of deliberative democracy, see Joshua Cohen, "Deliberation and Democratic Legitimacy," in *The Good Polity,* edited by Alan Hamlin (Oxford: Basil Blackwell, 1989). For the bearing of religion on public reason, see Kent Greenawalt's *Religious Conviction and Political Choice,* esp. chaps. 8 and 12; Robert Audi, " The Separation of Church and State and the Obligations of Citizenship," *Philosophy and Public Affairs* 18 (Summer 1989) and Paul Weithman's "The Separation of Church and State: Some Questions for Professor Audi,"*Philosophy and Public Affairs* 20 (Winter 1991), with Audi's reply in the same issue; and finally, Lawrence Solum's instructive "Faith and Justice," *DePaul Law Review* 39 (Summer 1990).

reason would take up these other questions and explain in more detail than I can here how they differ from constitutional essentials and questions of basic justice and why the restrictions imposed by public reason may not apply to them; or if they do, not in the same way, or so strictly.

Some will ask: why not say that all questions in regard to which citizens exercise their final and coercive political power over one another are subject to public reason? Why would it ever be admissible to go outside its range of political values? To answer: my aim is to consider first the strongest case where the political questions concern the most fundamental matters. If we should not honor the limits of public reason here, it would seem we need not honor them anywhere. Should they hold here, we can then proceed to other cases. Still, I grant that it is usually highly desirable to settle political questions by invoking the values of public reason. Yet this may not always be so.

2. Another feature of public reason is that its limits do not apply to our personal deliberations and reflections about political questions, or to the reasoning about them by members of associations such as churches and universities, all of which is a vital part of the background culture. Plainly, religious, philosophical, and moral considerations of many kinds may here properly play a role. But the ideal of public reason does hold for citizens when they engage in political advocacy in the public forum, and thus for members of political parties and for candidates in their campaigns and for other groups who support them. It holds equally for how citizens are to vote in elections when constitutional essentials and matters of basic justice are at stake. Thus, the ideal of public reason not only governs the public discourse of elections insofar as the issues involve those fundamental questions, but also how citizens are to cast their vote on these questions (§2.4). Otherwise, public discourse runs the risks of being hypocritical: citizens talk before one another one way and vote another.

We must distinguish, however, between how the ideal of public reason applies to citizens and how it applies to various officers of the government. It applies in official forums and so to legislators when they speak on the floor of parliament, and to the executive in its public acts and pronouncements. It applies also in a special way to the judiciary and above all to a supreme court in a constitutional democracy with judicial review. This is because the justices have to explain and justify their decisions as based on their understanding of the constitution and relevant statutes and precedents. Since acts of the legislative and the executive need not be justified in this way, the court's special role makes it the exemplar of public reason (§6).

§ 2. Public Reason and the Ideal of Democratic Citizenship

1. I now turn to what to many is a basic difficulty with the idea of public reason, one that makes it seem paradoxical. They ask: why should citizens in discussing and voting on the most fundamental political questions honor the limits of public reason? How can it be either reasonable or rational, when basic matters are at stake, for citizens to appeal only to a public conception of justice and not to the whole truth as they see it? Surely, the most fundamental questions should be settled by appealing to the most important truths, yet these may far transcend public reason!

I begin by trying to dissolve this paradox and invoke a principle of liberal legitimacy as explained in IV:1.2–3. Recall that this principle is connected with two special features of the political relationship among democratic citizens:

First, it is a relationship of persons within the basic structure of the society into which they are born and in which they normally lead a complete life.

Second, in a democracy political power, which is always coercive power, is the power of the public, that is, of free and equal citizens as a collective body.

As always, we assume that the diversity of reasonable religious, philosophical, and moral doctrines found in democratic societies is a permanent feature of the public culture and not a mere historical condition soon to pass away.

Granted all this, we ask: when may citizens by their vote properly exercise their coercive political power over one another when fundamental questions are at stake? Or in the light of what principles and ideals must we exercise that power if our doing so is to be justifiable to others as free and equal? To this question political liberalism replies: our exercise of political power is proper and hence justifiable only when it is exercised in accordance with a constitution the essentials of which all citizens may reasonably be expected to endorse in the light of principles and ideals acceptable to them as reasonable and rational. This is the liberal principle of legitimacy. And since the exercise of political power itself must be legitimate, the ideal of citizenship imposes a moral, not a legal, duty—the duty of civility—to be able to explain to one another on those fundamental questions how the principles and policies they advocate and vote for can be supported by the political values of public reason. This duty also involves a willingness to listen to others and a fairmindedness in deciding when accommodations to their views should reasonably be made.[4]

2. Some might say that the limits of public reason apply only in official forums and so only to legislators, say, when they speak on the floor of parliament, or to the executive and the judiciary in their public acts and decisions. If they honor public reason, then citizens are indeed given public reasons for the laws they are to comply with and for the policies society follows. But this does not go far enough.

Democracy involves, as I have said, a political relationship between citizens within the basic structure of the society into which they are born and within which they normally lead a complete life; it implies further an equal share in the coercive political power that citizens exercise over one another by voting

---

4. On this last, see the instructive discussion by Amy Gutmann and Dennis Thompson in their "Moral Conflict and Political Consensus," *Ethics* 101 (October 1990): 76–86.

and in other ways. As reasonable and rational, and knowing that they affirm a diversity of reasonable religious and philosophical doctrines, they should be ready to explain the basis of their actions to one another in terms each could reasonably expect that others might endorse as consistent with their freedom and equality. Trying to meet this condition is one of the tasks that this ideal of democratic politics asks of us. Understanding how to conduct oneself as a democratic citizen includes understanding an ideal of public reason.

Beyond this, the political values realized by a well-ordered constitutional regime are very great values and not easily overridden and the ideals they express are not to be lightly abandoned. Thus, when the political conception is supported by an overlapping consensus of reasonable comprehensive doctrines, the paradox of public reason disappears. The union of the duty of civility with the great values of the political yields the ideal of citizens governing themselves in ways that each thinks the others might reasonably be expected to accept; and this ideal in turn is supported by the comprehensive doctrines reasonable persons affirm. Citizens affirm the ideal of public reason, not as a result of political compromise, as in a modus vivendi, but from within their own reasonable doctrines.

3. Why the apparent paradox of public reason is no paradox is clearer once we remember that there are familiar cases where we grant that we should not appeal to the whole truth as we see it, even when it might be readily available. Consider how in a criminal case the rules of evidence limit the testimony that can be introduced, all this to insure the accused the basic right of a fair trial. Not only is hearsay evidence excluded but also evidence gained by improper searches and seizures, or by the abuse of defendants upon arrest and failing to inform them of their rights. Nor can defendants be forced to testify in their own defense. Finally, to mention a restriction with a quite different ground, spouses cannot be required to testify against one another, this to protect the great good of family life and to show public respect for the value of bonds of affection.

218

It may be objected that these examples are quite remote from the limits involved in relying solely on public reason. Remote perhaps but the idea is similar. All these examples are cases where we recognize a duty not to decide in view of the whole truth so as to honor a right or duty, or to advance an ideal good, or both. The examples serve the purpose, as many others would, of showing how it is often perfectly reasonable to forswear the whole truth and this parallels how the alleged paradox of public reason is resolved. What has to be shown is either that honoring the limits of public reason by citizens generally is required by certain basic rights and liberties and their corresponding duties, or else that it advances certain great values, or both. Political liberalism relies on the conjecture that the basic rights and duties and values in question have sufficient weight so that the limits of public reason are justified by the overall assessments of reasonable comprehensive doctrines once those doctrines have adapted to the conception of justice itself.[5]

4. On fundamental political questions the idea of public reason rejects common views of voting as a private and even personal matter. One view is that people may properly vote their preferences and interests, social and economic, not to mention their dislikes and hatreds. Democracy is said to be majority rule and a majority can do as it wishes. Another view, offhand quite different, is that people may vote what they see as right and true as their comprehensive convictions direct without taking into account public reasons.

Yet both views are similar in that neither recognizes the duty of civility and neither respects the limits of public reason in voting on matters of constitutional essentials and questions of basic justice. The first view is guided by our preferences and interests, the second view by what we see as the whole truth. Whereas public reason with its duty of civility gives a view about voting on fundamental questions in some ways reminiscent of Rousseau's *Social Contract*. He saw voting as ideally expressing

---

5. The process of adaptation was described in IV:6–7.

our opinion as to which of the alternatives best advances the common good.[6]

§ 3. Nonpublic Reasons

1. The nature of public reason will be clearer if we consider the differences between it and nonpublic reasons. First of all, there are many nonpublic reasons and but one public reason. Among the nonpublic reasons are those of associations of all kinds: churches and universities, scientific societies and professional groups. As we have said, to act reasonably and responsibly, corporate bodies, as well as individuals, need a way of reasoning about what is to be done. This way of reasoning is public with respect to their members, but nonpublic with respect to political society and to citizens generally. Nonpublic reasons comprise the many reasons of civil society and belong to what I have called the "background culture," in contrast with the public political culture. These reasons are social, and certainly not private.[7]

Now all ways of reasoning—whether individual, associational, or political—must acknowledge certain common elements: the concept of judgment, principles of inference, and rules of evidence, and much else, otherwise they would not be ways of reasoning but perhaps rhetoric or means of persuasion. We are concerned with reason, not simply with discourse. A way of reasoning, then, must incorporate the fundamental concepts and principles of reason, and include standards of correctness and criteria of justification. A capacity to master these ideas is part of common human reason. However, different procedures and methods are appropriate to different conceptions of themselves

6. *The Social Contract,* bk. IV, chap. II, para. 8.

7. The public vs. nonpublic distinction is not the distinction between public and private. This latter I ignore: there is no such thing as private reason. There is social reason—the many reasons of associations in society which make up the background culture; there is also, let us say, domestic reason—the reason of families as small groups in society—and this contrasts both with public and social reason. As citizens, we participate in all these kinds of reason and have the rights of equal citizens when we do so.

held by individuals and corporate bodies, given the different conditions under which their reasoning is carried out, as well as the different constraints to which their reasoning is subject. These constraints may arise from the necessity to protect certain rights or to achieve certain values.

To illustrate: the rules for weighing evidence in a court of law—the rules relating to hearsay evidence in a criminal trial and requiring that the defendant be shown guilty beyond a reasonable doubt—are suited to the special role of courts and needed to protect the right of the accused to a fair trial. Different rules of evidence are used by a scientific society; and different authorities are recognized as relevant or binding by different corporate bodies. Consider the different authorities cited in a church council discussing a point of theological doctrine, in a university faculty debating educational policy, and in a meeting of a scientific association trying to assess the harm to the public from a nuclear accident. The criteria and methods of these nonpublic reasons depend in part on how the nature (the aim and point) of each association is understood and the conditions under which it pursues its ends.

2. In a democratic society nonpublic power, as seen, for example, in the authority of churches over their members, is freely accepted. In the case of ecclesiastical power, since apostasy and heresy are not legal offenses, those who are no longer able to recognize a church's authority may cease being members without running afoul of state power.[8] Whatever comprehensive reli-

---

8. In this case we think of liberty of conscience as protecting the individual against the church. This is an example of the protection that basic rights and liberties secure for individuals generally. But equally, liberty of conscience and other liberties such as freedom of association protect churches from the intrusions of government and from other powerful associations. Both associations and individuals need protection, and so do families need protection from associations and government, as do the individual members of families from other family members (wives from their husbands, children from their parents). It is incorrect to say that liberalism focuses solely on the rights of individuals; rather, the rights it recognizes are to protect associations, smaller groups, and individuals, all from one another in an appropriate balance specified by its guiding principles of justice.

gious, philosophical, or moral views we hold are also freely accepted, politically speaking; for given liberty of conscience and freedom of thought, we impose any such doctrine on ourselves. By this I do not mean that we do this by an act of free choice, as it were, apart from all prior loyalties and commitments, attachments, and affections. I mean that, as free and equal citizens, whether we affirm these views is regarded as within our political competence specified by basic constitutional rights and liberties.

By contrast, the government's authority cannot be evaded except by leaving the territory over which it governs, and not always then. That its authority is guided by public reason does not change this. For normally leaving one's country is a grave step: it involves leaving the society and culture in which we have been raised, the society and culture whose language we use in speech and thought to express and understand ourselves, our aims, goals, and values; the society and culture whose history, customs, and conventions we depend on to find our place in the social world. In large part we affirm our society and culture, and have an intimate and inexpressible knowledge of it, even though much of it we may question, if not reject.

The government's authority cannot, then, be freely accepted in the sense that the bonds of society and culture, of history and social place of origin, begin so early to shape our life and are normally so strong that the right of emigration (suitably qualified) does not suffice to make accepting its authority free, politically speaking, in the way that liberty of conscience suffices to make accepting ecclesiastical authority free, politically speaking. Nevertheless, we may over the course of life come freely to accept, as the outcome of reflective thought and reasoned judgment, the ideals, principles, and standards that specify our basic rights and liberties, and effectively guide and moderate the political power to which we are subject. This is the outer limit of our freedom.[9]

9. Here I accept the Kantian (not Kant's) view that what we affirm on the basis of free and informed reason and reflection is affirmed freely; and that insofar as our

§ 4. The Content of Public Reason

1. I now turn to the content of public reason, having considered its nature and sketched how the apparent paradox of honoring its limits may be dissolved. This content is formulated by what I have called a "political conception of justice," which I assume is broadly liberal in character. By this I mean three things: first, it specifies certain basic rights, liberties, and opportunities (of the kind familiar from constitutional democratic regimes); second, it assigns a special priority to these rights, liberties, and opportunities, especially with respect to claims of the general good and of perfectionist values; and third, it affirms measures assuring all citizens adequate all-purpose means to make effective use of their basic liberties and opportunities. The two principles stated in I:1.1–2 fall under this general description. But each of these elements can be seen in different ways, so there are many liberalisms.

In saying a conception of justice is political I also mean three things (I:2): that it is framed to apply solely to the basic structure of society, its main political, social, and economic institutions as a unified scheme of social cooperation; that it is presented independently of any wider comprehensive religious or philosophical doctrine; and that it is elaborated in terms of fundamental political ideas viewed as implicit in the public political culture of a democratic society.

2. Now it is essential that a liberal political conception include, besides its principles of justice, guidelines of inquiry that specify ways of reasoning and criteria for the kinds of information relevant for political questions. Without such guidelines substantive principles cannot be applied and this leaves the political concep-

---

conduct expresses what we affirm freely, our conduct is free to the extent it can be. Freedom at the deepest level calls upon the freedom of reason, both theoretical and practical, as expressed in what we say and do. Limits on freedom are at bottom limits on our reason: on its development and education, its knowledge and information, and on the scope of the actions in which it can be expressed, and therefore our freedom depends on the nature of the surrounding institutional and social context.

tion incomplete and fragmentary. That conception has, then, two parts:

    a. first, substantive principles of justice for the basic structure; and

    b. second, guidelines of inquiry: principles of reasoning and rules of evidence in the light of which citizens are to decide whether substantive principles properly apply and to identify laws and policies that best satisfy them.

Hence liberal political values are likewise of two kinds:

    a. The first kind—the values of political justice—fall under the principles of justice for the basic structure: the values of equal political and civil liberty; equality of opportunity; the values of social equality and economic reciprocity; and let us add also values of the common good as well as the various necessary conditions for all these values.

    b. The second kind of political values—the values of public reason—fall under the guidelines for public inquiry, which make that inquiry free and public. Also included here are such political virtues as reasonableness and a readiness to honor the (moral) duty of civility, which as virtues of citizens help to make possible reasoned public discussion of political questions.

3. As we have said, on matters of constitutional essentials and basic justice, the basic structure and its public policies are to be justifiable to all citizens, as the principle of political legitimacy requires. We add to this that in making these justifications we are to appeal only to presently accepted general beliefs and forms of reasoning found in common sense, and the methods and conclusions of science when these are not controversial. The liberal principle of legitimacy makes this the most appropriate, if not the only, way to specify the guidelines of public inquiry. What other guidelines and criteria have we for this case?

This means that in discussing constitutional essentials and matters of basic justice we are not to appeal to comprehensive religious and philosophical doctrines—to what we as individuals or members of associations see as the whole truth—nor to elaborate economic theories of general equilibrium, say, if these are in dispute. As far as possible, the knowledge and ways of reasoning that ground our affirming the principles of justice and their application to constitutional essentials and basic justice are to rest on the plain truths now widely accepted, or available, to citizens generally. Otherwise, the political conception would not provide a public basis of justification.

As we consider later in §5, we want the substantive content and the guidelines of inquiry of a political conception, when taken together, to be complete. This means that the values specified by that conception can be suitably balanced or combined, or otherwise united, as the case may be, so that those values alone give a reasonable public answer to all, or to nearly all, questions involving the constitutional essentials and basic questions of justice. For an account of public reason we must have a reasonable answer, or think we can in due course find one, to all, or nearly all, those cases. I shall say a political conception is complete if it meets this condition.

4. In justice as fairness, and I think in many other liberal views, the guidelines of inquiry of public reason, as well as its principle of legitimacy, have the same basis as the substantive principles of justice. This means in justice as fairness that the parties in the original position, in adopting principles of justice for the basic structure, must also adopt guidelines and criteria of public reason for applying those norms. The argument for those guidelines, and for the principle of legitimacy, is much the same as, and as strong as, the argument for the principles of justice themselves. In securing the interests of the persons they represent, the parties insist that the application of substantive principles be guided by judgment and inference, reasons and evidence that the persons they represent can reasonably be expected to endorse. Should the parties fail to insist on this, they would not act responsibly as trustees. Thus we have the principle of legitimacy.

In justice as fairness, then, the guidelines of public reason and the principles of justice have essentially the same grounds. They are companion parts of one agreement. There is no reason why any citizen, or association of citizens, should have the right to use state power to decide constitutional essentials as that person's, or that association's, comprehensive doctrine directs. When equally represented, no citizen could grant to another person or association that political authority. Any such authority is, therefore, without grounds in public reason, and reasonable comprehensive doctrines recognize this.

5. Keep in mind that political liberalism is a kind of view. It has many forms, depending on the substantive principles used and how the guidelines of inquiry are set out. These forms have in common substantive principles of justice that are liberal and an idea of public reason. Content and idea may vary within these limits.

Accepting the idea of public reason and its principle of legitimacy emphatically does not mean, then, accepting a particular liberal conception of justice down to the last details of the principles defining its content. We may differ about these principles and still agree in accepting a conception's more general features. We agree that citizens share in political power as free and equal, and that as reasonable and rational they have a duty of civility to appeal to public reason, yet we differ as to which principles are the most reasonable basis of public justification. The view I have called "justice as fairness" is but one example of a liberal political conception; its specific content is not definitive of such a view.

The point of the ideal of public reason is that citizens are to conduct their fundamental discussions within the framework of what each regards as a political conception of justice based on values that the others can reasonably be expected to endorse and each is, in good faith, prepared to defend that conception so understood. This means that each of us must have, and be ready to explain, a criterion of what principles and guidelines we think other citizens (who are also free and equal) may reasonably be expected to endorse along with us. We must have some test we are ready to state as to when this condition is met. I have elsewhere suggested as a criterion the values expressed by the principles and guidelines that would be agreed to in the original position. Many will prefer another criterion.

Of course, we may find that actually others fail to endorse the principles and guidelines our criterion selects. That is to be expected. The idea is that we must have such a criterion and this alone already imposes very considerable discipline on public discussion. Not any value is reasonably said to meet this test, or to be a political value; and not any balance of political values is reasonable. It is inevitable and often desirable that citizens have different views as to the most appropriate political conception; for the public political culture is bound to contain different fundamental ideas that can be developed in different ways. An orderly contest between them over time is a reliable way to find which one, if any, is most reasonable.

§ 5. The Idea of Constitutional Essentials

1. We said above (§4.3) that to find a complete political conception we need to identify a class of fundamental questions for which the conception's political values yield reasonable answers. As these questions I propose the constitutional essentials and questions of basic justice. To explain:

There is the greatest urgency for citizens to reach practical agreement in judgment about the constitutional essentials. These are of two kinds:

    a. fundamental principles that specify the general structure of government and the political process: the powers of the legislature, executive and the judiciary; the scope of majority rule; and

    b. equal basic rights and liberties of citizenship that legislative majorities are to respect: such as the right to vote and to participate in politics, liberty of conscience, freedom of thought and of association, as well as the protections of the rule of law.

These things are a complex story; I merely hint at what is meant. There is, however, an important difference between the constitutional essentials under (a) which specify the general structure of government and the political process and the essentials under (b) which specify the equal basic rights and liberties of citizens.

2. Essentials of the first kind can be specified in various ways. Witness the difference between presidential and cabinet government. But once settled it is vital that the structure of government be changed only as experience shows it to be required by political justice or the general good, and not as prompted by the political advantage of one party or group that may at the moment have the upper hand. Frequent controversy over the structure of government, when it is not required by political justice and when the changes proposed tend to favor some parties over others, raises the stakes of politics and may lead to distrust and turmoil that undermines constitutional government.

By contrast, the essentials of the second kind concern basic rights and liberties and can be specified in but one way, modulo relatively small variations. Liberty of conscience and freedom of association, and the political rights of freedom of speech, voting, and running for office are characterized in more or less the same manner in all free regimes.

3. Observe further an important distinction between the principles of justice specifying the equal basic rights and liberties and the principles regulating basic matters of distributive justice, such as freedom of movement and equality of opportunity, social and economic inequalities, and the social bases of self-respect.

A principle specifying the basic rights and liberties covers the second kind of constitutional essentials. But while some principle of opportunity is surely such an essential, for example, a principle requiring at least freedom of movement and free choice of occupation, fair equality of opportunity (as I have specified it) goes beyond that and is not such an essential. Similarly, though a social minimum providing for the basic needs of all citizens is also an essential, what I have called the "difference principle" is more demanding and is not.[10]

4. The distinction between the principles covering the basic freedoms and those covering social and economic inequalities is not that the first expresses political values while the second does not. Both express political values. Rather, the basic structure of society has two coordinate roles, the principles covering the basic freedoms specifying the first role, the principles covering the social and economic inequalities specifying the second. In the first role that structure specifies and secures citizens' equal basic rights and liberties and institutes just political procedures. In the second it sets up the background institutions of social and economic justice appropriate to citizens as free and equal. The first role concerns how political power is acquired and the limits of its exercise. We hope to settle at least those questions by reference to political values that can provide a public basis of justification.

Whether the constitutional essentials covering the basic freedoms are satisfied is more or less visible on the face of constitutional arrangements and how these can be seen to work in practice. But whether the aims of the principles covering social and economic inequalities are realized is far more difficult to ascertain. These matters are nearly always open to wide differences of reasonable opinion; they rest on complicated inferences and intuitive judgments that require us to assess complex social and economic information about topics poorly understood. Thus, although questions of both kinds are to be discussed in terms of political values, we can expect more agreement about whether the principles for the basic rights and liberties are realized than about whether the principles for social and economic justice are

10. On fair equality of opportunity, see *Theory,* pp. 72f. On the difference principle, ibid., §13. Political discussions of the reasons for and against fair opportunity and the difference principle, though they are not constitutional essentials, fall under questions of basic justice and so are to be decided by the political values of public reason.

realized. This is not a difference about what are the correct principles but simply a difference in the difficulty of seeing whether the principles are achieved.

To conclude: there are four grounds for distinguishing the constitutional essentials specified by the basic freedoms from the principles governing social and economic inequalities.

a. The two kinds of principles specify different roles for the basic structure.

b. It is more urgent to settle the essentials dealing with the basic freedoms.

c. It is far easier to tell whether those essentials are realized.

d. It much easier to gain agreement about what the basic rights and liberties should be, not in every detail of course, but about the main outlines.

These considerations explain why freedom of movement and free choice of occupation and a social minimum covering citizens' basic needs count as constitutional essentials while the principle of fair opportunity and the difference principle do not.

Here I remark that if a political conception of justice covers the constitutional essentials and matters of basic justice—for the present this is all we aim for—it is already of enormous importance even if it has little to say about many economic and social issues that legislative bodies must regularly consider. To resolve these more particular and detailed issues it is often more reasonable to go beyond the political conception and the values its principles express, and to invoke nonpolitical values that such a view does not include. But so long as there is firm agreement on the constitutional essentials and established political procedures are reasonably regarded as fair, willing political and social cooperation between free and equal citizens can normally be maintained.

§ 6. The Supreme Court as Exemplar of Public Reason

1. At the beginning (§1.2) I remarked that in a constitutional regime with judicial review, public reason is the reason of its supreme court.[11] I now sketch two points about this: first, that public reason is well suited to be the court's reason in exercising its role as the highest judicial interpreter but not the final interpreter of the higher law;[12] and second, that the supreme court is the branch of government that serves as the exemplar of public reason. To clarify these points, I mention briefly five principles of constitutionalism.[13]

The first principle is Locke's distinction in the *Two Treatises* between the people's constituent power to establish a new regime and the ordinary power of officers of government and the electorate exercised in day-to-day politics. That constituent power of the people (II:134, 141) sets up a framework to regulate ordinary power, and it comes into play only when the existing regime has been dissolved.

The second distinction is between higher and ordinary law. Higher law is the expression of the people's constituent power and has the higher authority of the will of We the People, whereas ordinary legislation has the authority, and is the expression of, the ordinary power of Congress and of the electorate. Higher law binds and guides this ordinary power.

---

11. This is not a definition. I assume that in a well-ordered society the two more or less overlap. I am grateful to James Fleming for valuable guidance in formulating many points in this section.

12. Here I have found particularly helpful: Bruce Ackerman, "Constitutional Politics/Constitutional Law," *Yale Law Journal* 99 (December 1989), as well as his recent *We The People: Foundations* (Cambridge, Mass.: Harvard University Press, 1991), vol. I.

13. Here I draw upon John Agresto, *The Supreme Court and Constitutional Democracy* (Ithaca: Cornell University Press, 1984), esp. pp. 45–55; Stephen Holmes, "Gag Rules or the Politics of Omission," and "Precommitment and the Paradox of Democracy," both in *Constitutionalism and Democracy*, edited by Jon Elster and Rune Slagstad (Cambridge: Cambridge University Press, 1987); Jon Elster, *Ulysses and the Sirens* (Cambridge: Cambridge University Press, 1979), pp. 81–86, 88–103. There is nothing at all novel in my account.

As a third principle, a democratic constitution is a principled expression in higher law of the political ideal of a people to govern itself in a certain way. The aim of public reason is to articulate this ideal. Some of the ends of political society may be stated in a preamble—to establish justice and to promote the general welfare—and certain constraints are found in a bill of rights or implied in a framework of government—due process of law and equal protection of the laws. Together they fall under political values and its public reason. This principled expression of higher law is to be widely supported and for this and other reasons it is best not to burden it with many details and qualifications. It should also be possible to make visible in basic institutions its essential principles.[14]

A fourth principle is that by a democratically ratified constitution with a bill of rights, the citizen body fixes once and for all certain constitutional essentials, for example, the equal basic political rights and liberties, and freedom of speech and association, as well as those rights and liberties guaranteeing the security and independence of citizens, such as freedom of movement and choice of occupation, and the protections of the rule of law. This ensures that ordinary laws are enacted in a certain way by citizens as free and independent. It is through these fixed procedures that the people can express, even if they do not, their reasoned democratic will, and indeed without those procedures they can have no such will.

Fifth and last, in constitutional government the ultimate power cannot be left to the legislature or even to a supreme court, which is only the highest judicial interpreter of the constitution. Ultimate power is held by the three branches in a duly specified relation with one another with each responsible to the people.[15]

---

14. For these reasons, among others, I suppose that the principle of fair equality of opportunity and the difference principle are not constitutional essentials, though, as I have said, in justice as fairness they are matters of basic justice (§5.3).

15. In saying this I follow what I understand to be Lincoln's view as expressed in his remarks about Dred Scott (1857) in his speeches and in his debates with Douglas in *Lincoln: Speeches and Writings,* edited by Don Fehrenbacher (New York: Library of

Now admittedly, in the long run a strong majority of the electorate can eventually make the constitution conform to its political will. This is simply a fact about political power as such. There is no way around this fact, not even by entrenchment clauses that try to fix permanently the basic democratic guarantees. No institutional procedure exists that cannot be abused or distorted to enact statutes violating basic constitutional democratic principles.[16] The idea of right and just constitutions and basic laws is always ascertained by the most reasonable political conception of justice and not by the result of an actual political process. I return to a question this raises below (§6.4).

2. Thus, constitutional democracy is dualist: it distinguishes constituent power from ordinary power as well as the higher law of the people from the ordinary law of legislative bodies. Parliamentary supremacy is rejected.

A supreme court fits into this idea of dualist constitutional democracy as one of the institutional devices to protect the higher law.[17] By applying public reason the court is to prevent that law from being eroded by the legislation of transient majorities, or more likely, by organized and well-situated narrow interests skilled at getting their way. If the court assumes this role and effectively carries it out,[18] it is incorrect to say that it is straight-

---

America, 1989), vol. 1, pp. 392f., 450ff., 524ff., 714—17, 740f.; and in his First Inaugural (1861), ibid., vol. 2, 220f. For accounts of Lincoln's view see Alexander Bickel, *the Last Dangerous Branch* (New York: Bobbs-Merrill, 1962), pp. 65—69; 259—69; Agresto, *the supreme court,* esp. pp. 86—95, 105, 128f.; and Don Fehrenbacher, *Lincoln: In Text and Context* (Stanford; Stanford University Press, 1987), esp. pp. 20—23, 125ff., and 293.

16. Similarly, there is no procedure of inquiry, not even that of the investigations of science and scholarship that can be guaranteed in the long run to uncover the truth. As we commented at the end of III:8, we cannot define truth as given by the beliefs that would stand up even in an idealized consensus, however far extended.

17. See Ackerman, "Constitutional Politics/Constitutional Law," pp. 464f. and *We the People,* pp. 6–10.

18. It must be said that historically the court has often failed badly in this role. It upheld the Alien and Sedition Acts of 1798 and one need only mention Dred Scott (1857). It emasculated the Reconstruction amendments by interpreting them as a charter of capitalist liberty rather than the liberty of the freed slaves; and from Lochner (1905) through the early New Deal years it did much the same.

forwardly antidemocratic. It is indeed antimajoritarian with respect to ordinary law, for a court with judicial review can hold such law unconstitutional. Nevertheless, the higher authority of the people supports that. The court is not antimajoritarian with respect to higher law when its decisions reasonably accord with the constitution itself and with its amendments and politically mandated interpretations.

Suppose we agree that the three most innovative periods of our constitutional history are the founding, Reconstruction, and the New Deal.[19] Here it is important that all three seem to rely on, and only on, the political values of public reason. The constitution and its amendment process, the Reconstruction amendments that sought to remove the curse of slavery, and the modern activist so-called welfare state of the New Deal, all seem to fit that description, though it would take some time to show this. Yet accepting this as correct, and seeing the Court as the highest judicial though not the final interpreter of this body of higher law, the point is that the political values of public reason provide the Court's basis for interpretation. A political conception of justice covers the fundamental questions addressed by higher law and sets out the political values in terms of which they can be decided.[20]

Some will say, certainly, that parliamentary supremacy with no bill of rights at all is superior to our dualist regime. It offers firmer support for the values that higher law in the dualist scheme tries to secure. On the other hand, some may think it better that a constitution entrench a list of basic rights, as the German constitution does. It places those rights beyond amendment, even by the people and the German supreme court, and in enforcing those rights can be said to be undemocratic. Entrenchment has that consequence. Judged by the values of a reasonable

19. Here I follow Ackerman's account in "Constitutional Politics/Constitutional Law," at essentially pp. 486–515, and *We the People*, chaps. 3–6 passim.

20. See Samuel Freeman, "Original Meaning, Democratic Interpretation, and the Constitution," *Philosophy and Public Affairs* 21 (Winter 1992), pp. 26f. and 36f., where these matters are discussed.

political conception of justice, these regimes may be superior to a dualist regime in which these basic questions are settled by the higher law of We the People.[21]

Political liberalism as such, it should be stressed, does not assert or deny any of these claims and so we need not discuss them. Our point here is simply that, however these questions are decided, the content of a political conception of justice includes the values of public reason by appeal to which the merits of the three kinds of regime are to be judged.

3. Now I turn to a second point: the court's role is not merely defensive but to give due and continuing effect to public reason by serving as its institutional exemplar.[22] This means, first, that public reason is the sole reason the court exercises. It is the only branch of government that is visibly on its face the creature of that reason and of that reason alone. Citizens and legislators may properly vote their more comprehensive views when constitutional essentials and basic justice are not at stake; they need not justify by public reason why they vote as they do or make their grounds consistent and fit them into a coherent constitutional view over the whole range of their decisions. The role of the justices is to do precisely that and in doing it they have no other reason and no other values than the political. Beyond that they

21. Robert Dahl, in his *Democracy and Its Critics* (New Haven: Yale University Press, 1989), discusses the relative merits of these forms of democratic institutions. He is in some ways critical of the British parliamentary system (the "Westminster model") (pp. 156–57), and although he is also critical of judicial review (pp. 187–91), he thinks there is no one universally best way to solve the problem of how to protect fundamental rights and interests. He says: "In the absence of a universally best solution, specific solutions need to be adapted to the historical conditions and experiences, political culture, and concrete political institutions of a particular country" (p. 192). I incline to agree with this and thank Dennis Thompson for correcting my earlier misunderstanding of Dahl's view.

22. The judiciary with a supreme court is not the only institution that does this. It is essential that other social arrangements also do the same, as is done for example by an orderly public financing of elections and constraints on private funding that achieves the fair value of the political liberties, or at least significantly move the political process in that direction. See *Theory,* pp. 224–27 and VIII:7, 12 at pp. 324–31 and 356–63, respectively.

are to go by what they think the constitutional cases, practices, and traditions, and constitutionally significant historical texts require.

To say that the court is the exemplar of public reason also means that it is the task of the justices to try to develop and express in their reasoned opinions the best interpretation of the constitution they can, using their knowledge of what the constitution and constitutional precedents require. Here the best interpretation is the one that best fits the relevant body of those constitutional materials, and justifies it in terms of the public conception of justice or a reasonable variant thereof. In doing this it is expected that the justices may and do appeal to the political values of the public conception whenever the constitution itself expressly or implicitly invokes those values, as it does, for example, in a bill of rights guaranteeing the free exercise of religion or the equal protection of the laws. The court's role here is part of the publicity of reason and is an aspect of the wide, or educative, role of public reason.

The justices cannot, of course, invoke their own personal morality, nor the ideals and virtues of morality generally. Those they must view as irrelevant. Equally, they cannot invoke their or other people's religious or philosophical views. Nor can they cite political values without restriction. Rather, they must appeal to the political values they think belong to the most reasonable understanding of the public conception and its political values of justice and public reason. These are values that they believe in good faith, as the duty of civility requires, that all citizens as reasonable and rational might reasonably be expected to endorse.[23]

23. This account of what the justices are to do seems to be the same as Ronald Dworkin's view as stated say in "Hard Cases" in *Taking Rights Seriously* (Cambridge, Mass.: Harvard University Press, 1978) or in *Law's Empire* (Cambridge, Mass.: Harvard University Press, 1986), chap. 7, except for possibly one proviso. I have said that the justices in interpreting the constitution are to appeal to the political values covered by the public political conception of justice, or at least by some recognizable variant thereof. The values the justices can invoke are restricted to what is reasonably

But, as I have said (§4.5), the idea of public reason does not mean that judges agree with one another, any more than citizens do, in the details of their understanding of the constitution. Yet they must be, and appear to be, interpreting the same constitution in view of what they see as the relevant parts of the political conception and in good faith believe it can be defended as such. The court's role as the highest judicial interpreter of the constitution supposes that the political conceptions judges hold and their views of constitutional essentials locate the central range of the basic freedoms in more or less the same place. In these cases at least its decisions succeed in settling the most fundamental political questions.

4. Finally, the court's role as exemplar of public reason has a third aspect: to give public reason vividness and vitality in the public forum; this it does by its authoritative judgments on fundamental political questions. The court fulfills this role when it clearly and effectively interprets the constitution in a reasonable way; and when it fails to do this, as ours often has, it stands at the center of a political controversy the terms of settlement of which are public values.

The constitution is not what the Court says it is. Rather, it is what the people acting constitutionally through the other branches eventually allow the Court to say it is. A particular understanding

---

believed to be covered by that conception or its variants, and not by a conception of morality as such, not even of political morality. The latter I think too broad. Thus, though an appeal to a social minimum specified by basic needs is appropriate (accepting Frank Michelman's view as stated in "Welfare Rights and Constitutional Democracy," *Washington University Law Quarterly* 1979 (Summer 1979), an appeal cannot be made to the difference principle unless it appears as a guideline in a statute (§5.3). I believe Dworkin thinks that his requirement of fit alone leads to roughly the same conclusion, as he takes the requirement of fit to distinguish interpretation from invention and that a reasonable interpretation suffices to show what is already implicit in the law as articulated within the political conception, or one of its recognizable variants. He may be correct about this but I am unsure. I incline to require, in addition to fit, that in order for the court's decisions to be properly judicial decisions of law, that the interpretation fall within the public political conception of justice or a recognizeable variant thereof. I doubt that this view differs in substance from Dworkin's.

of the constitution may be mandated to the Court by amendments, or by a wide and continuing political majority, as it was in the case of the New Deal.[24] This raises the question whether an amendment to repeal the First Amendment, say, and to make a particular religion the state religion with all the consquences of that, or to repeal the Fourteenth Amendment with its equal protection of the laws, must be accepted by the Court as a valid amendment.[25] It is truistic to say, as I said above, that if the people act constitutionally such amendments are valid. But is it sufficient for the validity of an amendment that it be enacted by the procedure of Article V?[26] What reasons could the Court or the executive have (assuming the amendment was over its veto) for counting invalid an enactment meeting that condition?

Consider the following reasons: an amendment is not merely a change. One idea of an amendment is to adjust basic constitutional values to changing political and social circumstances, or to incorporate into the constitution a broader and more inclusive understanding of those values. The three amendments related to the Civil War all do this, as does the Nineteenth Amendment granting women the vote; and the Equal Rights Amendment attempted the same. At the Founding there was the blatant contradiction between the idea of equality in the Declaration of Independence and the Constitution and chattel slavery of a subjugated race; there were also property qualifications for voting and women were denied the suffrage altogether. Historically those amendments brought the Constitution more in line with

24. See Ackerman, "Constitutional Politics/Constitutional Law," pp. 510–15 and *We the People,* chap 5.

25. Ackerman suggests that a commitment to dualist democracy implies that the Court must accept the amendment as valid, whereas I want to deny this. While Ackerman says he would be proud to belong to the generation that entrenched the Bill of Rights, as that would give a more ideal regime, entrenchment, he thinks, is contrary to the idea of our dualist democracy. *We the People,* pp. 319–22.

26. I am indebted to Stephen Macedo for valuable discussion that led me to take up this question. See his *Liberal Virtues* (Oxford: Clarendon Press, 1990), pp. 182f. What I say is similar to what he says there.

its original promise.[27] Another idea of amendment is to adapt basic institutions in order to remove weaknesses that come to light in subsequent constitutional practice. Thus, with the exception of the Eighteenth, the other amendments concern either the institutional design of government, witness the Twenty-second, which allows the president to serve only two terms; or certain basic matters of policy, witness the Sixteenth, which grants Congress the power to levy income taxes. Such has been the role of amendments.

The Court could say, then, that an amendment to repeal the First Amendment and replace it with its opposite fundamentally contradicts the constitutional tradition of the oldest democratic regime in the world. It is therefore invalid. Does this mean that the Bill of Rights and the other amendments are entrenched? Well, they are entrenched in the sense of being validated by long historical practice. They may be amended in the ways mentioned above but not simply repealed and reversed. Should that happen, and it is not inconceivable that the exercise of political power might take that turn, that would be constitutional breakdown,[28] or revolution in the proper sense, and not a valid amendment of the constitution. The successful practice of its ideas and principles over two centuries place restrictions on what can now count as an amendment, whatever was true at the beginning.

Thus, in the midst of any great constitutional change, legitimate or otherwise, the Court is bound to be a center of controversy. Often its role forces political discussion to take a principled form so as to address the constitutional question in line with the political values of justice and public reason. Public discussion becomes more than a contest for power and position. This edu-

27. See the late Judith Shklar's lucid brief account of this history in her *American Citizenship: The Quest for Inclusion* (Cambridge, Mass.: Harvard University Press, 1991).

28. This is the term Samuel Freeman uses in his "Original Meaning, Democratic Interpretation, and the Constitution," pp. 41f., where he contrasts his view with Ackerman's. I am indebted to his discussion.

cates citizens to the use of public reason and its value of political justice by focusing their attention on basic constitutional matters.

To conclude these remarks on the Supreme Court in a constitutional regime with judicial review, I emphasize that they are not intended as a defense of such review, although it can perhaps be defended given certain historical circumstances and conditions of political culture. Rather, my aim has been to elaborate the idea of public reason, and in order to make this idea more definite, I have looked at the way in which the Court may serve as its exemplar. And while the Court is special in this respect, the other branches of government can certainly, if they would but do so, be forums of principle along with it in debating constitutional questions.[29]

§ 7. Apparent Difficulties with Public Reason

1. Recall from §4.3 that we look for a political conception whose combined values of justice and of public reason yield reasonable answers for all, or nearly all, fundamental political questions: those that involve constitutional essentials and matters of basic justice. I discuss several apparent difficulties.

One difficulty is that public reason often allows more than one reasonable answer to any particular question. This is because there are many political values and many ways they can be characterized. Suppose, then, that different combinations of values, or the same values weighted differently, tend to predominate in a particular fundamental case. Everyone appeals to political values but agreement is lacking and more than marginal differences persist. Should this happen, as it often does, some may say that public reason fails to resolve the question, in which case citizens may legitimately invoke principles appealing to nonpolitical values to resolve it in a way they find satisfactory.[30] Not everyone

---

29. For this last aspect, see Dworkin, "The Forum of Principle," in *A Matter of Principle* (Cambridge: Harvard University Press, 1985), pp. 70f.

30. Kent Greenawalt seems inclined to this view. See his detailed discussion in

would introduce the same nonpolitical values but at least all would have an answer suitable to them.

The ideal of public reason urges us not to do this in cases of constitutional essentials and matters of basic justice. Close agreement is rarely achieved and abandoning public reason whenever disagreement occurs in balancing values is in effect to abandon it altogether. Moreover, as we said in §4.5, public reason does not ask us to accept the very same principles of justice, but rather to conduct our fundamental discussions in terms of what we regard as a political conception. We should sincerely think that our view of the matter is based on political values everyone can reasonably be expected to endorse. For an electorate thus to conduct itself is a high ideal the following of which realizes fundamental democratic values not to be abandoned simply because full agreement does not obtain. A vote can be held on a fundamental question as on any other; and if the question is debated by appeal to political values and citizens vote their sincere opinion, the ideal is sustained.

2. A second difficulty concerns what is meant by voting our sincere opinion. Let us say that we honor public reason and its principle of legitimacy when three conditions are satisfied: a) we give very great and normally overriding weight to the ideal it prescribes; b) we believe public reason is suitably complete, that is, for at least the great majority of fundamental questions, possibly for all, some combination and balance of political values alone reasonably shows the answer; and finally c) we believe that the particular view we propose, and the law or policy based thereon, expresses a reasonable combination and balance of those values.

But now a problem arises: I have assumed throughout that citizens affirm comprehensive religious and philosophical doctrines and many will think that nonpolitical and transcendent values are the true ground of political values. Does this belief

_____

chaps. 6–7 of *Religious Convictions and Political Choice* (New York: Oxford University Press, 1988).

make our appeal to political values insincere? It does not. These comprehensive beliefs are fully consistent with the three conditions above stated. That we think political values have some further backing does not mean we do not accept those values or affirm the conditions of honoring public reason, any more than our accepting the axioms of geometry means that we do not accept the theorems. Moreover, we may accept the axioms as much because of the theorems they lead to as the other way around.[31]

In affirming the three conditions, we accept the duty to appeal to political values as the duty to adopt a certain form of public discourse. As institutions and laws are always imperfect, we may view that form of discourse as imperfect and in any case as falling short of the whole truth set out by our comprehensive doctrine. Also, that discourse can seem shallow because it does not set out the most basic grounds on which we believe our view rests. Yet we think we have strong reasons to follow it given our duty of civility to other citizens. After all, they share with us the same sense of its imperfection, though on different grounds, as they

---

31. This is an important point: namely, that we must distinguish the order of deduction from the order of support. Deductive argument lays out the order of how statements can be connected; axioms, or basic principles, are illuminating in setting out these connections in a clear and perspicuous way. A conception such as that of the original position is illuminating in the same way and enables us to present justice as fairness as having a certain unity. But the statements that justify a normative conception and make us confident that it is reasonable may, or may not, be high in the order of deduction. If we rank principles and convictions according to how strongly they support the doctrine that leads to them, then principles and convictions high in this order of support may be low in the order of deduction. The idea of reflective equilibrium allows that convictions of any level of generality may provide supporting reasons. So in a well presented doctrine the order of deduction, so far as there is one, may be clear; but the order of support is another matter and must be decided by due reflection. Even then, how do we tell? Once this distinction is made, there are no grounds for saying that people who affirm religious or philosophical views cannot be sincere in affirming public reason as well. It might be thought that religious people would balk at the distinction between the order of deduction and the order of support. Yet they need not, for in their case, beginning with the existence of God, the orders of deduction and support are the same. The conceptual distinction between those orders does not imply that they cannot be isomorphic.

hold different comprehensive doctrines and believe different grounds are left out of account. But it is only in this way, and by accepting that politics in a democratic society can never be guided by what we see as the whole truth, that we can realize the ideal expressed by the principle of legitimacy: to live politically with others in the light of reasons all might reasonably be expected to endorse.

What public reason asks is that citizens be able to explain their vote to one another in terms of a reasonable balance of public political values, it being understood by everyone that of course the plurality of reasonable comprehensive doctrines held by citizens is thought by them to provide further and often transcendent backing for those values. In each case, which doctrine is affirmed is a matter of conscience for the individual citizen. It is true that the balance of political values a citizen holds must be reasonable, and one that can be seen to be reasonable by other citizens; but not all reasonable balances are the same. The only comprehensive doctrines that run afoul of public reason are those that cannot support a reasonable balance of political values.[32] Yet given that the doctrines actually held support a rea-

---

32. As an illustration, consider the troubled question of abortion. Suppose first that the society in question is well-ordered and that we are dealing with the normal case of mature adult women. It is best to be clear about this idealized case first; for once we are clear about it, we have a guide that helps us to think about other cases, which force us to consider exceptional circumstances. Suppose further that we consider the question in terms of these three important political values: the due respect for human life, the ordered reproduction of political society over time, including the family in some form, and finally the equality of women as equal citizens. (There are, of course, other important political values besides these.) Now I believe any reasonable balance of these three values will give a woman a duly qualified right to decide whether or not to end her pregnancy during the first trimester. The reason for this is that at this early stage of pregnancy the political value of the equality of women is overriding, and this right is required to give it substance and force. Other political values, if tallied in, would not, I think, affect this conclusion. A reasonable balance may allow her such a right beyond this, at least in certain circumstances. However, I do not discuss the question in general here, as I simply want to illustrate the point of the text by saying that any comprehensive doctrine that leads to a balance of political values excluding that duly qualified right in the first trimester is to that extent unreasonable; and depending on details of its formulation, it may also be cruel and

243

sonable balance, how could anyone complain? What would be the objection? [33]

3. A third difficulty is to specify when a question is successfully resolved by public reason. Some think it leaves many questions without answers. Yet we want a political conception of justice to be complete: its political values should admit of a balance giving a reasonable answer for all or nearly all fundamental questions (§4.3). To discuss this matter, I mention several "problems of extension," as I have called them (I:3.4) as these may seem unanswerable from within a political conception.

As time does not permit an account of these questions, I recall what we said earlier (I:3.4) that there are at least four such problems. One is extending justice to cover our duties to future generations (under which falls the problem of just savings). Another is the problem of extending it to the concepts and principles that apply to international law and political relations between peoples—the traditional *jus gentium*. A third problem of extension is that of setting out the principles of normal health

---

oppressive; for example, if it denied the right altogether except in the case of rape and incest. Thus, assuming that this question is either a constitutional essential or a matter of basic justice, we would go against the ideal of public reason if we voted from a comprehensive doctrine that denied this right (see §2.4). However, a comprehensive doctrine is not as such unreasonable because it leads to an unreasonable conclusion in one or even in several cases. It may still be reasonable most of the time.

33. I believe the idea of public reason as explained here and elsewhere in the text is consistent with the view of Greenawalt in his *Religious Convictions and Political Choice*. That he thinks to the contrary is due, I think, to his interpreting philosophical liberalism and the requirements expressed by its ideal of liberal democracy as being far stronger than those of what I have called "political liberalism." For one thing, the requirements of public reason belong to an ideal of democratic citizenship and are limited to our conduct in the public political forum and how we are to vote on constitutional essentials and questions of basic justice. Moreover, as the text above brings out, public reason does not ask citizens "to pluck out their religious convictions" and to think about those questions as if "they started from scratch, disregarding what they presently take as basic premises of moral thought" (Greenawalt, p. 155). Indeed, this suggestion is altogether contrary to the idea of an overlapping consensus. I think the text is consistent with Greenawalt's discussion at pp. 153–56 in the important central chapter of the book and with what he says in pt. III, which deals with such matters as the appropriate political discussion in a liberal society.

care; and finally, we may ask whether justice can be extended to our relations to animals and the order of nature. As I have said (I:3.4), I believe that justice as fairness can be reasonably extended to cover the first three problems, although I can't discuss them here.

Instead, I simply express my conjecture that these three problems can be resolved in a similar way. Some views drawing on the tradition of the social contract, and justice as fairness is one, begin by taking for granted the full status of adult persons in the society in question (the members of its citizen body) and proceed from there: forward to other generations, outward to other societies, and inward to those requiring normal health care. In each case we start from the status of adult citizens and proceed subject to certain constraints to obtain a reasonable law. We can do the same with the claims of animals and the rest of nature; this has been the traditional view of Christian ages. Animals and nature are seen as subject to our use and wont.[34] This has the virtue of clarity and yields some kind of answer. There are numerous political values here to invoke: to further the good of ourselves and future generations by preserving the natural order and its life-sustaining properties; to foster species of animals and plants for the sake of biological and medical knowledge with its potential applications to human health; to protect the beauties of nature for purposes of public recreation and the pleasures of a deeper understanding of the world. The appeal to values of this kind gives what many have found a reasonable answer to the status of animals and the rest of nature.

Of course, some will not accept these values as alone sufficient to settle the case. Thus, suppose our attitude toward the world is one of natural religion: we think it utterly wrong to appeal solely to those values, and others like them, to determine our relations with the natural world. To do that is to see the natural order

---

34. See Keith Thomas, *Man and the Natural World* (New York: Pantheon, 1983), for the view of Christian ages in chap. 1, while later chapters trace the development of modern attitudes beginning with the eighteenth century.

from a narrowly anthropocentric point of view, whereas human beings should assume a certain stewardship toward nature and give weight to an altogether different family of values. In this case our attitude might be much the same as those who reject abortion on theological grounds. Yet there is this important difference: the status of the natural world and our proper relation to it is not a constitutional essential or a basic question of justice, as these questions have been specified (§5).[35] It is a matter in regard to which citizens can vote their nonpolitical values and try to convince other citizens accordingly. The limits of public reason do not apply.

4. Let us pull the threads together by stating when a fundamental question is resolved by public reason. Clearly, for public reason to yield a reasonable answer in a given case, it is not required that it yield the same answer that any chosen comprehensive doctrine would yield if we proceeded from it alone. In what sense, though, must the answer of public reason itself be reasonable?

In reply: the answer must be at least reasonable, if not the most reasonable, as judged by public reason alone. But beyond this, and thinking of the ideal case of a well-ordered society, we hope that answer lies within the leeway allowed by each of the reasonable comprehensive doctrines making up an overlapping consensus. By that leeway I mean the scope within which a doctrine can accept, even if reluctantly, the conclusions of public reason, either in general or in any particular case. A reasonable and effective political conception may bend comprehensive doctrines toward itself, shaping them if need be from unreasonable to reasonable. But even granting this tendency, political liberalism itself cannot argue that each of those comprehensive doctrines should find the conclusions of public reason nearly always within its leeway. To argue that transcends public reason.

---

35. Of course, these questions may become ones of constitutional essentials and basic justice once our duties and obligations to future generations and to other societies are involved.

All the same, we can maintain that the political conception is a reasonable expression of the political values of public reason and justice between citizens seen as free and equal. As such the political conception makes a claim on comprehensive doctrines in the name of those fundamental values, so that those who reject it run the risk of being unjust, politically speaking. Here recall what we said in II:3.3: namely, that in recognizing others' comprehensive views as reasonable, citizens also recognize that, in the absence of a public basis of establishing the truth of their beliefs, to insist on their comprehensive view must be seen by others as their insisting on their own beliefs. If we do so insist, others in self-defense can oppose us as using upon them unreasonable force.

§ 8. The Limits of Public Reason

1. A last question about the limits of public reason.[36] I have often referred to these limits. To this point they would appear to mean that, on fundamental political matters, reasons given explicitly in terms of comprehensive doctrines are never to be introduced into public reason. The public reasons such a doctrine supports may, of course, be given but not the supporting doctrine itself. Call this understanding of public reason the "exclusive view." But as against this exclusive view, there is another view allowing citizens, in certain situations, to present what they regard as the basis of political values rooted in their comprehensive doctrine, provided they do this in ways that strengthen the ideal of public reason itself. This understanding of public reason we may call the "inclusive view."

The question, then, is whether we should understand the ideal of public reason in accordance with the exclusive or the inclusive

---

36. I am greatly indebted to Amy Gutmann and Lawrence Solum for discussion and correspondence about these limits. At first I inclined to what I call the "exclusive view"; they persuaded me that this was too restrictive, as the examples of the abolitionists (which is Solum's) and of Martin Luther King, Jr., brings out. I have not begun to cover the complexities of this question as shown in their correspondence.

view. The answer turns on which view best encourages citizens to honor the ideal of public reason and secures its social conditions in the longer run in a well-ordered society. Accepting this, the inclusive view seems the correct one. For under different political and social conditions with different families of doctrine and practice, the ideal must surely be advanced and fulfilled in different ways, sometimes by what may look like the exclusive view, at others by what may look like the inclusive view. Those conditions determine, then, how the ideal is best attained, either in the short or the longer run. The inclusive view allows for this variation and is more flexible as needed to further the ideal of public reason.

2. To illustrate: let us suppose first the ideal case: the society in question is more or less well ordered. Its members recognize a firm overlapping consensus of reasonable doctrines and it is not stirred by any deep disputes. In this case the values of the political conception are familiar and citizens honor the ideal of public reason most clearly by appealing to those values. Other than the motives of ordinary politics, they have no great interest in introducing other considerations: their fundamental rights are already guaranteed and there are no basic injustices they feel bound to protest. Public reason in this well-ordered society may appear to follow the exclusive view. Invoking only political values is the obvious and the most direct way for citizens to honor the ideal of public reason and to meet their duty of civility.

A second case is when there is a serious dispute in a nearly well-ordered society in applying one of its principles of justice. Suppose that the dispute concerns the principle of fair equality of opportunity as it applies to education for all. Diverse religious groups oppose one another, one group favoring government support for public education alone, another group favoring government support for church schools as well. The first group views the latter policy as incompatible with the so-called separation of church and state, whereas the second denies this. In this situation those of different faiths may come to doubt the sincerity of one another's allegiance to fundamental political values.

One way this doubt might be put to rest is for the leaders of the opposing groups to present in the public forum how their comprehensive doctrines do indeed affirm those values. Of course, it is already part of the background culture to examine how various doctrines support, or fail to support, the political conception. But in the present kind of case, should the recognized leaders affirm that fact in the public forum, their doing so may help to show that the overlapping consensus is not a mere modus vivendi (IV:3). This knowledge surely strengthens mutual trust and public confidence; it can be a vital part of the sociological basis encouraging citizens to honor the ideal of public reason.[37] This being so, the best way to strengthen that ideal in such instances may be to explain in the public forum how one's comprehensive doctrine affirms the political values.

3. A very different kind of case arises when a society is not well ordered and there is a profound division about constitutional essentials. Consider the abolitionists who argued against the antebellum South that its institution of slavery was contrary to God's law. Recall that the abolitionists agitated for the immediate, uncompensated, and universal emancipation of the slaves as early as the 1830s, and did so, I assume, basing their arguments on religious grounds.[38] In this case the nonpublic reason

37. I am indebted to Lawrence Solum and Seana Shiffrin for stressing this point.
38. For an account of the abolitionists, see James McPherson, *The Struggle for Equality* (Princeton: Princeton University Press, 1964), pp. 1–8 and passim. *The Antislavery Argument,* edited by William Pease and Jane Pease (New York: Bobbs-Merrill, 1965) contains a number of abolitionists writings. Characteristic is this from William Ellery Channing's *Slavery,* 3d ed. (1836): "I come now to what is to my own mind the great argument against seizing and using a man as property. He cannot be property in the sight of God and justice, because he is a Rational, Moral, Immortal Being, because created in God's image, and therefore in the highest sense his child, because created to unfold godlike faculties, and to govern himself by a Divine Law written on his heart, and republished in God's word. From his very nature it follows, that so to seize him is to offer an insult to his Maker, and to inflict aggravated social wrong. Into every human being God has breathed an immortal spirit, more precious than the whole outward creation. . . . Did God create such a being to be owned as a tree or a brute?" (in Pease and Pease, *The Antislavery Argument,* pp. 115f.). While the abolitionists often argued in the usual way, appealing to political values and political considerations, I assume for purposes of the question that the religious basis of their views was always clear.

of certain Christian churches supported the clear conclusions of public reason. The same is true of the civil rights movement led by Martin Luther King, Jr., except that King could appeal—as the abolitionists could not—to the political values expressed in the Constitution correctly understood.[39]

Did the abolitionists go against the ideal of public reason? Let us view the question conceptually and not historically, and take for granted that their political agitation was a necessary political force leading to the Civil War and so to the destruction of the great evil and curse of slavery. Surely they hoped for that result and they could have seen their actions as the best way to bring about a well-ordered and just society in which the ideal of public reason could eventually be honored. Similar questions can be raised about the leaders of the civil rights movement. The abolitionists and King would not have been unreasonable in these conjectured beliefs if the political forces they led were among

39. Thus, King could, and often did, appeal to *Brown v. Board of Education,* the Supreme Court's decision of 1954 holding segregation unconstitutional. For King, "just law is a man-made code that squares with the moral law or the law of God. An unjust law is a code that is out of harmony with the moral law. To put it in the terms of Saint Thomas Aquinas, an unjust law is a human law that is not rooted in eternal and natural law. Any law that uplifts human personality is just. Any law that degrades human personality is unjust. All segregation statutes are unjust because segregation distorts the soul and damages the personality." In the next paragraph, a more concrete definition: "Unjust law is a code that the majority inflicts on a minority that is not binding on itself. This is difference made legal. . . . A just law is a code that a majority compels a minority to follow that it is willing to follow itself. This is sameness made legal." The following paragraph has: "An unjust law is a code inflicted on a minority which that minority had no part in enacting or creating because they did not have the unhampered right to vote" (from paragraphs 14–16, respectively, of *Letter from Birmingham City Jail* (April 1963), in *A Testament of Hope: The Essential Writings of Martin Luther King,* edited by J. M. Washington [San Francisco: Harper and Row, 1986], pp. 293f.). Other of King's writings and addresses can be cited to make the same point. For example his "Give us the Ballot," (ibid., pp. 197–200), his address of May 1957 on the third anniversary of *Brown* and "I Have a Dream," (ibid., pp. 217–23), his keynote address of the March on Washington for civil rights, August 1963, both given in Washington before the Lincoln Memorial. Religious doctrines clearly underlie King's views and are important in his appeals. Yet they are expressed in general terms: and they fully support constitutional values and accord with public reason.

250

the necessary historical conditions to establish political justice, as does indeed seem plausible in their situation.

On this account the abolitionists and the leaders of the civil rights movement did not go against the ideal of public reason; or rather, they did not provided they thought, or on reflection would have thought (as they certainly could have thought), that the comprehensive reasons they appealed to were required to give sufficient strength to the political conception to be subsequently realized. To be sure, people do not normally distinguish between comprehensive and public reasons; nor do they normally affirm the ideal of public reason, as we have expressed it. Yet people can be brought to recognize these distinctions in particular cases. The abolitionists could say, for example, that they supported political values of freedom and equality for all, but that given the comprehensive doctrines they held and the doctrines current in their day, it was necessary to invoke the comprehensive grounds on which those values were widely seen to rest.[40] Given those historical conditions, it was not unreasonable of them to act as they did for the sake of the ideal of public reason itself.[41] In this case, the ideal of public reason allows the inclusive view.

4. This brief discussion shows that the appropriate limits of public reason vary depending on historical and social conditions. While much more would have to be said to make this suggestion at all convincing, the main point is that citizens are to be moved to honor the ideal itself, in the present when circumstances permit, but often we may be forced to take a longer view. Under

40. It seems clear from n. 31 that Channing could easily do this. I am indebted to John Cooper for instructive discussion of points in this paragraph.

41. This suggests that it may happen that for a well-ordered society to come about in which public discussion consists mainly in the appeal to political values, prior historical conditions may require that comprehensive reasons be invoked to strengthen those values. This seems more likely when there are but a few and strongly held yet in some ways similar comprehensive doctrines and the variety of distinctive views of recent times has not so far developed. Add to these conditions another: namely, the idea of public reason with its duty of civility has not yet been expressed in the public culture and remains unknown.

different conditions with different current doctrines and practices, the ideal may be best achieved in different ways, in good times by following what at first sight may appear to be the exclusive view, in less good times by what may appear to be the inclusive view.

Here I assume that the political conception of justice and the ideal of honoring public reason mutually support one another. A well-ordered society publicly and effectively regulated by a recognized political conception fashions a climate within which its citizens acquire a sense of justice inclining them to meet their duty of civility and without generating strong interests to the contrary. On the other hand, the institutions of a well-ordered society are in turn supported once the ideal of public reason is firmly established in its citizens' conduct. But whether these assumptions are correct and can be founded on the moral psychology I sketched in II:7 are large questions I cannot take up here. It's clear, however, that should these assumptions be mistaken, there is a serious problem with justice as fairness as I have presented it. One must hope, as I have throughout, that the political conception and its ideal of public reason are mutually sustaining, and in this sense stable.

5. Looking back, I note a few main points. An ideal of public reason is an appropriate complement of a constitutional democracy, the culture of which is bound to be marked by a plurality of reasonable comprehensive doctrines. This is often said and in some form it is surely correct. Yet it is difficult to specify that ideal in a satisfactory way. In the attempt to do so, I have proposed the kinds of political questions to which public reason applies: namely, to questions concerning constitutional essentials and matters of basic justice (§1.1), and we have examined what these questions are (§5). As to whom public reason applies, we say that it applies to citizens when they engage in political advocacy in the public forum, in political campaigns for example and when they vote on those fundamental questions. It always applies to public and government officers in official forums, in their debates and votes on the floor of the legislature (§1.1). Public

reason applies especially to the judiciary in its decisions and as the one institutional exemplar of public reason (§6). The content of public reason is given by a political conception of justice: this content has two parts: substantive principles of justice for the basic structure (the political values of justice); and guidelines of inquiry and conceptions of virtue that make public reason possible (the political values of public reason) (§4.1–3).

I stress that the limits of public reason are not, clearly, the limits of law or statute but the limits we honor when we honor an ideal: the ideal of democratic citizens trying to conduct their political affairs on terms supported by public values that we might reasonably expect others to endorse. The ideal also expresses a willingness to listen to what others have to say and being ready to accept reasonable accommodations or alterations in one's own view. Public reason further asks of us that the balance of those values we hold to be reasonable in a particular case is a balance we sincerely think can be seen to be reasonable by others. Or failing this, we think the balance can be seen as at least not unreasonable in this sense: that those who oppose it can nevertheless understand how reasonable persons can affirm it. This preserves the ties of civic friendship and is consistent with the duty of civility. On some questions this may be the best we can do.[42]

All this allows some latitude, since not all reasonable balances are the same. The only comprehensive doctrines that do not accord with public reason on a given question are those that cannot support a reasonable balance of political values on the issues it raises (§7.2). Certain reasonable comprehensive views fail to do this in some cases but we must hope that none that endure over time in a well-ordered society is likely to fail in all or even in many cases.

The innovations, if any, in my account of public reason are possibly two: the first is the central place of the duty of civility as an ideal of democracy (§2.1–3); the second is that the content of

42. I am indebted to Robert Adams for instructive discussion of this point.

public reason be given by the political values and the guidelines of a political conception of justice (§4.1–4). The content of public reason is not given by political morality as such, but only by a political conception suitable for a constitutional regime. To check whether we are following public reason we might ask: how would our argument strike us presented in the form of a supreme court opinion?[43] Reasonable? Outrageous?

Finally, whether this or some other understanding of public reason is acceptable can be decided only by examining the answers it leads to over a wide range of the more likely cases. Also we should have to consider other ways in which religious beliefs and statements can have a role in political life. We might ask whether Lincoln's Proclamation of a National Fast Day in August of 1861 and his two Proclamations of Thanksgiving in October of 1863 and 1864 violate the idea of public reason. And what are we to say of the Second Inaugural with its prophetic (Old Testament) interpretation of the Civil War as God's punishment for the sin of slavery, and falling equally on North and South? I incline to think Lincoln does not violate public reason as I have discussed it and as it applied in his day—whether in ours is another matter—since what he says has no implications bearing on constitutional essentials or matters of basic justice. Or whatever implications it might have could surely be supported firmly by the values of public reason. I mention these questions only to indicate that much remains to be discussed. And of course not all liberal views would accept the idea of public reason as I have expressed it. Those that would accept some form of it, allowing for variations, we may call political liberalisms.

43. Think not of an actual court but of the court as part of a constitutional regime ideally conceived. I say this because some doubt that an actual supreme court can normally be expected to write reasonable decisions. Also, courts are bound by precedents in ways that public reason is not, and must wait for questions to come before them, and much else. But these points do not affect the propriety of the check suggested in the text.

PART THREE

Institutional
Framework

The Basic
Structure
as Subject[1]

§ 1. First Subject of Justice

An essential feature of the contractarian conception of justice is that the basic structure of society is the first subject of justice. The contract view begins by trying to work out a theory of justice for this special but plainly very important case; and the conception of justice that results has a certain regulative primacy with re-

1. This essay is a considerable revision of a paper with the same title presented at the meetings of the American Philosophical Association (Pacific Division) at Portland, Oregon in March 1977 and reprinted in the *American Philosophical Quarterly* 14 (April 1977). Sections 2 and 3 are new. I am indebted to Joshua Cohen, Joshua Rabinowitz, T. M. Scanlon, and Quentin Skinner for valuable discussions on the topic of this paper. To Burton Dreben I am grateful for many improvements; and to Thomas Hill and Hugo Bedau for their instructive comments.

spect to the principles and standards appropriate for other cases. The basic structure is understood as the way in which the major social institutions fit together into one system, and how they assign fundamental rights and duties and shape the division of advantages that arises through social cooperation. Thus the political constitution, the legally recognized forms of property, and the organization of the economy, and the nature of the family, all belong to the basic structure. The initial objective of the theory is to find a conception, the first principles of which provide reasonable guidelines for the classical and familiar questions of social justice in connection with this complex of institutions. These questions define the data, so to speak, for which the theory seeks an account. There is no attempt to formulate first principles that apply equally to all subjects. Rather, on this view, a theory must develop principles for the relevant subjects step by step in some appropriate sequence.

In this essay I should like to discuss why the basic structure is taken as the first subject of justice. Of course, it is perfectly legitimate to restrict the initial inquiry to the basic structure. We must begin somewhere, and this starting point may turn out to be justified by how well the theory that results hangs together. But there should be a more illuminating answer than this; and moreover one that draws upon the special features of the basic structure in contrast with other social arrangements, and connects these features with the characteristic role and content of the principles of justice themselves. I hope to give an answer that does precisely this.[2]

Now a social contract is a hypothetical agreement a) between all rather than some members of society, and it is b) between them as members of society (as citizens) and not as individuals who hold some particular position or role within it. In the Kant-

---

2. In *Theory* the basic structure was regarded as the primary subject and discussion focused on this case. See pp. 7ff. But the reasons for this choice of subject and its consequences were not sufficiently explained. Here I want to make good this lack.

ian form of this doctrine, which I shall call "justice as fairness,"
c) the parties are thought of as free and equal moral persons, and
d) the content of the agreement is the first principles that are to
regulate the basic structure. We take as given a short list of
conceptions of justice found in the tradition of moral philosophy
and then ask which of these conceptions the parties would agree
to when the alternatives are thus restricted. Assuming that we
have a clear enough idea of the circumstances necessary to insure
that any agreement reached is fair, the content of justice for the
basic structure can be ascertained, or at least approximated, by
the principles that would be adopted. (Of course, this presupposes the reasonableness of the tradition of moral philosophy;
but where else can we start?) Thus pure procedural justice is
invoked at the highest level: the fairness of the circumstances
transfers to fairness of the principles acknowledged.

I shall suggest the following: first, that once we think of the
parties to a social contract as free and equal (and rational) moral
persons, then there are strong reasons for taking the basic structure as the primary subject (4–5). Second, that in view of the
distinctive features of this structure, the initial agreement, and
the conditions under which it is made, must be understood in a
special way that distinguishes this agreement from all others (6–
7); and third, doing this allows a Kantian view to take account of
the profoundly social nature of human relationships. And finally,
that while a large element of pure procedural justice transfers to
the principles of justice, these principles must nevertheless em-
body an ideal form for the basic structure in the light of which
ongoing institutional processes are to be constrained and the
accumulated results of individual transactions continually adjusted (9).

§ 2. Unity by Appropriate Sequence

Before taking up these points, I should like to remark that
starting with the basic structure and then developing other prin-

ciples sequentially, gives justice as fairness a distinctive character.[3]

To illustrate this, consider first the contrast with utilitarianism: it is usually interpreted as a completely general theory. Certainly this is true of the classical doctrine as definitively formulated by Sidgwick.[4] The principle of utility applies equally to all social forms and to the actions of individuals; in addition, the assessment of character and dispositional traits, as well as the social practice of praising and blaming, are to be guided by it. To be sure, rule-utilitarianism recognizes that certain distinctions between subjects may raise special problems. But the distinction between rules and acts, besides being itself very general, is a categorial or metaphysical distinction, and not one within the class of social forms. It evokes the questions of how the principle of utility is to be applied across category differences; and the general way in which this question is treated by rule-utilitarianism preserves the contrast with the contract view.

Of course, utilitarian theory recognizes the peculiarities of different kinds of cases, but these peculiarities are treated as springing from various kinds of effects and causal relationships that have to be allowed for. Thus it is agreed, let's suppose, that the basic structure is an important complex of institutions, given the deep and pervasive nature of its social and psychological effects. It might be agreed also that it is useful to distinguish this structure from particular associations within it, as well as from the larger surrounding international system. These distinctions may be helpful in a systematic application of the standard of utility. In no case, however, is there a change of first principle, although, of course, a variety of secondary norms and precepts, derivative from utility, may be justified in view of the characteristic features of different problems. Thus, for utilitarianism, neither the number of individuals concerned, nor the institutional

3. I am grateful to Hugo Bedau for pointing out to me the need to emphasize this. In his comments on the earlier version of this paper he noted that the last paragraph of §2 of *Theory* is particularly misleading in this respect.

4. See *Methods of Ethics,* 7th ed. (London, 1907).

260

forms by which their decisions and activities are organized, affect the universal scope of the principle of utility: number and structure are relevant only indirectly through their effects on how the greatest net balance of satisfaction (summed over all persons affected) is most effectively attained.

The first principles of justice as fairness are plainly not suitable for a general theory.[5] These principles require (as stated later, in the first paragraph of §6) that the basic structure establish certain equal basic liberties for all and make sure that social and economic inequalities work for the greatest benefit of the least advantaged against a background of fair opportunity. In many if not most cases these principles give unreasonable directives. To illustrate: for churches and universities different principles are plainly more suitable. Their members usually affirm certain shared aims and purposes as essential guidelines to the most appropriate form of organization. The most we can say is this: because churches and universities are associations within the basic structure, they must adjust to the requirements that this structure imposes in order to establish background justice. Thus, churches and universities may be restricted in various ways, for example, by what is necessary to maintain the basic equal liberties (including liberty of conscience) and fair equality of opportunity.

At first sight the contract doctrine may appear hopelessly unsystematic: for how are the principles that apply to different subjects to be tied together? But there are other forms of theoretical unity than that defined by completely general first princi-

5. This fact is regarded as an objection to these principles by J. C. Harsanyi, "Can the Maximin Principle Serve as a Basis for Morality," *American Political Science Review* 69 (June 1975):594–606. I cannot reply adequately to Harsanyi's forceful objections here, but I note the following: the maximin principle was never proposed as a basis for morality; in the form of the difference principle it is one principle constrained by others that applies to the basic structure; and when this principle is seen in this limited role as a criterion of background justice, its implications in normal cases (see n. 10 below) are not, I believe, implausible. Finally, confining the application of the principles of justice to the basic structure does not imply, contrary to Harsanyi's suggestion (see p. 605), that only the number of persons involved determines which principles hold for a given case. On this, see the last paragraph in this section.

ples. It may be possible to find an appropriate sequence of kinds of subjects and to suppose that the parties to a social contract are to proceed through this sequence with the understanding that the principles of each later agreement are to be subordinate to those of all earlier agreements, or else adjusted to them by certain priority rules. The underlying unity is provided by the idea that free and equal moral persons are to construct reasonable and helpful guidelines for moral reflection in view of their need for such organizing principles and the role in social life that these principles and their corresponding subjects are presumed to have.

It should be noted here, to avoid misunderstanding, that in developing a conception of justice for the basic structure, or indeed for any subject, we do not assume that variation in numbers alone accounts for the appropriateness of different principles. Rather, it is differences in the structure and social role of institutions that is essential, although variations in number are sometimes a necessary condition, and encourage certain institutional forms. Thus a constitutional democracy is larger than a family: greater numbers are required to staff its component parts. But it is the distinct purposes and roles of the parts of the social structure, and how they fit together, that explains there being different principles for distinct kinds of subjects. Indeed, it seems natural to suppose that the distinctive character and autonomy of the various elements of society requires that, within some sphere, they act from their own principles designed to fit their peculiar nature.

§ 3. Libertarianism Has No Special Role for the Basic Structure

A completely general theory like utilitarianism is not the only kind of view that rejects the idea that special first principles are required for the basic structure. Consider for example the libertarian theory, which holds that only a minimal state limited to the narrow functions of protection against force, theft, fraud, enforcement of contracts, and so on, is justified; and that any

262

state with more comprehensive powers violates the rights of individuals. For our purposes here, perhaps the main features of this theory are these:[6]

The aim is to see how the minimal state could have arisen from a perfectly just situation by a series of steps each of which is morally permissible and violates no one's rights. If we can see how this could happen when everyone acts as they ought and why a no more extensive state could arise, then we shall have justified the minimal state, provided of course that the moral theory that identifies the initial situation as just, and defines the permissible departures from it, is correct. To this end, we assume that a state of nature once existed in which there was relative abundance and the actual configuration of people's holdings raised no moral questions. The existing configuration was just and all were adequately provided for. This state of nature is also characterized by the absence of any institution (such as the state) that enforces certain rules and thereby establishes an institutional basis for people's expectations as to how others will act.

Next, a libertarian theory defines certain basic principles of justice that govern the acquisition of holdings (the appropriation of previously unheld things) and the transfer of holdings from one person (or association) to another. Then a just configuration of holdings is defined recursively: a person is entitled to hold whatever is acquired in accordance with the principles of justice in acquisition and transfer, and no one is entitled to something except by repeated application of these principles. If one starts from a state of nature in which the existing array of holdings is just, and if everyone always acts subsequently in accordance with justice in acquisition and transfer, then all later configurations are likewise said to be just. It is maintained that the principles of just acquisition and transfer preserve the justice of holdings throughout the whole sequence of historical transactions, however extended in time. The only way injustice is thought to arise

6. I follow the account in Robert Nozick, *Anarchy, State, and Utopia* (New York: Basic Books, 1974).

is from deliberate violations of these principles, or from error and ignorance of what they require and the like.

Finally, and most relevant for our purposes here, a great variety of associations and modes of cooperation may form depending upon what individuals actually do and what agreements are reached. No special theory is needed to cover these transactions and joint activities: the requisite theory is already provided by the principles of justice in acquisition and transfer, suitably interpreted in the light of certain provisos. All forms of legitimate social cooperation are, then, the handiwork of individuals who voluntarily consent to them; there are no powers or rights lawfully exercised by associations, including the state, that are not rights already possessed by each individual acting alone in the initial just state of nature.

One noteworthy feature of this doctrine is that the state is just like any other private association. The state comes about in the same way as other associations and its formation in the perfectly as-if just historical process is governed by the same principles.[7] Of course, the state serves certain characteristic purposes, but this is true of associations generally. Moreover, the relation of individuals to the state (the legitimate minimal state) is just like their relation with any private corporation with which they have made an agreement. Thus political allegiance is interpreted as a private contractual obligation with, so to speak, a large and successful monopolistic firm: namely, the locally dominant protection agency. There is in general no uniform public law that applies equally to all persons, but rather a network of private agreements; this network represents the procedures the domi-

7. I distinguish here and elsewhere below between an as-if historical and an as-if nonhistorical process (or procedure). In both cases the process is hypothetical in the sense that the process has not actually occurred, or may not have occurred. But as-if historical processes can occur: they are not thought to be excluded by fundamental social laws or natural facts. Thus on the libertarian view, if everyone were to follow the principles of justice in acquisition and transfer, and they can follow them, then the as-if historical process leading to the formation of the state would be realized. By contrast, an as-if nonhistorical process, for example, the procedure leading up to the agreement in the original position, cannot take place. See below §6.

nant protection agency (the state) has agreed to use with its clients, as it were, and these procedures may differ from client to client depending on the bargain each was in a position to make with the dominant agency. No one can be compelled to enter into such an agreement and everyone always has the option of becoming an independent: we have the choice of being one of the state's clients, just as we do in the case of other associations. While the libertarian view makes important use of the notion of agreement, it is not a *social* contract theory at all; for a social contract theory envisages the original compact as establishing a system of common public law which defines and regulates political authority and applies to everyone as citizen. Both political authority and citizenship are to be understood through the conception of the social contract itself. By viewing the state as a private association the libertarian doctrine rejects the fundamental ideas of the contract theory, and so quite naturally it has no place for a special theory of justice for the basic structure.

By way of concluding these preliminary matters, the point of noting these differences with libertarian and utilitarian doctrines is to clarify by illustration and contrast the peculiar features of justice as fairness with its emphasis on the basic structure. Similar contrasts hold in regard to perfectionism and intuitionism and other familiar moral views. The problem here is to show why the basic structure has a special role and why it is reasonable to seek special principles to regulate it.

§ 4. The Importance of Background Justice

I shall begin by noting several considerations that might lead us to regard the basic structure as the first subject of justice, at least when we proceed within the framework of a Kantian social contract theory.

The first consideration is this: suppose we begin with the initially attractive idea that social circumstances and people's relationships to one another should develop over time in accordance with free agreements fairly arrived at and fully honored.

265

Straightaway we need an account of when agreements are free and the social circumstances under which they are reached are fair. In addition, while these conditions may be fair at an earlier time, the accumulated results of many separate and ostensibly fair agreements, together with social trends and historical contingencies, are likely in the course of time to alter citizens' relationships and opportunities so that the conditions for free and fair agreements no longer hold. The role of the institutions that belong to the basic structure is to secure just background conditions against which the actions of individuals and associations take place. Unless this structure is appropriately regulated and adjusted, an initially just social process will eventually cease to be just, however free and fair particular transactions may look when viewed by themselves.

We recognize this fact when we say, for example, that the distribution resulting from voluntary market transactions (even if all the ideal conditions for competitive efficiency obtain) is not, in general, fair unless the antecedent distribution of income and wealth, as well as the structure of the system of markets, is fair. The existing wealth must have been properly acquired and all must have had fair opportunities to earn income, to learn wanted skills, and so on. Again, the conditions necessary for background justice can be undermined, even though nobody acts unfairly or is aware of how the overall result of many separate exchanges affects the opportunities of others. There are no feasible rules that it is practicable to require economic agents to follow in their day-to-day transactions that can prevent these undesirable consequences. These consequences are often so far in the future, or so indirect, that the attempt to forestall them by restrictive rules that apply to individuals would be an excessive if not an impossible burden.

There are four points to emphasize in these familiar observations: first, we cannot tell by looking only at the conduct of individuals and associations in the immediate (or local) circumstances whether, from a social point of view, agreements reached are just or fair. For this assessment depends importantly on the features of the basic structure, on whether it succeeds in maintaining background justice. Thus whether wage agreements are fair rests, for example, on the nature of the labor market: excess market power must be prevented and fair bargaining power should obtain between employers and employees. But in addition, fairness depends on underlying social conditions, such as fair opportunity, extending backward in time and well beyond any limited view.

Second, fair background conditions may exist at one time and be gradually undermined even though no one acts unfairly when their conduct is judged by the rules that apply to transactions within the appropriately circumscribed local situation. The fact that everyone with reason believes that they are acting fairly and scrupulously honoring the norms governing agreements is not sufficient to preserve background justice. This is an important though obvious point: when our social world is pervaded by duplicity and deceit we are tempted to think that law and government are necessary only because of the propensity of individuals to act unfairly. But, to the contrary, the tendency is rather for background justice to be eroded even when individuals act fairly: the overall result of separate and independent transactions is away from and not toward background justice. We might say: in this case the invisible hand guides things in the wrong direction and favors an oligopolistic configuration of accumulations that succeeds in maintaining unjustified inequalities and restrictions on fair opportunity. Therefore, we require special institutions to preserve background justice, and a special conception of justice to define how these institutions are to be set up.

The preceding observation assumes, thirdly, that there are no feasible and practicable rules that it is sensible to impose on individuals that can prevent the erosion of background justice. This is because the rules governing agreements and individual transactions cannot be too complex, or require too much information to be correctly applied; nor should they enjoin individuals to engage in bargaining with many widely scattered third parties, since this would impose excessive transaction costs. The rules applying to agreements are, after all, practical and public directives, and not mathematical functions which may be as complicated as one can imagine. Thus any sensible scheme of rules will not exceed the capacity of individuals to grasp and follow them with sufficient ease, nor will it burden citizens with requirements of knowledge and foresight that they cannot normally meet. Individuals and associations cannot comprehend the ramifications of their particular actions viewed collectively, nor can they be expected to foresee future circumstances that shape and transform present tendencies. All of this is evident enough if we consider the cumulative effects of the purchase and sale of landed property and its transmission by bequest over generations. It is obviously not sensible to impose on parents (as heads of families) the duty to adjust their own bequests to what they estimate the effects of the totality of actual bequests will be on the next generation, much less beyond.

Thus, fourth and finally, we arrive at the idea of a division of labor between two kinds of social rules, and the different institutional forms in which these rules are realized. The basic structure comprises first the institutions that define the social background and includes as well those operations that continually adjust and compensate for the inevitable tendencies away from background fairness, for example, such operations as income and inheritance taxation designed to even out the ownership of property. This structure also enforces through the legal system another set of rules that govern the transactions and agreements between individuals and associations (the law of contract, and so on). The rules relating to fraud and duress, and the like, belong to these rules, and satisfy the requirements of simplicity and practicality. They are framed to leave individuals and associations free to act effectively in pursuit of their ends and without excessive constraints.

To conclude: we start with the basic structure and try to see how this structure itself should make the adjustments necessary to preserve background justice. What we look for, in effect, is an institutional division of labor between the basic structure and the rules applying directly to individuals and associations and to be followed by them in particular transactions. If this division of labor can be established, individuals and associations are then left free to advance their ends more effectively within the framework of the basic structure, secure in the knowledge that elsewhere in the social system the necessary corrections to preserve background justice are being made.

§ 5. How the Basic Structure Affects Individuals

Further reflections also point to the special role of the basic structure. So far we have seen that certain background conditions are necessary if transactions between individuals are to be fair: these conditions characterize the objective situation of individuals vis-à-vis one another. But what about the character and interests of individuals themselves? These are not fixed or given. A theory of justice must take into account how the aims and aspirations of people are formed; and doing this belong to the wider framework of thought in the light of which a conception of justice is to be explained.

Now everyone recognizes that the institutional form of society affects its members and determines in large part the kind of persons they want to be as well as the kind of persons they are. The social structure also limits people's ambitions and hopes in different ways; for they will with reason view themselves in part according to their position in it and take account of the means and opportunities they can realistically expect. So an economic regime, say, is not only an institutional scheme for satisfying existing desires and aspirations but a way of fashioning desires and aspirations in the future. More generally, the basic structure shapes the way the social system produces and reproduces over time a certain form of culture shared by persons with certain conceptions of their good.

Again, we cannot view the talents and abilities of individuals as fixed natural gifts. To be sure, even as realized there is presumably a significant genetic component. However, these abilities and talents cannot come to fruition apart from social conditions, and as realized they always take but one of many possible forms. Developed natural capacities are always a selection, a small selection at that, from the possibilities that might have been attained. In addition, an ability is not, for example, a computer in the head with a definite measurable capacity unaffected by social circumstances. Among the elements affecting the realization of natural capacities are social attitudes of encouragement and support and the institutions concerned with their training and use. Thus even a potential ability at any given time is not something unaffected by existing social forms and particular contingencies over the course of life up to that moment. So not only our final ends and hopes for ourselves but also our realized abilities and talents reflect, to a large degree, our personal history, opportunities, and social position. There is no way of knowing what we might have been had these things been different.

Finally, the preceding considerations must be viewed together with the fact that the basic structure most likely permits significant social and economic inequalities in the life prospects of citizens depending on their social origins, their realized natural endowments, and the chance opportunities and accidents that have shaped their personal history. Such inequalities, we may assume, are inevitable, or else necessary or highly advantageous in maintaining effective social cooperation. Presumably there are various reasons for this, among which the need for incentives is but one.

The nature of inequalities in life prospects can be clarified by contrasting them with other inequalities. Thus imagine a university in which there are three ranks of faculty and everyone stays in each rank the same length of time and receives the same salary. Then while there are inequalities of rank and salary at any given time, there is no inequality in life prospects between faculty members. The same may be true when members of an association adopt a rotation scheme for filling certain more highly privileged or rewarded positions, perhaps because they involve taking greater responsibility. If the scheme is designed so that, barring accidents, death, and the like, all serve the same time in these positions, there are again no inequalities in life prospects.

What the theory of justice must regulate is the inequalities in life prospects between citizens that arise from social starting positions, natural advantages, and historical contingencies. Even if these inequalities are not in some cases very great, their effect may be great enough so that over time they have significant cumulative consequences. The Kantian form of the contract doctrine focuses on these inequalities in the basic structure in the conviction that these inequalities are the most fundamental ones: once suitable principles are found to govern them and the requisite institutions are established, the problem of how to regulate other inequalities can be much more easily resolved.

§ 6. Initial Agreement as Hypothetical and Nonhistorical

In justice as fairness the institutions of the basic structure are just provided they satisfy the principles that free and equal moral persons, in a situation that is fair between them, would adopt for the purpose of regulating that structure. The main two principles read as follows: a) Each person has an equal right to the most extensive scheme of equal basic liberties compatible with a similar scheme of liberties for all. b) Social and economic inequalities are permissible provided that they are i) to the greatest expected benefit of the least advantaged; and ii) attached to positions and offices open to all under conditions of fair equality of opportunity.[8]

Let us consider how the special role of the basic structure affects the conditions of the initial agreement and necessitates that this agreement be understood as hypothetical and nonhistorical. Now by assumption the basic structure is the all-inclusive

---

8. These principles are discussed in *Theory*, §§11–13, and elsewhere. A summary statement, including the principle of just savings and priority rules, is given on pp. 302f.

social system that determines background justice. (Observe that I leave aside here the problem of justice between nations.[9]) Thus, first of all, any fair situation between individuals conceived as free and equal moral persons must be one that suitably evens out the contingencies within this system. Actual agreements reached when people know their present place in an ongoing society are influenced by disparate social and natural contingencies. The principles adopted depend on the actual course of events that takes place within its institutional structure. We cannot by actual agreements get beyond happenstance or specify a suitably independent standard.

It is also clear why, when we interpret the parties as free and equal moral persons, they are to reason as if they know very little about themselves (referring here to the restrictions of the veil of ignorance). For to proceed otherwise is still to allow the diverse and deep contingent effects to influence the principles that are to regulate their social relations as such persons. Thus we suppose that the parties do not know their place in society, their class position or social status, their good or ill fortune in the distribution of natural talents and abilities, all within the normal range.[10] Nor do the parties know their final aims and interests, or their particular psychological makeup.

---

9. The reason for doing this is that, as a first approximation, the problem of social justice concerns the basic structure as a closed background system. To start with the society of nations would seem merely to push one step further back the task of finding a theory of background justice. At some level there must exist a closed background system, and it is this subject for which we want a theory. We are better prepared to take up this problem for a society (illustrated by nations) conceived as a more or less self-sufficient scheme of social cooperation and as possessing a more or less complete culture. If we are successful in the case of a society, we can try to extend and to adjust our initial theory as further inquiry requires.

10. The normal range is specified as follows: since the fundamental problem of justice concerns the relations among those who are full and active participants in society, and directly or indirectly associated together over the course of a whole life, it is reasonable to assume that everyone has physical needs and psychological capacities within some normal range. Thus the problem of special health care and how to treat the mentally defective are aside. If we can work out a viable theory for the normal range, we can attempt to handle these other cases later.

Finally, in order to establish fairness between generations (for example, in the agreement on a principle of just savings), the parties, who are assumed to be contemporaries, do not know the present state of society. They have no information about the stock of natural resources or productive assets, or the level of technology beyond what can be inferred from the assumption that the circumstances of justice obtain. The relative good or ill fortune of their generation is unknown. For when contemporaries are influenced by a general description of the present state of society while agreeing how to treat each other, and the generations that come after them, they have not yet left out of account the results of historical accident and social contingency found within the basic structure. And so we arrive at a thicker rather than a thinner veil of ignorance: the parties are to be understood so far as possible solely as moral persons and in abstraction from contingencies. To be fair, the initial situation treats the parties symmetrically, for as moral persons they are equal: the same relevant properties qualify everyone. Beginning with a state of no information, we allow in just enough information to make the agreement rational, though still suitably independent from historical, natural, and social happenstance. Considerably more information would be compatible with impartiality but a Kantian view seeks more than this.[11]

Thus, it is evident why the social contract must be regarded as hypothetical and nonhistorical. The explanation is that the agreement in the original position represents the outcome of a rational process of deliberation under ideal and nonhistorical conditions that express certain reasonable constraints. There exists no practicable way actually to carry out this deliberative process and to be sure that it conforms to the conditions imposed. Therefore, the outcome cannot be ascertained by pure procedural justice as realized by deliberations of the parties on some actual occasion. Instead the outcome must be determined by reasoning analyti-

11. For this way of putting the distinction between a thicker and a thinner veil of ignorance I am indebted to Joshua Rabinowitz.

cally: that is, the original position is to be characterized with sufficient exactness so that it is possible to work out from the nature of the parties and the situation they confront which conception of justice is favored by the balance of reasons. The content of justice must be discovered by reason: that is, by solving the agreement problem posed by the original position.

To preserve the present-time of entry interpretation, all questions of justice are dealt with by constraints that apply to contemporaries. Consider the case of just savings: since society is a system of cooperation between generations over time, a principle for savings is required. Rather than imagine a (hypothetical and nonhistorical) direct agreement between all generations, the parties can be required to agree to a savings principle subject to the further condition that they must want all *previous* generations to have followed it. Thus the correct principle is that which the members of any generation (and so all generations) would adopt as the one their generation is to follow and as the principle they would want preceding generations to have followed (and later generations to follow), no matter how far back (or forward) in time.[12]

That the initial situation is hypothetical and nonhistorical poses no difficulty once its theoretical purpose is correctly understood. On the present-time of entry interpretation, we can, as it were, enter that situation at any moment simply by conducting our moral reasoning about first principles in accordance with the stipulated procedural constraints. We have considered judg-

12. This formulation of the conditions for the agreement on a just savings principle differs from that in *Theory,* pp. 128f. and 291f. There it is not required that the parties must want the previous generations to have followed the principle they adopt as contemporaries. Therefore, assuming that generations are mutually disinterested, nothing constrains them from refusing to make any savings at all. To cope with this difficulty it was stipulated that the parties care for their descendants. While this is a reasonable stipulation, the requirement above has the virtue that it removes the difficulty without changing the motivation assumption. It also preserves the present time of entry interpretation of the original position and coheres with the strict compliance condition and ideal theory generally. I am indebted to Thomas Nagel and Derek Parfit for this revision; it is also proposed by Jane English, who notes the connection with ideal theory. See her "Justice Between Generations," p. 98.

ments at many levels of generality, from the more particular to the most abstract. So if we affirm the judgments expressed by these constraints, and therefore the values embodied in the idea of fairness between equal moral persons when first principles for the basic structure are to be adopted, then we must accept the limitations on conceptions of justice that result. The initial situation is an attempt to represent and to unify the formal and general elements of our moral thought in a manageable and vivid construction in order to use these elements to determine which first principles of justice are the most reasonable.

I conclude by remarking that once we note the distinctive role of the basic structure and abstract from the various contingencies within it in order to find an appropriate conception of justice to regulate it, something like the notion of the original position seems inevitable. It is a natural extension of the idea of the social contract when the basic structure is taken as the primary subject of justice.

§ 7. Special Features of the Initial Agreement

At this point I consider why the initial agreement has features that distinguish it from any other agreement. Once again, the explanation lies in the distinctive role of the basic structure: we must distinguish between particular agreements made and associations formed within this structure, and the initial agreement and membership in society as a citizen. Consider first particular agreements: typically these are based on the parties' known (or probable) assets and abilities, opportunities, and interests, as these have been realized within background institutions. We may assume that each party, whether an individual or an association, has various alternatives open to them, that they can compare the likely advantages and disadvantages of these alternatives, and act accordingly. Under certain conditions someone's contribution to a joint venture, or to an ongoing association, can be estimated: one simply notes how the venture or association would fare without that person's joining, and the difference measures their worth to the venture or association. The attractiveness of joining to the individuals is ascertained by a comparison with their opportunities. Thus particular agreements are reached in the context of existing and foreseeable configurations of relationships within the basic structure; and it is these configurations that provide a basis for contractual calculations.

The context of a social contract is strikingly different, and must allow for three facts, among others: namely, that membership in our society is given, that we cannot know what we would have been like had we not belonged to it (perhaps the thought itself lacks sense), and that society as a whole has no ends or ordering of ends in the way that associations and individuals do. The bearing of these facts is clear once we try to regard the social contract as an ordinary agreement and ask how deliberations leading up to it would proceed. Since membership in their society is given, there is no question of the parties comparing the attractions of other societies. Moreover, there is no way to identify someone's potential contribution to society who is not yet a member of it; for this potentiality cannot be known and is, in any case, irrelevant to their present situation. Not only this, but from the standpoint of society as a whole vis-à-vis any one member, there is no set of agreed ends by reference to which the potential social contributions of an individual could be assessed. Associations and individuals have such ends, but not a well-ordered society; although it has the aim of giving justice to all its citizens, this is not an aim that ranks their expected contributions and on that basis determines their social role or their worth from a social standpoint. The notion of an individual's contribution to society viewed as an association (so that society is entitled to offer terms for joining derived from the aims of those already members of the association) has no place in a Kantian view. It is necessary, therefore, to construe the social contract in a special way that distinguishes it from other agreements.

In justice as fairness this is done by constructing the notion of the original position. This construction must reflect the fundamental contrasts just noted and it must supply the missing ele-

276

ments in order that a rational agreement can be reached. Consider in turn the three facts in the preceding paragraph. In connection with the first, the parties in the original position suppose that their membership in their society is fixed. This presumption reflects the fact that we are born into our society and within its framework realize but one of many possible forms of our person; the question of our entering another society does not arise. The task of the parties, therefore, is to agree on principles for the basic structure of the society in which it is assumed that they will lead their life. While the principles adopted will no doubt allow for emigration (subject to suitable qualifications), they will not permit arrangements that would be just only if emigration were allowed. The attachments formed to persons and places, to associations and communities, as well as cultural ties, are normally too strong to be given up, and this fact is not to be deplored. Thus the right to emigrate does not affect what counts as a just basic structure, for this structure is to be viewed as a scheme into which people are born and are expected to lead a complete life.

Turning now to the second fact noted above, observe that the veil of ignorance not only establishes fairness between equal moral persons, but by excluding information about the parties' actual interests and abilities, it corresponds to the way in which, apart from our place and history in society, even our potential abilities cannot be known and our interests and character are still to be formed. Thus, the initial situation suitably recognizes that our nature as reasonable and responsible beings apart from society includes but a potential for a whole range of possibilities. Third and finally, there are no social ends except those established by the principles of justice themselves, or else authorized by them; but these principles have yet to be adopted.

Nevertheless, although the calculations that typically influence agreements within society have no place in the original position, other aspects of this initial situation provide the setting for rational deliberation. Thus the alternatives are not opportunities to join other societies, but instead a list of conceptions of justice to regulate the basic structure of one's own society. The parties' interests and preferences are given by their desire for primary goods.[13] Their particular final ends and aims indeed are already formed, although not known to them; and it is these already formed interests, as well as the conditions necessary to preserve moral personality, that they seek to protect by ranking conceptions on the basis of their preference (in the original position) for primary goods. Finally, the availability of general social theory gives a sufficient basis for estimating the feasibility and consequences of alternative conceptions of justice. In view of these aspects of the original position, the idea of the social contract as a rational undertaking can be maintained despite the unusual nature of this agreement.

§ 8. The Social Nature of Human Relationships

Consider now three ways in which the social aspect of human relationships is reflected in the content of the principles of justice themselves. First, the difference principle (which governs economic and social inequalities) does not distinguish between what is acquired by individuals as members of society and what would have been acquired by them had they not been members.[14] Indeed, no sense can be made of the notion of that part of an individual's social benefits that exceed what would have been their situation in another society or in a state of nature. We can, if we like, in setting up the argument from the original

13. These goods are defined as things that, from the standpoint of the original position, it is rational for the parties to want whatever their final ends (which are unknown to them). They serve as generalized means, so to speak, for realizing all, or most all, rational systems of aims. See *Theory*, pp. 92–95, 396f., 433f.

14. One aim of §§7–8 is to indicate a reply to David Gauthier's illuminating critique of the difference principle, "Justice and Natural Endowment," *Social Theory and Practice* 3 (1974):3–26. I refer to his discussion here because his argument depends on being able to distinguish between what is acquired by individuals as members of society and what would have been acquired by them in a state of nature. If this distinction has no useful meaning, then I believe that the way is cleared to meeting Gauthier's objection. Of course, much more needs to be said. In any case, I fully agree with his remarks on pp. 25f. and much of my discussion is designed to show how a Kantian contract view can be stated to accord with them.

position, introduce the state of nature in relation to the so-called nonagreement point. This point can be defined as general egoism and its consequences, and this can serve as the state of nature.[15] But these conditions do not identify a definite state. All that is known in the original position is that each of the conceptions of justice available to the parties have consequences superior to general egoism. There is no question of determining anyone's contribution to society, or how much better off each is than they would have been had they not belonged to it, and then adjusting the social benefits of citizens by reference to these estimates. Although we may draw this kind of distinction in the case of associations within society, the parallel calculations when adopting principles for the basic structure have no foundation. Neither our situation in other societies, nor in a state of nature, have any role in assessing conceptions of justice. And clearly these notions are not relevant in applying the two principles of justice.

Second, and related to the preceding, the two principles of justice regulate how entitlements are acquired in return for contributions to associations, or to other forms of cooperation, within the basic structure. As we have seen, these contributions are evaluated on the basis of the particular aims of individuals and associations; and what people have contributed is influenced partly by their efforts and achievements, and partly by social circumstances and happenstance. Contributions can only be defined as contributions to this or that association in this or that situation. Such contributions reflect an individual's marginal usefulness to some particular group. These contributions are not to be mistaken for contributions to society itself, or for the worth to society of its members as citizens. The sum of an individual's entitlements, or even of their uncompensated contributions to associations within society, is not to be regarded as a contribution to society. Within a Kantian view there is no place for the idea of an individual's contribution to society that parallels that of an individual's contribution to associations within society. Insofar as

15. See *Theory,* pp. 136, 147; cf. 80.

we compare the worth of citizens at all, their worth in a just and well-ordered society is always equal;[16] and this equality is reflected in the system of basic liberties and fair opportunities, and in the operations of the difference principle.[17]

Third, and last, recall that in a Kantian view the parties are regarded as free and equal moral persons. To say that they are moral persons is to say that they have a conception of the good (a system of final ends) and a capacity to understand a conception of justice and to follow it in their life (a sense of justice). Now the freedom of moral persons can be interpreted under two headings: first, as free persons, they regard themselves as having a highest-order interest in regulating all their other interests, even their fundamental ones, by reason, that is, by rational and reasonable principles that are expressive of their autonomy. Moreover, free persons do not think of themselves as indissolubly tied to any particular final end, or family of such ends, but regard themselves as always capable of appraising and revising their aims in the light of reasonable considerations. Second, we assume that free persons are responsible for their interests and ends: they are able to control and revise their wants and desires, and as circumstance requires, they accept the responsibility for doing so.[18]

Now freedom as applied to social institutions means a certain pattern of rights and liberties; and equal freedom means that certain basic liberties and opportunities are equal and that social and economic inequalities are regulated by principles suitably adjusted to preserve the fair value of these liberties. From the preceding definitions of freedom as applied to moral persons and to social forms, it is plain that free and equal persons are not

16. The worth of citizens in a well-ordered society is always equal because in such a society everyone is assumed to comply with just institutions and to fulfill their duties and obligations moved, when appropriate, by a sufficiently strong sense of justice. Inequalities do not arise from unequal moral worth; their explanation lies elsewhere.

17. See below, the second paragraph of §9.

18. These remarks are stated a bit more fully in "Reply to Alexander and Musgrave," *Quarterly Journal of Economics* 88 (November 1974):639–43.

defined as those whose social relations answer to the very principles that would be agreed to in the original position. For to say
this would undermine the argument for these principles that is
grounded on their being the principles that would be adopted.
But once the parties are described in terms that have an institutional expression, then, given the role of the basic structure, it is
no accident that the first principles of justice apply directly to
the basic structure. The freedom and equality of moral persons
require some public form, and the content of the two principles
fulfills this expectation. And this stands in contrast, for example,
to classical utilitarianism, which takes as basic the capacity for
pleasure and pain, or for certain intrinsically valuable experiences, defined in such a way that no particular institutional expression is required, although of course certain social forms are
superior to others as more effective means to achieve a greater
net balance of happiness, or a greater sum of value.

§ 9. Ideal Form for the Basic Structure

We now come to the fourth and last point (see the end of §1):
namely, that although society may reasonably rely on a large
element of pure procedural justice in determining distributive
shares, a conception of justice must incorporate an ideal form for
the basic structure in the light of which the accumulated results
of ongoing social processes are to be limited and adjusted.[19]

Now in view of the special role of the basic structure, it is
natural to ask the following question: by what principle can free
and equal moral persons accept the fact that social and economic
inequalities are deeply influenced by social fortune, and natural
and historical happenstance? Since the parties regard themselves
as such persons, the obvious starting point is for them to suppose
that all social primary goods, including income and wealth, should
be equal: everyone should have an equal share. But they must

19. On pure procedural justice, see *Theory*, pp. 84–89, 310–15; and also pp. 64,
66, 72ff., 79, 274–80, 305–10.

take organizational requirements and economic efficiency into account. Thus it is unreasonable to stop at equal division. The basic structure should allow organizational and economic inequalities so long as these improve everyone's situation, including that of the least advantaged, provided these inequalities are consistent with equal liberty and fair equality of opportunity. Because they start from equal shares, those who benefit least (taking equal division as the benchmark) have, so to speak, a veto. And thus the parties arrive at the difference principle. Here equal division is accepted as the benchmark because it reflects how people are situated when they are represented as free and equal moral persons. Among such persons, those who have gained more than others are to do so on terms that improve the situation of those who have gained less. These intuitive considerations indicate why the difference principle is the appropriate criterion to govern social and economic inequalities.

To understand the difference principle several matters have to be kept in mind. First, the two principles of justice as they work in tandem incorporate an important element of pure procedural justice in the actual determination of distributive shares. They apply to the basic structure and its system for acquiring entitlements; within appropriate limits, whatever distributive shares result are just. A fair distribution can be arrived at only by the actual working of a fair social process over time in the course of which, in accordance with publicly announced rules, entitlements are earned and honored. These features define pure procedural justice. Therefore, if it is asked in the abstract whether one distribution of a given stock of things to definite individuals with known desires and preferences is more just than another, then there is simply no answer to the question.[20]

Thus the principles of justice, in particular the difference principle, apply to the main public principles and policies that regulate social and economic inequalities. They are used to adjust the system of entitlements and earnings and to balance the

20. Ibid., p. 88.

282

familiar everyday standards and precepts which this system employs. The difference principle holds, for example, for income and property taxation, for fiscal and economic policy. It applies to the announced system of public law and statutes and not to particular transactions or distributions, nor to the decisions of individuals and associations, but rather to the institutional background against which these transactions and decisions take place. There are no unannounced and unpredictable interferences with citizens' expectations and acquisitions. Entitlements are earned and honored as the public system of rules declares. Taxes and restrictions are all in principle foreseeable, and holdings are acquired on the known condition that certain transfers and redistributions will be made. The objection that the difference principle enjoins continuous corrections of particular distributions and capricious interference with private transactions is based on a misunderstanding.

Again, the two principles of justice do not insist that the actual distribution conform at any given time (or over time) to any observable pattern, say equality, or that the degree of inequality computed from the distribution fall within a certain range, say of values of the Gini coefficient.[21] What is enjoined is that (permissible) inequalities should make a certain functional contribution to the expectations of the least favored, where this functional contribution results from the working of the system of entitlements set up in public institutions. The aim, however, is not to eliminate contingencies from social life, for some contingencies are inevitable. Thus even if an equal distribution of natural assets seemed more in keeping with the equality of free persons, the question of redistributing these assets (were this conceivable) does not arise, since it is incompatible with the integrity of the person. Nor need we make any specific assumptions about how great natural variations are; we only suppose that, as realized in later life, they are influenced by many kinds of happenstance.

21. For this and other measures of inequality, see A. K. Sen, *On Economic Inequality* (New York: W. W. Norton, 1973), chap. 2.

Institutions must organize social cooperation so that they encourage constructive efforts. We have a right to our natural
abilities and a right to whatever we become entitled to by taking
part in a fair social process. The problem, of course, is how to
characterize such a process. The two principles express the idea
that no one should have less than they would receive in an equal
division of primary goods, and that when the fruitfulness of social
cooperation allows for a general improvement, then the existing
inequalities are to work to the benefit of those whose position
has improved the least, taking equal division as the benchmark.

The two principles also specify an ideal form for the basic
structure in the light of which ongoing institutional and procedural processes are constrained and adjusted. Among these constraints are the limits on the accumulation of property (especially
if private property in productive assets exists) that derive from
the requirements of the fair value of political liberty and fair
equality of opportunity, and the limits based on considerations
of stability and excusable envy, both of which are connected to
the essential primary good of self-respect.[22] We need such an
ideal to guide the adjustments necessary to preserve background
justice. As we have seen (in §4), even if everyone acts fairly as
defined by the rules that it is both reasonable and practicable to
impose on individuals, the upshot of many separate transactions
will eventually undermine background justice. This is obvious
once we view society, as we must, as involving cooperation over
generations. Thus even in a well-ordered society, adjustments in
the basic structure are always necessary. And so an institutional
division of labor must be established between the basic structure
and the rules applying directly to particular transactions. Individuals and associations are left free to advance their ends within
the framework of background institutions which carry out the
operations required to maintain a just basic structure.

The need for a structural ideal to specify constraints and to
guide adjustments does not depend upon injustice. Even with

22. See *Theory*, pp. 224–27, 277f., 534–37, 543–46.

284

strict compliance with all reasonable and practical rules, such adjustments are continually required. The fact that actual political and social life is often pervaded by much injustice merely underlines this necessity. A purely procedural theory that contained no structural principles for a just social order would be of no use in our world, where the political goal is to eliminate injustice and to guide change toward a fair basic structure. A conception of justice must specify the requisite structural principles and point to the overall direction of political action. In the absence of such an ideal form for background institutions, there is no rational basis for continually adjusting the social process so as to preserve background justice, nor for eliminating existing injustice. Thus ideal theory, which defines a perfectly just basic structure, is a necessary complement to nonideal theory without which the desire for change lacks an aim.

§ 10. Reply to Hegel's Criticism

This completes my discussion of the four points stated at the end of §1. One result of what has been said is a reply to idealism. The problem is this: in order to work out a Kantian conception of justice it seems desirable to detach the structure of Kant's doctrine from its background in transcendental idealism and to give it a procedural interpretation by means of the construction of the original position. (This detachment is important if for no other reason than that it should enable us to see how far a procedural interpretation of Kant's view within a reasonable empiricist framework is possible.) But to achieve this aim we have to show that the original position construction, which uses the idea of the social contract, is not open to the cogent objections that idealists raised to the contract tradition of their day.

Thus Hegel thought that this doctrine confused society and the state with an association of private persons; that it permitted the general form and content of public law to be determined too much by the contingent and specific private interests and personal concerns of individuals; and that it could make no sense of the fact that it is not up to us whether we are born into and belong to our society. For Hegel the doctrine of social contract was an illegitimate and uncritical extension of ideas at home in and limited to (what he called) "civil society." A further objection was that the doctrine failed to recognize the social nature of human beings and depended on attributing to them certain fixed natural abilities and specific desires independent from, and for theoretical purposes prior to, society.[23]

I have attempted to reply to these criticisms first by maintaining that the primary subject of justice is the basic structure of society, which has the fundamental task of establishing background justice (§§4–5). And while this contention may offhand appear to be a concession, it nevertheless is not: the original position can still be characterized so that it establishes a fair agreement situation between free and equal moral persons and one in which they can reach a rational agreement. This characterization depends upon conceiving of free and equal moral persons in a certain way and interpreting their wants and needs (for purposes of the argument in the original position) in terms of an account of primary goods. To be sure, we must distinguish the agreement on a conception of justice from all other agreements, but this requirement is not surprising: we should expect the agreement that settles principles for the basic structure to have features that mark it off from all agreements made within that structure (§§6–7). Finally, I have indicated how justice as fairness can accommodate the social nature of human beings (§8). At the same time, since it proceeds from a suitably individualistic basis (the original position is conceived as fair between free and equal moral persons), it is a moral conception that provides an appropriate place for social values without sacrificing the freedom and integrity of the person.

It may be that other contract views cannot answer the idealist critique. Historical process doctrines such as those of Hobbes

23. See *The Philosophy of Right,* translated by T. M. Knox (Oxford: Clarendon Press, 1942), pp. 58f., 70f., 156f., 186.

and Locke, or the libertarian view, although importantly very different from one another, all seem open to objection. First, since the social contract is made by people in a state of nature (in the case of Hobbes and Locke), or individuals agree to become a client of the dominant protection agency (on the libertarian scheme), it appears inevitable that the terms of these agreements, or the circumstances that they ratify, are bound to be substantially affected by contingencies and accidents of the as-if just historical process which has no tendency to preserve or to move toward background justice. This difficulty is strikingly illustrated by Locke's doctrine. He assumes that not all members of society following the social compact have equal political rights: citizens have the right to vote in virtue of owning property so that the propertyless have no vote and no right to exercise political authority.[24] Presumably the diverse accumulations of the as-if just historical process over generations has left many without property through no fault of their own; and although the social contract and the subsequent entrusteeship of political authority is perfectly rational from their standpoint, and does not contradict their duty to God, it does not secure for them these basic political rights. From a Kantian viewpoint, Locke's doctrine improperly subjects the social relationships of moral persons to historical and social contingencies that are external to, and eventually undermine, their freedom and equality. The constraints that Locke imposes on the as-if historical process are not strong enough to characterize a conception of background justice acceptable to free and equal moral persons. This can be brought out by supposing that the social compact is to be made immediately following the creation of human beings as free and equal persons in the state of nature. Assuming that their situation with respect to one another suitably represents their freedom and equality, and also that (as Locke holds) God has not conferred on anyone the right to exercise political authority, they will presumably acknowledge principles that assure equal basic (including political) rights for

24. See *Second Treatise of Government,* reading together §§140 and 158.

all throughout the later historical process. This reading of Locke's view makes it an as-if nonhistorical doctrine when we suppose that during the relevant period of time people were too widely scattered for any agreement to be reached. That Locke seems not to have considered this alternative possibility brings out the historical aspect of his theory.[25]

I have also suggested that any contract theory must recognize that a division of labor is necessary between the operations of the basic structure in maintaining background justice and the definition and enforcement by the legal system of the rules that apply directly to individuals and associations, and govern their particular transactions. Finally, there is no use in a Kantian contract theory for the contrast between the situation of individuals in the state of nature and their situation in society. This kind of comparison belongs solely to agreements struck within the framework of background institutions and has no role in determining basic rights of the members of society. Moreover, any benchmark of comparison between the relative advantages of citizens must be founded on their present relationships and the way in which social institutions work now, and not on how the actual (or some as-if just) historical sequence of transactions extending backward over generations has improved (or would improve) everyone's circumstances in comparison with the initial (or some hypothetical) state of nature.

My aim here is not to criticize other contract theories. To do that would require a separate discussion. Rather, I have tried to explain why justice as fairness takes the basic structure as the first subject of justice and attempts to develop a special theory for this case. Given the unique features and role of this structure, the idea of an agreement must be appropriately transformed if the intent of the Kantian form of the contract doctrine is to be realized. I have sought to show how the necessary transformations can be made.

25. For this way of seeing the historical aspect of Locke's theory I am indebted to Quentin Skinner.

The Basic
Liberties and
Their Priority[1]

It was pointed out by H. L. A. Hart
that the account in my book *A Theory of Justice* of the basic liberties and
their priority contains, among other

1. This is a much revised and longer version of
the Tanner Lecture given at the University of
Michigan in April 1981. I am grateful to the
Tanner Foundation and the Department of Philosophy at the University of Michigan for the
opportunity to give this lecture. I should like to
take this occasion to express my gratitude to H.
L. A. Hart for writing his critical review (see n.
2) to which I attempt a partial reply. I have tried
to sketch replies to what I believe are the two
most fundamental difficulties he raises; and this
has led to several important changes in my account of liberty. For many valuable comments
and suggestions for how to meet the difficulties
Hart raises, I am much indebted to Joshua Rabinowitz.

In making this revision I am indebted to Samuel Scheffler and Anthony Kronman for their
comments immediately following the lecture and
for later conversations. Scheffler's comments have
led me to recast entirely and greatly to enlarge

failings, two serious gaps. In this lecture I shall outline, and can do no more than outline, how these gaps can be filled. The first gap is that the grounds upon which the parties in the original position adopt the basic liberties and agree to their priority are not sufficiently explained.[2] This gap is connected with a second, which is that when the principles of justice are applied at the constitutional, legislative, and judicial stages, no satisfactory criterion is given for how the basic liberties are to be further specified and adjusted to one another as social circumstances are made known.[3] I shall try to fill these two gaps by carrying through the revisions already introduced in my Dewey Lectures. I shall outline how the basic liberties and the grounds for their priority can be founded on the conception of citizens as free and equal persons in conjunction with an improved account of primary goods.[4] These revisions bring out that the basic liberties and their priority rest on a conception of the person that would be recognized as liberal and not, as Hart thought, on considerations of rational interests alone.[5] Nevertheless, the structure and content of justice as fairness is still much the same; except for an

---

the original version of what are now §§5 and 6. Kronman's comments have been particularly helpful in revising §7. I must also thank Burton Dreben, whose instructive advice and discussion have led to what seem like innumerable changes and revisions.

I remark as a preface that my account of the basic liberties and their priority, when applied to the constitutional doctrine of what I call "a well-ordered society," has a certain similarity to the well-known view of Alexander Meiklejohn (see n. 12). There are, however, these important differences. First, the kind of primacy Meiklejohn gives to the political liberties and to free speech is here given to the family of basic liberties as a whole; second, the value of self-government, which for Meiklejohn often seems overriding, is counted as but one important value among others; and finally, the philosophical background of the basic liberties is very different.

2. H. L. A. Hart, "Rawls on Liberty and Its Priority," *University of Chicago Law Review* 40(3) (Spring 1973):551–55 (hereafter Hart); reprinted in *Reading Rawls,* edited by Norman Daniels (New York: Basic Books, 1975), pp. 249–52 (hereafter Daniels).

3. Hart, pp. 542–50; see Daniels, pp. 239–44.

4. See "Kantian Constructivism in Moral Theory," *Journal of Philosophy* 77(9) (September 1980):519–30.

5. Hart, p. 555; Daniels, p. 252.

important change of phrase in the first principle of justice, the statement of the two principles of justice is unchanged and so is the priority of the first principle over the second.

§ 1. The Initial Aim of Justice as Fairness

Before taking up the two gaps in the account of the basic liberties, a few preliminary matters should be noted. First, the two principles of justice read as follows:

> a. Each person has an equal right to a fully adequate scheme of equal basic liberties which is compatible with a similar scheme of liberties for all.
>
> b. Social and economic inequalities are to satisfy two conditions. First, they must be attached to offices and positions open to all under conditions of fair equality of opportunity; and second, they must be to the greatest benefit of the least advantaged members of society.

The change in the first principle of justice mentioned above is that the words "a fully adequate scheme" replace the words "the most extensive total system" which were used in *Theory*.[6] This change leads to the insertion of the words "which is" before "compatible." The reasons for this change are explained later and the notion of a fully adequate scheme of basic liberties is discussed in §8. For the moment I leave this question aside.

A further preliminary matter is that the equal basic liberties in the first principle of justice are specified by a list as follows: freedom of thought and liberty of conscience; the political liberties and freedom of association, as well as the freedoms specified by the liberty and integrity of the person; and finally, the rights and liberties covered by the rule of law. No priority is assigned to liberty as such, as if the exercise of something called "liberty"

---

6. The phrase "the most extensive" is used in the main statements of the principles of justice on pp. 60, 250, and 302. The phrase "total system" is used in the second and third of these statements.

has a preeminent value and is the main if not the sole end of political and social justice. There is, to be sure, a general presumption against imposing legal and other restrictions on conduct without sufficient reason. But this presumption creates no special priority for any particular liberty. Hart noted, however, that in *Theory* I sometimes used arguments and phrases which suggest that the priority of liberty as such is meant; although, as he saw, this is not the correct interpretation.[7] Throughout the history of democratic thought the focus has been on achieving certain specific liberties and constitutional guarantees, as found, for example, in various bills of rights and declarations of the rights of man. The account of the basic liberties follows this tradition.

Some may think that to specify the basic liberties by a list is a makeshift which a philosophical conception of justice should do without. We are accustomed to moral doctrines presented in the form of general definitions and comprehensive first principles. Note, however, that if we can find a list of liberties which, when made part of the two principles of justice, leads the parties in the original position to agree to these principles rather than to the other principles of justice available to them, then what we may call "the initial aim" of justice as fairness is achieved. This aim is to show that the two principles of justice provide a better understanding of the claims of freedom and equality in a democratic society than the first principles associated with the traditional doctrines of utilitarianism, with perfectionism, or with intuitionism. It is these principles, together with the two principles of justice, which are the alternatives available to the parties in the original position when this initial aim is defined.

Now a list of basic liberties can be drawn up in two ways. One way is historical: we survey the constitutions of democratic states

---

7. Hart gives a perceptive discussion of whether the first principle of justice means by "liberty" what I have called "liberty as such." This question arises because in the first statement of the principle on p. 60, and elsewhere, I use the phrase "basic liberty," or simply "liberty" when I should have used "basic liberties." With Hart's discussion I agree, on the whole; see pp. 537–41; Daniels, pp. 234–37.

and put together a list of liberties normally protected, and we examine the role of these liberties in those constitutions which have worked well. While this kind of information is not available to the parties in the original position, it is available to us—to you and me who are setting up justice as fairness—and therefore this historical knowledge may influence the content of the principles of justice which we allow the parties as alternatives.[8] A second way is to consider which liberties are essential social conditions for the adequate development and full exercise of the two powers of moral personality over a complete life. Doing this connects the basic liberties with the conception of the person used in justice as fairness, and I shall come back to these important matters in §§3–6.

Let us suppose that we have found a list of basic liberties which achieves the initial aim of justice as fairness. This list we view as a starting point that can be improved by finding a second list such that the parties in the original position would agree to the two principles with the second list rather than the two principles with the initial list. This process can be continued indefinitely, but the discriminating power of philosophical reflection at the level of the original position may soon run out. When this happens we should settle on the last preferred list and then specify that list further at the constitutional, legislative, and judicial stages, when general knowledge of social institutions and of society's circumstances is made known. It suffices that the considerations adduced from the standpoint of the original position determine the general form and content of the basic liberties and explain the adoption of the two principles of justice, which alone among the alternatives incorporate these liberties and assign them priority. Thus, as a matter of method, nothing need be lost by using a step-by-step procedure for arriving at a list of liberties and their further specification.

A final remark concerning the use of a list of liberties. The

8. See "Kantian Constructivism in Moral Theory," Lect. I, pp. 533–34, Lect. III, pp. 567–68.

argument for the priority of liberty, like all arguments from the original position, is always relative to a given enumeration of the alternatives from which the parties are to select. One of these alternatives, the two principles of justice, contains as part of its specification a list of basic liberties and their priority. The source of the alternatives is the historical tradition of moral and political philosophy. We are to regard the original position and the characterization of the deliberations of the parties as a means of selecting principles of justice from alternatives already presented. And this has the important consequence that to establish the priority of liberty it is not necessary to show that the conception of the person, combined with various other aspects of the original position, suffices of itself to derive a satisfactory list of liberties and the principles of justice which assign them priority. Nor is it necessary to show that the two principles of justice (with the priority of liberty included) would be adopted from any enumeration of alternatives however amply it might be supplemented by other principles.[9] I am concerned here with the initial aim of justice as fairness, which, as defined above, is only to show that the principles of justice would be adopted over the other traditional alternatives. If this can be done, we may then proceed to further refinements.

§ 2. The Special Status of Basic Liberties

After these preliminaries, I begin by noting several features of the basic liberties and their priority. First, the priority of liberty means that the first principle of justice assigns the basic liberties, as given by a list, a special status. They have an absolute weight with respect to reasons of public good and of perfectionist values.[10] For example, the equal political liberties cannot be denied

9. On this point, see *Theory*, p. 581.

10. The phrases "public good" and "perfectionist values" are used to refer to the notions of goodness in the teleological moral doctrines of utilitarianism and perfectionism, respectively. Thus, these notions are specified independently of a notion of right, for example, in utilitarianism (and in much of welfare economics also) as the

to certain social groups on the grounds that their having these liberties may enable them to block policies needed for economic efficiency and growth. Nor could a discriminatory selective service act be justified (in time of war) on the grounds that it is the least socially disadvantageous way to raise an army. The claims of the basic liberties cannot be overridden by such considerations.

Since the various basic liberties are bound to conflict with one another, the institutional rules which define these liberties must be adjusted so that they fit into a coherent scheme of liberties. The priority of liberty implies in practice that a basic liberty can be limited or denied solely for the sake of one or more other basic liberties, and never, as I have said, for reasons of public good or of perfectionist values. This restriction holds even when those who benefit from the greater efficiency, or together share the greater sum of advantages, are the same persons whose liberties are limited or denied. Since the basic liberties may be limited when they clash with one another, none of these liberties is absolute; nor is it a requirement that, in the finally adjusted scheme, all the basic liberties are to be equally provided for (whatever that might mean). Rather, however these liberties are adjusted to give one coherent scheme, this scheme is secured equally for all citizens.

In understanding the priority of the basic liberties we must distinguish between their restriction and their regulation.[11] The priority of these liberties is not infringed when they are merely regulated, as they must be, in order to be combined into one scheme as well as adapted to certain social conditions necessary for their enduring exercise. So long as what I shall call "the central range of application" of the basic liberties is provided for,

---

satisfaction of the desires, or interests, or preferences of individuals. See further, *Theory*, pp. 24–26.

11. This distinction is familiar and important in constitutional law. See, for example, Lawrence Tribe, *American Constitutional Law* (Mineola, N.Y.: The Foundation Press, 1978), chap. 12, §2, where it is applied to freedom of speech as protected by the First Amendment. In *Theory* I failed to make this distinction at crucial points in my account of the basic liberties. I am indebted to Joshua Rabinowitz for clarification on this matter.

the principles of justice are fulfilled. For example, rules of order are essential for regulating free discussion.[12] Without the general acceptance of reasonable procedures of inquiry and precepts of debate, freedom of speech cannot serve its purpose. Not everyone can speak at once, or use the same public facility at the same time for different ends. Instituting the basic liberties, just as fulfilling various desires, calls for scheduling and social organization. The requisite regulations are not to be mistaken for restrictions on the content of speech, for example, for prohibitions against arguing for certain religious, philosophical, or political doctrines, or against discussing questions of general and particular fact which are relevant in assessing the justice of the basic structure of society. The public use of our reason[13] must be regulated, but the priority of liberty requires this to be done, so far as possible, to preserve intact the central range of application of each basic liberty.

It is wise, I think, to limit the basic liberties to those that are truly essential in the expectation that the liberties which are not basic are satisfactorily allowed for by the general presumption when the discharge of the burden of proof is decided by the other requirements of the two principles of justice. The reason for this limit on the list of basic liberties is the special status of these liberties. Whenever we enlarge the list of basic liberties we risk weakening the protection of the most essential ones and recreating within the scheme of liberties the indeterminate and unguided balancing problems we had hoped to avoid by a suitably circumscribed notion of priority. Therefore, I shall assume throughout, and not always mention, that the basic liberties on

12. See Alexander Meiklejohn, *Free Speech and Its Relation to Self-Government* (New York: Harper and Row, 1948), chap. 1, §6, for a well-known discussion of the distinction between rules of order and rules abridging the content of speech.

13. The phrase "the public use of our reason" is adapted from Kant's essay "What Is Enlightenment?" (1784), where it is introduced in the fifth paragraph; Academy edition of the *Gesammelte Schriften,* vol. 8 (1912), pp. 36–37. Kant contrasts the public use of reason, which is free, to the private use, which may not be free. I do not mean to endorse this view.

the list always have priority, as will often be clear from the arguments for them.

The last point about the priority of liberty is that this priority is not required under all conditions. For our purposes here, however I assume that it is required under what I shall call "reasonably favorable conditions," that is, under social circumstances which, provided the political will exists, permit the effective establishment and the full exercise of these liberties. These conditions are determined by a society's culture, its traditions and acquired skills in running institutions, and its level of economic advance (which need not be especially high), and no doubt by other things as well. I assume as sufficiently evident for our purposes, that in our country today reasonably favorable conditions do obtain, so that for us the priority of the basic liberties is required. Of course, whether the political will exists is a different question entirely. While this will exists by definition in a well-ordered society, in our society part of the political task is to help fashion it.

Following the preceding remarks about the priority of liberty, I summarize several features of the scheme of basic liberties. First: as I have indicated, I assume that each such liberty has what I shall call a "central range of application." The institutional protection of this range of application is a condition of the adequate development and full exercise of the two moral powers of citizens as free and equal persons. I shall elaborate this remark in the next sections. Second, the basic liberties can be made compatible with one another, at least within their central range of application. Put another way, under reasonably favorable conditions, there is a practicable scheme of liberties that can be instituted in which the central range of each liberty is protected. But that such a scheme exists cannot be derived solely from the conception of the person as having the two moral powers, nor solely from the fact that certain liberties, and other primary goods as all-purpose means, are necessary for the development and exercise of these powers. Both of these elements must fit into a workable constitutional arrangement. The historical experience of democratic institutions and reflection on the principles of constitutional design suggest that a practicable scheme of liberties can indeed be found.

I have already remarked that the scheme of basic liberties is not specified in full detail by considerations available in the original position. It is enough that the general form and content of the basic liberties can be outlined and the grounds of their priority understood. The further specification of the liberties is left to the constitutional, legislative, and judicial stages. But in outlining this general form and content we must indicate the special role and central range of application of the basic liberties sufficiently clearly to guide the process of further specification at later stages. For example, among the basic liberties of the person is the right to hold and to have the exclusive use of personal property. The role of this liberty is to allow a sufficient material basis for a sense of personal independence and self-respect, both of which are essential for the development and exercise of the moral powers. Two wider conceptions of the right of property as a basic liberty are to be avoided. One conception extends this right to include certain rights of acquisition and bequest, as well as the right to own means of production and natural resources. On the other conception, the right of property includes the equal right to participate in the control of means of production and natural resources, which are to be socially owned. These wider conceptions are not used because they cannot, I think, be accounted for as necessary for the development and exercise of the moral powers. The merits of these and other conceptions of the right of property are decided at later stages when much more information about a society's circumstances and historical traditions is available.[14]

Finally, it is not supposed that the basic liberties are equally

14. As an elaboration of this paragraph, see the discussion in *Theory*, pp. 270–74, 280–82, of the question of private property in democracy versus socialism. The two principles of justice by themselves do not settle this question.

important or prized for the same reasons. Thus one strand of the liberal tradition regards the political liberties as of less intrinsic value than freedom of thought and liberty of conscience, and the civil liberties generally. What Constant called "the liberties of the moderns" are prized above "the liberties of the ancients."[15] In a large modern society, whatever may have been true in the city-state of classical times, the political liberties are thought to have a lesser place in most persons' conceptions of the good. The role of the political liberties is perhaps largely instrumental in preserving the other liberties.[16] But even if this view is correct, it is no bar to counting certain political liberties among the basic liberties and protecting them by the priority of liberty. For to assign priority to these liberties they need only be important enough as essential institutional means to secure the other basic liberties under the circumstances of a modern state. And if assigning them this priority helps to account for the judgments of priority that we are disposed to affirm after due reflection, then so far so good.

§ 3. Conceptions of Person and Social Cooperation

I now consider the first gap in the account of liberty. Recall that this gap concerns the grounds upon which the parties in the original position accept the first principle of justice and agree to the priority of its basic liberties as expressed by the ranking of the first principle of justice over the second. To fill this gap I shall introduce a certain conception of the person together with a companion conception of social cooperation.[17] Consider first the conception of the person: there are many different aspects of

15. See Constant's essay, "De la Liberté des Anciens comparée à celle des modernes" (1819).

16. For an important recent statement of this view, see Isaiah Berlin's "Two Concepts of Liberty" (1958), reprinted in *Four Essays on Liberty* (Oxford: Oxford University Press, 1969); see, for example, pp. 165–66.

17. In this and the next section I draw upon my "Kantian Constructivism in Moral Theory," n. 4, to provide the necessary background for the argument to follow.

our nature that can be singled out as particularly significant depending on our aim and point of view. This fact is witnessed by the use of such expressions as *Homo politicus, Homo oeconomicus,* and *Homo faber.* In justice as fairness the aim is to work out a conception of political and social justice which is congenial to the most deep-seated convictions and traditions of a modern democratic state. The point of doing this is to see whether we can resolve the impasse in our recent political history; namely, that there is no agreement on the way basic social institutions should be arranged if they are to conform to the freedom and equality of citizens as persons. Thus, from the start the conception of the person is regarded as part of a conception of political and social justice. That is, it characterizes how citizens are to think of themselves and of one another in their political and social relationships as specified by the basic structure. This conception is not to be mistaken for an ideal for personal life (for example, an ideal of friendship) or as an ideal for members of some association, much less as a moral ideal such as the Stoic ideal of a wise man.

The connection between the notion of social cooperation and the conception of the person which I shall introduce can be explained as follows. The notion of social cooperation is not simply that of coordinated social activity efficiently organized and guided by publicly recognized rules to achieve some overall end. Social cooperation is always for mutual benefit and this implies that it involves two elements: the first is a shared notion of fair terms of cooperation, which each participant may reasonably be expected to accept, provided that everyone else likewise accepts them. Fair terms of cooperation articulate an idea of reciprocity and mutuality: all who cooperate must benefit, or share in common burdens, in some appropriate fashion judged by a suitable benchmark of comparison. This element in social cooperation I call "the reasonable." The other element corresponds to "the rational": it refers to each participant's rational advantage; what, as individuals, the participants are trying to advance. Whereas the notion of fair terms of cooperation is

300

shared, participants' conceptions of their own rational advantage in general differ. The unity of social cooperation rests on persons agreeing to its notion of fair terms.

Now the appropriate notion of fair terms of cooperation depends on the nature of the cooperative activity itself: on its background social context, the aims and aspirations of the participants, how they regard themselves and one another as persons, and so on. What are fair terms for joint partnerships and for associations, or for small groups and teams, are not suitable for social cooperation. For in this case we start by viewing the basic structure of society as a whole as a form of cooperation. This structure comprises the main social institutions—the constitution, the economic regime, the legal order and its specification of property and the like, and how these institutions cohere into one system. What is distinctive about the basic structure is that it provides the framework for a self-sufficient scheme of cooperation for all the essential purposes of human life, which purposes are served by the variety of associations and groups within this framework. Since I suppose the society in question is closed, we are to imagine that there is no entry or exit except by birth and death; thus persons are born into society taken as a self-sufficient scheme of cooperation, and we are to conceive of persons as having the capacity to be normal and fully cooperating members of society over a complete life. It follows from these stipulations that while social cooperation can be willing and harmonious, and in this sense voluntary, it is not voluntary in the sense that our joining or belonging to associations and groups within society is voluntary. There is no alternative to social cooperation except unwilling and resentful compliance, or resistance and civil war.

Our focus, then, is on persons as capable of being normal and fully cooperating members of society over a complete life. The capacity for social cooperation is taken as fundamental, since the basic structure of society is adopted as the first subject of justice. The fair terms of social cooperation for this case specify the content of a political and social conception of justice. But if persons are viewed in this way, we are attributing to them two

301

powers of moral personality. These two powers are the capacity for a sense of right and justice (the capacity to honor fair terms of cooperation and thus to be reasonable), and the capacity for a conception of the good (and thus to be rational). In greater detail, the capacity for a sense of justice is the capacity to understand, to apply, and normally to be moved by an effective desire to act from (and not merely in accordance with) the principles of justice as the fair terms of social cooperation. The capacity for a conception of the good is the capacity to form, to revise, and rationally to pursue such a conception, that is, a conception of what we regard for us as a worthwhile human life. A conception of the good normally consists of a determinate scheme of final ends and aims, and of desires that certain persons and associations, as objects of attachments and loyalties, should flourish. Also included in such a conception is a view of our relation to the world—religious, philosophical, or moral—by reference to which these ends and attachments are understood.

The next step is to take the two moral powers as the necessary and sufficient condition for being counted a full and equal member of society in questions of political justice. Those who can take part in social cooperation over a complete life, and who are willing to honor the appropriate fair terms of cooperation, are regarded as equal citizens. Here we assume that the moral powers are realized to the requisite minimum degree and paired at any given time with a determinate conception of the good. Given these assumptions, variations and differences in natural gifts and abilities are subordinate: they do not affect persons' status as equal citizens and become relevant only as we aspire to certain offices and positions, or belong to or wish to join certain associations within society. Thus political justice concerns the basic structure as the encompassing institutional framework within which the natural gifts and abilities of individuals are developed and exercised, and the various associations in society exist.

So far I have said nothing about the content of fair terms of cooperation, or what concerns us here, about the basic liberties and their priority. To approach this question, let's sum up by saying: fair terms of social cooperation are terms upon which as equal persons we are willing to cooperate in good faith with all members of society over a complete life. To this let us add: to cooperate on a basis of mutual respect. Adding this clause makes explicit that fair terms of cooperation can be acknowledged by everyone without resentment or humiliation (or for that matter bad conscience) when citizens regard themselves and one another as having to the requisite degree the two moral powers which constitute the basis of equal citizenship. Against this background the problem of specifying the basic liberties and grounding their priority can be seen as the problem of determining appropriate fair terms of cooperation on the basis of mutual respect. Until the wars of religion in the sixteenth and seventeenth centuries these fair terms were narrowly drawn: social cooperation on the basis of mutual respect was regarded as impossible with those of a different faith; or (in terms I have used) with those who affirm a fundamentally different conception of the good. As a philosophical doctrine, liberalism has its origin in those centuries with the development of the various arguments for religious toleration.[18] In the nineteenth century the liberal doctrine was formulated in its main essentials by Constant, Tocqueville, and Mill for the context of the modern democratic state, which they saw to be imminent. A crucial assumption of liberalism is that equal citizens have different and indeed incommensurable and irreconcilable conceptions of the good.[19] In a modern democratic society the existence of such diverse ways of life is seen as a normal condition which can only be removed by

18. For an instructive survey of these arguments, see Allen, *A History of Political Thought in the Sixteenth Century*, pp. 73–103, 231–46, 302–31, 428–30; and also his *English Political Thought, 1603–1660* (London: Methuen, 1938), pp. 199–249. The views in Locke's *Letter on Toleration* (1689) or in Montesquieu's *The Spirit of Laws* (1748) have a long prehistory.

19. This assumption is central to liberalism as stated by Berlin in "Two Concepts of Liberty," pp. 167–71. I believe it is implicit in the writers cited but cannot go into the matter here. For a more recent statement, see Ronald Dworkin, "Liberalism," in *Public and Private Morality*, edited by Stuart Hampshire (Cambridge: Cambridge University Press, 1978).

the autocratic use of state power. Thus liberalism accepts the plurality of conceptions of the good as a fact of modern life, provided, of course, these conceptions respect the limits specified by the appropriate principles of justice. It tries to show both that a plurality of conceptions of the good is desirable and how a regime of liberty can accommodate this plurality so as to achieve the many benefits of human diversity.

My aim in this lecture is to sketch the connection between the basic liberties with their priority and the fair terms of social cooperation among equal persons as described above. The point of introducing the conception of the person I have used, and its companion conception of social cooperation, is to try to carry the liberal view one step further: that is, to root its assumptions in two underlying philosophical conceptions and then to indicate how the basic liberties with their priority can be regarded as belonging among the fair terms of social cooperation where the nature of this cooperation answers to the conditions these conceptions impose. The social union is no longer founded on a conception of the good as given by a common religious faith or philosophical doctrine, but on a shared public conception of justice appropriate to the conception of citizens in a democratic state as free and equal persons.

§ 4. The Original Position

In order to explain how this might be done I shall now summarize very briefly what I have said elsewhere about the role of what I have called "the original position" and the way in which it models the conception of the person.[20] The leading idea is that the original position connects the conception of the person and its companion conception of social cooperation with certain specific principles of justice. (These principles specify what I have earlier called "fair terms of social cooperation.") The connection

20. On the original position, see *Theory,* the entries in the index; for how this position models the conception of the person, see further "Kantian Constructivism in Moral Theory."

304

between these two philosophical conceptions and specific principles of justice is established by the original position as follows: the parties in this position are described as rationally autonomous representatives of citizens in society. As such representatives, the parties are to do the best they can for those they represent subject to the restrictions of the original position. For example, the parties are symmetrically situated with respect to one another and they are in that sense equal; and what I have called "the veil of ignorance" means that the parties do not know the social position, or the conception of the good (its particular aims and attachments), or the realized abilities and psychological propensities, and much else, of the persons they represent. And, as I have already remarked, the parties must agree to certain principles of justice on a short list of alternatives given by the tradition of moral and political philosophy. The agreement of the parties on certain definite principles establishes a connection between these principles and the conception of the person represented by the original position. In this way the content of fair terms of cooperation for persons so conceived is ascertained.

Two different parts of the original position must be carefully distinguished. These parts correspond to the two powers of moral personality, or to what I have called "the capacity to be reasonable" and "the capacity to be rational." While the original position as a whole represents both moral powers, and therefore represents the full conception of the person, the parties as rationally autonomous representatives of persons in society represent only the rational: the parties agree to those principles which they believe are best for those they represent as seen from these persons' conception of the good and their capacity to form, revise, and rationally to pursue such a conception, so far as the parties can know these things. The reasonable, or persons' capacity for a sense of justice, which here is their capacity to honor fair terms of social cooperation, is represented by the various restrictions to which the parties are subject in the original position and by the conditions imposed on their agreement. When the principles of justice which are adopted by the parties are affirmed and acted upon by equal citizens in society, citizens then act with full autonomy. The difference between full autonomy and rational autonomy is this: rational autonomy is acting solely from our capacity to be rational and from the determinate conception of the good we have at any given time. Full autonomy includes not only this capacity to be rational but also the capacity to advance our conception of the good in ways consistent with honoring the fair terms of social cooperation; that is, the principles of justice. In a well-ordered society in which citizens know they can count on each other's sense of justice, we may suppose that a person normally wants to act justly as well as to be recognized by others as someone who can be relied upon as a fully cooperating member of society over a complete life. Fully autonomous persons therefore publicly acknowledge and act upon the fair terms of social cooperation moved by the reasons specified by the shared principles of justice. The parties, however, are only rationally autonomous, since the constraints of the reasonable are simply imposed from without. Indeed, the rational autonomy of the parties is merely that of artificial agents who inhabit a construction designed to model the full conception of the person as both reasonable and rational. It is equal citizens in a well-ordered society who are fully autonomous because they freely accept the constraints of the reasonable, and in so doing their political life reflects that conception of the person which takes as fundamental their capacity for social cooperation. It is the full autonomy of active citizens which expresses the political ideal to be realized in the social world.[21]

Thus we can say that the parties in the original position are, as

21. I use the distinction between the two parts of the original position which correspond to the reasonable and the rational as a vivid way to state the idea that this position models the *full* conception of the person. I hope that this will prevent several misinterpretations of this position, for example, that it is intended to be morally neutral, or that it models only the notion of rationality, and therefore that justice as fairness attempts to select principles of justice purely on the basis of a conception of rational choice as understood in economics or decision theory. For a Kantian view, such an attempt is out of the question and is incompatible with its conception of the person.

rational representatives, rationally autonomous in two respects. First, in their deliberations they are not required to apply, or to be guided by, any prior or antecedent principles of right and justice. Second, in arriving at an agreement on which principles of justice to adopt from the alternatives available, the parties are to be guided solely by what they think is for the determinate good of the persons they represent, so far as the limits on information allow them to determine this. The agreement in the original position on the two principles of justice must be an agreement founded on rationally autonomous reasons in this sense. Thus, in effect, we are using the rationally autonomous deliberations of the parties to select from given alternatives the fair terms of cooperation between the persons they represent.

Much more would have to be said adequately to explain the preceding summary. But here I must turn to the considerations that move the parties in the original position. Of course, their overall aim is to fulfill their responsibility and to do the best they can to advance the determinate good of the persons they represent. The problem is that given the restrictions of the veil of ignorance, it may seem impossible for the parties to ascertain these persons' good and therefore to make a rational agreement on their behalf. To solve this problem we introduce the notion of primary goods and enumerate a list of various things which fall under this heading. The main idea is that primary goods are singled out by asking which things are generally necessary as social conditions and all-purpose means to enable persons to pursue their determinate conceptions of the good and to develop and exercise their two moral powers. Here we must look to social requirements and the normal circumstances of human life in a democratic society. That the primary goods are necessary conditions for realizing the moral powers and are all-purpose means for a sufficiently wide range of final ends presupposes various general facts about human wants and abilities, their characteristic phases and requirements of nurture, relations of social interdependence, and much else. We need at least a rough account of rational plans of life which shows why they normally have a certain structure and depend upon the primary goods for their formation, revision, and execution. What are to count as primary goods is not decided by asking what general means are essential for achieving the final ends which a comprehensive empirical or historical survey might show that people usually or normally have in common. There may be few if any such ends; and those there are may not serve the purposes of a conception of justice. The characterization of primary goods does not rest on such historical or social facts. While the determination of primary goods invokes a knowledge of the general circumstances and requirements of social life, it does so only in the light of a conception of the person given in advance.

The five kinds of primary goods enumerated in *Theory* (accompanied by an indication of why each is used) are the following:

a. The basic liberties (freedom of thought and liberty of conscience, and so on): these liberties are the background institutional conditions necessary for the development and the full and informed exercise of the two moral powers (particularly in what later, in §8, I shall call "the two fundamental cases"); these liberties are also indispensable for the protection of a wide range of determinate conceptions of the good (within the limits of justice).

b. Freedom of movement and free choice of occupation against a background of diverse opportunities: these opportunities allow the pursuit of diverse final ends and give effect to a decision to revise and change them, if we so desire.

c. Powers and prerogatives of offices and positions of responsibility: these give scope to various self-governing and social capacities of the self.

d. Income and wealth, understood broadly as all-purpose means (having an exchange value): income and wealth are needed to achieve directly or indirectly a wide range of ends, whatever they happen to be.

e. The social bases of self-respect: these bases are those

aspects of basic institutions normally essential if citizens are to have a lively sense of their own worth as persons and to be able to develop and exercise their moral powers and to advance their aims and ends with self-confidence.[22]

Observe that the two principles of justice assess the basic structure of society according to how its institutions protect and assign some of these primary goods, for example, the basic liberties, and regulate the production and distribution of other primary goods, for example, income and wealth. Thus, in general, what has to be explained is why the parties use this list of primary goods and why it is rational for them to adopt the two principles of justice.

In this lecture I cannot discuss this general question. Except for the basic liberties, I shall assume that the grounds for relying on primary goods are clear enough for our purposes. My aim in the following sections is to explain why, given the conception of the person which characterizes the citizens the parties represent, the basic liberties are indeed primary goods, and moreover why the principle which guarantees these liberties is to have priority over the second principle of justice. Sometimes the reason for this priority is evident from the explanation of why a liberty is basic, as in the case of equal liberty of conscience (discussed in §§5–6). In other cases the priority derives from the procedural role of certain liberties and their fundamental place in regulating the basic structure as a whole, as in the case of the equal political liberties (discussed in §8). Finally, certain basic liberties are indispensable institutional conditions once other basic liberties are guaranteed; thus freedom of thought and freedom of association are necessary to give effect to liberty of conscience and the political liberties. (This connection is sketched in the case of free political speech and the political liberties in §§10–12). My discussion is very brief and simply illustrates the kinds of grounds the parties have for counting certain liberties as basic. By consid-

---

22. For a fuller account of primary goods, see my "Social Unity and Primary Goods."

ering several different basic liberties, each grounded in a somewhat different way, I hope to explain the place of the basic liberties in justice as fairness and the reasons for their priority.

§ 5. Priority of Liberties, I: Second Moral Power

We are now ready to survey the grounds upon which the parties in the original position adopt principles which guarantee the basic liberties and assign them priority. I cannot here present the argument for such principles in a rigorous and convincing manner, but shall merely indicate how it might proceed.

Let us note first that given the conception of the person, there are three kinds of considerations the parties must distinguish when they deliberate concerning the good of the persons they represent. There are considerations relating to the development and the full and informed exercise of the two moral powers, each power giving rise to considerations of a distinct kind; and, finally, considerations relating to a person's determinate conception of the good. In this section I take up the considerations relating to the capacity for a conception of the good and to a person's determinate conception of the good. I begin with the latter. Recall that while the parties know that the persons they represent have determinate conceptions of the good, they do not know the content of these conceptions; that is, they do not know the particular final ends and aims these persons pursue, nor the objects of their attachments and loyalties, nor their view of their relation to the world—religious, philosophical, or moral—by reference to which these ends and loyalties are understood. However, the parties do know the general structure of rational persons' plans of life (given the general facts about human psychology and the workings of social institutions) and hence the main elements in a conception of the good as just enumerated. Knowledge of these matters goes with their understanding and use of primary goods as previously explained.

To fix ideas, I focus on liberty of conscience and survey the grounds the parties have for adopting principles which guarantee

310

this basic liberty as applied to religious, philosophical, and moral views of our relation to the world.[23] Of course, while the parties cannot be sure that the persons they represent affirm such views, I shall assume that these persons normally do so, and in any event the parties must allow for this possibility. I assume also that these religious, philosophical, and moral views are already formed and firmly held, and in this sense given. Now if but one of the alternative principles of justice available to the parties guarantees equal liberty of conscience, this principle is to be adopted. Or at least this holds if the conception of justice to which this principle belongs is a workable conception. For the veil of ignorance implies that the parties do not know whether the beliefs espoused by the persons they represent is a majority or a minority view. They cannot take chances by permitting a lesser liberty of conscience to minority religions, say, on the possibility that those they represent espouse a majority or dominant religion and will therefore have an even greater liberty. For it may also happen that these persons belong to a minority faith and may suffer accordingly. If the parties were to gamble in this way, they would show that they did not take the religious, philosophical, or moral convictions of persons seriously, and, in effect, did not know what a religious, philosophical, or moral conviction was.

Note that, strictly speaking, this first ground for liberty of conscience is not an argument. That is, one simply calls attention to the way in which the veil of ignorance combined with the parties' responsibility to protect some unknown but determinate and affirmed religious, philosophical, or moral view gives the parties the strongest reasons for securing this liberty. Here it is fundamental that affirming such views and the conceptions of the good to which they give rise is recognized as non-negotiable, so to speak. They are understood to be forms of belief and conduct the protection of which we cannot properly abandon or be per-

---

23. In this and the next two paragraphs I state in a somewhat different way the main consideration given for liberty of conscience in *Theory*, §33.

suaded to jeopardize for the kinds of considerations covered by the second principle of justice. To be sure, there are religious conversions, and persons change their philosophical and moral views. But presumptively these conversions and changes are not prompted by reasons of power and position, or of wealth and status, but are the result of conviction, reason, and reflection. Even if in practice this presumption is often false, this does not affect the responsibility of the parties to protect the integrity of the conception of the good of those they represent.

It is clear, then, why liberty of conscience is a basic liberty and possesses the priority of such a liberty. Given an understanding of what constitutes a religious, philosophical, or moral view, the kinds of considerations covered by the second principle of justice cannot be adduced to restrict the central range of this liberty. If someone denies that liberty of conscience is a basic liberty and maintains that all human interests are commensurable, and that between any two there always exists some rate of exchange in terms of which it is rational to balance the protection of one against the protection of the other, then we have reached an impasse. One way to continue the discussion is to try to show that the scheme of basic liberties as a family is part of a coherent and workable conception of justice appropriate for the basic structure of a democratic regime and, moreover, a conception that is congruent with its most essential convictions.

Let us now turn to considerations relating to the capacity for a conception of the good. This capacity was earlier defined as a capacity to form, to revise, and rationally to pursue a determinate conception of the good. Here there are two closely related grounds, since this capacity can be viewed in two ways. In the first way, the adequate development and exercise of this capacity, as circumstances require, is regarded as a means to a person's good; and as a means it is not (by definition) part of this person's determinate conception of the good. Persons exercise this power in rationally pursuing their final ends and in articulating their notions of a complete life. At any given moment this power serves the determinate conception of the good then affirmed; but the role of this power in forming other and more rational conceptions of the good and in revising existing ones must not be overlooked. There is no guarantee that all aspects of our present way of life are the most rational for us and not in need of at least minor if not major revision. For these reasons the adequate and full exercise of the capacity for a conception of the good is a means to a person's good. Thus, on the assumption that liberty of conscience, and therefore the liberty to fall into error and to make mistakes, is among the social conditions necessary for the development and exercise of this power, the parties have another ground for adopting principles that guarantee this basic liberty. Here we should observe that freedom of association is required to give effect to liberty of conscience; for unless we are at liberty to associate with other like-minded citizens, the exercise of liberty of conscience is denied. These two basic liberties go in tandem.

The second way of regarding the capacity for a conception of the good leads to a further ground for liberty of conscience. This ground rests on the broad scope and regulative nature of this capacity and the inherent principles that guide its operations (the principles of rational deliberation). These features of this capacity enable us to think of ourselves as affirming our way of life in accordance with the full, deliberate, and reasoned exercise of our intellectual and moral powers. And this rationally affirmed relation between our deliberative reason and our way of life itself becomes part of our determinate conception of the good. This possibility is contained in the conception of the person. Thus, in addition to our beliefs being true, our actions right, and our ends good, we may also strive to appreciate *why* our beliefs are true, our actions right, and our ends good and suitable for us. As Mill would say, we may seek to make our conception of the good "our own"; we are not content to accept it ready-made from our society or social peers.[24] Of course, the conception we affirm

24. See J. S. Mill, *On Liberty*, chap. 3, par. 5, where he says, "To a certain extent it is admitted, that our understanding should be our own; but there is not the same willingness to admit that our desires and impulses should be our own likewise; or that to possess impulses of our own, and of any strength, is anything but a peril and a snare." See the whole of pars. 2–9 on the free development of individuality.

need not be peculiar to us, or a conception we have, as it were, fashioned for ourselves; rather, we may affirm a religious, philosophical, or moral tradition in which we have been raised and educated, and which we find, at the age of reason, to be a center of our attachments and loyalties. In this case what we affirm is a tradition that incorporates ideals and virtues which meet the tests of our reason and which answer to our deepest desires and affections. Of course, many persons may not examine their acquired beliefs and ends but take them on faith, or be satisfied that they are matters of custom and tradition. They are not to be criticized for this, for in the liberal view there is no political or social evaluation of conceptions of the good within the limits permitted by justice.

In this way of regarding the capacity for a conception of the good, this capacity is not a means to but is an essential part of a determinate conception of the good. The distinctive place in justice as fairness of this conception is that it enables us to view our final aims and loyalties in a way that realizes to the full extent one of the moral powers in terms of which persons are characterized in this political conception of justice. For this conception of the good to be possible we must be allowed, even more plainly than in the case of the preceding ground, to fall into error and to make mistakes within the limits established by the basic liberties. In order to guarantee the possibility of this conception of the good, the parties, as our representatives, adopt principles which protect liberty of conscience.

The preceding three grounds for liberty of conscience are related as follows. In the first, conceptions of the good are regarded as given and firmly rooted; and since there is a plurality of such conceptions, each, as it were, non-negotiable, the parties recognize that behind the veil of ignorance the principles of justice which guarantee equal liberty of conscience are the only principles which they can adopt. In the next two grounds, conceptions of the good are seen as subject to revision in accordance with deliberative reason, which is part of the capacity for a conception of the good. But since the full and informed exercise

314

of this capacity requires the social conditions secured by liberty of conscience, these grounds support the same conclusion as the first.

§ 6. Priority of Liberties, II: First Moral Power

Finally we come to the considerations relating to the capacity for a sense of justice. Here we must be careful. The parties in the original position are rationally autonomous representatives and as such are moved solely by considerations relating to what furthers the determinate conceptions of the good of the persons they represent, either as a means or as a part of these conceptions. Thus, any grounds that prompt the parties to adopt principles that secure the development and exercise of the capacity for a sense of justice must accord with this restriction. Now we saw in the preceding section that the capacity for a conception of the good can be part of, as well as a means to, someone's determinate conception of the good, and that the parties can invoke reasons based on each of these two cases without violating their rationally autonomous role. The situation is different with the sense of justice: for here the parties cannot invoke reasons founded on regarding the development and exercise of this capacity as part of a person's determinate conception of the good. They are restricted to reasons founded on regarding it solely as a means to a person's good.

To be sure, we assume (as do the parties) that citizens have the capacity for a sense of justice, but this assumption is purely formal. It means only that whatever principles the parties select from the alternatives available, the persons the parties represent will be able to develop, as citizens in society, the corresponding sense of justice to the degree to which the parties' deliberations, informed by commonsense knowledge and the theory of human nature, show to be possible and practicable. This assumption is consistent with the parties' rational autonomy and the stipulation that no antecedent notions or principles of justice are to guide (much less constrain) the parties' reasoning as to which alternative to select. In view of this assumption, the parties know that their agreement is not in vain and that citizens in society will act upon the principles agreed to with an effectiveness and regularity of which human nature is capable when political and social institutions satisfy, and are publicly known to satisfy, these principles. But when the parties count, as a consideration in favor of certain principles of justice, the fact that citizens in society will effectively and regularly act upon them, the parties can do so only because they believe that acting from such principles will serve as effective means to the determinate conceptions of the good of the persons they represent. These persons as citizens are moved by reasons of justice as such, but the parties as rational autonomous representatives are not.

With these precautions stated, I now sketch three grounds, each related to the capacity for a sense of justice, that prompt the parties to adopt principles securing the basic liberties and assign them priority. The first ground rests on two points: first, on the great advantage to everyone's conception of the good of a just and stable scheme of cooperation; and second, on the thesis that the most stable conception of justice is the one specified by the two principles of justice, and this is the case importantly because of the basic liberties and the priority assigned to them by these principles.

Clearly, the public knowledge that everyone has an effective sense of justice and can be relied upon as a fully cooperating member of society is a great advantage to everyone's conception of the good.[25] This public knowledge, and the shared sense of justice which is its object, is the result of time and cultivation, easier to destroy than to build up. The parties assess the traditional alternatives in accordance with how well they generate a publicly recognized sense of justice when the basic structure is known to satisfy the corresponding principles. In doing this they view the developed capacity for a sense of justice as a means to

25. Here I restate the reasoning for the greater stability of justice as fairness found in *Theory*, §76.

the good of those they represent. That is, a scheme of just social cooperation advances citizens' determinate conceptions of the good; and a scheme made stable by an effective public sense of justice is a better means to this end than a scheme which requires a severe and costly apparatus of penal sanctions, particularly when this apparatus is dangerous to the basic liberties.

The comparative stability of the traditional principles of justice available to the parties is a complicated matter. I cannot summarize here the many considerations I have examined elsewhere to support the second point, the thesis that the two principles of justice are the most stable. I shall only mention one leading idea: namely, that the most stable conception of justice is one that is clear and perspicuous to our reason, congruent with and unconditionally concerned with our good, and rooted not in abnegation but in affirmation of our person.[26] The conclusion argued for is that the two principles of justice answer better to these conditions than the other alternatives precisely because of the basic liberties taken in conjunction with the fair value of the political liberties (discussed in the next section) and the difference principle. For example, that the two principles of justice are unconditionally concerned with everyone's good is shown by the equality of the basic liberties and their priority, as well as by the fair value of the political liberties. Again, these principles are clear and perspicuous to our reason because they are to be public and mutually recognized, and they enjoin the basic liberties directly—on their face, as it were.[27] These liberties do not depend upon conjectural calculations concerning the greatest net balance of social interests (or of social values). In justice as fairness such calculations have no place. Observe that this argument for the first ground conforms to the precautions stated in the opening paragraphs of this section. For the parties in adopting the principles of justice which most effectively secure the development

26. See ibid., pp. 498f.
27. In saying that the principles of justice enjoin the basic liberties directly and on their face, I have in mind the various considerations mentioned in ibid. in connection with what I called "embedding"; see pp. 160f., 261–63, 288–89, and 326–27.

and exercise of the sense of justice are moved not from the desire to realize this moral power for its own sake, but rather view it as the best way to stabilize just social cooperation and thereby to advance the determinate conceptions of the good of the persons they represent.

The second ground, not unrelated to the first, proceeds from the fundamental importance of self-respect.[28] It is argued that self-respect is most effectively encouraged and supported by the two principles of justice, again precisely because of the insistence on the equal basic liberties and the priority assigned them, although self-respect is further strengthened and supported by the fair value of the political liberties and the difference principle.[29] That self-respect is also confirmed by other features of the two principles besides the basic liberties only means that no single feature works alone. But this is to be expected. Provided the basic liberties play an important role in supporting self-respect, the parties have grounds founded on these liberties for adopting the two principles of justice.

Very briefly, the argument is this. Self-respect is rooted in our self-confidence as a fully cooperating member of society capable of pursuing a worthwhile conception of the good over a complete life. Thus self-respect presupposes the development and exercise of both moral powers and therefore an effective sense of justice. The importance of self-respect is that it provides a secure sense of our own value, a firm conviction that our determinate conception of the good is worth carrying out. Without self-respect nothing may seem worth doing, and if some things have value for us, we lack the will to pursue them. Thus, the parties give great weight to how well principles of justice support self-re-

28. Self-respect is discussed in *Theory*, §67. For its role in the argument for the two principles of justice, see pp. 178–83. For the equal political liberties as a basis of self-respect, see pp. 234, 544–46.

29. The fair value of the political liberties is discussed in ibid., pp. 224–28, 233–34, 277–79, and 356. In the discussion of the equal political liberties as a basis of self-respect on pp. 544–46, the fair value of these liberties is not mentioned. It should have been. See also §§7 and 12 below.

spect, otherwise these principles cannot effectively advance the determinate conceptions of the good of those the parties represent. Given this characterization of self-respect, we argue that self-respect depends upon and is encouraged by certain public features of basic social institutions, how they work together and how people who accept these arrangements are expected to (and normally do) regard and treat one another. These features of basic institutions and publicly expected (and normally honored) ways of conduct are the social bases of self-respect (listed earlier in §4 as the last kind of primary goods).

It is clear from the above characterization of self-respect that these social bases are among the most essential primary goods. Now these bases are importantly determined by the public principles of justice. Since only the two principles of justice guarantee the basic liberties, they are more effective than the other alternatives in encouraging and supporting the self-respect of citizens as equal persons. It is the content of these principles as public principles for the basic structure which has this result. This content has two aspects, each paired with one of the two elements of self-respect. Recall that the first element is our self-confidence as a fully cooperating member of society rooted in the development and exercise of the two moral powers (and so as possessing an effective sense of justice); the second element is our secure sense of our own value rooted in the conviction that we can carry out a worthwhile plan of life. The first element is supported by the basic liberties which guarantee the full and informed exercise of both moral powers. The second element is supported by the public nature of this guarantee and the affirmation of it by citizens generally, all in conjunction with the fair value of the political liberties and the difference principle. For our sense of our own value, as well as our self-confidence, depends on the respect and mutuality shown us by others. By publicly affirming the basic liberties citizens in a well-ordered society express their mutual respect for one another as reasonable and trustworthy, as well as their recognition of the worth all citizens attach to their way of life. Thus the basic liberties enable the two principles of justice to meet more effectively than the other alternatives the requirements for self-respect. Once again, note that at no point in the parties' reasoning are they concerned with the development and exercise of the sense of justice for its own sake; although, of course, this is not true of fully autonomous citizens in a well-ordered society.

The third and last ground relating to the sense of justice I can only indicate here. It is based on that conception of a well-ordered society I have called "a social union of social unions."[30] The idea is that a democratic society well-ordered by the two principles of justice can be for each citizen a far more comprehensive good than the determinate good of individuals when left to their own devices or limited to smaller associations. Participation in this more comprehensive good can greatly enlarge and sustain each person's determinate good. The good of social union is most completely realized when everyone participates in this good, but only some may do so and perhaps only a few.

The idea derives from von Humboldt. He says:

> Every human being . . . can act with only one dominant faculty at a time: or rather, one whole nature disposes us at any given time to some single form of spontaneous activity. It would, therefore, seem to follow that man is inevitably destined to a partial cultivation, since he only enfeebles his energies by directing them to a multiplicity of objects. But man has it in his power to avoid one-sidedness, by attempting to unite distinct and generally separately exercised faculties of his nature, by bringing into spontaneous cooperation, at each period of his life, the dying sparks of one activity, and those which the future will kindle, and endeavoring to increase and diversify the powers with which he works, by harmoniously combining them instead of looking for mere variety of objects for their separate exercise. What is achieved in the case of the individual, by the union of past and future with the present, is produced in society by the mutual cooperation of its different

30. This notion is discussed in *Theory*, §79. There I didn't connect it with the basic liberties and their priority as I attempt to do here.

members; for in all stages of his life, each individual can achieve only one of those perfections, which represent the possible features of human character. It is through social union, therefore, based on the internal wants and capabilities of its members, that each is enabled to participate in the rich collective resources of all the others.[31]

To illustrate the idea of social union, consider a group of gifted musicians, all of whom have the same natural talents and who could, therefore, have learned to play equally well every instrument in the orchestra. By long training and practice they have become highly proficient on their adopted instrument, recognizing that human limitations require this; they can never be sufficiently skilled on many instruments, much less play them all at once. Thus, in this special case in which everyone's natural talents are identical, the group achieves, by a coordination of activities among peers, the same totality of capacities latent in each. But even when these natural musical gifts are not equal and differ from person to person, a similar result can be achieved provided these gifts are suitably complementary and properly coordinated. In each case, persons need one another, since it is only in active cooperation with others that any one's talents can be realized, and then in large part by the efforts of all. Only in the activities of social union can the individual be complete.

In this illustration the orchestra is a social union. But there are as many kinds of social unions as there are kinds of human activities which satisfy the requisite conditions. Moreover, the basic structure of society provides a framework within which each of these activities may be carried out. Thus we arrive at the idea of society as a social union of social unions once these diverse kinds of human activities are made suitably complementary and can be properly coordinated. What makes a social union of social unions possible is three aspects of our social nature. The

31. This passage is quoted in ibid., pp. 523–24n. It is from *The Limits of State Action*, edited by J. W. Burrow (Cambridge: Cambridge University Press, 1969), pp. 16–17.

first aspect is the complementarity between various human talents which makes possible the many kinds of human activities and their various forms of organization. The second aspect is that what we might be and do far surpasses what we can do and be in any one life, and therefore we depend on the cooperative endeavors of others, not only for the material means of well-being, but also to bring to fruition what we might have been and done. The third aspect is our capacity for an effective sense of justice which can take as its content principles of justice which include an appropriate notion of reciprocity. When such principles are realized in social institutions and honored by all citizens, and this is publicly recognized, the activities of the many social unions are coordinated and combined into a social union of social unions.

The question is: which principles available to the parties in the original position are the most effective in coordinating and combining the many social unions into one social union? Here there are two desiderata: first, these principles must be recognizably connected with the conception of citizens as free and equal persons, which conception should be implicit in the content of these principles and conveyed on their face, as it were. Second, these principles, as principles for the basic structure of society, must contain a notion of reciprocity appropriate to citizens as free and equal persons engaged in social cooperation over a complete life. If these desiderata are not satisfied, we cannot regard the richness and diversity of society's public culture as the result of everyone's cooperative efforts for mutual good; nor can we appreciate this culture as something to which we can contribute and in which we can participate. For this public culture is always in large part the work of others; and therefore to support these attitudes of regard and appreciation citizens must affirm a notion of reciprocity appropriate to their conception of themselves and be able to recognize their shared public purpose and common allegiance. These attitudes are best secured by the two principles of justice precisely because of the recognized public purpose of giving justice to each citizen as a free and equal person on a basis of mutual respect. This purpose is manifest in the public affirmation of the equal basic liberties in the setting of the two principles of justice. The ties of reciprocity are extended over the whole of society and individual and group accomplishments are no longer seen as so many separate personal or associational goods.

Finally, observe that in this explanation of the good of social union, the parties in the original position need have no specific knowledge of the determinate conception of the good of the persons they represent. For whatever these persons' conceptions of the good are, their conceptions will be enlarged and sustained by the more comprehensive good of social union provided that their determinate conceptions lie within a certain wide range and are compatible with the principles of justice. Thus this third ground is open to the parties in the original position, since it meets the restrictions imposed on their reasoning. To advance the determinate good of those they represent, the parties adopt principles which secure the basic liberties. This is the best way to establish the comprehensive good of social union and the effective sense of justice which makes it possible. I note in passing that the notion of society as a social union of social unions shows how it is possible for a regime of liberty not only to accommodate a plurality of conceptions of the good but also to coordinate the various activities made possible by human diversity into a more comprehensive good to which everyone can contribute and in which each can participate. Observe that this more comprehensive good cannot be specified by a conception of the good alone but also needs a particular conception of justice, namely, justice as fairness. Thus this more comprehensive good presupposes this conception of justice and it can be attained provided the already given determinate conceptions of the good satisfy the general conditions stated above. On the assumption that it is rational for the parties to suppose these conditions fulfilled, they can regard this more comprehensive good as enlarging the good of the persons they represent, whatever the determinate conceptions of the good of these persons may be.

This completes the survey of the grounds upon which the

parties in the original position adopt the two principles of justice which guarantee the equal basic liberties and assign them priority as a family. I have not attempted to cover all the grounds that might be cited, nor have I tried to assess the relative weights of those I have discussed. My aim has been to survey the most important grounds. No doubt the grounds connected with the capacity for a conception of the good are more familiar, perhaps because they seem more straightforward and, offhand, of greater weight; but I believe that the grounds connected with the capacity for a sense of justice are also important. Throughout I have had occasion to emphasize that the parties, in order to advance the determinate conceptions of the good of the persons they represent, are led to adopt principles that encourage the development and allow for the full and informed exercise of the two moral powers. Before discussing how the basic liberties are to be specified and adjusted at later stages (that is, before discussing what I earlier called "the second gap"), I must consider an important feature of the first principle of justice which I have referred to several times, namely, the fair value of the political liberties. Considering this feature will bring out how the grounds for the basic liberties and their priority depend on the content of the two principles of justice as an interrelated family of requirements.

§ 7. Basic Liberties not Merely Formal

We can summarize the preceding sections as follows: given first, that the procedure of the original position situates the parties symmetrically and subjects them to constraints that express the reasonable, and second, that the parties are rationally autonomous representatives whose deliberations express the rational, each citizen is fairly represented in the procedure by which the principles of justice to regulate the basic structure of society are selected. The parties are to decide between the alternative principles moved by considerations derived solely from the good of the persons they represent. For the reasons we have just surveyed, the parties favor principles which protect a wide range of determinate (but unknown) conceptions of the good and which best secure the political and social conditions necessary for the adequate development and the full and informed exercise of the two moral powers. On the assumption that the basic liberties and their priority secure these conditions (under reasonably favorable circumstances), the two principles of justice, with the first principle prior to the second, are the principles agreed to. This achieves what I earlier called "the initial aim" of justice as fairness. But to this it will rightly be objected that I have not considered the provisions made for the material means required for persons to advance their good. Whether principles for the basic liberties and their priority are acceptable depends upon the complementing of such principles by others that provide a fair share of these means.

The question at hand is this: how does justice as fairness meet the long-standing problem that the basic liberties may prove to be merely formal, so to speak?[32] Many have argued, particularly radical democrats and socialists, that while it may appear that citizens are effectively equal, the social and economic inequalities likely to arise if the basic structure includes the basic liberties and fair equality of opportunity are too large. Those with greater responsibility and wealth can control the course of legislation to their advantage. To answer this question, let us distinguish between the basic liberties and the worth of these liberties as follows:[33] the basic liberties are specified by institutional rights and duties that entitle citizens to do various things, if they wish, and that forbid others to interfere. The basic liberties are a framework of legally protected paths and opportunities. Of course, ignorance and poverty, and the lack of material means generally, prevent people from exercising their rights and from taking ad-

32. I am indebted to Norman Daniels for raising the question I try to resolve in this section. See his "Equal Liberty and Unequal Worth of Liberty," in Daniels, pp. 253–81. I am grateful to Joshua Rabinowitz for extensive comments and discussion.

33. The rest of this paragraph and the next elaborate the paragraph which begins on p. 204 of *Theory*.

vantage of these openings. But rather than counting these and similar obstacles as restricting a person's liberty, we count them as affecting the worth of liberty, that is, the usefulness to persons of their liberties. Now in justice as fairness, this usefulness is specified in terms of an index of the primary goods regulated by the second principle of justice. It is not specified by a person's level of well-being (or by a utility function) but by these primary goods, claims to which are treated as claims to special needs defined for the purposes of a political conception of justice. Some primary goods such as income and wealth are understood as all-purpose material means for citizens to advance their ends within the framework of the equal liberties and fair equality of opportunity.

In justice as fairness, then, the equal basic liberties are the same for each citizen and the question of how to compensate for a lesser liberty does not arise. But the worth, or usefulness, of liberty is not the same for everyone. As the difference principle permits, some citizens have, for example, greater income and wealth and therefore greater means of achieving their ends. When this principle is satisfied, however, this lesser worth of liberty is compensated for in this sense: the all-purpose means available to the least advantaged members of society to achieve their ends would be even less were social and economic inequalities, as measured by the index of primary goods, different from what they are. The basic structure of society is arranged so that it maximizes the primary goods available to the least advantaged to make use of the equal basic liberties enjoyed by everyone. This defines one of the central aims of political and social justice.

This distinction between liberty and the worth of liberty is, of course, merely a definition and settles no substantive question.[34] The idea is to combine the equal basic liberties with a principle for regulating certain primary goods viewed as all-purpose means for advancing our ends. This definition is a first step in combining

34. The paragraph which begins on p. 204 of *Theory* can unfortunately be read so as to give the contrary impression.

liberty and equality into one coherent notion. The appropriateness of this combination is decided by whether it yields a workable conception of justice which fits, on due reflection, our considered convictions. But to achieve this fit with our considered convictions, we must take an important further step and treat the equal political liberties in a special way. This is done by including in the first principle of justice the guarantee that the political liberties, and only these liberties, are secured by what I have called their "fair value."[35]

To explain: this guarantee means that the worth of the political liberties to all citizens, whatever their social or economic position, must be approximately equal, or at least sufficiently equal, in the sense that everyone has a fair opportunity to hold public office and to influence the outcome of political decisions. This notion of fair opportunity parallels that of fair equality of opportunity in the second principle of justice.[36] When the parties in the original position adopt the priority of liberty, they understand that the equal political liberties are treated in this special way. When we judge the appropriateness of this combination of liberty and equality into one notion, we must keep in mind the distinctive place of the political liberties in the two principles of justice.

It is beyond the scope of a philosophical doctrine to consider in any detail the kinds of arrangements required to insure the fair value of the equal political liberties, just as it is beyond its scope to consider the laws and regulations required to ensure competition in a market economy. Nevertheless, we must recognize that the problem of guaranteeing the fair value of the political liberties is of equal if not greater importance than making sure that markets are workably competitive. For unless the fair value of these liberties is approximately preserved, just back-

35. While the idea of the fair value of the equal political liberties is an important aspect of the two principles of justice as presented in *Theory*, this idea was not sufficiently developed or explained. It was, therefore, easy to miss its significance. The relevant references are given in n. 29 above.

36. For fair equality of opportunity in ibid., see pp. 72–74 and §14.

ground institutions are unlikely to be either established or maintained. How best to proceed is a complex and difficult matter; and at present the requisite historical experience and theoretical understanding may be lacking, so that we must advance by trial and error. But one guideline for guaranteeing fair value seems to be to keep political parties independent of large concentrations of private economic and social power in a private-property democracy, and of government control and bureaucratic power in a liberal socialist regime. In either case, society must bear at least a large part of the cost of organizing and carrying out the political process and must regulate the conduct of elections. The guarantee of fair value for the political liberties is one way in which justice as fairness tries to meet the objection that the basic liberties are merely formal.

Now this guarantee of the fair value of the political liberties has several noteworthy features. First, it secures for each citizen a fair and roughly equal access to the use of a public facility designed to serve a definite political purpose, namely, the public facility specified by the constitutional rules and procedures which govern the political process and control the entry to positions of political authority. As we shall discuss later (in §9), these rules and procedures are to be a fair process, designed to yield just and effective legislation. The point to note is that the valid claims of equal citizens are held within certain standard limits by the notion of a fair and equal access to the political process as a public facility. Second, this public facility has limited space, so to speak. Hence, those with relatively greater means can combine together and exclude those who have less in the absence of the guarantee of fair value of the political liberties. We cannot be sure that the inequalities permitted by the difference principle will be sufficiently small to prevent this. Certainly, in the absence of the second principle of justice, the outcome is a foregone conclusion; for the limited space of the political process has the consequence that the usefulness of our political liberties is far more subject to our social position and our place in the distribution of income and wealth than the usefulness of our other basic liberties. When we also consider the distinctive role of the political process in determining the laws and policies to regulate the basic structure, it is not implausible that these liberties alone should receive the special guarantee of fair value. This guarantee is a natural focal point between merely formal liberty on the one side and some kind of wider guarantee for all basic liberties on the other.

The mention of this natural focal point raises the question of why a wider guarantee is not included in the first principle of justice. While there is a problem as to what a wider guarantee of fair value would mean, the answer to this question is, I believe, that such a guarantee is either irrational or superfluous or socially divisive. Thus, let us first understand it as enjoining the equal distribution of all primary goods and not only the basic liberties. This principle I assume to be rejected as irrational, since it does not permit society to meet certain essential requirements of social organization, and to take advantage of considerations of efficiency, and much else. Second, this wider guarantee can be understood to require that a certain fixed bundle of primary goods is to be secured to each citizen as a way publicly to represent the ideal of establishing the equal worth of everyone's liberties. Whatever the merits of this suggestion, it is superfluous in view of the difference principle. For any fraction of the index of primary goods enjoyed by the least advantaged can already be regarded in this manner. Third and last, this guarantee can be understood as requiring the distribution of primary goods according to the content of certain interests regarded as especially central, for example, the religious interest. Thus, some persons may count among their religious obligations going on pilgrimages to distant places or building magnificent cathedrals or temples. To guarantee the equal worth of religious liberty is now understood to require that such persons receive special provision to enable them to meet these obligations. On this view, then, their religious needs, as it were, are greater for the purposes of political justice, whereas those whose religious beliefs oblige them to make but modest demands on material means do not receive such provision; their religious needs are much less. Plainly, this kind of guarantee is socially divisive, a receipt for religious controversy if not civil strife. Similar consequences result, I believe, whenever the public conception of justice adjusts citizens' claims to social resources so that some receive more than others depending on the determinate final ends and loyalties belonging to their conceptions of the good. Thus, the principle of proportionate satisfaction is likewise socially divisive. This is the principle to distribute the primary goods regulated by the difference principle so that the fraction K (where $0 < K \leq 1$), which measures the degree to which a citizen's conception of the good is realized, is the same for everyone, and ideally maximized. Since I have discussed this principle elsewhere, I shall not do so here.[37] It suffices to say that one main reason for using an index of primary goods in assessing the strength of citizens' claims in questions of political justice is precisely to eliminate the socially divisive and irreconcilable conflicts which such principles would arouse.[38]

Finally, we should be clear why the equal political liberties are treated in a special way as expressed by the guarantee of their fair value. It is not because political life and the participation by everyone in democratic self-government is regarded as the preeminent good for fully autonomous citizens. To the contrary, assigning a central place to political life is but one conception of the good among others. Given the size of a modern state, the exercise of the political liberties is bound to have a lesser place in the conception of the good of most citizens than the exercise of the other basic liberties. The guarantee of fair value for the political liberties is included in the first principle of justice because it is essential in order to establish just legislation and also to make sure that the fair political process specified by the constitution is open to everyone on a basis of rough equality. The idea is to incorporate into the basic structure of society an effective political procedure which mirrors in that structure the fair representation of persons achieved by the original position. It is the fairness of this procedure, secured by the guarantee of the

37. See "Fairness to Goodness," *Philosophical Review* 84 (October 1975):551–53.
38. See further "Social Unity and Primary Goods," §§4–5.

fair value of the political liberties, together with the second principle of justice (with the difference principle), which provides the answer as to why the basic liberties are not merely formal.

§ 8. A Fully Adequate Scheme of Basic Liberties

I now turn to how the second gap may be filled. Recall that this gap arises because once we have a number of liberties which must be further specified and adjusted to one another at later stages, we need a criterion for how this is to be done. We are to establish the best, or at least a fully adequate, scheme of basic liberties, given the circumstances of society. Now, in *Theory* one criterion suggested seems to be that the basic liberties are to be specified and adjusted so as to achieve the most extensive scheme of these liberties. This criterion is purely quantitative and does not distinguish some cases as more significant than others; moreover, it does not generally apply and is not consistently followed. As Hart noted, it is only in the simplest and least significant cases that the criterion of greatest extent is both applicable and satisfactory.[39] A second proposed criterion in *Theory* is that in the ideal procedure of applying the principles of justice, we are to take up the point of view of the representative equal citizen and to adjust the scheme of liberties in the light of this citizen's rational interests as seen from the point of view of the appropriate later stage. But Hart thought that the content of these interests was not described clearly enough for the knowledge of their content to serve as a criterion.[40] In any case, the two criteria seem to conflict, and the best scheme of liberties is not said to be the most extensive.[41]

39. See Hart, pp. 542–43; Daniels, pp. 239–40.
40. Hart pp. 543–47; Daniels, pp. 240–44.
41. See *Theory*, p. 250, where I have said in the statement of the priority rule that "a less extensive liberty must strengthen the total system of liberty shared by all." Here the "system of liberty" refers to the "system of equal basic liberties," as found in the statement of the first principle on the same page.

I must clear up this ambiguity concerning the criterion. Now it is tempting to think that the desired criterion should enable us to specify and adjust the basic liberties in the best, or the optimum, way. And this suggests in turn that there is something that the scheme of basic liberties is to maximize. Otherwise, how could the best scheme be identified? But in fact, it is implicit in the preceding account of how the first gap is filled that the scheme of basic liberties is not drawn up so as to maximize anything, and, in particular, not the development and exercise of the moral powers.[42] Rather, these liberties and their priority are to guarantee equally for all citizens the social conditions essential for the adequate development and the full and informed exercise of these powers in what I shall call "the two fundamental cases."

The first of these cases is connected with the capacity for a sense of justice and concerns the application of the principles of justice to the basic structure of society and its social policies. The political liberties and freedom of thought are discussed later under this heading. The second fundamental case is connected with the capacity for a conception of the good and concerns the application of the principles of deliberative reason in guiding our conduct over a complete life. Liberty of conscience and freedom of association come in here. What distinguishes the fundamental cases is the comprehensive scope and basic character of the subject to which the principles of justice and of deliberative reason must be applied. The notion of a fundamental case en-

42. I take it as obvious that acting from the best reasons, or from the balance of reasons as defined by a moral conception, is not, in general, to maximize anything. Whether something is maximized depends on the nature of the moral conception. Thus, neither the pluralistic intuitionism of W. D. Ross as found in *The Right and the Good* (Oxford: Clarendon Press, 1930), nor the liberalism of Isaiah Berlin as found in *Four Essays on Liberty,* specifies something to be maximized. Neither for that matter does the economists' utility function specify anything to be maximized, in most cases. A utility function is simply a mathematical representation of households' or economic agents' preferences, assuming these preferences to satisfy certain conditions. From a purely formal point of view, there is nothing to prevent an agent who is a pluralistic intuitionist from having a utility function. (Of course, it is well known that an agent with a lexicographical preference-ordering does not have a utility function.)

ables us later to define a notion of the significance of a liberty, which helps us to outline how the second gap is to be filled.[43]

The upshot will be that the criterion at later stages is to specify and adjust the basic liberties so as to allow the adequate development and the full and informed exercise of both moral powers in the social circumstances under which the two fundamental cases arise in the well-ordered society in question. Such a scheme of liberties I shall call "a fully adequate scheme." This criterion coheres with that of adjusting the scheme of liberties in accordance with the rational interests of the representative equal citizen, the second criterion mentioned earlier. For it is clear from the grounds on which the parties in the original position adopt the two principles of justice that these interests, as seen from the appropriate stage, are best served by a fully adequate scheme. Thus the second gap is filled by carrying through the way the first gap is filled.

Now there are two reasons why the idea of a maximum does not apply to specifying and adjusting the scheme of basic liberties. First, a coherent notion of what is to be maximized is lacking. We cannot maximize the development and exercise of two moral powers at once. And how could we maximize the development and exercise of either power by itself? Do we maximize, other things equal, the number of deliberate affirmations of a conception of the good? That would be absurd. Moreover, we have no notion of a maximum development of these powers. What we do have is a conception of a well-ordered society with certain general features and certain basic institutions. Given this conception, we form the notion of the development and exercise of these powers which is adequate and full relative to the two fundamental cases.

The other reason why the idea of a maximum does not apply is that the two moral powers do not exhaust the person, for persons also have a determinate conception of the good. Recall

43. For clarification of the notion of a fundamental case I am indebted to Susan Wolf.

that such a conception includes an ordering of certain final ends and interest, attachments and loyalties to persons and associations, as well as a view of the world in the light of which these ends and attachments are understood. If citizens had no determinate conceptions of the good which they sought to realize, the just social institutions of a well-ordered society would have no point. Of course, grounds for developing and exercising the moral powers strongly incline the parties in the original position to adopt the basic liberties and their priority. But the great weight of these grounds from the standpoint of the parties does not imply that the exercise of the moral powers on the part of the citizens in society is either the supreme or the sole form of good. Rather, the role and exercise of these powers (in the appropriate instances) is a condition of good. That is, citizens are to act justly and rationally, as circumstances require. In particular, their just and honorable (and fully autonomous) conduct renders them, as Kant would say, worthy of happiness; it makes their accomplishments wholly admirable and their pleasures completely good.[44] But it would be madness to maximize just and rational actions by maximizing the occasions which require them.

§ 9. How Liberties Fit into One Coherent Scheme

Since the notion of a fully adequate scheme of basic liberties has been introduced, I can outline how the scheme of basic liberties is specified and adjusted at later stages. I begin by arranging the basic liberties so as to show their relation to the two moral powers and to the two fundamental cases in which these powers are exercised. The equal political liberties and freedom of thought are to secure the free and informed application of the principles of justice, by means of the full and effective exercise of citizens' sense of justice, to the basic structure of

44. It is a central theme of Kant's doctrine that moral philosophy is not the study of how to be happy but of how to be worthy of happiness. This theme is found in all his major works beginning with the *First Critique;* see A806, B834.

society. (The political liberties, assured their fair value and other relevant general principles, properly circumscribed, may of course supplement the principles of justice.) These basic liberties require some form of representative democratic regime and the requisite protections for the freedom of political speech and press, freedom of assembly, and the like. Liberty of conscience and freedom of association are to secure the full and informed and effective application of citizens' powers of deliberative reason to their forming, revising, and rationally pursuing a conception of the good over a complete life. The remaining (and supporting) basic liberties—the liberty and integrity of the person (violated, for example, by slavery and serfdom, and by the denial of freedom of movement and occupation) and the rights and liberties covered by the rule of law—can be connected to the two fundamental cases by noting that they are necessary if the preceding basic liberties are to be properly guaranteed. Altogether the possession of these basic liberties specifies the common and guaranteed status of equal citizens in a well-ordered democratic society.[45]

Given this arrangement of the basic liberties, the notion of the *significance* of a particular liberty, which we need to fill the second gap, can be explained in this way: a liberty is more or less significant depending on whether it is more or less essentially involved in, or is a more or less necessary institutional means to protect, the full and informed and effective exercise of the moral powers in one (or both) of the two fundamental cases. Thus, the

---

45. The arrangement in this paragraph is designed to emphasize the role of the two fundamental cases and to connect these cases with the two moral powers. Thus this arrangement belongs to a particular conception of justice. Other arrangements may be equally useful for other purposes. Vincent Blasi, in his instructive essay "The Checking Value in FIrst Amendment Theory," *Weaver Constitutional Law Series*, no. 3 (American Bar Foundation, 1977), classifies First Amendment values under three headings: individual autonomy, diversity, and self-government, in addition to what he calls "the checking value." This value focuses on the liberties protected by the First Amendment as a way of controlling the misconduct of government. I believe the arrangement in the text covers these distinctions. The discussion in §7 and below in §§10–12 indicates my agreement with Blasi on the importance of the checking value.

weight of particular claims to freedom of speech, press, and discussion are to be judged by this criterion. Some kinds of speech are not specially protected and others may even be offenses, for example, libel and defamation of individuals, so-called fighting words (in certain circumstances), and even political speech when it becomes incitement to the imminent and lawless use of force. Of course, why these kinds of speech are offenses may require careful reflection, and will generally differ in each case. Libel and defamation of private persons (as opposed to political figures) has no significance at all for the public use of reason to judge and regulate the basic structure, and it is in addition a private wrong; while incitements to the imminent and lawless use of force, whatever the significance of the speakers' overall political views, are too disruptive of the democratic process to be permitted by the rules of order of political debate. A well-designed constitution tries to constrain the political leadership to govern with sufficient justice and good sense so that among a reasonable people such incitements to violence will seldom occur and never be serious. So long as the advocacy of revolutionary and even seditious doctrines is fully protected, as it should be, there is no restriction on the content of political speech, but only regulations as to time and place, and the means used to express it.

It is important to keep in mind that in filling the second gap the first principle of justice is to be applied at the stage of the constitutional convention. This means that the political liberties and freedom of thought enter essentially into the specification of a just political procedure. Delegates to such a convention (still regarded as representatives of citizens as free and equal persons but now assigned a different task) are to adopt, from among the just constitutions that are both just and workable the one that seems most likely to lead to just and effective legislation. (Which constitutions and legislation are just is settled by the principles of justice already agreed to in the original position.) This adoption of a constitution is guided by the general knowledge of how political and social institutions work, together with the general

336

facts about existing social circumstances. In the first instance, then, the constitution is seen as a just political procedure which incorporates the equal political liberties and seeks to assure their fair value so that the processes of political decision are open to all on a roughly equal basis. The constitution must also guarantee freedom of thought if the exercise of these liberties is to be free and informed. The emphasis is first on the constitution as specifying a just and workable political procedure so far without any explicit constitutional restrictions on what the legislative outcome may be. Although delegates have a notion of just and effective legislation, the second principle of justice, which is part of the content of this notion, is not incorporated into the constitution itself. Indeed, the history of successful constitutions suggests that principles to regulate economic and social inequalities, and other distributive principles, are generally not suitable as constitutional restrictions. Rather, just legislation seems to be best achieved by assuring fairness in representation and by other constitutional devices.

The initial emphasis, then, is on the constitution as specifying a just and workable political procedure without any constitutional restrictions on legislative outcomes. But this initial emphasis is not, of course, final. The basic liberties associated with the capacity for a conception of the good must also be respected and this requires additional constitutional restrictions against infringing equal liberty of conscience and freedom of association (as well as the remaining and supporting basic liberties). Of course, these restrictions are simply the result of applying the first principle of justice at the stage of the constitutional convention. But if we return to the idea of starting from the conception of persons as capable of being normal and fully cooperating members of society and of respecting its fair terms of cooperation over a complete life, then these restrictions can be viewed in another light. If the equal basic liberties of some are restricted or denied, social cooperation on the basis of mutual respect is impossible. For we saw that fair terms of social cooperation are terms upon which as equal persons we are willing to cooperate with all members of society over a complete life. When fair terms are not honored, those mistreated will feel resentment or humiliation, and those who benefit must either recognize their fault and be troubled by it, or else regard those mistreated as deserving their loss. On both sides, the conditions of mutual respect are undermined. Thus, the basic liberties of liberty of conscience and freedom of association are properly protected by explicit constitutional restrictions. These restrictions publicly express on the constitution's face, as it were, the conception of social cooperation held by equal citizens in a well-ordered society.

So much for a bare outline of how the second gap is filled, at least at the constitutional stage. In the next section I shall briefly discuss freedom of speech in order to illustrate how this gap is filled in the case of a particular basic liberty. But before doing this it should be noted that all legal rights and liberties other than the basic liberties as protected by the various constitutional provisions (including the guarantee of the fair value of the political liberties) are to be specified at the legislative stage in the light of the two principles of justice and other relevant principles. This implies, for example, that the question of private property in the means of production or their social ownership and similar questions are not settled at the level of the first principles of justice, but depend upon the traditions and social institutions of a country and its particular problems and historical circumstances.[46] Moreover, even if by some convincing philosophical argument—at least convincing to us and a few like-minded others—we could trace the right of private or social ownership back to first principles or to basic rights, there is a good reason for working out a conception of justice which does not do this. For as we saw earlier, the aim of justice as fairness as a political conception is to resolve the impasse in the democratic tradition as to the way in which social institutions are to be arranged if they are to conform to the freedom and equality of citizens as moral persons. Philosophical argument alone is most

46. For references in *Theory* on this point, see n. 14 above.

unlikely to convince either side that the other is correct on a question like that of private or social property in the means of production. It seems more fruitful to look for bases of agreement implicit in the public culture of a democratic society and there-fore in its underlying conceptions of the person and of social cooperation. Certainly these conceptions are obscure and may possibly be formulated in various ways. That remains to be seen. But I have tried to indicate how these conceptions may be under-stood and to describe the way in which the notion of the original position can be used to connect them with definite principles of justice found in the tradition of moral philosophy. These princi-ples enable us to account for many if not most of our fundamen-tal constitutional rights and liberties, and they provide a way to decide the remaining questions of justice at the legislative stage. With the two principles of justice on hand, we have a possible common court of appeal for settling the question of property as it arises in the light of current and foreseeable social circum-stances.

In sum, then, the constitution specifies a just political proce-dure and incorporates restrictions which both protect the basic liberties and secure their priority. The rest is left to the legisla-tive stage. Such a constitution conforms to the traditional idea of democratic government while at the same time it allows a place for the institution of judicial review.[47] This conception of the constitution does not found it, in the first instance, on principles of justice, or on basic (or natural) rights. Rather, its foundation is in the conceptions of the person and of social cooperation most likely to be congenial to the public culture of a modern democratic society.[48] I should add that the same idea is used each time in the stages I discuss. That is, at each stage the reasonable frames and subordinates the rational; what varies is the task of

---

47. For a valuable discussion of judicial review in the context of the conception of justice as fairness, see Frank I. Michelman, "In Pursuit of Constitutional Welfare Rights: One View of Rawls' *Theory of Justice,*" *University of Pennsylvania Law Review* 121(5) (May 1973):991–1019.

48. See "Kantian Constructivism in Moral Theory," pp. 518–19.

the rational agents of deliberation and the constraints to which they are subject. Thus the parties in the original position are rationally autonomous representatives constrained by the reasonable conditions incorporated into the original position; and their task is to adopt principles of justice for the basic structure. Whereas delegates to a constitutional convention have far less leeway, since they are to apply the principles of justice adopted in the original position in selecting a constitution. Legislators in a parliamentary body have less leeway still, because any laws they enact must accord both with the constitution and the two principles of justice. As the stages follow one another and as the task changes and becomes less general and more specific, the constraints of the reasonable become stronger and the veil of ignorance becomes thinner. At each stage, then, the rational is framed by the reasonable in a different way. While the constraints of the reasonable are weakest and the veil of ignorance thickest in the original position, at the judicial stage these constraints are strongest and the veil of ignorance thinnest. The whole sequence is a schema for working out a conception of justice and guiding the application of its principles to the right subject in the right order. This schema is not, of course, a description of any actual political process, and much less of how any constitutional regime may be expected to work. It belongs to a conception of justice, and although it is related to an account of how democracy works, it is not such an account.

§ 10. Free Political Speech

The preceding outline of how the second gap is filled is extremely abstract. To see in more detail how to proceed, I discuss in this and the next section the freedom of political speech and press which falls under the basic liberty of freedom of thought and the first fundamental case. Doing this will illustrate how the basic liberties are further specified and adjusted at later stages, and the way the significance of a particular liberty is given by its role in a fully adequate scheme. (For the notion of significance, see the second paragraph of §9.)

I begin by noting that the basic liberties not only limit one another but they are also self-limiting.[49] The notion of significance shows why this is so. To explain: the requirement that the basic liberties are to be the same for everyone implies that we can obtain a greater liberty for ourselves only if the same greater liberty is granted to others. For example, while we might want to include in our freedom of (political) speech rights to the unimpeded access to public places and to the free use of social resources to express our political views, these extensions of our liberty, when granted to all, are so unworkable and socially divisive that they would actually greatly reduce the effective scope of freedom of speech. These consequences are recognized by delegates to a constitutional convention who are guided by the rational interest of the representative equal citizen in a fully adequate scheme of basic liberties. Thus, the delegates accept reasonable regulations relating to time and place, and the access to public facilities, always on a footing of equality. For the sake of the most significant liberties, they abandon any special claims to the free use of social resources. This enables them to establish the rules required to secure an effective scope for free political speech in the fundamental case. Much the same reasoning shows why the basic liberty of liberty of conscience is also self-limiting. Here too reasonable regulations would be accepted to secure intact the central range of this liberty, which includes the freedom and integrity of the internal life of religious associations and the liberty of persons to determine their religious affiliations in social conditions that are free.

Let us now turn to freedom of political speech as a basic liberty, and consider how to specify it into more particular liber-

49. Hart argues that a strictly quantitative criterion of how to specify and adjust the basic liberties cannot account for this fact, or so I interpret his argument, pp. 550–51; Daniels, pp. 247–48. I agree that some qualitative criterion is necessary and the notion of significance is to serve this role.

ties so as to protect its central range. Recall that we are concerned with the fundamental case of the application of the principles of justice (and other general principles as appropriate) to the basic structure of society and its social policies. We think of these principles as applied by free and equal citizens of a democratic regime by the exercise of their sense of justice. The question is: what more particular liberties, or rules of law, are essential to secure the free, full, and informed exercise of this moral power?

Here as before I proceed not from a general definition that singles out these liberties but from what the history of constitutional doctrine shows to be some of the fixed points within the central range of the freedom of political speech. Among these fixed points are the following: there is no such thing as the crime of seditious libel; there are no prior restraints on freedom of the press, except for special cases; and the advocacy of revolutionary and subversive doctrines is fully protected. The three fixed points mark out and cover by analogy much of the central range of freedom of political speech. Reflection on these constitutional rules brings out why this is so.

Thus, as Kalven has said, a free society is one in which we cannot defame the government; there is no such offense:

> The absence of seditious libel as a crime is the true pragmatic test of freedom of speech. This I would argue is what free speech is about. Any society in which seditious libel is a crime is, no matter what its other features, not a free society. A society can, for example, either treat obscenity as a crime or not a crime without thereby altering its basic nature as a society. It seems to me it cannot do so with seditious libel. Here the response to this crime defines the society.[50]

Kalven is not saying, I think, that the absence of seditious libel is the whole of freedom of political speech; rather, it is a necessary condition and indeed a condition so necessary that, once

50. See *The Negro and the First Amendment* (Chicago: University of Chicago Press, 1966), p. 16.

342

securely won, the other essential fixed points are much easier to establish. The history of the use by governments of the crime of seditious libel to suppress criticism and dissent and to maintain their power demonstrates the great significance of this particular liberty to any fully adequate scheme of basic liberties.[51] So long as this crime exists the public press and free discussion cannot play their role in informing the electorate. And, plainly, to allow the crime of seditious libel would undermine the wider possibilities of self-government and the several liberties required for its protection. Thus the great importance of *New York Times v. Sullivan* in which the Supreme Court not only rejected the crime of seditious libel but declared the Sedition Act of 1798 unconstitutional now, whether or not it was unconstitutional at the time it was enacted. It has been tried, so to speak, by the court of history and found wanting.[52]

The denial of the crime of seditious libel is closely related to the two other fixed points noted above. If this crime does exist, it can serve as a prior restraint and may easily include subversive advocacy. But the Sedition Act of 1798 caused such resentment that once it lapsed in 1801, the crime of seditious libel was never revived. Within our tradition there has been a consensus that the discussion of general political, religious, and philosophical doctrines can never be censored. Thus the leading problem of the freedom of political speech has focused on the question of subversive advocacy, that is, on advocacy of political doctrines an essential part of which is the necessity of revolution, or the use of unlawful force and the incitement thereto as a means of political change. A series of Supreme Court cases from *Schenck* to *Brandenburg* has dealt with this problem; it was in *Schenck* that Holmes formulated the well-known "clear and present danger rule," which was effectively emasculated by the way it was under-

51. See Blasi, "The Checking Value in First Amendment Theory," pp. 529–44, where he discusses the history of the use of seditious libel to show the importance of the checking value of the liberties secured by the First Amendment.

52. *New York Times v. Sullivan,* 376 U.S. 254 (1964) at 276. See Kalven's discussion of this case, *The Negro and the First Amendment,* pp. 56–64.

stood and applied in *Dennis*. Thus I shall briefly discuss the problem of subversive advocacy to illustrate how the more particular liberties are specified under freedom of political speech.

Let us begin by noting why subversive advocacy becomes the central problem once there is agreement that all general discussion of doctrine as well as of the justice of the basic structure and its policies is fully protected. Kalven rightly emphasizes that it is with such advocacy that the grounds for restricting political speech seem most persuasive, yet at the same time these grounds run counter to the fundamental values of a democratic society.[53] Free political speech is not only required if citizens are to exercise their moral powers in the first fundamental case, but free speech together with the just political procedure specified by the constitution provides an alternative to revolution and the use of force which can be so destructive to the basic liberties. There must be some point at which political speech becomes so closely connected with the use of force that it may be properly restricted. But what is this point?

In *Gitlow* the Supreme Court held that subversive advocacy was not protected by the First Amendment when the legislature had determined that advocating the overthrow of organized government by force involves the danger of substantive evils which the state through its police power may prevent. The Court presumed that the legislature's determination of the danger was correct, in the absence of strong grounds to the contrary. *Brandenburg,* which is now controlling and therefore ends the story for the moment, overrules *Gitlow* (implied by its explicit overruling of *Whitney*). Here the Court adopts the principle that "the constitutional guarantees of free speech and press do not permit a State to forbid or to proscribe advocacy of the use of force or of law violation except where such advocacy is directed to inciting or producing imminent lawless action and is likely to incite

53. Here and throughout this section and the next I am much indebted to Kalven's discussion of subversive advocacy in *A Worthy Tradition: Freedom of Speech in America* (New York: Harper and Row, 1987). I am most grateful to James Kalven for letting me read the relevant part of the manuscript of this very important work.

or produce such action." [54] Observe that the proscribed kind of speech must be both intentional and directed to producing imminent lawless action as well as delivered in circumstances which make this result likely.

While *Brandenburg* leaves several important questions unanswered, it is much better constitutional doctrine than what preceded it, especially when it is read together with *New York Times v. Sullivan* and the later *New York Times v. United States*.[55] (These three cases between them cover the three fixed points previously mentioned.) The reason is that *Brandenburg* draws the line to protected speech so as to recognize the legitimacy of subversive advocacy in a constitutional democracy. It is tempting to think of political speech which advocates revolution as similar to incitement to an ordinary crime such as arson or assault, or even to causing a dangerous stampede, as in Holmes's utterly trivial example of someone falsely shouting "Fire!" in a crowded theater. (This example is trivial because it has point only against the view, defended by no one, that all speech of whatever kind is protected, perhaps because it is thought that speech is not action and only action is punishable.[56]) But revolution is a very special crime; while even a constitutional regime must have the legal right to punish violations of its laws, these laws even when enacted by due process may be more or less unjust, or may appear to be so to significant groups in society who find them

54. *Brandenburg v. Ohio,* 395 U.S. 444 (1969) at 447.

55. *New York Times v. United States,* 403 U.S. 713. See also *Near v. Minnesota,* 283 U.S. 697, the major earlier case on prior restraint.

56. A similar critical view of Holmes's example is found in Kalven, *A Worthy Tradition.* Thomas Emerson, in *The System of Freedom of Expression* (New York: Random House, 1970), attempts to give an account of free speech based on a distinction between speech and action, the one protected, the other not. But as T. M. Scanlon points out in his "A Theory of Freedom of Expression," *Philosophy and Public Affairs* 1(2) (Winter 1972):207–8, a view of this kind puts the main burden on how this distinction is to be made and is bound to depart widely from the ordinary use of the words "speech" and "conduct." For an instructive and sympathetic account of how such a view might be developed, see Alan Fuchs, "Further Steps toward a General Theory of Freedom of Expression," *William and Mary Law Review* 18 (Winter 1976).

oppressive. Historically, the question of when resistance and revolution are justified is one of the deepest political questions. Most recently, the problems of civil disobedience and conscientious refusal to military service, occasioned by what was widely regarded as an unjust war, have been profoundly troubling and are still unresolved. Thus, although there is agreement that arson, murder, and lynching are crimes, this is not the case with resistance and revolution whenever they become serious questions even in a moderately well-governed democratic regime (as opposed to a well-ordered society, where by definition the problem does not arise). Or more accurately, they are agreed to be crimes only in the legal sense of being contrary to law, but to a law that in the eyes of many has lost its legitimacy. That subversive advocacy is widespread enough to pose a live political question is a sign of an impending crisis rooted in the perception of significant groups that the basic structure is unjust and oppressive. It is a warning that they are ready to entertain drastic steps because other ways of redressing their grievances have failed.

All this is long familiar. I mention these matters only to recall the obvious: that subversive advocacy is always part of a more comprehensive political view; and in the case of so-called criminal syndicalism (the statutory offense in many of the historical cases), the political view was socialism, one of the most comprehensive political doctrines ever formulated. As Kalven observes, revolutionaries don't simply shout: "Revolt! Revolt!" They give reasons.[57] To repress subversive advocacy is to suppress the discussion of these reasons, and to do this is to restrict the free and informed public use of our reason in judging the justice of the basic structure and its social policies. And thus the basic liberty of freedom of thought is violated.

As a further consideration, a conception of justice for a democratic society presupposes a theory of human nature. It does so, first, in regard to whether the ideals expressed by its conceptions of the person and of a well-ordered society are feasible in view of the capacities of human nature and the requirements of social

57. See Kalven, *A Worthy Tradition*.

346

life.[58] And second, and most relevant here, it presupposes a theory of how democratic institutions are likely to work and of how fragile and unstable they are likely to be. The Court said in *Gitlow:*

> That utterances inciting to the overthrow of organized government by unlawful means, present a sufficient danger of substantive evil to bring their punishment within the range of legislative discretion, is clear. Such utterances, by their very nature, involve danger to the public peace and to the security of the State. . . . And the immediate danger is none the less real and substantial, because the effect of a given utterance cannot be accurately foreseen. A single revolutionary spark may kindle a fire that, smouldering for a time, may burst into a sweeping and destructive conflagration.[59]

This passage suggests a view, not unlike that of Hobbes, of the very great fragility and instability of political arrangements. Even in a democratic regime, it supposes that volatile and destructive social forces may be set going by revolutionary speech, to smolder unrecognized below the surface calm of political life only to break out suddenly with uncontrollable force that sweeps all before it. If free political speech is guaranteed, however, serious grievances do not go unrecognized or suddenly become highly dangerous. They are publicly voiced; and in a moderately well-governed regime they are at least to some degree taken into account. Moreover, the theory of how democratic institutions work must agree with Locke that persons are capable of a certain natural political virtue and do not engage in resistance and revolution unless their social position in the basic structure is seriously unjust and this condition has persisted over some period of time and seems to be removable by no other means.[60] Thus the basic institutions of a moderately well-governed democratic

---

58. See "Kantian Constructivism in Moral Theory," pp. 534–35.

59. *Gitlow v. New York,* 268 U.S. 652 (1925) at 669.

60. See Locke's Second Treatise of Government, §§223–30. For the idea of natural political virtue in Locke, see Peter Laslett's introduction to his critical edition: *John Locke, Two Treatises of Government* (Cambridge: Cambridge University Press, 1960), pp. 108–11.

society are not so fragile or unstable as to be brought down by subversive advocacy alone. Indeed, a wise political leadership in such a society takes this advocacy as a warning that fundamental changes may be necessary; and what changes are required is known in part from the more comprehensive political view used to explain and justify the advocacy of resistance and revolution.

It remains to connect the preceding remarks with the deliberations of delegates in a constitutional convention who represent the rational interest of equal citizens in a fully adequate scheme of basic liberties. We simply say that these remarks explain why the delegates would draw the line between protected and unprotected political speech not (as *Gitlow* does) at subversive advocacy as such but (as *Brandenburg* does) at subversive advocacy when it is both directed to inciting imminent and unlawful use of force and likely to achieve this result. The discussion illustrates how the freedom of political speech as a basic liberty is specified and adjusted at later stages so as to protect its central range, namely the free public use of our reason in all matters that concern the justice of the basic structure and its social policies.

§ 11. The Clear and Present Danger Rule

In order to fill out the preceding discussion of free political speech I shall make a few observations about the so-called clear and present danger rule. This rule is familiar and has an importance place in the history of constitutional doctrine. It may prove instructive to ask why it has fallen into disrepute. I shall assume throughout that the rule is intended to apply to political speech, and in particular to subversive advocacy, to decide when such speech and advocacy may be restricted. I assume also that the rule concerns the content of speech and not merely its regulation, since as a rule for regulating speech, it raises altogether different questions and may often prove acceptable.[61]

---

61. My account of the clear and present danger rule has been much influenced by Kalven, *A Worthy Tradition,* and by Meiklejohn's *Free Speech and Its Relation to Self-Government,* chap. 2.

Let us begin by considering Holmes's original formulation of the rule in *Schenck*. It runs as follows: "The question in every case is whether the words are used in such circumstances and are of such a nature as to create a clear and present danger that they will bring about the substantive evils that Congress has a right to prevent. It is a question of proximity and degree."[62] This rule has a certain similarity with *Brandenburg;* we have only to suppose that the words "clear and present danger" refer to imminent lawless action. But this similarity is deceptive, as we can see by noting the reasons why Holmes's rule, and even Brandeis's statement of it in *Whitney,* proves unsatisfactory. One reason is that the roots of the rule in Holmes's formulation are in his account of the law of attempts in his book *The Common Law*.[63] The law of attempts tries to bridge the gap between what the defendant did and the completed crime as defined by statute. In attempts, and similarly in the case of free speech, actions with no serious consequences can be ignored. The traditional view of attempts required specific intent to do the particular offense. For Holmes intent was relevant only because it increased the likelihood that what the agent does will cause actual harm. When applied to free speech this view has the virtue of tolerating innocuous speech and does not justify punishment for thoughts alone. But it is an unsatisfactory basis for the constitutional protection of political speech, since it leads us to focus on how dangerous the speech in question is, as if by being somehow dangerous, speech becomes an ordinary crime.

The essential thing, however, is the kind of speech in question and the role of this kind of speech in a democratic regime. And *of course* political speech which expresses doctrines we reject, or find contrary to our interests, all too easily strikes us as dangerous. A just constitution protects and gives priority to certain kinds of speech in virtue of their significance in what I have

62. *Schenck v. United States*, 249 U.S. 47 at 52.
63. For the significance of this origin of the rule, see Yosal Rogat, "Mr. Justice Holmes: The Judge as Spectator," *University of Chicago Law Review* 31 (Winter 1964):215–17.

called "the two fundamental cases." Because Holmes's rule ignores the role and significance of political speech, it is not surprising that he should have written the unanimous opinions upholding the convictions of *Schenck* and *Debs* and dissented in *Abrams* and *Gitlow*. It might appear that he perceived the political speech of the socialists Schenck and Debs as sufficiently dangerous when the country was at war, while he dissented in *Abrams* and *Gitlow* because he perceived the political activities of the defendants as harmless.

This impression is strengthened by the fact that the words which follow the statement of the rule (cited above) are these: "When a nation is at war many things that might be said in time of peace are such a hindrance to its effort that their utterance will not be endured as long as men fight and that no Court could regard them as protected by any constitutional right. It seems to be admitted that if an actual obstruction of the recruiting service were proved, liability for words that produced that effect might be enforced."

If we look at Holmes's opinion in *Debs,* the socialist candidate for the presidency is not accused of encouraging or inciting imminent and lawless violence, and so of creating a clear and present danger in that sense. As reported in the Court's opinion, Debs in a public speech simply attacked the war as having been declared by the master class for its own ends and maintained that the working class had everything to lose, including their lives, and so on. Holmes finds it sufficient to uphold the sentence of ten years' imprisonment that one purpose of the speech "was to oppose not only war in general but this war, and that the opposition was so expressed that its natural and intended effect would be to obstruct recruiting. If that was intended, and if, in all the circumstances, that would be the probable effect, it would not be protected by reason of its being part of a general program and expressions of a general and conscientious belief."[64] Here the natural and intended effect to which Holmes refers is surely that

64. *Debs v. United States,* 249 U.S. 211 at 215.

350

those who heard or read about Debs's speech would be convinced or encouraged by what he said and resolve to conduct themselves accordingly. It must be the consequences of political conviction and resolve which Holmes sees as the clear and present danger. Holmes is little troubled by the constitutional question raised in *Debs,* even though the case involves a leader of a political party, already four times its candidate for the presidency. Holmes devotes little time to it. He is content to say in one sentence, which immediately follows the passage just quoted, that *Schenck* settles the matter. This sentence reads: "The chief defences upon which the defendant seemed willing to rely were the denial that we have dealt with and that based upon the First Amendment to the Constitution, disposed of in Schenck v. United States." Holmes is here referring to the fact that Debs had maintained that the statute under which he was indicted is unconstitutional as interfering with free speech contrary to the First Amendment.

Brandeis's concurring opinion in *Whitney* is another matter. Along with Hand's opinion in *Masses,* it was one of the memorable steps in the development of doctrine. Early in the opinion Brandeis states that the right of free speech, the right to teach, and the right to assembly are "fundamental rights" protected by the First Amendment. These rights, even though fundamental, are not absolute; their exercise is subject to restriction "if the particular restriction proposed is required in order to protect the State from destruction or serious injury, political, economic, or moral."[65] He then proceeds to refer to the *Schenck* formulation of the clear and present danger rule and seeks to fix more exactly the standard by which it is to be applied; that is, to say when a danger is clear, how remote it may be and yet be held present, and what degree of evil is necessary to justify a restriction of free speech.

The strength of Brandeis's opinion lies in its recognition of

65. 274 U.S. 357 at 373. For Hand's opinion in *Masses,* see *Masses Publishing v. Patten,* 244 Fed. 535 (S.D.N.Y. 1917).

the role of free political speech in a democratic regime and the connection he establishes between this role and the requirement that the danger must be imminent and not merely likely sometime in the future. The idea is that the evil should be "so imminent that it may befall before there is opportunity for full discussion. If there is time to expose through discussion the falsehoods and fallacies to avert the evil by the processes of education, the remedy to be applied is more speech, not enforced silence. Only an emergency can justify repression. Such must be the rule if authority is to be reconciled with freedom."[66] Later on he says, referring to advocacy and not incitement: "The fact that speech is likely to result in some violence or in the destruction of property is not enough to justify its suppression. There must be the probability of serious injury to the State. Among free men the deterrents ordinarily applied to prevent crime are education and punishment for violations of the law, not abridgement of the rights of free speech and assembly."[67] And finally, in rejecting the grounds of the majority opinion, Brandeis concludes: "I am unable to assent to the suggestion in the opinion of the Court that assembling with a political party, formed to advocate the desirability of a proletarian revolution by mass action at some date necessarily far in the future, is not a right within the protection of the Fourteenth Amendment."[68] All of this and much else is plainly an advance in fixing the standard by which the clear and present danger rule is to be applied.

Yet in *Dennis* the Court interprets the rule in such a way as to emasculate it as a standard for protecting free political speech. For here the Court adopts Hand's formulation of the rule which runs as follows: "In each case [courts] must ask whether the gravity of the 'evil' discounted by its improbability, justifies such an invasion of free speech as is necessary to avoid the danger."[69] Expressed this way the rule does not require that the evil be

66. Ibid., at 377.
67. Ibid., at 378.
68. Ibid., at 379.
69. 341 U.S. 494 at 510, citing 183 F. 2d. at 212.

352

imminent. Even though the evil is remote, it may be enough that it is great and sufficiently probable. The rule now reads like a maxim of decision theory appropriate to a constitutional doctrine that justifies all decisions by what is necessary to maximize the net sum of social advantages, or the net balance of social values. Given this background conception, it can seem simply irrational to require that the danger be in any strict sense imminent. This is because the principle to maximize the net sum of social advantages (or the net balance of social values) does not allow us to give any greater weight to what is imminent than what the improbability and the value of future advantages permit. Free political speech is assessed as a means and as an end in itself along with everything else. Thus Brandeis's idea that the danger must be imminent because free speech is the constitutionally approved way to protect against future danger may appear irrational in many situations and sometimes even suicidal. His account of free speech needs to be further elaborated in order to make it convincing. This is because the clear and present danger rule originates from a different view than the constitutional doctrine he is attempting to develop.[70] What is required is to specify more sharply the kind of situation which can justify the restriction of free political speech. Brandeis refers to protecting "the state from destruction," and from "serious injury, political, economic, and moral." These phrases are too loose and cover too much ground. Let us see how Brandeis's view might be elaborated to accord with the priority of liberty.

The essential thing is to recognize the difference between

70. The basis of Brandeis's own view is best expressed, I think, in the well-known paragraph which begins: "Those who won our independence believed that the final end of the State was to make men free to develop their faculties; and that in its government the deliberative forces should prevail over the arbitrary." This paragraph ends: "Believing in the power of reason as applied through public discussion, they eschewed the silence coerced by law—the argument of force in its worst form. Recognizing the occasional tyrannies of governing majorities, they amended the Constitution so that free speech and assembly should be guaranteed." It is no criticism of this fine paragraph to recognize that by itself it does not remedy the defect of Brandeis's formulation of the clear and present danger rule.

what I shall call "a constitutional crisis of the requisite kind" and an emergency in which there is a present or foreseeable threat of serious injury, political, economic, and moral, or even of the destruction of the state. For example, the fact that the country is at war and such an emergency exists does not entail that a constitutional crisis of the requisite kind also exists. The reason is that to restrict or suppress free political speech, including subversive advocacy, always implies at least a partial suspension of democracy. A constitutional doctrine which gives priority to free political speech and other basic liberties must hold that to impose such a suspension requires the existence of a constitutional crisis in which free political institutions cannot effectively operate or take the required measures to preserve themselves. A number of historical cases illustrate that free democratic political institutions have operated effectively to take the necessary measures in serious emergencies without restricting free political speech; and in some cases where such restrictions have been imposed they were unnecessary and made no contribution whatever to meeting the emergency. It is not enough for those in authority to say that a grave danger exists and that they are taking effective steps to prevent it. A well-designed constitution includes democratic procedures for dealing with emergencies. Thus as a matter of constitutional doctrine the priority of liberty implies that free political speech cannot be restricted unless it can be reasonably argued from the specific nature of the present situation that there exists a constitutional crisis in which democratic institutions cannot work effectively and their procedures for dealing with emergencies cannot operate.

In the constitutional doctrine proposed, then, it is of no particular moment whether political speech is dangerous, since political speech is by its nature often dangerous, or may often appear to be dangerous. This is because the free public use of our reason applies to the most fundamental questions, and the decisions made may have grave consequences. Suppose a democratic people, engaged in a military rivalry with an autocratic power, should decide that the use of nuclear weapons is so contrary to the

354

principles of humanity that their use must be forsworn and significant steps taken unilaterally toward reducing these weapons, this done in the hope that the other power might be persuaded to follow. This could be a highly dangerous decision; but surely that is irrelevant to whether it should be freely discussed and whether the government is constitutionally obligated to carry out this decision once it is properly made. The dangerousness of political speech is beside the point; it is precisely the danger involved in making this decision which must be freely discussed. Wasn't it dangerous to hold free elections in 1862–64 in the midst of a civil war?

Focusing on the danger of political speech flawed the clear and present danger rule from the start. It failed to recognize that for free political speech to be restricted, a constitutional crisis must exist requiring the more or less temporary suspension of democratic political institutions, solely for the sake of preserving these institutions and other basic liberties. Such a crisis did not exist in 1862–64; and if not then, surely at no other time before or since. There was no constitutional crisis of the requisite kind when *Schenck, Debs,* or *Dennis* were decided, no political conditions which prevented free political institutions from operating. Never in our history has there been a time when free political speech, and in particular subversive advocacy, could be restricted or suppressed. And this suggests that in a country with a vigorous tradition of democratic institutions, a constitutional crisis need never arise unless its people and institutions are simply overwhelmed from the outside. For practical purposes, then in a well-governed democratic society under reasonably favorable conditions, the free public use of our reason in questions of political and social justice would seem to be absolute.

Of course, the preceding remarks do not provide a systematic explanation of the distinction between a constitutional crisis of the requisite kind and an emergency in which there is a threat of serious injury, political, economic, and moral. I have simply appealed to the fact, or to what I take to be a fact, that we can recognize from a number of cases in our history that there is the distinction I have indicated and that often we can tell when it applies. Here I cannot go into a systematic explanation. I believe, however, that the notion of a constitutional crisis of this kind is an important part of an account of free political speech, and that when we explain this notion we must start from an account of free political speech which assigns it priority. In justice as fairness this kind of speech falls under the basic liberties, and while these liberties are not absolute, they can be restricted in their content (as opposed to being regulated in ways consistent with maintaining a fully adequate scheme) only if this is necessary to prevent a greater and more significant loss, either directly or indirectly, to these liberties. I have tried to illustrate how in the case of political speech, we try to identify the more essential elements in the central range of application of this basic liberty. We then proceed to further extensions up to the point where a fully adequate provision for this liberty is achieved, unless this liberty has already become self-limiting or conflicts with more significant extensions of other basic liberties. As always, I assume that these judgments are made by delegates and legislators from the point of view of the appropriate stage in the light of what best advances the rational interest of the representative equal citizen in a fully adequate scheme of basic liberties. If we insist on using the language of the clear and present danger rule, we must say, first, that the substantive evils which the legislature seeks to prevent must be of a highly special kind, namely, the loss of freedom of thought itself, or of other basic liberties, including here the fair value of the political liberties; and second, that there must be no alternative way to prevent these evils than the restriction of free speech. This formulation of the rule goes with the requirement that a constitutional crisis of the requisite kind is one in which free political institutions cannot operate or take the steps required to preserve themselves.

§ 12. Maintaining the Fair Value of Political Liberties

I now wish to supplement the preceding discussion of political speech in two ways. First, it needs to be emphasized that the basic liberties constitute a family, and that it is this family that has priority and not any single liberty by itself, even if, practically speaking, one or more of the basic liberties may be absolute under certain conditions. In this connection I shall very briefly note the manner in which political speech may be regulated in order to preserve the fair value of the political liberties. I do this not, of course, to try to resolve this difficult problem, but to illustrate why the basic liberties need to be adjusted to one another and cannot be specified individually. Second, it is helpful in clarifying the notion of the basic liberties and their significance to survey several (nonbasic) liberties associated with the second principle of justice. This serves to bring out how the significance of a liberty (whether basic or nonbasic) is tied to its political and social role within a just basic structure as specified by the two principles of justice.

I begin in this section with the problem of maintaining the fair value of the equal political liberties. Although (as I said in §7) it is beyond the scope of a philosophical doctrine to consider in any detail how this problem is to be solved, such a doctrine must explain the grounds upon which the necessary institutions and rules of law can be justified. Let us assume, for reasons stated earlier, that public financing of political campaigns and election expenditures, various limits on contributions and other regulations are essential to maintain the fair value of the political liberties.[71] These arrangements are compatible with the central role of free political speech and press as a basic liberty provided that the following three conditions hold. First, there are no restrictions on the content of speech; the arrangements in question are, therefore, regulations which favor no political doctrine over any other. They are, so to speak, rules of order for elections and are required to establish a just political procedure in which the fair value of the equal political liberties is maintained.

A second condition is that the instituted arrangements must not impose any undue burdens on the various political groups in society and must affect them all in an equitable manner. Plainly,

71. See §7.

what counts as an undue burden is itself a question, and in any particular case is to be answered by reference to the purpose of achieving the fair value of the political liberties. For example, the prohibition of large contributions from private persons or corporations to political candidates is not an undue burden (in the requisite sense) on wealthy persons and groups. Such a prohibition may be necessary so that citizens similarly gifted and motivated have roughly an equal chance of influencing the government's policy and of attaining positions of authority irrespective of their economic and social class. It is precisely this equality which defines the fair value of the political liberties. On the other hand, regulations that restrict the use of certain public places for political speech might impose an undue burden on relatively poor groups accustomed to this way of conveying their views since they lack the funds for other kinds of political expression.

Finally, the various regulations of political speech must be rationally designed to achieve the fair value of the political liberties. While it would be too strong to say that they must be the least restrictive regulations required to achieve this end—for who knows what the least restrictive among the equally effective regulations might be—nevertheless, these regulations become unreasonable once considerably less restrictive and equally effective alternatives are both known and available.

The point of the foregoing remarks is to illustrate how the basic liberties constitute a family, the members of which have to be adjusted to one another to guarantee the central range of these liberties in the two fundamental cases. Thus, political speech, even though it falls under the basic liberty of freedom of thought, must be regulated to insure the fair value of the political liberties. These regulations do not restrict the content of political speech and hence may be consistent with its central role. It should be noted that the mutual adjustment of the basic liberties is justified on grounds allowed by the priority of these liberties as a family, no one of which is in itself absolute. This kind of adjustment is markedly different from a general balancing of interests which permits considerations of all kinds—political, economic, and social—to restrict these liberties, even regarding their content, when the advantages gained or injuries avoided are thought to be great enough. In justice as fairness the adjustment of the basic liberties is grounded solely on their significance as specified by their role in the two fundamental cases, and this adjustment is guided by the aim of specifying a fully adequate scheme of these liberties.

In the preceding two sections I recalled a part of development of doctrine from *Schenck* to *Brandenburg,* a development with a happy ending. By contrast, *Buckley* and its sequel *First National Bank* are profoundly dismaying.[72] In *Buckley* the Court held unconstitutional various limits on expenditures imposed by the Election Act Amendment of 1974. These limits applied to expenditures in favor of individual candidates, to expenditures by candidates from their own funds, and to total expenditures in the course of a campaign. The Court said that the First Amendment cannot tolerate such provisions since they place direct and substantial restrictions on political speech.[73] For the most part the Court considers what it regards as the primary government interest served by the act, namely, the interest in preventing corrup-

---

72. *Buckley v. Valeo,* 424 U.S. 1 (1976), and *First National Bank v. Bellotti,* 435 U.S. 765 (1978). For discussions of *Buckley,* see Tribe, *American Constitutional Law,* chap. 13, pp. 800–11; and Skelly Wright, "Political Speech and the Constitution: Is Money Speech?," *Yale Law Journal* 85(8) (July 1976):1001–21. For an earlier discussion, see M. A. Nicholson, "Campaign Financing and Equal Protection," *Stanford Law Review* 26 (April 1974):815–54. In *First National Bank* the Court, by a 5-to-4 decision, invalidated a Massachusetts criminal law which prohibited expenditures by banks and corporations for the purpose of influencing the outcome of voting on referendum proposals, unless these proposals materially affected the property, business, or assets of the corporation. The statute specified that no referendum question solely concerning the taxation of individuals came under this exception. In a dissent joined by Brennan and Marshall, Justice White said that the fundamental error of the majority opinion was its failure to recognize that the government's interest in prohibiting such expenditures by banks and corporations derives from the First Amendment—in particular, from the value of promoting free political discussion by preventing corporate domination; see 435 U.S. 765 (1978) at 803–4. My discussion in the text is in sympathy with this dissenting opinion, and also with White's dissent in *Buckley* at 257–66, and with Marshall's at 287–90.

73. *Buckley v. Valeo,* at 58–59.

tion of the electoral process, and the appearance of such corruption. The Court also considers two so-called ancillary interests of the act, namely, the interest in limiting the increasing costs of political campaigns and the interest in equalizing the relative ability of citizens to affect the outcome of elections. Here I am concerned solely with the legitimacy of this second ancillary interest, since it is the only one which falls directly under the notion of the fair value of the political liberties. Moreover, I leave aside, as irrelevant for our purposes, the question whether the measures enacted by Congress were rationally framed to fulfill this interest in an effective way.

What is dismaying is that the present Court seems to reject altogether the idea that Congress may try to establish the fair value of the political liberties. It says: "The concept that the government may restrict the speech of some elements in our society in order to enhance the relative voice of others is wholly foreign to the First Amendment."[74] The Court then proceeds to cite its own precedents, holding that the First Amendment was designed to secure the widest possible dissemination of information from diverse and opposed sources, and to assure the unrestricted exchange of ideas for bringing about political and social changes favored by the people.[75] But none of the cases cited involves the fundamental question of the fair value of the political liberties.[76] Moreover, the Court's opinion focuses too much on the so-called primary interest in eliminating corruption and the appearance of corruption. The Court fails to recognize the essential point that the fair value of the political liberties is required for a just political procedure, and that to insure their fair value it is necessary to prevent those with greater property and wealth, and the greater skills of organization which accompany them, from controlling the electoral process to their advantage. The way in which this is accomplished need not involve

74. Ibid., at 48–49.
75. Ibid., at 49–51.
76. See Tribe, *American Constitutional Law,* p. 806.

bribery and dishonesty or the granting of special favors, however common these vices may be. Shared political convictions and aims suffice. In *Buckley* the Court runs the risk of endorsing the view that fair representation is representation according to the amount of influence effectively exerted. On this view, democracy is a kind of regulated rivalry between economic classes and interest groups in which the outcome should properly depend on the ability and willingness of each to use its financial resources and skills, admittedly very unequal, to make its desires felt.

It is surprising, however, that the Court should think that attempts by Congress to establish the fair value of the political liberties must run afoul of the First Amendment. In a number of earlier decisions the Court has affirmed the principle of one person, one vote, sometimes relying on Article I, Section 2 of the Constitution, at other times on the Fourteenth Amendment. It has said of the right to vote that it is the "preservative of all rights," and in *Wesberry* it stated: "Other rights, even the most basic, are illusory if the right to vote is undermined." [77] In *Reynolds* the Court recognized that this right involves more than the right simply to cast a vote which is counted equally. The Court said: "Full and effective participation by all citizens in state government requires . . . that each citizen has an equally effective voice in the election of members of the state legislature." [78] Later in the opinion it said: "Since achieving of fair and effective representation for all citizens is concededly the basic aim of legislative apportionment, we conclude that the Equal Protection Clause guarantees the opportunity for equal participation by voters in the election of state legislators." [79] Thus, what is fundamental is a political procedure which secures for all citizens a full and equally effective voice in a fair scheme of representation. Such a scheme is fundamental because the adequate protection of other basic rights depends on it. Formal equality is not enough.

77. *Wesberry v. Sanders,* 376 U.S. 1 (1964) at 17.
78. *Reynolds v. Sims,* 377 U.S. 533 (1964) at 565.
79. Ibid., at 565–66.

It would seem to follow that the aim of achieving a fair scheme of representation can justify limits on and regulations of political speech in elections, provided that these limits and regulations satisfy the three conditions mentioned earlier. For how else is the full and effective voice of all citizens to be maintained? Since it is a matter of one basic liberty against another, the liberties protected by the First Amendment may have to be adjusted in the light of other constitutional requirements, in this case the requirement of the fair value of the political liberties. Not to do so is to fail to see a constitution as a whole and to fail to recognize how its provisions are to be taken together in specifying a just political procedure as an essential part of a fully adequate scheme of basic liberties.

As already noted (in §7), what kinds of electoral arrangements are required to establish the fair value of the political liberties is an extremely difficult question. It is not the task of the Court to say what these arrangements are, but to make sure that the arrangements enacted by the legislature accord with the Constitution. The regulations proposed by Congress and struck down in *Buckley* would quite possibly have been ineffective; but in the present state of our knowledge they were admissible attempts to achieve the aim of a fair scheme of representation in which all citizens could have a more full and effective voice. If the Court means what it says in *Wesberry* and *Reynolds*, *Buckley* must sooner or later give way. The First Amendment no more enjoins a system of representation according to influence effectively exerted in free political rivalry between unequals than the Fourteenth Amendment enjoins a system of liberty of contract and free competition between unequals in the economy, as the Court thought in the Lochner era.[80] In both cases the results of the free play of the electoral process and of economic competition are acceptable only if the necessary conditions of background justice are fulfilled. Moreover, in a democratic regime it is important that the fulfillment of these conditions be publicly recognized.

80. *Lochner v. New York,* 198 U.S. 45 (1905).

362

This is more fundamental than avoiding corruption and the appearance of corruption; for without the public recognition that background justice is maintained, citizens tend to become resentful, cynical, and apathetic. It is this state of mind that leads to corruption as a serious problem, and indeed makes it uncontrollable. The danger of *Buckley* is that it risks repeating the mistake of the Lochner era, this time in the political sphere where, for reasons the Court itself has stated in the cases cited above, the mistake could be much more grievous.

§ 13. Liberties Connected with the Second Principle

To clarify further the notion of the significance of the basic liberties I shall briefly discuss several liberties associated with the second principle of justice. The examples I consider are related to advertising; and although some of these liberties are quite important, they are not basic liberties, since they do not have the requisite role and significance in the two fundamental cases.

We may distinguish three kinds of advertising according to whether the information conveyed concerns political questions, openings for jobs and positions, or the nature of products for sale. Political advertising I shall not discuss; I assume that it can be regulated for the reasons just considered in the preceding section, provided that the regulations in question satisfy the conditions already indicated. Let us turn, then, to advertisements of openings for jobs and positions. These contain information important in maintaining fair equality of opportunity. Since the first part of the second principle of justice requires that social and economic inequalities are to be attached to offices and positions open to everyone under conditions of fair equality of opportunity, this kind of advertising is associated with this part of the principle and it is granted protection accordingly. Thus, announcements of jobs and positions can be forbidden to contain statements which exclude applicants of certain designated ethnic and racial groups, or of either sex, when these limitations are contrary to fair equality of opportunity. The notion of fair equality of opportunity, like that of a basic liberty, has a central range of application which consists of various liberties together with certain conditions under which these liberties can be effectively exercised. The advertising of employment opportunities may be restricted and regulated to preserve intact this central range. Just as in the case of basic liberties, I assume that this range of application can be preserved in ways consistent with the other requirements of justice, and in particular with the basic liberties. Observe here that the restrictions in question, in contrast with the basic liberties, may be restrictions on content.

In the case of the advertising of products, let us distinguish two kinds. The first kind is advertising which contains information about prices and the features of products used by knowledgeable purchasers as criteria of evaluation. Assuming that the two principles of justice are best satisfied by a substantial use of a system of free competitive markets, economic policy should encourage this kind of advertising. This is true whether the economy is that of a private-property democracy or a liberal socialist regime. In order for markets to be workably competitive and efficient, it is necessary for consumers to be well informed about both prices and the relevant features of available products. The law may impose penalties for inaccurate or false information, which it cannot do in the case of freedom of thought and liberty of conscience; and for the protection of consumers the law can require that information about harmful and dangerous properties of goods be clearly described on the label, or in some other suitable manner. In addition, it may be forbidden for firms, or for trade and professional associations, to make agreements to limit or not to engage in this kind of advertising. The legislature may require, for example, that prices and accurate information about commodities be readily accessible to the public. Such measures help to maintain a competitive and efficient system of markets and enable consumers to make more intelligent and informed decisions.

A second kind of advertising of products is market-strategic advertising, which is found in imperfect and oligopolistic markets dominated by relatively few firms. Here the aim of a firm's expenditures on advertising may be either aggressive, for example, to expand its volume of sales or its share of the market; or the aim may be defensive: firms may be forced to advertise in order to preserve their position in the industry. In these cases consumers are usually unable to distinguish between the products of firms except by rather superficial and unimportant properties; advertising tries to influence consumers' preferences by presenting the firm as trustworthy through the use of slogans, eye-catching photographs, and so on, all designed to form or to strengthen the habit of buying the firm's products. Much of this kind of advertising is socially wasteful, and a well-ordered society that tries to preserve competition and to remove market imperfections would seek reasonable ways to limit it. The funds now devoted to advertising can be released for investment or for other useful social ends. Thus, the legislature might, for example, encourage agreements among firms to limit expenditures on this kind of advertising through taxes and by enforcing such contracts as legally valid. I am not concerned here with how practicable such a policy would be, but solely with illustrating how in this case the right to advertise, which is a kind of speech, can be restricted by contract, and therefore this right is not inalienable, in contrast to the basic liberties.

I must digress a moment to explain this last point. To say that the basic liberties are inalienable is to say that any agreement by citizens which waives or violates a basic liberty, however rational and voluntary this agreement may be, is void *ab initio;* that is, it has no legal force and does not affect any citizen's basic liberties. Moreover, the priority of the basic liberties implies that they cannot be justly denied to anyone, or to any group of persons, or even to all citizens generally, on the grounds that such is the desire, or overwhelming preference, of an effective political majority, however strong and enduring. The priority of liberty excludes such considerations from the grounds that can be entertained.

A commonsense explanation of why the basic liberties are

inalienable might say, following an idea of Montesquieu, that the basic liberties of each citizen are a part of public liberty, and therefore in a democratic state a part of sovereignty. The Constitution specifies a just political procedure in accordance with which this sovereignty is exercised subject to limits which guarantee the integrity of the basic liberties of each citizen. Thus agreements which alienate these liberties cannot be enforced by law, which consists only of enactments of sovereignty. Montesquieu believed that to sell one's status as a citizen (and, let us add, any part of it) is an act so extravagant that we cannot attribute it to anyone. He thought that its value to the seller must be beyond all price.[81] In justice as fairness, the sense in which this is so can be explained as follows. We use the original position to model the conception of free and equal persons as both reasonable and rational, and then the parties as rationally autonomous representatives of such persons select the two principles of justice which guarantee the basic liberties and their priority. The grounds upon which the parties are moved to guarantee these liberties, together with the constraints of the reasonable, explain why the basic liberties are, so to speak, beyond all price to persons so conceived. For these liberties are beyond all price to the representatives of citizens as free and equal persons when these representatives adopt principles of justice for the basic structure in the original position. The aims and conduct of citizens in society are therefore subordinate to the priority of these liberties, and thus in effect subordinate to the conception of citizens as free and equal persons.

This explanation of why the basic liberties are inalienable does not exclude the possibility that even in a well-ordered society some citizens may want to circumscribe or alienate one or more of their basic liberties. They may promise to vote for a certain political party or candidate; or they may enter into a relationship with a party or candidate such that it is a breach of trust not to vote in a certain way. Again, members of a religious association

81. *The Spirit of the Laws,* B 15, chap. 2.

366

may regard themselves as having submitted in conscience to religious authority, and therefore as not free, from the standpoint of that relationship, to question its pronouncements. Relationships of this kind are obviously neither forbidden nor in general improper.[82]

The essential point here is that the conception of citizens as free and equal persons is not required in a well-ordered society as a personal or associational or moral ideal (see §3, first paragraph). Rather it is a political conception affirmed for the sake of establishing an effective public conception of justice. Thus the institutions of the basic structure do not enforce undertakings which waive or limit the basic liberties. Citizens are always at liberty to vote as they wish and to change their religious affiliations. This, of course, protects their liberty to do things which they regard, or which they may come to regard, as wrong, and which indeed may be wrong. (Thus, they are at liberty to break promises to vote in a certain way, or to apostatize.) This is not a contradiction but simply a consequence of the role of the basic liberties in this political conception of justice.

After this digression, we can sum up by saying that the protection for different kinds of advertising varies depending on whether it is connected with political speech, or with maintaining fair equality of opportunity, or with preserving a workably competitive and efficient system of markets. The conception of the person in justice as fairness ascribes to the self a capacity for a certain hierarchy of interests; and this hierarchy is expressed by the nature of the original position (for example, by the way the reasonable frames and subordinates the rational) and by the priorities in the two principles of justice. The second principle of justice is subordinate to the first since the first guarantees the

---

82. There are many other reasons why citizens in certain situations or at certain times might not put much value on the exercise of some of their basic liberties and might want to do an action which limited these liberties in various ways. Unless these possibilities affect the agreement of the parties in the original position (and I hold that they do not), they are irrelevant to the inalienability of the basic liberties. I am indebted to Arthur Kuflik for discussion on this point.

basic liberties required for the full and informed exercise of the two moral powers in the two fundamental cases. The role of the second principle of justice is to ensure fair equality of opportunity and to regulate the social and economic system so that social resources are properly used and the means to citizens' ends are produced efficiently and fairly shared. Of course, this division of role between the two principles of justice is but part of a guiding framework for deliberation; nevertheless, it brings out why the liberties associated with the second principles are less significant in a well-ordered society than the basic liberties secured by the first.

§ 14. The Role of Justice as Fairness

I conclude with several comments. First, I should emphasize that the discussion of free speech in the last four sections is not intended to advance any of the problems that actually face constitutional jurists. My aim has been solely to illustrate how the basic liberties are specified and adjusted to one another in the application of the two principles of justice. The conception of justice to which these principles belong is not to be regarded as a method of answering the jurist's questions, but as a guiding framework, which if jurists find it convincing, may orient their reflections, complement their knowledge, and assist their judgment. We must not ask too much of a philosophical view. A conception of justice fulfills its social role provided that persons equally conscientious and sharing roughly the same beliefs find that, by affirming the framework of deliberation set up by it, they are normally led to a sufficient convergence of judgment necessary to achieve effective and fair social cooperation. My discussion of the basic liberties and their priority should be seen in this light.

In this connection recall that the conception of justice as fairness is addressed to that impasse in our recent political history shown in the lack of agreement on the way basic institutions are to be arranged if they are to conform to the freedom and equality of citizens as persons. Thus justice as fairness is addressed not so much to constitutional jurists as to citizens in a constitutional regime. It presents a way for them to conceive of their common and guaranteed status as equal citizens and attempts to connect a particular understanding of freedom and equality with a particular conception of the person thought to be congenial to the shared notions and essential convictions implicit in the public culture of a democratic society. Perhaps in this way the impasse concerning the understanding of freedom and equality can at least be intellectually clarified if not resolved. It is particularly important to keep in mind that the conception of the person is part of a conception of political and social justice. That is, it characterizes how citizens are to think of themselves and of one another in their political and social relationships, and, therefore, as having the basic liberties appropriate to free and equal persons capable of being fully cooperating members of society over a complete life. The role of a conception of the person in a conception of political justice is distinct from its role in a personal or associational ideal, or in a religious or moral way of life. The basis of toleration and of social cooperation on a footing of mutual respect in a democratic regime is put in jeopardy when these distinctions are not recognized; for when this happens and such ideals and ways of life take a political form, the fair terms of cooperation are narrowly drawn, and free and willing cooperation between persons with different conceptions of the good may become impossible. In this lecture I have tried to strengthen the liberal view (as a philosophical doctrine) by indicating how the basic liberties and their priority belong to the fair terms of cooperation between citizens who regard themselves and one another according to a conception of free and equal persons.

Finally, an observation about the concluding paragraphs of Hart's essay to which my discussion owes so much. Hart is quite rightly unconvinced by the grounds explicitly offered in *Theory* for the priority of the basic liberties. He suggests that the apparently dogmatic course of my argument for this priority may be explained by my tacitly imputing to the parties in the original position a latent ideal of my own. This latent ideal, he thinks, is that of a public-spirited citizen who prizes political activity and service to others so highly that the exchange of the opportunities for such activities for mere material good and contentment would be rejected. Hart goes on to say that this idea is, of course, one of the main ideals of liberalism; but the difficulty is that my argument for "the priority of liberty purports to rest on interests, not on ideals, and to demonstrate that the general priority of liberty reflects a preference for liberty over other goods which every self-interested person who is rational would have."[83] Now Hart is correct in saying that the priority of liberty cannot be argued for by imputing this ideal of the person to the parties in the original position; and he is right also in supposing that a conception of the person in some sense liberal underlies the argument for the priority of liberty. But this conception is the altogether different conception of citizens as free and equal persons; and its does not enter justice as fairness by imputation to the parties. Rather, it enters through the constraints of the reasonable imposed on the parties in the original position as well as in the revised account of primary goods. This conception of the person as free and equal also appears in the recognition by the parties that the persons they represent have the two moral powers and a certain psychological nature. How these elements lead to the basic liberties and their priority is sketched in §§5 and 6, and there the deliberations of the parties were rational and based on the determinate good of the persons represented. This conception of the person can be said to be liberal (in the sense of the philosophical doctrine) because it takes the capacity for social cooperation as fundamental and attributes to persons the two moral powers which make such cooperation possible. These powers specify the basis of equality. Thus citizens are regarded as having a certain natural political virtue without which the hopes for a regime of liberty may be unrealistic. Moreover, persons are assumed to have different and incommensurable

83. Hart, p. 555; Daniels, p. 252.

conceptions of the good so that the unity of social cooperation rests on a public conception of justice which secures the basic liberties. Yet despite this plurality of conceptions of the good, the notion of society as a social union of social unions shows how it is possible to coordinate the benefits of human diversity into a more comprehensive good.

While the grounds I have surveyed for the basic liberties and their priority have been drawn from and develop considerations found in *Theory,* I failed to bring them together in that work. Furthermore, the grounds I cited for this priority were not sufficient, and in some cases even incompatible with the kind of doctrine I was trying to work out.[84] I hope that the argument in this lecture is an improvement, thanks to Hart's critical discussion.

---

84. Here I refer to the errors in pars. 3–4 of §82 of *Theory,* the section in which the grounds for the priority of liberty are discussed explicitly. Two main errors are first, that I did not enumerate the most important grounds in a clear way; and second, in par. 3, pp. 542–43, that I should not have used the notion of the diminishing marginal significance of economic and social advantages relative to our interest in the basic liberties, which interest is said to become stronger as the social conditions for effectively exercising these liberties are more fully realized. Here the notion of marginal significance is incompatible with the notion of a hierarchy of interests used in par. 4, p. 543. It is this latter notion, founded on a certain conception of the person as a free and equal person, which is required by a Kantian view. The marginal changes I could have spoken of in par. 3 are the marginal, or step-by-step, changes reflected in the gradual realization of the social conditions which are necessary for the full and effective exercise of the basic liberties. But these changes are a different matter altogether from the marginal significance of interests.

Reply to Habermas

First, I want to thank Jürgen Habermas for his generous discussion and acute comments on my work, and for his setting the stage for me

This article originally appeared in the *Journal of Philosophy* 92 (March 1995) immediately following Jürgen Habermas's "Reconciliation Through the Public Use of Reason: Remarks on John Rawls's Political Liberalism." For republication I have made some minor editorial but not substantive changes. For clarity I use lecture, section, and paragraph numbers, or lecture, section, and page numbers when referring to my own work, and page numbers when referring to Habermas's. I am much indebted to many people who have helped me with this reply since I started thinking about it several years ago at the suggestion of Sidney Morgenbesser. Thomas McCarthy has given me indispensable guidance and shared with me his deep knowledge of Habermas's views from early on; several discussions with Gerald Doppelt were highly instructive at the start. In later conversations, Kenneth Baynes was always generous with his advice and counsel. I am also much indebted to Samuel Freeman and Wilfried Hinsch, and to Erin Kelly and David Peritz for their valuable assistance and comments throughout. I owe special thanks to Burton Dreben who has been a wonderful critic at every turn, especially in §2, in which I hope I to reply to the instructive criticisms he raises. Doing this offers me an ideal context in which to explain the meaning of *political liberalism* and to contrast it with Habermas's own powerful philosophical doctrine. I must thank him also for forcing me to rethink things I have said. In doing this I have come to realize that my formulations have often been not only unclear and misleading, but also inaccurate and inconsistent with my own thoughts. I have benefited greatly by trying to face up to his objections and express my view so that its main claims are made perspicuous and more exact.

My reply to Habermas begins in §1 by reviewing two main differences between his views and mine, which in good part are the result of our diverse aims and motivations. With this done, I try to reply to his more central criticisms, though for reasons of space I focus largely on what I believe are the most important ones in parts II and III of his paper. We agree on many philosophical points, though there are basic differences I try to make clear, especially in §§1 and 2 below. Throughout, I take for granted some acquaintance with his writings, and so much of my discussion consists of reminders of what he says.

§ I. Two Main Differences

Of the two main differences between Habermas's position and mine, the first is that his is comprehensive while mine is an account of the political and is limited to that. The first difference is the more fundamental as it sets the stage for and frames the second. This concerns the contrasts between our *devices of representation,* as I call them: his is the ideal discourse situation as part of his theory of communicative action, and mine is the original position. These have different aims and roles, as well as distinctive features serving different purposes.

---

have finally got right the three ideas of justification. The reply is far better as a result of their unflagging interest and suggestions. To others I indicate my indebtedness as we proceed.

1. I think of political liberalism [1] as a doctrine that falls under the category of the political. It works entirely within that domain and does not rely on anything outside it. The more familiar view of political philosophy is that its concepts, principles and ideals, and other elements are presented as consequences of comprehensive doctrines—religious, metaphysical, and moral. By contrast, political philosophy, as understood in political liberalism, consists largely of different political conceptions of right and justice viewed as *freestanding*. So while political liberalism is of course liberal, some political conceptions of right and justice belonging to political philosophy in this sense may be conservative or radical; conceptions of the divine right of kings, or even of dictatorship, may also belong to it. Although in the last two cases the corresponding regimes would lack the historical, religious, and philosophical justifications with which we are acquainted, they could have freestanding conceptions of political right and justice—however implausible,[2] and so fall within political philosophy.

1. I do not know of any liberal writers of an earlier generation who have clearly put forward the doctrine of political liberalism. Yet it is not a novel doctrine. Two contemporaries who share with me this general view, if not all its parts, and who developed it entirely independently, are Charles Larmore—see for example his "Political Liberalism," *Political Theory* 18, no. 3 (August 1990); and the late Judith Shklar—see her "The Liberalism of Fear," in Nancy Rosenblum, ed., *Liberalism and the Moral Life* (Cambridge: Harvard University Press, 1989). At least two aspects of it are also found in Bruce Ackerman's *Social Justice in the Liberal State* (New Haven: Yale University Press, 1980). On pp. 357–61, Ackerman states the relative autonomy of political discussion governed by his principle of neutrality and then considers various ways of arriving at this idea of political discourse. To be mentioned here also is the related view of Joshua Cohen in his account of deliberative democracy; see his "Deliberation and Democratic Legitimacy," in Alan Hamlin and Philip Pettit, eds., *The Good Polity* (Cambridge: Blackwell, 1989), and his "Notes on Deliberative Democracy" (unpublished, 1989). It is a great puzzle to me why political liberalism was not worked out much earlier: it seems such a natural way to present the idea of liberalism, given the fact of reasonable pluralism in political life. Does it have deep faults that preceding writers may have found in it that I have not seen and these led them to dismiss it?

2. This raises the question whether the doctrine of the divine rights of kings or of dictatorship could be plausible without in some way moving outside the political. Does the answer throw any light on the conditions leading to democracy?

374

Thus, of the various freestanding political conceptions of justice within political philosophy, some are liberal and some are not. I think of justice as fairness as working out a liberal political conception of justice for a democratic regime: one that might be endorsed—so it is hoped—by all reasonable comprehensive doctrines that exist in a democracy regulated by it or some similar view. Other liberal political conceptions have somewhat different principles and elements, but I assume that in each case their principles specify certain rights, liberties, and opportunities, assign them a certain priority with respect to other claims, and make provisions for all citizens to make essential and effective use of their freedoms.[3]

The central idea is that political liberalism moves within the category of the political and leaves philosophy as it is. It leaves untouched all kinds of doctrines—religious, metaphysical, and moral—with their long traditions of development and interpretation. Political philosophy proceeds apart from all such doctrines, and presents itself in its own terms as freestanding. Hence, it cannot argue its case by invoking any comprehensive doctrines, or by criticizing or rejecting them, so long of course as those doctrines are reasonable, politically speaking (II:3). When attributed to persons, the two basic elements of the conception of the reasonable are, first, a willingness to propose fair terms of social cooperation that others as free and equal also might endorse—and to act on these terms, provided others do, even contrary to one's own interest; and second, a recognition of the burdens of judgment (II:2–3) and acceptance of their consequences for one's attitude (including toleration) toward other comprehensive doctrines. Political liberalism abstains from assertions about the domain of comprehensive views except as necessary when these views are unreasonable and reject all variations of the basic essentials of a democratic regime. That is part of leaving philosophy as it is.

3. These conceptions are distinct from the familiar liberalisms of Immanuel Kant and J. S. Mill. Their views clearly go well beyond the political, relying on ideas of autonomy and individuality as moral values belonging to a comprehensive doctrine.

In line with these aims, political liberalism characterizes a political conception of justice by three features:

a. It applies in the first instance to the basic structure of society (assumed in the case of justice as fairness to be a democratic society). This structure consists of the main political, economic, and social institutions, and how they fit together as one unified system of social cooperation.

b. It can be formulated independently of any particular comprehensive doctrine, religious, philosophical, or moral. While we suppose that it may be derived from, or supported by, or otherwise related to one or more comprehensive doctrines (indeed, we hope it can be thus related to many such doctrines), it is not presented as depending upon, or as presupposing, any such view.

c. Its fundamental ideas—such ideas in political liberalism as those of political society as a fair system of social cooperation, of citizens as reasonable and rational, and free and equal—all belong to the category of the political and are familiar from the public political culture of a democratic society and its traditions of interpretation of the constitution and basic laws, as well as of its leading historical documents and widely known political writings.

These features illustrate the way in which a political conception of justice is freestanding (I:2).

2. Habermas's position, on the other hand, is a comprehensive doctrine that covers many things far beyond political philosophy. Indeed, the aim of his theory of communicative action is to give a general account of meaning, reference, and truth or validity both for theoretical reason and for the several forms of practical reason. It rejects naturalism and emotivism in moral argument and aims to give a full defense of both theoretical and practical reason. Moreover, Habermas often criticizes religious and metaphysical views without taking much time to argue against them in detail; rather, he lays them aside—or occasionally dismisses them—as unusable and without credible independent

merit in light of his philosophical analysis of the presuppositions of rational discourse and communicative action.

I mention two passages in *Faktizität und Geltung*.[4] From the preface:

> Discourse theory attempts to reconstruct this self-understanding [that of a universalistic moral consciousness and the liberal institutions of the democratic state] in a way that empowers its intrinsic normative meaning and logic to resist both scientific reductions and aesthetic assimilations. . . . After a century that more than any other has taught us the horror of existing unreason, the last remains of an essentialist trust in reason are destroyed.[5] Yet modernity, now aware of its contingencies, depends all the more on a procedural reason, that is, on a reason that puts itself on trial. The critique of reason is its own work: this Kantian double meaning is due to the radically anti-Platonic insight that there is neither a higher nor a deeper reality to which we could appeal—we who find ourselves already situated in our linguistically structured forms of life (FG 11).

Now, read as not appealing to religious or metaphysical doctrines, political liberalism could say something parallel to this passage regarding political justice,[6] but there would be a fundamental difference. For in presenting a freestanding political conception and not going beyond that, it is left entirely open to citizens and associations in civil society to formulate their own

---

4. Frankfurt am Main: Suhrkamp, 1992 (hereafter FG with citations and *Between Facts and Norms* in the text). William Rehg has prepared a translation of the entire work, and I am grateful to him and Thomas McCarthy for giving me a copy (*Between Facts and Norms* [Cambridge: MIT Press, forthcoming]). Without it I could not have acquired an understanding of this long and complex work. Since I refer to this work a number of times, I do so simply by giving the page reference to the German text.

5. There are two odd phrases in this passage: 'existing unreason', and 'essentialist trust in reason'. Yet Habermas has 'existierender Unvernunft' and 'essentialischen Vernunftvertrauens', respectively, so Rehg's translation is correct. By the former phrase I assume Habermas means the existence of human institutions and conduct that violate reason (*Vernunft*), and by the latter, the trust in the capacity of our reason to grasp the (Platonic) essences correctly.

6. This is the sense of the remark, justice as fairness: political not metaphysical.

ways of going beyond, or of going deeper, so as to make that political conception congruent with their comprehensive doctrines. Political liberalism never denies or questions these doctrines in any way, so long as they are politically reasonable. That Habermas himself takes a different stand on this basic point is part of his comprehensive view: he would appear to say that all higher or deeper doctrines lack any logical force on their own. He rejects what he calls an essentialist Platonic idea of reason, asserting that such an idea must be replaced by a procedural reason that puts itself on trial and is the judge of its own critique.

In another passage in chapter 5 of *Between Facts and Norms,* after an explanation of how the ideal discourse situation proceeds, he stresses that the principle of discourse requires that norms and values must be judged from the point of view of the first-person plural.

> The practice of argumentation recommends itself for such a jointly practiced, universalized role taking. As the reflexive form of communicative action, it distinguishes itself socio-ontologically, one might say, by a complete reversibility of participant perspectives, which unleashes the higher-level intersubjectivity of the deliberating collective. In this way, Hegel's concrete universal [*Sittlichkeit*]⁷ is sublimated into a communicative structure purified of all substantial elements (FG 280).

Thus, according to Habermas, the substantial elements of Hegel's view of *Sittlichkeit,* an apparently metaphysical doctrine of ethical life (one among many possible examples), are—so far as they are valid—fully sublimated into (I interpret him to mean expressible, or articulated, by) the theory of communicative action with its procedural presuppositions of ideal discourse. Habermas's own doctrine, I believe, is one of logic in the broad Hegelian sense: a philosophical analysis of the presuppositions of rational discourse (of theoretical and practical reason) which

---

7. I assume this concrete universal is a reference to Hegel's idea of *Sittlichkeit,* as expounded in his *Philosophy of Right.*

378

includes within itself all the allegedly substantial elements of religious and metaphysical doctrines. His logic is metaphysical in the following sense: it presents an account of what there is[8]— human beings engaged in communicative action in their life-world. As to what 'substance' and 'substantial' mean, I would conjecture that Habermas intends something like the following: people often think that their basic way of doing things—their communicative action with its presuppositions of ideal discourse, or their conception of society as a fair system of cooperation between citizens who are free and equal—needs a foundation beyond itself discerned by a Platonic reason that grasps the essences, or else is rooted in metaphysical substances. In thought, we reach behind or deeper to a religious or metaphysical doctrine for a firm foundation. This reality is also expected to provide moral motivation.[9] Without these foundations everything may seem to us to waver and we experience a kind of vertigo—a feeling of being lost without a place to stand. But Habermas holds that "In the vertigo of this freedom there is no longer any fixed point outside the democratic procedure itself— a procedure whose meaning is already summed up in the system of rights" (FG 229).[10] (I return to this view of Habermas at the end of §5.)

The preceding comments bear on Habermas's last two paragraphs (131). Here he says we each see our own views as more

8. I think of metaphysics as being at least a general account of what there is, including fundamental, fully general statements—for example, the statements 'every event has a cause' and 'all events occur in space and time', or can be related thereto. So viewed, W. V. Quine also is a metaphysician. To deny certain metaphysical doctrines is to assert another such doctrine.

9. On these points, see his remarks on Ronald Dworkin, FG 86ff.

10. Another example is what Habermas says (130) that once both public and private autonomy (I discuss these in §§3 and 4) are incorporated in law and political institutions in accordance with the discourse-theoretic account of democracy, "it becomes clear that the normative substance of basic liberal rights is already contained in the indispensable medium for the legal institutionalization of the public reason of sovereign citizens." The word for *vertigo* in the quotation in the text is *der Taumel* which can mean: reeling, giddiness, or, figuratively, delirium, ecstasy, frenzy. Rehg's 'vertigo' seems appropriate here.

modest than the other's. He sees his view as more modest than mine, since it is purportedly a procedural doctrine that leaves questions of substance to be decided by the outcome of actual free discussions engaged in by free and rational, real and live participants—as opposed to the artificial creatures of the original position. He proposes, he says, to limit moral philosophy to the clarification of the moral point of view and to the procedure of democratic legitimation, and to the analysis of the conditions of rational discourses and negotiation. In contrast, he thinks that my view takes on a more ambitious task, since it hopes to formulate a political conception of justice for the basic structure of a democracy, all of which involves fundamental substantive conceptions, which raise larger questions that only the actual discourse of real participants can decide.

At the same time, Habermas thinks I see my view as more modest than his: it aims to be solely a political conception and not a comprehensive one. He believes, though, that I fail in doing this. My conception of political justice is not really freestanding, as I would like it to be, because whether I like it or not, he thinks that the conception of the person in political liberalism goes beyond political philosophy. Moreover, he claims that political constructivism involves the philosophical questions of rationality and truth. And he may also think that, along with Immanual Kant, I express a conception of a priori and metaphysical reason laying down in justice as fairness principles and ideals so conceived.

I deny these things. The philosophical conception of the person is replaced in political liberalism by the political conception of citizens as free and equal. As for political constructivism, its task is to connect the content of the political principles of justice with the conception of citizens as being reasonable and rational. The argument is set out in III:1–3. It does not rely on a Platonic and Kantian reason—or if so, does so in the same way Habermas does. No sensible view can possibly get by without the reasonable and rational as I use them. If this argument involves Plato's

380

and Kant's view of reason, so does the simplest bit of logic and mathematics. I come back to this in §2.

3. As I have said, the stage for the second difference between Habermas's position and mine is prepared for by the first. This is because the differences between the two analytical devices of representation—the ideal discourse situation and the original position[11]—reflect their different locations, one in a comprehensive doctrine, the other limited to the political.

The original position is an analytical device used to formulate a conjecture. The conjecture is that when we ask—What are the most reasonable principles of political justice for a constitutional democracy whose citizens are seen as free and equal, reasonable and rational?—the answer is that these principles are given by a device of representation in which rational parties (as trustees of citizens, one for each) are situated in reasonable conditions and constrained by these conditions absolutely. Thus, free and equal citizens are envisaged as themselves reaching agreement about these political principles under conditions that represent those citizens as both reasonable and rational. That the principles so agreed to are indeed the most reasonable ones is a conjecture, since it may of course be incorrect. We must check it against the fixed points of our considered judgments at different levels of generality. We also must examine how well these principles can be applied to democratic institutions and what their results would be, and hence ascertain how well they fit in practice with our considered judgments on due reflection.[12] In either direction, we may be led to revise our judgments.

Habermas's theory of communicative action yields the analyti-

11. I have not always been clear about this and thought for a time that a more useful comparison might be between the ideal discourse situation and the position of citizens in civil society, you and me. On the latter, see "Kantian Constructivism in Moral Theory," the *Journal of Philosophy* 77 (September 1980): 533f.; and I:4.6. I am indebted to Jon Mandle for valuable correspondence on this topic.

12. See fn. 16 at the end of this section for further remarks on reflective equilibrium.

cal device of the ideal discourse situation, which offers an account of the truth and validity of judgments of both theoretical and practical reason. It tries to lay out completely the presuppositions of rational and free discussion as guided by the strongest reasons such that, if all requisite conditions were actually realized and fully honored by all active participants, their rational consensus would serve as a warrant for truth or validity. Alternatively, to claim that a statement of whatever kind is true, or a normative judgment valid, is to claim that it could be accepted by participants in a discourse situation to the extent that all the required conditions expressed by the ideal obtained. As I have remarked, his doctrine is one of logic in the broad Hegelian sense: a philosophical analysis of the presuppositions of rational discourse which includes within itself all the apparent substantial elements of religious and metaphysical doctrines.

From what point of view are the two devices of representation to be discussed? And from what point of view does the debate between them take place? Always, we must be attentive to where we are and whence we speak. To all these questions the answer is the same: all discussions are from the point of view of citizens in the culture of civil society, which Habermas calls the *public sphere*.[13] There, we as citizens discuss how justice as fairness is to be formulated, and whether this or that aspect of it seems acceptable—for example, whether the details of the set-up of the

13. See FG, ch. 8; and the considerably earlier (1962) *The Structural Transformation of the Public Sphere,* T. Burger, trans. (Cambridge: MIT Press, 1989). Here terminology can get in the way. The public reason of political liberalism may be confused with Habermas's public sphere but they are not the same. Public reason in this text is the reasoning of legislators, executives (presidents, for example), and judges (especially those of a supreme court, if there is one). It includes also the reasoning of candidates in political elections and of party leaders and others who work in their campaigns, as well as the reasoning of citizens when they vote on constitutional essentials and matters of basic justice. The ideal of public reason does not have the same requirements in all these cases. As for Habermas's public sphere, since it is much the same as what I call in I: 2.3 the background culture, public reason with its duty of civility does not apply. We agree on this. I am not clear whether he accepts this ideal (129–30). Some of his statements in FG (see 18, 84, 152, 492, 534f.) certainly seem to suggest it and I believe it would not be consistent with his view, but regrettably I cannot discuss the question here.

original position are properly laid out and whether the principles selected are to be endorsed. In the same way, the claims of the ideal of discourse and of its procedural conception of democratic institutions are considered. Keep in mind that this background culture contains comprehensive doctrines of all kinds that are taught, explained, debated one against another, and argued about—indefinitely without end as long as society has vitality and spirit. It is the culture of the social, not of the publicly political. It is the culture of daily life with its many associations: its universities and churches, learned and scientific societies; endless political discussions of ideas and doctrines are commonplace everywhere.

The point of view of civil society includes all citizens. Like Habermas's ideal discourse situation, it is a dialogue; indeed, an omnilogue.[14] There are no experts: a philosopher has no more authority than other citizens. Those who study political philosophy may sometimes know more about some things, but so may anyone else. Everyone appeals equally to the authority of human reason present in society. So far as other citizens pay attention to it, what is written may become part of the ongoing public discussion—*A Theory of Justice*[15] along with the rest—until it

---

14. I blame this term on Christine Korsgaard. Habermas sometimes says that the original position is monological and not dialogical; that is because all the parties have, in effect, the same reasons and so they elect the same principles. This is said to have the serious fault of leaving it to "the philosopher" as an expert and not to citizens of an ongoing society to determine the political conception of justice. See Habermas's *Moralbewusstsein and kommunikatives Handeln* (Frankfurt am Main: Suhrkamp, 1983). The third essay is entitled: "Diskursethik: Notizen zu einen Begründungsprogramm." I refer to the English translation entitled *Moral Consciousness and Communicative Action,* C. Lenhardt and S. W. Nicholsen, trans. (Cambridge: MIT Press, 1990) and refer to the third essay as "Notes." The reply I make to his objection ("Notes," pp. 66ff.) is that it is you and I—and so all citizens over time, one by one and in associations here and there—who judge the merits of the original position as a device of representation and the principles it yields. I deny that the original position is monological in a way that puts in doubt its soundness as a device of representation. There is also his *Erläuterungen zur Discursethik* (Frankfurt am Main: Suhrkamp, 1991); a translation by Ciaran Cronin with his introduction is entitled *Justification and Application* (Cambridge: MIT Press, 1993).

15. Cambridge: Harvard, 1971 (hereafter *Theory*).

eventually disappears. Citizens' debates may, but need not, be reasonable and deliberative, and they are protected at least in a decent democratic regime, by an effective law of free speech. Argument may occasionally reach a fairly high level of openness and impartiality, as well as show a concern for truth—or when the discussion concerns the political, for reasonableness. How high a level it reaches depends, obviously, on the virtues and intelligence of the participants.

The argument is normative and concerned with ideals and values, though in political liberalism it is limited to the political, while in discourse ethics it is not. By addressing this audience of citizens in civil society, as any democratic doctrine must, justice as fairness spells out various fundamental political conceptions— those of society as a fair system of cooperation, of citizens as free and equal, and of a well-ordered society—and then hopes to combine them into a reasonable and complete political conception of justice for the basic structure of a constitutional democracy. That is its primary aim: to be presented to and understood by the audience in civil society for its citizens to consider. The overall criterion of the reasonable is general and wide reflective equilibrium;[16] whereas we have seen that in Habermas's view

16. I add here two remarks about wide and general reflective equilibrium. Wide reflective equilibrium (in the case of one citizen) is the reflective equilibrium reached when that citizen has carefully considered alternative conceptions of justice and the force of various arguments for them. More specifically, the citizen has considered the leading conceptions of political justice found in our philosophical tradition (including views critical of the concept of justice itself) and has weighed the force of the different philosophical and other reasons for them. We suppose this citizen's general convictions, first principles, and particular judgments are at last in line. The reflective equilibrium is wide, given the wide-ranging reflection and possibly many changes of view that have preceded it. Wide and not narrow reflective equilibrium (in which we take note of only our own judgments) is plainly the important philosophical concept.

Recall that a well-ordered society is a society effectively regulated by a public political conception of justice. Think of each citizen in such a society as having achieved wide reflective equilibrium. Since citizens recognize that they affirm the same public conception of political justice, reflective equilibrium is also general: the same conception is affirmed in everyone's considered judgments. Thus, citizens have achieved general and wide, or what we may refer to as full, reflective equilibrium. In such a society, not only is there a public point of view from which all citizens can

the test of moral truth or validity is fully rational acceptance in the ideal discourse situation, with all requisite conditions satisfied. Reflective equilibrium resembles his test in this respect: it is a point at infinity we can never reach, though we may get closer to it in the sense that through discussion, our ideals, principles, and judgments seem more reasonable to us and we regard them as better founded than they were before.

§ 2. Overlapping Consensus and Justification

1. In his second section, Habermas raises two questions.[17] The first question is whether an overlapping consensus adds to the justification of a political conception of justice already taken to be justified as reasonable. Put another way, he asks whether the doctrines belonging to the consensus further strengthen and deepen the justification of a freestanding conception; or whether they merely constitute a necessary condition of social stability (119–22). By these questions I take Habermas to ask, in effect: What bearing do doctrines within an overlapping consensus have on the justification of the political conception—once citizens see that conception as both reasonable and freestanding?

The second question concerns how political liberalism uses the term 'reasonable': Does the term express the validity of political and moral judgments or does the term merely express a reflective attitude of enlightened tolerance (123–26)?

Habermas's two questions are intimately related. The answer to both lies in the way in which political liberalism specifies three different kinds of justification and two kinds of consensus, and then connects these with the idea of stability for the right reasons, and with the idea of legitimacy. I begin with the three kinds

---

adjudicate their claims of political justice, but also this point of view is mutually recognized as affirmed by them all in full reflective equilibrium. This equilibrium is fully intersubjective: that is, each citizen has taken into account the reasoning and arguments of every other citizen.

17. I have gained much from valuable discussion with Wilfried Hinsch and Peter de Marneffe on earlier drafts of this section.

of justification in the following order: first, *pro tanto* justification of the political conception; second, full justification of that conception by an individual person in society; and finally, public justification of the political conception by political society. I then explain the other ideas as we proceed.

Consider *pro tanto* justification. In public reason the justification of the political conception takes into account only political values, and I assume that a political conception properly laid out is complete (IV:4.3, VI:7.2). That is, the political values specified by it can be suitably ordered, or balanced, so that those values alone give a reasonable answer by public reason to all or nearly all questions concerning constitutional essentials and basic justice. This is the meaning of *pro tanto* justification. By examining a wide range of political questions to see whether a political conception can always provide a reasonable answer we can check to see if it seems to be complete. But since political justification is *pro tanto,* it may be overridden by citizens' comprehensive doctrines once all values are tallied up.

Second, full justification is carried out by an individual citizen as a member of civil society. (We assume that each citizen affirms both a political conception and a comprehensive doctrine.[18]) In this case, the citizen accepts a political conception and fills out its justification by embedding it in some way into the citizen's comprehensive doctrine as either true or reasonable, depending on what that doctrine allows. Some may consider the political conception fully justified even though it is not accepted by other people. Whether our view is endorsed by them is not given sufficient weight to suspend its full justification in our own eyes.

Thus it is left to each citizen, individually or in association with others, to say how the claims of political justice are to be ordered, or weighed, against nonpolitical values. The political conception gives no guidance in such questions, since it does not

18. Some citizens might not have a comprehensive doctrine, except possibly a null doctrine, such as agnosticism or skepticism.

say how nonpolitical values are to be counted. This guidance belongs to citizens' comprehensive doctrines. Recall that a political conception of justice is not dependent on any particular comprehensive doctrine, including even agnostic ones. But even though a political conception of justice is freestanding, that does not mean that it cannot be embedded in various ways—or mapped, or inserted as a module[19]—into the different doctrines citizens affirm.

Third and last is public justification by political society. This is a basic idea of political liberalism and works in tandem with the other three ideas: those of a reasonable overlapping consensus, stability for the right reasons, and legitimacy. Public justification happens when all the reasonable members of political society carry out a justification of the shared political conception by embedding it in their several reasonable comprehensive views. In this case, reasonable citizens take one another into account as having reasonable comprehensive doctrines that endorse that political conception, and this mutual accounting shapes the moral quality of the public culture of political society. A crucial point here is that while the public justification of the political conception for political society depends on reasonable comprehensive doctrines, this justification does so only in an indirect way. That is, the express contents of these doctrines have no normative role in public justification; citizens do not look into the content of others' doctrines, and so remain within the bounds of the political. Rather, they take into account and give some weight to only the fact—the existence—of the reasonable overlapping consensus itself.[20]

19. This phrase was used twice in I:2.2, IV: 3.1. One might also mention the way in which, in algebra, a group may be included as a subgroup in each group of a certain class of groups.

20. Here I assume that the existence of reasonable comprehensive doctrines and of their forming an overlapping consensus are facts about the political and cultural nature of a pluralist democratic society, and these facts can be used like any other such facts. Reference to these facts, or making assumptions about them, is not reliance on the religious, metaphysical, or moral contents of such doctrines.

This basic case of public justification[21] is one in which the shared political conception is the common ground and all reasonable citizens taken collectively (but not acting as a corporate body[22]) are held in general and wide reflective equilibrium in affirming the political conception on the basis of their several reasonable comprehensive doctrines. Only when there is a reasonable overlapping consensus can political society's political conception of justice be publicly—though never finally—justified. Granting that we should give weight to the considered convictions of other reasonable citizens, this is because general and wide reflective equilibrium with respect to a public justification gives the best justification of the political conception that we can have at any given time.[23] There is, then, no public justification for political society without a reasonable overlapping consensus, and such a justification also connects with the ideas of

21. I refer to public justification as a basic case for political liberalism because of its role in that doctrine and of its connection with the ideas of a reasonable overlapping consensus, stability for the right reasons, and legitimacy. That idea of justification is a part of the rebuilding of a fundamental conception of *Theory* III, and expressed in section 79 on the conception of a social union of social unions and its companion idea of stability, which depends on the congruence of the right and the good. (On this last, see Samuel Freeman's account in the *Chicago-Kent Law Review* 69, no. 3 (1994): 619–68, sects. I–II.) This conception depends, however, on everyone's holding the same comprehensive doctrine and so it is no longer viable as a political ideal once we recognize the fact of reasonable pluralism, which characterizes the public culture of the political society required by the two principles of justice. Now we face a different problem and the ideas of a reasonable overlapping consensus and the rest are used instead. Once we see the different nature of the task, the reasons for the introduction of these further ideas fall into place. We see why, for example, political justification must be *pro tanto*. One is not replying to objections but rather trying to fix a basic inherent conflict (recognized later) between the cultural conditions needed for justice as fairness to be a comprehensive doctrine and the requirements of freedom guaranteed by the two principles of justice. With this understood, I believe the complexities—if such they are—are no longer surprising.

22. By this I mean that there is no political body that acts by vote on the political conception. That is contrary to the idea of the reasonable. The conception of political justice can no more be voted on than can the axioms, principles, and rules of inference of mathematics or logic.

23. See my remarks in fn. 16 above in §1.

stability for the right reasons as well as of legitimacy. These last ideas I now set out more fully.

First, I distinguish two different ideas of consensus, as misunderstanding here would be fatal. One idea of consensus comes from everyday politics where the task of the politician is to find agreement. Looking to various existing interests and claims, the politician tries to put together a coalition or policy that all or a sufficient number can support to gain a majority. This idea of consensus is the idea of an overlap that is already present or latent, and could be articulated by the politician's skill in bringing together existing interests the politician knows intimately. The very different idea of consensus in political liberalism—the idea I call a *reasonable overlapping consensus*—is that the political conception of justice is worked out first as a freestanding view that can be justified *pro tanto* without looking to, or trying to fit, or even knowing what are, the existing comprehensive doctrines (I:6.4). It tries to put no obstacles in the path of all reasonable doctrines endorsing a political conception by eliminating from this conception any idea which goes beyond the political, and which not all reasonable doctrines could reasonably be expected to endorse (to do that violates the idea of reciprocity). When the political conception meets these conditions and is also complete, we hope the reasonable comprehensive doctrines affirmed by reasonable citizens in society can support it, and that in fact it will have the capacity to shape those doctrines toward itself (IV:6–7).

Consider the political sociology of a reasonable overlapping consensus: since there are far less doctrines than citizens, the latter may be grouped according to the doctrine they hold. More important than the simplification allowed by this numerical fact is that citizens are members of various associations into which, in many cases, they are born, and from which they usually, though not always, acquire their comprehensive doctrines (IV:6). The doctrines that different associations hold and propagate—as examples, think of religious associations of all kinds—play a basic social role in making public justification possible. This is how citizens may acquire their comprehensive doctrines. Moreover, these doctrines have their own life and history apart from their current members and endure from one generation to the next. The consensus of these doctrines is importantly rooted in the character of various associations and this is a basic fact about the political sociology of a democratic regime—crucial in providing a deep and enduring basis for its social unity.

In a democratic society marked by reasonable pluralism, showing that stability for the right reasons is at least possible is also part of public justification.[24] The reason is that when citizens affirm reasonable though different comprehensive doctrines, seeing whether an overlapping consensus on the political conception is possible is a way of checking whether there are sufficient reasons for proposing justice as fairness (or some other reasonable doctrine) which can be sincerely defended before others without criticizing or rejecting their deepest religious and philosophical commitments.[25] If we can make the case that there are adequate reasons for diverse reasonable people jointly to affirm justice as fairness as their working political conception, then the conditions for their legitimately exercising coercive political power over one another—something we inevitably do as citizens by voting, if in no other way—are satisfied (IV:1.3–4). The argument, if successful, would show how we can reasonably affirm and appeal to a political conception of justice as citizens' shared basis of reasons, all the while supposing that others no less reasonable than we may also affirm and recognize that same basis. Despite the fact of reasonable pluralism, the conditions for democratic legitimacy are fulfilled.[26]

24. Here I am speaking from within political liberalism. Whether a citizen will say the same within that citizen's comprehensive doctrine depends on the doctrine.

25. As I noted in §1, Habermas's comprehensive doctrine violates this.

26. In this paragraph, I am indebted to Thomas Hill's discussion in Los Angeles, April 1994, of how the concern with stability connects with the ideas of public justification and overlapping consensus. He stressed aspects of the matter I had not so clearly addressed.

Given a political society with such a reasonable consensus, political liberalism says that as citizens of this society we have achieved the deepest and most reasonable basis of social unity available to us in a modern democracy.[27] This unity yields stability for the right reasons, explained as follows:[28]

    a. The basic structure of society is effectively regulated by the most reasonable political conception of justice.

    b. This political conception of justice is endorsed by an overlapping consensus comprised of all the reasonable comprehensive doctrines in society and these are in an enduring majority with respect to those rejecting that conception.

    c. Public political discussions, when constitutional essentials and matters of basic justice are at stake, are always (or nearly always) reasonably decidable on the basis of the reasons specified by the most reasonable political conception of justice, or by a reasonable family of such conceptions.

Two comments. One is that this basis of social unity is the most reasonable since the political conception of justice is the most reasonable one—endorsed, or in some way supported by, all reasonable (or the reasonable) comprehensive doctrines in society. A second comment is that this basis of social unity is the

27. In I:1.3–4, the aim of the view so named is not, I now think, stated in the best way. There the text seems to focus on how stability can be achieved under conditions of reasonable pluralism but that question has an uninteresting Hobbesian answer. Rather, this text tries to answer the question as to the most reasonable basis of social unity given the fact of reasonable pluralism; see PL IV: Preface, V:7.1–2. Once we answer this question, we can also answer the other two questions I asked: What is the most appropriate conception of justice for specifying the fair terms of social cooperation between citizens of a democratic regime regarded as free and equal? What is the basis of toleration, given the fact of reasonable pluralism as the inevitable outcome of free institutions?

28. Once stability for the right reasons is attained and supports this basis of social unity, political liberalism hopes to satisfy the traditional liberal demand to justify the social world in a manner acceptable "at the tribunal of each person's understanding." So Jeremy Waldron put it in his *Liberal Rights* (New York: Cambridge University Press, 1993), p. 61.

deepest because the fundamental ideas of the political conception are endorsed by the reasonable comprehensive doctrines, and these doctrines represent what citizens regard as their deepest convictions—religious, philosophical, and moral. From this follows stability for the right reasons. The contrast is a society in which when citizens are grouped by their full justifications, their political conceptions are not embedded in or connected with a shared political conception. In this case there is only a *modus vivendi,* and society's stability depends on a balance of forces in contingent and possibly fluctuating circumstances.

These explanations of the three kinds of justification may seem to raise a grave question. One might ask: If political justification is always *pro tanto,* how can public justification of the political conception of justice be carried out? The answer, of course, is given by the existence and public knowledge of a reasonable overlapping consensus. In this case, citizens embed their shared political conception in their reasonable comprehensive doctrines. Then we hope that citizens will judge (by their comprehensive view) that political values either outweigh or are normally (though not always) ordered prior to whatever nonpolitical values may conflict with them.[29]

If this seems unrealistic to hope for, two things indicate why it may not be. First, those holding a reasonable comprehensive doctrine must ask themselves on what political terms they are ready to live with other such doctrines in an ongoing free society. Since reasonable citizens hold reasonable doctrines (II:3.1), they are ready to offer or endorse a political conception of justice to specify the terms of fair political cooperation. Hence, they may

---

29. There are several statements to this effect in IV:5. If one fails to note this background condition of a reasonable overlapping consensus, the assertion in the text taken alone appears to express a comprehensive moral point of view that ranks the duties owed to just basic institutions ahead of all other human commitments. How otherwise is it possible that values of the political, a subdomain of all values, normally outweighs whatever other values may conflict with them? A troubling assertion, however, occurs only when one forgets that a reasonable overlapping consensus is assumed to obtain and that the text is commenting on the public justification of the political conception carried out by the members of society.

well judge from within their reasonable comprehensive doctrines that political values are very great values to be realized in the framework of their political and social existence, and a shared public life on terms that all reasonable parties may reasonably be expected to endorse.

Second, we finally come to the idea of legitimacy: reasonable citizens understand this idea to apply to the general structure of political authority (IV:1.2–3). They know that in political life unanimity can rarely if ever be expected on a basic question, and so a democratic constitution must include procedures of majority or other plurality voting to reach decisions. It is unreasonable not to propose or endorse any such arrangements. Let us say, then, that the exercise of political power is legitimate only when it is exercised in fundamental cases in accordance with a constitution, the essentials of which all reasonable citizens as free and equal might reasonably be expected to endorse. Thus, citizens recognize the familiar distinction between accepting as (sufficiently) just and legitimate a constitution with its procedures for fair elections and legislative majorities, and accepting as legitimate (even when not just[30]) a particular statute or a decision in a particular matter of policy.[31] (I come back to the idea of legitimacy in §5.3.)

So Quakers, being pacifists, refuse to engage in war, yet they also support a constitutional regime and accept the legitimacy of majority or other plurality rule. While they refuse to serve in a war that a democratic people may reasonably decide to wage, they will still affirm democratic institutions and the basic values they represent. They do not think that the possibility of a people's voting to go to war is a sufficient reason for opposing democratic government.

One might ask why the Quaker's religious doctrine prohib-

30. It is unreasonable to expect in general that human statutes and laws should be strictly just by our lights. I cannot discuss here the extent of reasonable deviation allowed.

31. Stuart Hampshire rightly stresses this point; see his review of this text in the *New York Review of Books* (August 12, 1993), p. 44.

iting their engaging in war does not put their allegiance in doubt. Yet our religion may enjoin many things. It may require our support of constitutional government as that which, of all feasible political regimes, is most in accord with the religious injunction to be equally concerned with the basic rights and fundamental interests of others as well as our own. As with any reasonable doctrine, many political and nonpolitical values are represented and ordered within it. With that granted, allegiance to a just and enduring constitutional government may win out within the religious doctrine.[32] This illustrates how political values can be overriding in upholding the constitutional system itself, even if particular reasonable statutes and decisions may be rejected, and as necessary protested by civil disobedience or conscientious refusal.

What we have said elaborates the idea of a justified and freestanding political conception and enables us to answer Habermas's first question: whether the idea of an overlapping consensus adds to the justification of the political conception, or simply lays out a necessary condition of social stability. The answer to his first question is given by the third idea of justification—that of public justification—and by how it connects with the three further ideas of a reasonable overlapping consensus, stability for the right reasons, and legitimacy.

2. We can now briefly discuss Habermas's second question: Does political liberalism use the term 'reasonable' to express the truth or validity of moral judgments, or simply to express a reflective attitude toward tolerance?

I have nothing to add beyond what has been said already. Political liberalism does not use the concept of moral truth applied to its own political (always moral) judgments. Here it says that political judgments are reasonable or unreasonable; and it lays out political ideals, principles, and standards as criteria of the reasonable. These criteria in turn are connected with the

32. The same considerations, duly modified, hold in the case of those who reject abortion rights supported by a democratic regime.

394

two basic features of reasonable persons as citizens: first, their willingness to propose and to abide by, if accepted, what they think others as equal citizens with them might reasonably accept as fair terms of social cooperation; and, second, their willingness to recognize the burdens of judgment and accept the consequences thereof. For the political purpose of discussing questions of constitutional essentials and basic justice, political liberalism views this idea of the reasonable as sufficient. The use of the concept of truth is not rejected or questioned, but left to comprehensive doctrines to use or deny, or use some other idea instead. And finally, the reasonable does, of course, express a reflective attitude to toleration, since it recognizes the burdens of judgment, and this in turn leads to liberty of conscience and freedom of thought (II:2–4).

Yet Habermas maintains that political liberalism cannot avoid the questions of truth and the philosophical conception of the person (131). I have indicated before that I do not see why not. Political liberalism avoids reliance on both of these ideas and substitutes others—the reasonable, in one case, and the conception of persons as citizens viewed as free and equal, in the other. When in civil society we set up justice as fairness, or indeed any political conception, these ideas are always described and expressed by conceptions and principles within the political conception itself. Until this way of proceeding is shown unsatisfactory, or to fail in certain ways, political liberalism need not give ground. I grant that the idea of the reasonable needs a more thorough examination than this text offers. Yet I believe the main lines of the distinction between the reasonable and both the true and the rational are clear enough to show the plausibility of the idea of social unity secured by a reasonable overlapping consensus. Certainly people will continue to raise questions of truth and the philosophical idea of the person and to tax political liberalism with not discussing them. In the absence of particulars, these complaints fall short of being objections.

§ 3. Liberties of the Moderns Versus the Will of the People

1. In this section, I begin my reply to Habermas's objection as raised in III before the summary of his own view (130–31); in the next section, I complete my reply beginning with what he says in that summary. The objections concern the correct relation among two familiar classes of basic rights and liberties—the so-called liberties of the ancients and the liberties of the moderns. Habermas agrees that I share Jean-Jacques Rousseau's and Kant's hopes of deriving both kinds of rights from the same root. This is shown in the fact that both kinds of liberties appear equally in the first principle of justice, which is adopted in the original position. That these liberties have the same root means, he thinks, that the liberties of the moderns cannot be imposed as external constraints on the political process of citizens' self-determination. He then refers to the two-stage (*Zweistufig*) character (127–28) of the political conception of justice as fairness, by which I take him to mean that this conception starts with the hypothetical situation of the original position where principles of justice are selected once and for all by the parties as equals subject to the veil of ignorance, and next moves to citizens' regular application of those same principles under the actual conditions of political life.[33] The two-stage character of the political conception leads, he believes, to the liberal rights of the moderns having a priori features that demote the democratic process to an inferior status (127–28). This last statement I wish to deny.

Habermas also grants that I start from the idea of political autonomy and model it at the level of the original position. But while the form of this autonomy is given what he calls "virtual existence" in that position and so in theory, that form of autonomy does not "fully unfold in the heart of the justly constituted society." The reason for this is stated in a long passage I shall cite nearly entirely though in three parts, commenting on each part separately. I refer to the passage beginning with 'For the higher

33. I am indebted to Frank Michelman for clarification on this point.

the veil of ignorance' (128) and ending with the words 'prior to all political will formation' (129). This passage is the basis of my discussion of the relations among the basic liberties. It contains some puzzling statements and I fear I may not understand him. All the same, the passage raises deep questions about how our views are related.

2. I begin with an apparent misunderstanding of the idea of what I call the *four-stage sequence,* and even if only that, I should explain it. This sentence goes:

> For the higher the veil of ignorance is raised and the more Rawls's citizens take on flesh and blood, the more deeply they find themselves subject to principles and norms that have been anticipated in theory and have already become institutionalized beyond their control (128).

Two essential points. First, the four-stage sequence describes neither an actual political process, nor a purely theoretical one. Rather, it is part of justice as fairness and constitutes part of a framework of thought that citizens in civil society who accept justice as fairness are to use in applying its concepts and principles. It sketches what kinds of norms and information are to guide our political judgments of justice, depending on their subject and context.

We begin in the original position where the parties select principles of justice; next, we move to a constitutional convention where—seeing ourselves as delegates—we are to draw up the principles and rules of a constitution in the light of the principles of justice already on hand. After this we become, as it were, legislators enacting laws as the constitution allows and as the principles of justice require and permit;[34] and finally, we

---

34. Here there is a formidable complication that I can only mention here, namely, that there is an important distinction between legislation dealing with constitutional essentials and basic justice, and legislation dealing with political bargaining between the various interests in civil society which takes place through their representatives. The latter kind of legislation is required to have a framework of fair bargaining both in the legislature and in civil society. The complication is formidable because it is a difficult task to spell out the criteria needed for drawing this distinction and illustrating it by instructive cases.

assume the role of judges interpreting the constitution and laws as members of the judiciary. Different levels and kinds of information are available at each stage and in each case designed to enable us to apply the (two) principles intelligently, making rational but not partial decisions favoring our own interests or the interests of those to whom we are attached, such as our friends or religion, our social position or political party.

This framework extends the idea of the original position, adapting it to different settings as the application of principles requires. In judging a constitution, say, we are to follow the principles of justice as well as general information about our society, the kind framers of a constitution would want to know—which is then permitted us, but not particular information about ourselves and our attachments, as indicated above. This kind of relevant information, assuming sufficient intelligence and powers of reason, is thought to ensure that our judgment is impartial and reasonable, and following the principles of justice, is to guide us in framing a just constitution and similarly for the other stages (*Theory*, §31). Here I skip over a difficult question: What is the relevant information when the existing society contains grave injustices as societies always do, as American society did in 1787–91 [35] (and still does)—such as slavery and denying suffrage to women and those who did not meet property qualifications? Some think that no constitution excluding slavery could have been adopted at that time, so is that knowledge relevant? *Theory* takes the view that all such information is irrelevant and assumes that a just constitution is realizable. After working out what that constitution is under what I call *reasonably favorable conditions,* it sets up the aim of long-term political reform once, from the point of view of civil society, it turns out that a just constitution cannot be fully realized. In Habermas's terms, it is a project to be carried out (FG 163).

35. I use these dates to include the whole period from the constitutional convention through the ratification of the Bill of Rights. In this and the next sections, I am grateful to James Fleming for this and many other valuable suggestions bearing on constitutional law, all of which I have gladly followed.

398

The second point, related to the preceding one, is that when citizens in political offices or civil society use this framework, the institutions they find themselves under are not the work of a political philosopher who has institutionalized them in theory beyond citizens' control. Rather, those institutions are the work of past generations who pass them on to us as we grow up under them. We assess them when we come of age and act accordingly. All this seems obvious once the purpose and use of the four-stage sequence is made clear.[36] What may cause misunderstanding is the thought that, using an abstract idea like the original position as a device of representation and imagining the parties to understand their selection of principles to hold in perpetuity, justice as fairness apparently supposes that citizens' conception of justice can be fixed once and for all. This overlooks the crucial point that we are in civil society and that the political conception of justice, like any other conception, is always subject to being checked by our reflective considered judgments. Using the idea of perpetuity here is a way of saying that when we imagine rational (not reasonable) parties to select principles, it is a reasonable condition to require them to do so assuming their selection is to hold in perpetuity. Our ideas of justice are in this way fixed: we cannot change them to suit our rational interests and knowledge of circumstances as we please.[37] Checking them by our considered judgments is, of course, another matter.

3. The next aspect of Habermas's objection raises a question about the meaning of political autonomy and how it is realized. The question is well expressed by the idea that under a just constitution citizens "cannot reignite the radical democratic embers of the original position in the civic life of their society"

---

36. On the two points of this and the preceding paragraph, see *Theory*, §31, pp. 196f. and 200f.

37. In the last two paragraphs, I hope to address Habermas's concerns about the framework of the four-stage sequence. I thank McCarthy and Michelman for instructive discussion.

(128). The idea is put more fully in the second part of the passage. So after 'beyond their control' we have:

> In this way, the theory deprives the citizens of too many of the insights that they would have to assimilate anew in each generation. From the perspective of the theory of justice, the act of founding the democratic constitution cannot be repeated under the institutional conditions of an already constituted just society, and the process of realizing the system of basic rights cannot be assured on an ongoing basis. It is not possible for citizens to experience this process as open and incomplete, as the shifting historical circumstances nonetheless demand. They cannot reignite the radical democratic embers of the original position in the civic life of their society, for from their perspective all of the *essential* discourses of legitimation have already taken place within the theory; and they find the results of the theory already sedimented in the constitution. Because the citizens cannot conceive of the constitution as a *project,* the public use of reason does not actually have the significance of a present exercise of political autonomy but merely promotes the nonviolent *preservation of political stability* (128).

First a remark about the meaning of autonomy. In political liberalism, autonomy is understood as political and not as moral autonomy (II:6). The latter is a much wider idea and belongs to comprehensive doctrines of the kind associated with Kant and Mill. Political autonomy is specified in terms of various political institutions and practices, as well as expressed in certain political virtues of citizens in their thought and conduct—their discussions, deliberations, and decisions—in carrying out a constitutional regime. It suffices for political liberalism.

With this remark in mind, it is not clear what is meant by saying that citizens in a just society cannot "reignite the radical democratic embers of the original position in civic life." We are bound to ask: Why not? For we have seen above in considering the four-stage sequence that citizens continually discuss questions of political principles and social policy. Moreover, we may assume that any actual society is more or less unjust—usually

400

gravely so—and such debates are all the more necessary. No (human) theory could possibly anticipate all the requisite considerations bearing on these problems under existing circumstances, nor could the needed reforms have already been foreseen for improving present arrangements. The ideal of a just constitution is always something to be worked toward. On these points, Habermas would seem to agree:

> The justification of civil disobedience relies on a dynamic understanding of the constitution as an unfinished project. From this long term perspective, the democratic constitutional state does not represent a finished structure but is a delicate and above all a fallible and revisable undertaking, whose purpose is to realize the system of rights *anew* in changing circumstances, that is, to interpret the system of rights better, to institutionalize it more appropriately, and to draw out its contents more radically. This is the perspective of citizens who are actively involved in realizing the system of rights and who want to overcome the tension between social facticity and validity, aware of different contexts (FG 464).

Habermas seems to think that justice as fairness is somehow incompatible with what he says here. He refers (in the first passage mentioned) to an already just society (which includes, I assume, a just constitution and basic structure) and also to the "*essential* discourses of legitimation." He says that the constitution cannot be conceived as a project—as something yet to be achieved—and so public reason cannot involve the exercise of political autonomy but only the preservation of political stability. Perhaps he means that citizens can be politically autonomous only if they are autonomous from top to bottom—that is, by giving themselves a constitution issuing from their fundamental debates, from their "essential discourses of legitimation," and similarly in all lower-order enactments. Yet it is doubtful that he might think that in a well-ordered society as described ideally in justice as fairness, radical democratic embers cannot be reignited because citizens cannot actually give themselves what they view as a just constitution when they already have one.

If this is the difficulty, however, it is easy to address. To make clearer the idea of political autonomy we say, first, that citizens gain full political autonomy when they live under a reasonably just constitution securing their liberty and equality, with all of the appropriate subordinate laws and precepts regulating the basic structure, and when they also fully comprehend and endorse this constitution and its laws, as well as adjust and revise them as changing social circumstances require, always suitably moved by their sense of justice and the other political virtues. To this we add, second, that whenever the constitution and laws are in various ways unjust and imperfect, citizens with reason strive to become more autonomous by doing what, in their historical and social circumstances, can be reasonably and rationally seen to advance their full autonomy. Thus in this case, a just regime is a project as Habermas says, and justice as fairness agrees.

Even when the constitution is just, however, we are bound to ask: Why can citizens not be fully autonomous? Are the citizens of Rousseau's society of *The Social Contract* never fully autonomous because the Legislator originally gave them their just constitution under which they have grown up? Why should that memorable deed long past make any difference when they now comprehend the just constitution, and intelligently and wisely execute it?[38] How could the Legislator's wisdom deprive citizens of the insights they have assimilated for themselves over generations? Why can those insights not be assimilated by citizens from their reflections and experience with these institutions and as they come to understand the grounds of the constitution's design? Does Kant's *Groundwork* deprive us of our achieving the insights of the moral law by reflecting on that work? Surely not. Why is understanding the justice of the constitution any different?

Moreover, not every generation is called upon to carry through to a reasonable conclusion all the essential discourses of

38. See *The Social Contract*, bk. II, ch. 7.

legitimation and then successfully to give itself a new and just constitution. Whether a generation can do this is determined not by itself alone but by a society's history: that the founders of 1787–91 could be the founders was not determined solely by them but by the course of history up until that time. In this sense, those already living in a just constitutional regime cannot found a just constitution, but they can fully reflect on it, endorse it, and so freely execute it in all ways necessary. What is especially significant about our actually giving ourselves a just constitution that is reasonable and rational when we already have one and fully understand and act on it? While political autonomy expresses our freedom, no more than with any other kind of freedom is it reasonable to maximize acts thereof, but only so to act when it is appropriate. Perhaps though Habermas would object to the four-stage sequence as a framework for reflection even when it is interpreted as I have explained in §3.2 above; he may see its series of increasingly thinner veils of ignorance as too confining and restrictive.

4. I turn to the third and last part of the passage (128–29), supplemented by a later statement. Habermas grants that the consequences he spells out were not my intention, though he thinks my views do have that result. This is shown

> by the rigid boundary between the political and the nonpublic identities of the citizens. According to Rawls, this boundary is set by basic liberal rights that constrain democratic self-legislation, and with it the sphere of the political, *from the beginning,* that is, prior to all political will formation (128–29).

The supplementary passage (129) runs as follows:

> These two identities then constitute the reference points for two domains [one characterized by political values, the other by nonpublic values], the one constituted by rights of political participation and communication, the other protected by basic liberal rights. The constitutional protection of the private sphere [I would say the nonpublic sphere] in this way enjoys priority while 'the role of the political liberties is . . . largely

403

instrumental in preserving the other liberties'.[39] Thus, with reference to the political value sphere, a prepolitical domain of liberties is delimited which is withdrawn from the reach of democratic self-legislation (129).

I begin with the meaning of the italicized phrase near the end of the first quotation. Habermas says that *'from the beginning'* means prior to all will formation. If so, then what he says is not accurate to justice as fairness for this reason. From the point of view of citizens in the background culture, I have supposed that at the stage of the constitutional convention, after having selected the principles of justice in the original position, we adopt a constitution that, with its Bill of Rights and other provisions, restricts majority legislation in how it may burden such basic liberties as liberty of conscience and freedom of speech and

39. Here Habermas quotes from VIII: 2:299, "Basic Liberties and Their Priority." The point of the paragraph from which his citation is taken is to say that not all basic liberties are important or prized for the same reasons. I mention that one strand of the liberal tradition prizes what Benjamin Constant called "the liberties of the moderns" above the "liberties of the ancients," and in which the role of the political liberties is perhaps largely instrumental in preserving the other liberties. Then I say that "even if this view is correct, it is no bar to counting certain political liberties among the basic liberties and protecting them by the priority of liberty. For to assign priority to these liberties they need only be important enough as essential institutional means to secure the other basic liberties. . . ." I do not say that the political liberties are solely instrumental, nor that they have no place in the lives of most people. Indeed, I would insist that the political liberties have intrinsic political value in at least two ways: first, in playing a significant or even a predominant role in the lives of many citizens engaged in one way or another in political life; and, second, they are, when honored, one of the social bases of citizens' self-respect and in this way, among others, a primary good. See V:6, and also *Theory* 233f., where I say: "Of course, the grounds for self-government are not solely instrumental." Then, after noting briefly the role of the political liberties in promoting citizens' self-respect, the moral quality of civic life, the exercise of our moral and intellectual sensibilities, and the like, I conclude by remarking: "[These considerations] show that equal liberty is not solely a means." (In this passage I actually say 'self-esteem' and not 'self-respect' but I now realize, thanks to David Sachs, that self-esteem and self-respect are different ideas. I should have selected one term as appropriate and stuck with it, style be damned.) I meant to take no stand there on what the features of the public political space should be for the role of the people. This is a question that belongs to a constitutional convention, in the sense of the four-stage sequence, and I saw it not at issue.

thought. In this way it restricts popular sovereignty as expressed in the legislature. In justice as fairness, these basic liberties are not in a prepolitical domain; nonpublic values are not viewed, as they might be in some comprehensive doctrine (such as rational intuitionism or natural law), as ontologically prior and for that reason prior to political values. Some citizens no doubt hold such a view, but that is another matter. It is not part of justice as fairness. This conception allows—but does not require—the basic liberties to be incorporated into the constitution and protected as constitutional rights on the basis of citizens' deliberations and judgments over time. Endorsing a constitution restricting majority rule need not, then, be prior to the will of the people and in this way it need not express an external constraint on popular sovereignty. It is the will of the people expressed in democratic procedures such as ratifications of a constitution and enacting amendments. So much is clear once we see the four-stage sequence as a framework in a device of representation to order our political judgments as citizens.

All this can be made clearer by the distinction between constitutional and normal politics as I survey in VI:6.[40] We assume the idea of a dualist constitutional democracy found in John Locke: it distinguishes the people's constituent power to form, ratify,

40. Here I draw upon Ackerman's instructive *We The People, Volume I: Foundations* (Cambridge: Harvard University Press, 1991). A conception of constitutional democracy, however, can be dualist in the general sense of the text above without endorsing Ackerman's more specific sense of dualism that allows for "structural amendments" to the constitution outside of formal amending procedures of Article V. A political movement like the New Deal may be importantly influential in shifting the dominant interpretations that judges, say, give of the constitution, but amendments are something else again. I would also not accept his distinction between dualism and rights foundationalism (as he understands them). He thinks that dualism requires, although rights foundationalism does not, that any amendment in accordance with the procedures of Article V be constitutionally valid. In 238f. I argue otherwise. I cannot discuss these matters and aim to say only what bears on Habermas's concern. See further Freeman, "Original Meaning, Democratic Interpretation, and the Constitution," *Philosophy and Public Affairs* 21 (Winter 1992): 3–42; and Fleming, "Constructing the Substantive Constitution," *Texas Law Review* 72 (December 1993): 211–304; 287*n*380, 290*n*400. I am grateful to Fleming for valuable advice and correspondence clarifying these matters, from which I have learned much.

and amend a constitution from the ordinary power of legislators and executives in everyday politics; and it distinguishes also the higher law of the people from the ordinary law of legislative bodies (231ff.). Parliamentary supremacy is rejected. The three most innovative periods in American constitutional history are, let us say, the founding of 1787–91, Reconstruction, and in a different way the New Deal.[41] In all these periods, fundamental political debates were widespread and they offer three examples of when the electorate confirmed or motivated the constitutional changes that were proposed and finally accepted. Surely these cases show that the constitutional protection of basic rights is not prior to what Habermas calls will formation. It suffices to mention James Madison's guiding the Bill of Rights through Congress in June to September of 1789, as the Anti-Federalists had been promised; and had they not been, the constitution might not have been ratified.[42]

The four-stage sequence fits, then, with idea that the liberties of the moderns are subject to the constituent will of the people. Put in terms of that sequence, the people—or better, those citizens if any who affirm justice as fairness—are making a judgment at the stage of a constitutional convention. I believe that Habermas thinks that in my view the liberties of the moderns are a kind of natural law, and therefore, as in the case of Kant on his interpretation, they are external substantive ideas and so impose restrictions on the public will of the people.[43] Rather, justice as fairness is a political conception of justice, and while of course a moral conception, it is not an instance of a natural law doctrine. It neither denies nor asserts any such view. In my reply I have simply observed that from within that political conception of justice, the liberties of the moderns do not impose the prior

41. Here I follow Ackerman.
42. See Stanley Elkins and Eric McKittrick, *The Age of Federalism* (New York: Oxford, 1993), pp. 58–75.
43. He mentions me and Kant as natural law theorists, FG 110.

restrictions on the people's constituent will as Habermas objects.[44]

If this is right, then Habermas may have no objection to justice as fairness but may reject the constitution to which he thinks it leads, and which I think may secure both the ancient and modern liberties. He might suppose that since the illustrative ideas used in *Theory,* chapter IV, are taken from the United States constitution, the constitution that justice as fairness would justify is similar; and so it must be open to the same objections. He and I are not, however, debating the justice of the United States constitution as it is, but rather whether justice as fairness allows and is consistent with the popular sovereignty he cherishes. I have urged that it is. And I would have, as he does, objections deriving (in my case) from the two principles of justice to our present constitution and society's basic structure as a system of social cooperation. To mention three: the present system woefully fails in public financing for political elections, leading to a grave imbalance in fair political liberties; it allows a widely disparate distribution of income and wealth that seriously undermines fair opportunities in education and employment, all of which undermine economic and social equality; and absent also are provisions for important constitutional essentials such as health care for many who are uninsured. Yet these urgent matters do not concern the philosophical topics Habermas raises, such as the device of the original position and its relation to

44. This accords with Michelman's view in his essay "Law's Republic," *The Yale Law Journal* 97 (July 1988): 1493–1537, pp. 1499f., when he says: "I take American constitutionalism—as manifest in academic constitutional theory, in the professional practice of lawyers and judges, and in the ordinary self-understanding of Americans at large—to rest on two premises regarding political freedom: first, that the American people are politically free insomuch as they are governed by themselves collectively, and second, that the American people are politically free in that they are governed by laws rather than men. I take it that no earnest, non-disruptive participant in American constitutional debate is quite free to reject either of these two professions of belief. I take them to be premises whose problematic relation to each other, and therefore whose meaning, are subject to an endless contestation."

discourse theory, the two principles of justice and the four-stage sequence, and the connection between ancient and modern liberties.

Habermas may affirm ideas somewhat analogous to those of Jefferson, who seems to have been deeply troubled by this question. In his letter to Samuel Kercheval of 1816, Jefferson discusses his ideas for the reform of the constitution of Virginia and lays out the elements of his ward scheme, which divides counties into wards small enough so that all citizens can attend and voice their opinion on matters at the ward level up to the county and higher levels. These wards, together with presumably some kind of hierarchy of consultation, are to provide that necessary public space for the people to express themselves as equal citizens, a provision lacking in both the Virginian and American constitutions. Recall Jefferson's idea (also in this letter) of holding a constitutional convention every nineteen or twenty years, so that each generation could choose its own constitution, past generations having no rights in this respect.[45] I mention Jefferson's views only because they may cast light on Habermas's remark about reigniting the radical democratic embers in a just society.

I also hold that the most appropriate design of a constitution

45. See *Thomas Jefferson: Writings,* Merrill Peterson, ed. (New York: Viking, 1984), pp. 1399f. and 1401f., respectively. See also his letter to James Madison, September 6, 1789, in which he says that *"the earth belongs in usufruct to the living,* and that the dead have neither rights or powers over it" (ibid., p. 959). One generation of men cannot bind another. In this connection, Hannah Arendt refers to the seemingly insolvable perplexity of a revolutionary spirit that strives to establish a constitutional government. The perplexity is how to house a revolutionary spirit within a permanent regime. She also suggests that Jeffersons' antagonism toward those who regard constitutions with sanctimonious reverence rests on a feeling of outrage about the injustice that his generation alone should be able "to begin the world over again," a phrase from Thomas Paine's *Common Sense;* see her *On Revolution* (New York: Viking, 1963), p. 235. Yet this feeling of injustice is entirely misplaced and cannot sensibly be entertained. (I might as well spend my life whining that I am not Kant, Shakespeare, or Mozart.) As for the perplexity of finding an appropriate public political space for giving scope to the political autonomy of the people, I believe, as the text above says, that the question is one of constitutional design; any feeling of insolvable perplexity is illusory, not that Arendt would disagree.

is not a question to be settled by considerations of political philosophy alone, but depends on understanding the scope and limits of political and social institutions and how they can be made to work effectively. These things depend on history and how institutions are arranged. Of course, here the concept of truth applies. I come back to the question of constitutional design in §4.3.

§4. The Roots of the Liberties

1. The first part of Habermas's objection about the liberties that I addressed in §3 is connected with the short summary[46] near the end of his criticisms, bearing on what he calls the dialectical relation between private and public autonomy (130–31). I complete my reply by discussing this summary, which includes statements from the central argument of FG,[47] the essential parts of which are given mainly in chapters 3–4 of that work. It is also returned to in chapter 9, as well as in the "Postscript."[48] For this reason, I begin by reviewing some remarks from the latter in completing my reply to his objection to what he refers to as liberalism as a historical doctrine.[49]

Habermas thinks that throughout the history of political philosophy, both liberal and civic republican writers have failed to understand the internal relation between public and private autonomy. For example, he claims that liberal writers typically

46. The summary begins with the words 'A theory of justice' (130) and ends with the words 'in the present context' (131).

47. See David Rasmussen's review in *Philosophy and Social Criticism*, 20, no. 4 (1994):21–44, p. 41.

48. The "Postscript" (dated September 1993) was added to a later printing (*Auflage*) of FG 661–80. A translation by Rehg is now in *Philosophy and Social Criticism*, 20, no. 4 (October 1994): 135–50. I thank Rasmussen for sending me the page proofs of this.

49. I refer to Rehg's translation of the *Postscript* by section and paragraph number. The main section summarizing the central argument is in III. It has eight paragraphs: the first four state the central argument, while the next four reply to two critics, Otfried Höffe and Larmore, each in two paragraphs.

regard the relation between these two forms of autonomy in such a way that private autonomy, as specified by the liberties of the moderns, is founded on human rights, for example, the rights to life, liberty, and (personal[50]) property, and on an "anonymous"[51] rule of law. On the other hand, the public (political) autonomy of citizens is derived from the principle of popular sovereignty and expressed in democratic law. In the philosophical tradition, he thinks the relations between the two kinds of autonomy are marked by "an unresolved competition" ("Postscript" III:1).

This fault is seen in the fact that, since the nineteenth century, liberalism has invoked the great danger of the tyranny of majority rule and has simply postulated the priority of human rights as a constraint on popular sovereignty. For its part, civic republicanism in the tradition of Aristotle has all along granted priority to the ancient over the modern liberties. Contrary to Locke and Kant, Habermas denies that the rights of the moderns are moral rights based either on natural law or a moral conception such as the categorical imperative. He claims that by basing those rights on morality, liberalism subjects the legal order to an external ground, thereby placing constraints on legitimate democratic law; whereas the view of Rousseau and civic republicanism bases ancient liberties on the ethical values of a specific community with its ethos of the common good, rooting those liberties on particular and parochial values.

Moving between what he views as these two errors, Habermas sees the liberties of public autonomy and the liberties of private autonomy as "co-original" and of "equal weight," with neither being prior to or imposed on the other (FG 135). The point is that the internal connection between public and private auton-

50. I insert this because justice as fairness does not include the right to ownership of the means of production; see *Theory* 270–74.

51. The translator's term. The German is "eine anonyme *Herrschaft der Gesetze*," by which I believe he means the rule of law as such. That is, it is anonymous or nameless (in economics it can mean goods lacking a brand name); it is not the law of a king or a legislative body.

omy, which even Kant and Rousseau wished to formulate but missed the crucial insight to express, removes the unresolved competition between the two forms of autonomy. For once the internal connection between them is understood, we see that they mutually presuppose one another (130): since, given that connection, if we have one form of autonomy we have the other—and neither need be imposed. On the discourse-theoretic conception of democracy, harmony and balance reign and both are fully achieved.[52]

Habermas does not question that human rights can be justified as moral rights. His point is that once we think of them as belonging to positive law, which is always coercive and sanctioned by state power, they cannot be imposed by an external agency on the legislature of a democratic regime. This is surely correct: suppose (we wildly imagine) that the Prussian chancellor of Kant's day, with the support of the King, acts to ensure that all laws enacted are in accord with Kant's principle of the social contract.[53] If so, free and equal citizens would—let us say on due reflection—agree with them. Since citizens do not themselves freely discuss, vote on, and enact these laws, however, citizens are not politically autonomous and cannot thus regard themselves. On the other hand, Habermas says that even a democratic people as sovereign legislator, and fully autonomous politically, must not enact anything that violates those human rights. Here he thinks liberalism faces a dilemma ("Postscript" III:2), the resolution of which has long escaped political philosophy and puts the liberties in unresolved competition. The alleged dilemma, I think, is that while human rights cannot be externally imposed on the exercise of public autonomy in a democratic regime, that autonomy—however great—cannot legitimately violate those rights by its laws ("Postscript" III:2).

52. The preceding three paragraphs offer an interpretation of "Postscript," III:1. See also FG 129–35, 491ff.

53. See *Metaphysics of Morals,* Doctrine of Rights, sects. 47, 52, and Remark D in the general remarks after sect. 49; and "Theory and Practice," Akademie Edition VIII:289f., 297f.

2. Against what Habermas seems to say here, I shall simply defend liberalism as I understand it. Thus, I deny, first, that liberalism leaves political and private autonomy in unresolved competition; second, that the alleged dilemma liberalism is said to face is not a true dilemma, since the two propositions are plainly correct; and I maintain, third, that in liberalism properly interpreted, as I hope it to be in justice as fairness and in other liberal doctrines going back to Locke, public and private autonomy are also both co-original and of equal weight (to use Habermas's terms), with neither externally imposed on the other. I begin with the last.

I lay out three parallels between justice as fairness and Habermas's view in order to make clear that in liberalism properly interpreted, public and private autonomy are co-original and of equal weight. They show, I believe, that justice as fairness as well as other liberal views recognize what he calls the internal connection, or the mutual presupposition, between the ancient and modern liberties as much as he does by his discourse-theoretic view. I begin with the sentence that concludes the first paragraph of the summary: [54]

> The basic question then is: Which rights must free and equal persons mutually accord [*gegenseitig einräumen*] one another if they wish to regulate their coexistence by the legitimate means of positive and coercive law (130)?

Habermas takes this question as the starting point for his interpretation of the self-understanding democracy (FG 109).

Now is this statement not parallel to, though not of course the same as, what is happening in civil society when citizens discuss and accept (for those who do) the merits of the original position

---

54. This sentence is parallel to a sentence in "Postscript" II:2.3: "The leading question of modern natural law can be reformulated under new discourse-theoretic premises: What rights must citizens mutually cede to one another if they decide to constitute themselves in as a voluntary association of legal consociates and legitimately to regulate their living together by means of positive law?"

and the principles presumptively selected there?[55] Are the parties as citizens' trustees not selecting principles of justice to specify the scheme of (basic) liberties which best protect and further citizens' fundamental interests and which they then concede to one another? Here, also, the ancient and the modern liberties are co-original and of equal weight with neither given pride of place over the other. The liberties of both public and private autonomy are given side by side and unranked in the first principle of justice. These liberties are co-original for the further reason that both kinds of liberty are rooted in one or both of the two moral powers, respectively in the capacity for a sense of justice and the capacity for a conception of the good. As before, the two powers themselves are not ranked and both are essential aspects of the political conception of the person, each power with its own higher-order interest.[56]

3. A second parallel in justice as fairness is that it also has a two-stage construction much as does Habermas's view.[57] The parallel is that those in civil society who accept justice as fairness use the original position as a device of representation to determine the rights of citizens who recognize each other as equals and whose rights are to be secured by a democratic regime. Then, with the two principles of justice on hand (with the emphasis on the first principle), we move (in accordance with the four-stage sequence (§3.2) as delegates to a constitutional convention. At this point, just as in Habermas's view, we "advance

55. As we have seen, it is an important matter where these discussions take place. In justice as fairness, they take place among citizens in civil society—the point of view of you and me. I suppose the same holds in Habermas's case.

56. There is a third higher-order interest given by the determinate conception of the good that people have at any given time. But since this interest is subject to the higher-order interests of the two moral powers and therefore must be both reasonable and rational, I do not discuss this interest further here.

57. The idea of a two-stage construction is implicit in the summary argument (129–30), and it is briefly described using that phrase 'eine zweistufige Reconstruktion ("Postscript" III:8). I am unclear about how a construction differs from a reconstruction. Is it relevant here?

to the constitutional disciplining of the presupposed state power" ("Postscript" III:8). In justice as fairness, we adopt in thought and subsequent practice a constitution in which, as I have said, we may or may not embed the basic liberties, thereby subjecting parliamentary legislation to certain constitutional constraints as one of the ways to discipline and regulate the presupposed state power. This power is presupposed in justice as fairness, because from the start (§1) we are dealing with principles and ideals for the basic structure of society and its main political and social institutions, already taken to exist in some form.

When Habermas says that liberal rights are not originary in his view but rather emerge from a transformation of the liberties reciprocally ceded ("Postscript" III:8), the context shows that he is referring to rights against the state in the form of rights embedded in a constitution: say, the rights of the American Bill of Rights or of the German *Grundgesetz*. He is not discussing the individual rights persons initially cede to each other at his first step.[58] These latter rights are originary in the sense that it is there that we begin, just as we might say that the basic rights covered by the first principle of justice are originary. The basic liberties of these principles may be cited, along with a view about how legislatures and social institutions work, as reasons for embedding those liberties in a written constitution in a constitutional convention; or, in Habermas's words, they may be so transformed. The basic liberties (parallel to his initially ceded rights) are original (in his sense), but the constraints on legislation are not. He does not question that those liberties may also be appropriately related to the order of moral rights. Rather, his view is (and I agree) that the obtaining of this relation is of itself not sufficient in a democratic society to make enforcing them legitimate as law. Nor would he question that the reasonable belief of citizens in that relation is among the good reasons for their arguing for enacting certain private rights in democratic debate.

58. I am indebted to McCarthy for understanding of this point.

414

If all this is right, Habermas is not differing with justice as fairness or with Frank Michelman, whom he counts as a civic republican, or indeed with many other liberalisms. Both his view and ours (along with much of American constitutional doctrine) agree that whether the modern liberties are incorporated into the constitution is a matter to be decided by the constituent power of a democratic people,[59] a familiar line of constitutional doctrine stemming from George Lawson via Locke.[60] I think Habermas's view about liberalism does not fit this historical tradition.

Moreover, a question of real significance, as stated in §3, is whether these liberties are better secured and protected by their being incorporated into a constitution. The question is one of constitutional design. Of course, its answer presupposes principles of right and justice, but it also requires historical study and a grasp of the workings of democratic institutions under particular patterns of historical, cultural, and social conditions. In justice as fairness, this is a judgment to be made in a constitutional convention, with the pros and cons assessed from that point of view. Differences of opinion here depend in a good part on how we weigh the historical evidence for the effectiveness of constitutional protections and whether they have drawbacks of their own, such as debilitating effects on democracy itself. However attractive at first sight it may appear to be to constrain legislation, examination of the evidence, historical cases, and political and social thought may suggest otherwise. The point is that constitutional design is not a question to be settled only by a philosophical conception of democracy—liberal or discourse-theoretic or any other—nor by political and social study alone in the absence

59. For Locke's view of the people's constituent power, see *Second Treatise:* 134, 141. I might add that this fits the Federalist doctrine of the people. See Gordon Wood's splendid account in *The Creation of the American Republic, 1776–1787* (New York: Norton, 1969); chs. 7–9 and 13 give a good part of the picture.

60. On this see Julian Franklin, *Sovereignty of the People* (New York: Cambridge University Press, 1978), tracing Locke's view in the *Second Treatise* to Lawson's treatise of the 1650s.

of a case by case examination of instances, and also taking into account the particular political history and the democratic culture of the society in question. So I maintain that in liberalism (and in Habermas's view as well) there is no unresolved competition between ancient and modern liberties but rather a matter of weighing the evidence one way or the other. The case is on all fours with the question (discussed in *A Theory of Justice*) of private-property democracy versus liberal socialism (*Theory* 270–74).

I deny, then, that liberalism leaves political and private autonomy in unresolved competition. That is my first claim. The second is that the dilemma liberalism supposedly faces is a true dilemma, since, as I have said, the two propositions are correct. One says: no moral law can be externally imposed on a sovereign democratic people; and the other says: the sovereign people may not justly (but may legitimately [61]) enact any law violating those rights. These statements simply express the risk for political justice of all government, democratic or otherwise; for there is no human institution—political or social, judicial or ecclesiastical—that can guarantee that legitimate (or just) laws are always enacted and just rights always respected. To this add: certainly, and never to be questioned, a single person may stand alone and be right in saying that law and government are wrong and unjust. No special doctrine of the co-originality and equal weight of the two forms of autonomy is needed to explain this fact. It is hard to believe that all major liberal and civic republican writers did not understand this. It bears on the age-old question of how best to unite power with law to achieve justice.

4. A third parallel between justice as fairness and the idea that public and private autonomy are both co-original and of equal weight is the following. I believe that for Habermas the internal connection between the two forms of autonomy lies in the way that the discourse theory reconstructs the legitimacy of democratic law. In justice as fairness, the two forms of autonomy are

61. Legitimacy allows leeway for this; see §5 below.

416

also internally connected, in the sense that their connection lies in the way that conception is put together as an ideal. The source of its system of basic rights and liberties traces back to the idea of society as a fair system of social cooperation, and of citizens' rational representatives selecting the terms of cooperation subject to reasonable conditions. As participants engaged in such cooperation, citizens are said to have the requisite two moral powers with the three higher-order interests that enable them to take part in a society so conceived. These powers are the capacities for a sense of justice and a conception of the good. The first is paired with the reasonable—the capacity to propose and act on fair terms of social cooperation assuming others do; the second with the rational [62]—the capacity to have a rational and coherent conception of the good to be pursued only within the bounds of those fair terms.

From here the idea is to connect the basic liberties into a fully adequate system of the two kinds of liberties. This is done in six steps, which I only indicate here:

a. Specify for all citizens the social conditions for the adequate development and the full and informed exercise of the two moral powers in the two fundamental cases (VIII: 8:332).[63]

b. Identify the rights and liberties required to protect and allow the exercise of those two powers in the two fundamental cases. The first case concerns the application of the principles of justice to the basic structure of society and its social policies. Political liberty and freedom of political speech and thought are essential here. The second case concerns the application of deliberative reason in guiding one's conduct over a complete life. Liberty of conscience

---

62. I mention here that the concept of the rational here is wider and deeper than the concept of it used in the original position, where it has a narrower meaning. I cannot pursue the difference here.

63. This refers to "Basic Liberties and Their Priority" (1982), included unchanged as VIII.

and freedom of thought more generally enter here with freedom of association (VIII: 8:332).

c. Since the liberties are bound to conflict, and none is absolute with respect to the others, we must check whether the central range of each liberty can be simultaneously realized in a workable basic structure (VIII: 2:297f.). The point here is that we cannot simply say they can be: it must be shown by specifying the central range of these liberties and how they can be reconciled in workable institutions satisfying the two principles of justice.[64]

d. Use two ways—one historical and the other theoretical—of drawing up the list of basic liberties. In the historical, we look to constitutions of democratic societies, make a list of the liberties normally protected, and examine their role in democracies that historically have worked well. In the theoretical, we consider which liberties are crucial for the adequate development and exercise of the two moral powers over a complete life (VIII: 1:292f.).

e. Introduce primary goods (which include the basic liberties and fair opportunities) in order to further specify the details of the principles of justice so as to render them workable under normal social conditions. The basic rights, liberties, and opportunities we know are equal, and citizens are to have sufficient all-purpose means to make effective use of them. But what are these rights and liberties and means more specifically for those principles to be usable? The primary goods answer this question (V:3–4). With this done, the principles can direct us under reasonably favorable conditions to establish in due course, beginning from

64. The aim of *Theory* is to sketch these institutions. It says on p. 195 that the aim of part II (Institutions) is to illustrate the content of the principles of justice by describing a basic structure of institutions that satisfies them. They define, as the text says, a workable political conception, that is, one that can be set up in actual institutions and made to work given what citizens can be expected to know and how they can be expected to be motivated, with this last discussed in part III. I mention this because Habermas says in FG, ch. 2.2, that *Theory* is abstract and ignores these matters.

where society is now, a just system of political and social institutions that protects the central range of all the liberties, both ancient and modern.

f. Show finally that these principles would be adopted in the original position by the trustees of citizens in society regarded as free and equal, and as having the two moral powers with a determinate conception of the good.

In this way, the families of each of the two forms of autonomy have been internally connected by means of the construction of justice as fairness as a political conception of justice. This form of liberalism, then, does not leave the liberties in unresolved competition. Actual cases often present conflicts among the liberties and no scheme of constitutional or other design can altogether avoid this, no more on Habermas's view than any other, not that he would deny this.

As for the question of what are the differences between Habermas's view and mine concerning the co-originality and equal weight of public and private autonomy, I am uncertain. While his view is comprehensive (§1), we both have a normative ideal of democracy that grounds an internal connection between the two forms of autonomy, and these ideals are parallel in several ways. His ideal seems to me sketched too broadly to foresee to what family of liberties the ideal discourse procedure would lead. Indeed, it seems unclear whether it could lead to any very specific conclusion at all.[65]

5. A final question. Taking Habermas at his literal word, he may think that the internal relation between the two forms of autonomy depends on "the normative content of the *mode of exercising political autonomy*" (FG 133). Now, why the emphasis on the political? Does he really mean to imply that political autonomy has the primary and basic role, having said that the two kinds of autonomy are co-original and of equal weight? Why does it not go equally both ways in his conception?

---

65. Admittedly, I have not done much of this myself, but certain basic liberties and the cases to which they applied were discussed a bit in VIII, "Basic Liberties."

In any case, justice as fairness holds that, even if the liberties of private autonomy can be internally connected with and grounded on political autonomy, those liberties are not grounded solely in that relation. This is because the liberties of the moderns in justice as fairness have their own distinctive basis in the second moral power with its determinate (though in the original position, unknown) conception of the good. Moreover, the second moral power and the two higher-order interests associated with it express independently, in the system of basic liberties, the protections and freedoms of persons as members of civil society with its social, cultural, and spiritual life. This part of society contains institutions and associations of all kinds, cultural organizations and scientific societies, universities and churches, and media of one form or another, all without end. The value and worth of these activities in the eyes of citizens whose activities they are constitute at least a sufficient, if not a vital basis for the rights of private autonomy. For as Habermas grants (FG 165), political democracy depends for its enduring life upon the liberal background culture that sustains it. This culture will not sustain it, however, unless the institutions of democracy are seen by reasonable citizens as supporting what they regard to be appropriate forms of good, as specified by their comprehensive doctrines and permitted by political justice. So even if the internal relation to the political liberties gave a sufficient discourse-theoretic derivation for the civic liberties, that would not prevent the latter from having another, at least equally sufficient, justification, as I believe they do.

Habermas's seeming emphasis on the political (if he does intend it) is plausible at all only if it is supposed that the idea of civic humanism is true: that is, the activity in which human beings achieve their fullest realization, their greatest good, is in the activities of political life. Plainly, engaging in political life can be a reasonable part of many people's conceptions of the good and for some it may indeed be a great good, as great statesmen such as George Washington and Abraham Lincoln testify. Still, justice as fairness rejects any such declaration; and to make the good of civil society subordinate to that of public life it views as mistaken.

§5. Procedural Versus Substantive Justice

1. In this section, I conclude my defense of liberalism (of political liberalism in my case) by replying to Habermas's objection that justice as fairness is substantive rather than procedural. Recall that he says that his procedural theory

> focuses exclusively on the procedural aspects of the public use of reason and derives the system of rights from the idea of its [legitimate[66]] legal institutionalization. It can leave more questions open [than justice as fairness] because it entrusts more to the *process* of rational opinion and will formation. Philosophy shoulders different theoretical burdens when, as on Rawls's conception, it claims to elaborate the ideal of a just society, while the citizens then use this idea as a platform from which to judge existing arrangements and policies (131).

I see my reply as a defense of liberalism since any liberal view must be substantive, and it is correct in being so. Moreover, I do not see why Habermas's view is not also substantive, even though the substantive elements may differ.

I begin by explaining that I take the distinction between procedural and substantive justice to be, respectively, the distinction between the justice (or fairness) of a procedure and the justice (or fairness) of its outcome.[67] Both kinds of justice exemplify certain values, of the procedure and the outcome, respectively; and both kinds of values go together in the sense that the justice of a procedure always depends (leaving aside the special case of gambling) on the justice of its likely outcome, or on substantive justice. Thus, procedural and substantive justice are connected and not separate. This still allows that fair procedures have values

66. Do we not need legitimate here?

67. Here I follow Hampshire's distinction in his review, p. 44, cited above in footnote 31.

intrinsic to them—for example, a procedure having the value of impartiality by giving all an equal chance to present their case.[68]

The connection between procedural and substantive justice may be illustrated by recalling briefly two clear cases involving procedural justice.[69] The first is perfect procedural justice as illustrated by the common-sense procedure of dividing a cake. The procedure illustrates perfect procedural justice only because it always gives the accepted fair outcome: equal division. If it failed to give a fair outcome, it would not be a procedure for justice, but for something else. The same is true of a criminal trial, which is a case of imperfect procedural justice. It is imperfect because no trial procedure, however just and effective the law arranges it—with its rules of evidence and the rights and duties of the parties, all reasonably laid out—can be guaranteed to convict the accused if and only if the accused has committed the crime. Yet in the same way as before, the procedure of a criminal trial would not be just—not a procedure for a fair trial—unless it was intelligently drawn up so that the procedure gives the correct decision, at least much of the time. We know there will be some errors, partly from setting a high standard for

68. I am much indebted to Cohen's, "Pluralism and Proceduralism," *Chicago-Kent Law Review* 69 (1994): 589–618. This is a thorough and penetrating discussion of this question and I draw on it at many points. Its overall theme is that, since procedural justice depends on substantive justice, an overlapping consensus on substantive matters is, in general, no more utopian than agreement on procedural justice: a constitutional consensus already implies much agreement on substantive matters. Thus, Cohen rejects the objection to substantive justice that procedural justice is, in general, less demanding, since it is independent of substantive justice. This fits well with the view in IV: 6–7 that there are tendencies pushing a constitutional to an overlapping consensus. I did not use Cohen's argument there as it escaped me altogether. The topic of procedural justice is also nicely discussed by Charles Beitz in his *Political Equality* (Princeton: Princeton University Press, 1989), ch. 4. There he presents a thesis I follow here: that the justice of procedural justice depends in part on the justice of the outcomes. For critiques along these lines of John Hart Ely's *Democracy and Distrust* (Cambridge: Harvard University Press, 1981), see Dworkin, *A Matter of Principle* (Cambridge: Harvard University Press, 1985), ch. 2, pp. 57–69; and Laurence Tribe, *Constitutional Choices* (Cambridge: Harvard University Press, 1985), ch. 2: "The Pointless Flight from Substance," pp. 9–20.

69. I discussed these (including gambling) in *Theory* 84–87.

determining guilt and trying to avoid convicting innocent people, and partly from inevitable human fallibility and unlikely contingencies in the evidence. Yet these errors cannot be too frequent, otherwise the trial procedure ceases to be just.

Sometimes it may look as if the dispute is about procedural and substantive justice but it turns out not to be. Both sides agree that procedural justice depends on substantive justice and differ about something else. Consider pluralist democratic views urging some form of majority-rule democracy and rejecting constitutional democracy with its institutional devices—such as the separation of powers, supermajorities on certain matters, a bill of rights, or judicial review—as incompatible with democratic rule or otherwise unnecessary. These views see majority rule as a fair procedure specified in public political institutions for resolving political and social conflicts. Some features of the procedure are definitive of democracy and specify aspects of the procedure itself: for example, the right to vote, majority rule, freedom of political speech, the right to run for and to hold political office. A democratic government to be democratic must incorporate these rights; they are essential elements that specify its institutions.[70]

The debate between majoritarians and constitutionalists arises importantly over basic rights and liberties that are not obviously part of the recognized procedure of government—for example, nonpolitical speech and freedom of religious, philosophical, and moral thought, and liberty of conscience and the free exercise of religion. None of these are definitive of the democratic procedure. Given the definition of majority rule, the issue between majoritarians and constitutionalists is whether it provides a fair procedure and protects these other rights and liberties.

Majoritarians say that majority rule is fair and includes all the rights necessary for it to yield just legislation and reasonable outcomes. Constitutionalists say that majority rule is not accept-

70. See Robert Dahl, *Democracy and Its Critics* (New Haven: Yale University Press, 1989), pp. 167ff.

able. Unless constitutionally recognized restrictions on majority legislation and other elements are in place, the basic liberties and other freedoms will not be properly protected. Nor will democracy be firmly supported and gain the willing consent of its people. To this the majoritarians reply that they fully accept the fundamental significance of nonpolitical speech, liberty of thought and conscience, and the free exercise of religion. They maintain rather that constitutional restrictions are unnecessary, and in a genuinely democratic society and culture those rights and liberties will be respected by the electorate. They say that for a people to honor restrictions on the basic liberties, we must depend in any case on the spirit of the electorate, and that to rely on constitutional devices has debilitating effects on democracy itself.

Both majoritarians and constitutionalists may[71] agree that the debate turns on whether majority democracy is just in its outcomes or is substantially just. Majoritarians do not claim that democracy is purely procedural: they know that they cannot defend it against constitutionalists without holding that it is not only just in its outcomes, but that constitutional devices are unnecessary and would, if anything, make those outcomes worse.[72] The dispute hinges on fundamental questions about how political institutions actually work and rests on our rough knowledge of these things.

2. After this detour, can Habermas say that his view is only procedural? To be sure, he thinks of the discourse-theoretic idea as restricted to an analysis of the moral point of view and the procedure of democratic legitimation. And he leaves substantial questions calling for answers "here and now" to be settled by the more or less enlightened discussions of citizens (131). But none of this means that he can avoid relying on substantive content.

---

71. I say 'may' here because some may hold the majority-rule principle to be itself the final and governing norm. I am not considering that case.

72. I think this is the kind of argument Dahl intends to make in his *Democracy and Its Critics.* He is not denying the great significance of the nonpolitical rights and liberties; rather, he questions, as a general political view, the effectiveness and need for the familiar constitutional devices; see chs. 11–13.

424

He recognizes that once idealizations are attributed to the discourse procedure, elements of content are thereby embedded in it (FG 18). Moreover, the ideal procedure so formed is essential in his account of democracy, since a basic thought is that the process of public discussion can be guaranteed to have reasonable outcomes only to the extent that it realizes the conditions of ideal discourse. The more equal and impartial, the more open that process is and the less participants are coerced; also, the more they will be ready to be guided by the force of the better argument. Then it is more likely that truly generalizable interests will be accepted by all persons relevantly affected. Here are five values that offhand seem to be values of the procedure— impartiality and equality, openness (no one and no relevant information is excluded) and lack of coercion, and unanimity— which in combination guide discussion to generalizable interests to the agreement of all participants. This outcome is certainly substantive, since it refers to a situation in which citizens' generalizable interests are fulfilled. Moreover, any of the previous five values are related to substantive judgments once the reason those values are included as part of the procedure is that they are necessary to render the outcomes just or reasonable. In that case, we have shaped the procedure to accord with our judgment of those outcomes.

Further, Habermas holds that the outcomes of public reason working through democratic procedures are reasonable and legitimate. For example, he says that equal distribution of the liberties can be fulfilled by a democratic procedure supporting the assumption that the "outcomes of political will formation are reasonable" ("Postscript" III:3–4). This said, he presupposes an idea of reasonableness to assess those outcomes, and his view is substantive. It is common oversight (which I do not say he makes) to think that procedural legitimacy (or justice) tries for less and can stand on its own without substantive justice: it cannot.[73]

73. See Cohen's discussion of Hampshire's *Innocence and Experience* (Cambridge: Harvard University Press, 1989) in his "Pluralism and Proceduralism," pp. 589–94, 599f., 607–10.

In fact, I believe that Habermas recognizes that his view is substantive, since he only says it is more modest than mine, and that it leaves "more questions open because it entrusts more to the *process* of rational [reasonable] opinion and will formation." He does not say that his view leaves all substantive questions open to discussion. In the final paragraph of *Between Facts and Norms* he grants that his account cannot be merely formal:[74]

> Like the rule of law itself, [the procedural legal paradigm] retains a dogmatic core: the idea of autonomy according to which human beings act as free subjects only insofar as they obey just those statutes they give to themselves in accordance with their intersubjectively acquired insights. One must admit this is 'dogmatic' only in a harmless sense. For this idea expresses a tension between facticity and validity, a tension that is 'given' with the fact of the linguistic constitution of sociocultural forms of life, which is to say that *for us,* who have developed our identity in such a form of life, it cannot be circumvented (FG 536f.).

Some matters presumably have been settled by philosophical analysis of the moral point of view and the procedure of democratic legitimation. Since it is a matter of more or less, we need an intricate examination in which the substantive elements in both views are set out, compared, and in some way measured.[75] This calls for a comparison of exactly what questions each view leaves open for discussion and under what conditions. I cannot attempt such a comparison here.

Finally, as I pointed out in §1, citizens in civil society do not simply use the idea of justice as fairness "as a platform [handed to them by the philosopher as expert] from which to judge

74. I thank Baynes for calling my attention to the importance of this final passage.

75. This agrees with McCarthy who says, in comparing Habermas's view and mine, that for Habermas the difference between procedural and substantive justice is a matter of degree. See his "Kantian Constructivism and Reconstructivism: Rawls and Habermas in Dialogue," *Ethics* 105, no. 1 (October 1994): 44–63, p. 59, fn. 13. I thank Baynes also for instructive correspondence including this point. In his discussion of FG for the Cambridge University Press *Companion to Habermas* (forthcoming) he has further comments on this question.

426

existing arrangements and policies." In justice as fairness there are no philosophical experts. Heaven forbid! But citizens must, after all, have some ideas of right and justice in their thought and some basis for their reasoning. And students of philosophy take part in formulating these ideas but always as citizens among others.

3. Before concluding, I mention a way in which Habermas's view can be seen as focusing "exclusively on the procedural aspects of the public use of reason" (131). It is suggested by his regular use of the idea of legitimacy rather than justice. I mention it here, not because it is his (I think it is not), but as an idea having its own interest. Suppose we aim to lay out democratic political institutions so that they are legitimate, and so that the political decisions taken and the laws enacted pursuant to them are also legitimate. This puts the focus on the idea of legitimacy—and not justice.

To focus on legitimacy rather than justice may seem like a minor point, as we may think 'legitimate' and 'just' the same. A little reflection shows they are not. A legitimate king or queen may rule by just and effective government, but then they may not; and certainly not necessarily justly even though legitimately. Their being legitimate says something about their pedigree: how they came to their office. It refers to whether they were the legitimate heir to the throne in accordance with the established rules and traditions of, for example, the English or the French crown.

A significant aspect of the idea of legitimacy is that it allows a certain leeway in how well sovereigns may rule and how far they may be tolerated. The same holds under a democratic regime. It may be legitimate and in line with long tradition originating when its constitution was first endorsed by the electorate (the people) in a special ratifying convention. Yet it may not be very just, or hardly so, and similarly for its laws and policies. Laws passed by solid majorities are counted legitimate, even though many protest and correctly judge them unjust or otherwise wrong.

427

Thus, legitimacy is a weaker idea than justice and imposes weaker constraints on what can be done. It is also institutional, though there is of course an essential connection with justice. Note first that democratic decisions and laws are legitimate, not because they are just but because they are legitimately enacted in accordance with an accepted legitimate democratic procedure. It is of great importance that the constitution specifying the procedure be sufficiently just, even though not perfectly just, as no human institution can be that. But it may not be just and still be legitimate, provided it is sufficiently just in view of the circumstances and social conditions. A legitimate procedure gives rise to legitimate laws and policies made in accordance with it; and legitimate procedures may be customary, long established, and accepted as such. Neither the procedures nor the laws need be just by a strict standard of justice, even if, what is also true, they cannot be too gravely unjust. At some point, the injustice of the outcomes of a legitimate democratic procedure corrupts its legitimacy, and so will the injustice of the political constitution itself. But before this point is reached, the outcomes of a legitimate procedure are legitimate whatever they are. This gives us purely procedural democratic legitimacy and distinguishes it from justice, even granting that justice is not specified procedurally. Legitimacy allows an undetermined range of injustice that justice might not permit.

While the idea of legitimacy is clearly related to justice, it is noteworthy that its special role in democratic institutions (noted briefly in §2) is to authorize an appropriate procedure for making decisions when the conflicts and disagreements in political life make unanimity impossible or rarely to be expected. Thus, it counts many different forms of procedure with different size pluralities as yielding legitimate decisions depending on the case: from various kinds of committees and legislative bodies to general elections and elaborate constitutional procedures for amending a constitution. A legitimate procedure is one that all may reasonably accept as free and equal when collective decisions must be made and agreement is normally lacking. The burdens

428

of judgment lead to that even with reason and good will on all sides.[76]

4. There are serious doubts, however, about this idea of procedural legitimacy. It is quite plausible for a reasonably well-ordered society, for with well-framed and decent democratic institutions, reasonable and rational citizens will enact laws and policies that would almost always be legitimate though not, of course, always just. Yet this assurance of legitimacy would gradually weaken to the extent that the society ceased to be well ordered. This is because, as we saw, legitimacy of legislative enactments depends on the justice of the constitution (of whatever form, written or not), and the greater its deviation from justice, the more likely the injustice of outcomes. Laws cannot be too unjust if they are to be legitimate. Constitutional political procedures may indeed be—under normal and decent circumstances—purely procedural with respect to legitimacy. In view of the imperfection of all human political procedures, there can be no such procedure with respect to political justice and no procedure could determine its substantive content. Hence, we always depend on our substantive judgments of justice.[77]

Another serious doubt is that in practice a constitutional de-

---

76. I am indebted to Hinsch for valuable discussion about the meaning and role of legitimacy, and its distinction from the idea of justice; see his *Habilitationschrift* (1995) on democratic legitimacy. I am indebted also to David Estlund for his valuable unpublished paper on this concept as it is used in this text, especially IV–VI.

77. I think Habermas would agree with this distinction between political justice and legitimacy, since at one point he discusses the legitimacy both of particular enactments and of the constitution itself, both of which depend on justice, or on justification. Or as he says in *The Theory of Communicative Action, Volume 2: System and Lifeworld*, McCarthy, trans. (Boston: Beacon, 1987), p. 178: "the principle of enactment and the principle of justification reciprocally require one another. The legal system as a whole needs to be anchored in the basic principles of legitimation." Habermas appears here to argue against Max Weber, who understood legitimacy as acceptance by a people of its political and social institutions. Acceptance alone without justification Habermas rightly holds is not enough, since it allows for far too much. I would add only (Habermas I think would agree) that these institutions need not be perfectly just, and may, depending on the situation, be unjust and still be legitimate. I thank Peritz, whose understanding of Habermas has been invaluable, for pointing me to this reference.

mocracy could never arrange its political procedures and debates close enough to Habermas's communicative ideal of discourse to be confident that its legislation did not exceed the leeway legitimacy permits. Actual political conditions under which parliaments and other bodies conduct their business necessitate great departures from that ideal. One is the pressure of time: discussion must be regulated by rules of order, and must in due course come to an end; votes must be taken. Not everyone can survey and evaluate all the evidence and often it is too much even to read and understand. Legislators not infrequently must decide and vote largely in the dark, or else in accordance with what their not always impartial party leaders and constituents want. Even when well-designed political procedures moderate these and other defects, we cannot sensibly expect any legislative procedure, even if normally procedural with respect to legitimacy, to be so with respect to justice. The distance will always be far too great.

Habermas's description of the procedure of reasoning and argument in ideal discourses is also incomplete. It is not clear what forms of argument may be used, yet these importantly determine the outcome. Are we to think, as he seems to suggest, that each person's interests are to be given equal consideration in ideal discourse? What are the relevant interests? Or are all interests to be counted, as is sometimes done in applying the principle of equal consideration? This might yield a utilitarian principle to satisfy the greatest balance of interests. On the other hand, the deliberative conception of democracy (to which Habermas shows much sympathy) restricts the reasons citizens may use in supporting legislation to reasons consistent with the recognition of other citizens as equals. Here lies the difficulty with arguments for laws supporting discrimination.[78] The essential idea is that deliberative democracy, and political liberalism also, limit relevant human interests to fundamental interests of certain

78. See Cohen's review of Dahl's *Democracy and Its Critics*, in *Journal of Politics* 53, no. 1 (October 1991): 221–25, p. 223f.

kinds, or to primacy goods, and require that reasons be consistent with citizens' mutual recognition as equals. The point is that no institutional procedure without such substantive guidelines for admissible reasons can cancel the maxim "garbage in, garbage out." While the conditions of a constitutional democracy tend to force groups to advocate more compromising and reasonable views if they are to be influential, the mix of views and reasons in a vote in which citizens lack awareness of such guidelines may easily lead to injustice, even though the outcome of the procedure is legitimate.

Finally, the enactments and legislation of all institutional procedures should always be regarded by citizens as open to question. It is part of citizens' sense of themselves, not only collectively but also individually, to recognize political authority as deriving from them and that they are responsible for what it does in their name. Political authority is not mysterious, nor is it to be sanctified by symbols and rituals citizens cannot understand in terms of their common purposes. Obviously, Habermas would not disagree with this. It means, however, that our considered judgments with their fixed points—such as the condemned institutions of slavery and serfdom, religious persecution, the subjection of the working classes, the oppression of women, and the unlimited accumulation of vast fortunes, together with the hideousness of cruelty and torture, and the evil of the pleasures of exercising domination—stand in the background as substantive checks showing the illusory character of any allegedly purely procedural ideas of legitimacy and political justice.

I have gone into these matters in this section to explain why I am not ready to change my mind and feel unmoved by the objection that justice as fairness is substantive and not procedural. For as I understand these ideas, it could not be otherwise. I believe that Habermas's doctrine is also substantive in the sense that I have described, and indeed that he would not deny this. Therefore, his is procedural in a different way. I conjecture, looking back at §1 where I cited two passages from *Between Facts and Norms,* that by the terms 'substantive' and 'substantial' he means either elements of religious and metaphysical doctrines, or those incorporated in the thought and culture of particular communities and traditions, or possibly both. His main idea, I surmise, is that once the form and structure of the presuppositions of thought, reason, and action—both theoretical and practical—are properly laid out and analyzed by his theory of communicative action, then all the alleged substantial elements of those religious and metaphysical doctrines and the traditions of communities have been absorbed (or sublimated) into the form and structure of those presuppositions. This means that to the extent that those elements have validity and force in moral justification in matters of right and justice,[79] their force is fully captured and can be defended by reasoning of that form and structure; for those presuppositions are formal and universal, the conditions of the kinds of reason in all thought and action.[80] Justice as fairness is substantive, not in the sense I described (though it is that), but in the sense that it springs from and belongs to the tradition of liberal thought and the larger community of political culture of democratic societies. It fails then to be properly formal and truly universal, and thus to be part of the quasi-transcendental presuppositions (as Habermas sometimes says) established by the theory of communicative action.

Justice as fairness as a political doctrine wants no part of any such comprehensive account of the form and structural presuppositions of thought and action. Rather, as I have said, it aims to leave these doctrines as they are and criticizes them only insofar as they are unreasonable, politically speaking.[81] Otherwise, I have tried to defend the kind of liberalism found in justice as

79. Habermas is not speaking of ethics, or of the ethical values of individuals and groups. These may be pursued within the scope of legitimate and justified law.

80. For example, in the first essay of *Justification and Application,* entitled "On the Pragmatic, the Ethical, and the Moral Employments of Practical Reason," he sets out the form of four kinds of practical reason; see pp. 1–17.

81. A related objection is made by Larmore in a penetrating review of Habermas's FG in the *Deutsche Zeitschrift für Philosophie* 41 (1993): 321–27. A longer English version is to appear in the *European Journal of Philosophy* (April 1995).

fairness against Habermas's acute criticisms. Thus, I have tried to show that in the liberalism of justice as fairness, the modern liberties are not prepolitical and prior to all will formation. I stated further that there is an internal connection in justice as fairness between the public and private autonomy and that both are co-original.

I should likewise resist the tendency, also found in some American civic republican legal thought, to find as the basis of private autonomy (the liberties of the moderns) solely its (their) connection with public autonomy (the liberties of the ancients); as I indicated in §4.3, private autonomy has a further sufficient basis in the second moral power. To keep the ancient and the modern liberties properly co-original and co-equal, we need to recognize that neither is derivative from or reducible to the other. Another possible difference with Habermas I mentioned is institutional, the question of constitutional design; though it is not an object of his criticism, I emphasize that it is not in any case to be settled by philosophy alone (I do not suppose he would say it is), which can only, as always, help to provide the political principles of critical and informed judgment.

§ 6. Conclusion

There is one related question that I have not discussed in detail, and that is the question of how exactly the political institutions associated with constitutional democracy can be understood to be consistent with the idea of popular sovereignty. If we associate popular sovereignty with something like majority rule following free, open, and wide discussion, then there is at least an apparent difficulty. This difficulty may be an aspect of what Habermas is referring to when he says that "[t]he form of political autonomy . . . does not fully unfold in the heart of the justly constituted society" (128). The consistency of constitutional democracy with popular sovereignty I indicated with the idea of dualist democracy as discussed in §3.4, where a discussion of it could naturally arise. It is too great a question to have undertaken in my reply: it requires an account and explanation of the special features of the institutions for the exercise of the constituent power of a democratic people in making constitutional decisions, as opposed to the institutions of ordinary democratic politics within the framework set up by those decisions. But I want to express recognition of the question here.[82]

In concluding his introductory remarks, Habermas says that since he shares the intentions of justice as fairness and sees its essential conclusions as correct, he wishes his dissent to remain within the bounds of a family quarrel. His doubts are confined to whether I state my view in the most compelling way; and so far as his criticisms are to present serious challenges, he means his intensifying of objections to be seen as offering an occasion in which justice as fairness can show its strengths. I heartily accept Habermas's criticisms so graciously offered and I have attempted to meet the challenge they present. In formulating my replies, I repeat what I said at the beginning that I have been forced to think through and reexamine many aspects of my view, and now believe I understand it better than I once did. For that I shall always be in Habermas's debt.

82. I thank Dworkin, Thomas Nagel, and Lawrence Sager for pressing this question. I am grateful to Sager for instructive later discussion.

Index

This index contains, in addition to the standard kinds of entries, a brief analytical description of the contents of each section in the text, with the name of the entry the same (modulo definite and indefinite articles) as the section's title in the table of contents. I should like to thank Erin Kelly, William Bristow, and Paula Frederick for their unflagging assistance in preparing it; and I am much indebted to Erin Kelly for her greatly needed assistance with the paperback edition.

Abolitionists, lii, 249ff.

Abortion: disputed question of, lvff.; footnote pp. 243f. corrected, lvf$n$; question of decided in public reason by reasonable ordering or balance of political values, 243nf., 246

Abrams v. United States, 250 US 616 (1919), 350

Ackerman, Bruce, 231n, 233n, 234n, 238n, 239n, 374n, 405n, 406n

Adams, Robert, 253n

Addressing two fundamental questions, I:1, 4–11: first such question focuses on settling conflict of two democratic traditions, Locke vs. Rousseau, 4f.; two principles of justice stated, 5f., 271; three features of content of political liberalism, 6, 156f.; three aspects of two principles of justice as egalitarian, 6f.; how political philosophy might find public basis of justification, 8–11; justice as fairness as practical, 9f.;

Index

Addressing two questions (*Cont.*)
as free standing, 10, 12f., 40, 144f.;
hopes to answer second such question by finding political conception with support of reasonable overlapping consensus, 10f.

Agresto, John, 231*n*, 233*n*

Albritton, Rogers, 124*n*

Allen, J. W., 148*n*, 303*n*

Amendments to constitution: validity of, 237ff.

Animals: what is owed to as problem of extension, defined, 21, 244ff.

Apparent difficulties with public reason, VI:7, 240–47; (1) public reason allows more than one answer, 240f.; (2) how to specify meaning of voting our sincere opinion, 241–44; (3) how to say when a question is resolved by and problems of extension, 244ff.; what is owed to animals and nature: limits of public reason do not apply, 245f.; threads pulled together: how public reason must itself be reasonable, 246f.

Aquinas, St. Thomas, 134, 250*n*

Arendt, Hannah, 206*n*, 408*n*

Aristotelian principle, 203*n*, 207

Aristotle, 131, 134, 410

Arneson, Richard, 182*n*, 185*n*

Arrow, K. J.: his objection to primary goods discussed, xlviii*n*, 182f., 185*n*

Association: distinguished from both a community and democratic society, 40–43; practical and purposive distinguished, 42n

Audi, Robert, xxxv, 214*n*

St. Augustine, Bishop of Hippo, 234

Autonomy: political vs. moral, xlivf.; rational vs. full distinguished, 28, 72–81; defined as doctrinal autonomy and how based on practical reason, 98; autonomy of citizens, politically speaking, 98; of a political doctrine, 98f.; definition of Kant's conception of constitutive autonomy, 99f., 125

Background culture of civil society: defined as containing comprehensive doctrines of all kinds, 14, 151*n*, 211*n*; as culture of the social, not of the political, 14; more rigorous standards for reasonable doctrines may be stated in, 60*n*; questions taken off the political agenda discussed in, 151*n*; concern about consequences for if neutrality of effect is abandoned, 194*n*; churches and universities vital part of, 215; as containing nonpublic reasons of civil society, 220; not the same as Habermas's public sphere, 382*n*

Background, or basic, institutions, 11, 229; actual agreements embedded in, 23; role in establishing social world enabling us to become free and equal citizens, 41, 43, 77; *see also* Lecture VII:3–5

Baier, Kurt: idea of constitutional consensus, 149, 158*n*

Barry, Brian, 17*n*, 31*n*

Basic justice, matters of: not constitutional essentials but to be settled by political values alone, 228ff.

Basic liberties, fully adequate scheme of, VIII:8, 331–34: need criterion of to fill Hart's second gap, namely, how to adjust basic liberties when they conflict at later stages, 331; proposed criterion uses idea of a scheme of liberties essential for the adequate development and full exercise of the two moral powers in two fundamental cases, 325, 332f.; scheme does not maximize anything, 333ff.; *see also* Fundamental cases

Basic liberties, not merely formal, VIII:7, 324–31: principles for basic liberties acceptable only if complemented by principles assuring fair share of material means, 325; basic liberties and worth of liberty distinguished, 325; worth specified by index of primary goods regulated by

436

Index

Index

Maintaining fair value (*Continued*)
ditions of background justice are
fulfilled, 362f.

Mandle, Jon, 381*n*

Marshall, John, 359*n*

Masses Publishing v. Patten, 244 Fed.
535 (1917), (S.D.N.Y. 1917), 351

Maximum, idea of, 333f.

McCarthy, Thomas, 192*n*, 372*n*,
377*n*, 399*n*, 414*n*, 426*n*

McKittrick, Eric, 406*n*

McPherson, James, 249*n*

Medieval Christianity, xxvf., 37

Meiklejohn, Alexander, 290*n*, 296*n*,
348*n*

Melden, A. I., 212*n*

Meyers, Marvin, liv*n*

Michelman, Frank, xxxv, 166*n*, 237*n*,
339*n*, 396*n*, 399*n*, 407*n*, 415

Mill, J. S., xlv, 7*n*, 37, 78, 98, 139*n*,
145 159, 169, 199f., 211*n*, 303,
313, 375*n*, 400

Model case of a reasonable overlapping consensus, 145f., 147, 155,
169ff.

Modern moral and political philosophy, xxv

Module, political conception of justice as, 12f., 145

modus vivendi, xxxixf., lviii; versus
overlapping consensus, xxxixf., xli;
how might develop into an overlapping consensus, xlii; defined, 146f.

Morgenbesser, Sidney, 372*n*

Montesquieu, Charles de, 303*n*, 366

Moore, G. E., 63*n*

Moral powers, two: defined, 19, 81,
103f., 108; modeled in constructivist procedure, 103f.; exercise of experienced as good, 202f.; second
moral power not grounded solely
on political autonomy, 420f.

Moral psychology: philosophical, not
psychological: II:8, 86–88; that of
parties in the original position not
an account of, 28; that of justice as

fairness drawn from itself as political conception, 86f.; not a psychology originating in science, 86f.; human nature and its natural psychology as permissive, 87; ideal of
citizenship must be intelligible and
one people can be moved to honor,
87; political philosophy of constitutional regime autonomous in two
ways, 87f

Murray, Father John Courtney, lvii*n*

Musgrave, R, A., 181*n*

Mutual advantage, idea of: defined,
16f., 50; contrasted with idea of reciprocity, 16f., 50

Mutual good of mutual justice, 208

Nagel, Thomas, xxxiii, xlviii*n*, 20*n*,
61*n*, 84*n*, 90*n*, 96*n*, 121*n*, 144*n*,
214*n*, 274*n*, 434*n*; on the burdens
of judgment and fragmentation of
value, 57*n*; on impersonal point of
view, 116; on content and validity
of argument, 120*n*; on justice as
fairness as individualistic, 196*n*

Nardin, Terry, 42*n*

Natural religion, 245f.

Nature: what is owed to as problem
of extension, 21, 245f.

Near v. Minnesota, 283 U.S. 697
(1931), 345*n*

Needs of citizens, *see* Primary goods
as citizens' needs

Neiman, Susan, 101*n*

Neither community nor association,
I:7, 40–43; *see also* Idea of well-ordered society

Neutral values: defined, 191f.; examples of, 191; procedural neutrality
vs. neutrality of aim, or neutrality
of effect (influence), 191–94

Nevins, Allan, 45*n*

New Deal, 234

New York Times v. Sullivan, 376 U.S.
254 (1964), 343, 345

Index

Political philosophy (*Continued*)
basis for settling fundamental questions, 8f.; uses abstract conceptions, 44ff.; does not withdraw from society and the world, 45f.; autonomous in two ways, 87f.; aim of in the dominant tradition, 135; no experts in, 383f.; 426f

Political relationship in a constitutional regime, connection with reciprocity and public reason, li; features of, defined, 67f., 135f.; 216; give rise to question of legitimacy, 136, 217f.; identifies domain of the political, 137, 216

Political society, how conceived, 12 , 18ff., 26, 67f., 201–6; *see also* Neither association nor community; and Idea of well-ordered society

Political values of justice and public reason, 30, 139, 223f., 236, 245; express liberal ideal, 139f.

Political virtues, 121f., 139, 147, 171, 194f., 207f., 347. 400, 402; as necessary, xlvif.; examples of, 122, 157, 163, 194f, 347; their basis in moral psychology and role of public recognition, 163; how identified and justified, 195; in education of children, 199f.

Political wisdom: defined, 156

Possibilities of construction, 123ff.

Powers of Reason: defined as judgment, thought, and inference, 19, 81, 220; necessary for exercise of the moral powers, 81; *see also* Guidelines of public reason

Practical reason: defined in contrast with theoretical reason, 93, 117; its principles viewed as self-originating and self-authenticating, 100; as alone competent to settle the scope of its own authority, 101, 120n; two aspects of, 107f.; conceptions of society and person as ideas of, 107f., 110; public role of principles

of justice as idea of, 110; its role in objectivity of judgments, 119

Price, Richard, 91n, 92n

Primary goods and interpersonal comparisons, V:3, 178–87: 6n; two ways of making index of 39f.; list of these goods, 76, 181; introduced to resolve problem posed by veil of ignorance, 75f., 307; based on political conception of persons, 75f., 178; how problem of interpersonal comparisons arises, 179f.; these goods give idea of rational advantage independent of any comprehensive doctrine, 180; identify partial similarity of permissible conceptions of the good, 180; as practical public basis of interpersonal comparisons, 181; as recognizing limits of the political and the practicable, 182; whether can handle four main kinds of variations in citizens' capacities, 183–86; preferences and tastes our own responsibility, 185f.; use of assumes ends and preferences revisable in light of expectations of, 186; assumes workable public criteria and an ideal of the person, 186f.; role in parallel to Habermas's view, 418f.

Primary goods as citizens' needs, V:4, 187–90: connected with citizens' higher-order interests, 106, 178, 186; when basic institutions allow sufficient space for ways of life worthy of citizens' support, 187, 198n, 209f.; not intended as measure of overall psychological well-being, success, or intrinsic worth of ends, 187f.; specify citizens' needs within political conception, 178f., 188, 207; index of provides best available standard of justification of competing claims given reasonable pluralism, 188f.; account of includes idea of social division of responsibility, 189f.; desires and

454

Index

second stage, 65, 141f.; as purely practical matter, 142ff.; the stability required of justice as fairness depends on forces that secure it, 142f.; rests on how it addresses each citizen's public reason, 142f; only so is it a basis of legitimacy, 143f.; *see also* Stability and Stability for the right reasons

Questions and forums of public reason, VI:1, 213–16: public reason defined, 213, 214; part of a liberal conception of justice, 213f.; limits of public reason specified to apply to constitutional essentials and matters of basic justice, not to all political questions, 214f.; to what persons they apply and in what forums, 214f.; they do apply to voting 214ff.; apply in different ways to citizens and government officers, 215f.

Quine, W. V., 379n

Quinn, Warren, 117n, 118n, 119n

Rabinowitz, Joshua, 273n, 289n, 325n

Railton, Peter, 91n

Raphael, D. D., 91n

Rasmussen, David, 409n

Rational autonomy: artificial not political, II:5, 72–77: defined as resting on persons' intellectual and moral powers, 28, 72; shown in their capacity to form, revise, and pursue a conception of the good, 72; modeled by making original position a case of pure procedural justice, 72f.; parties' deliberations model rational autonomy, 73; this done by nature of their deliberations and the interests they consider as given by three higher-order interests, 73f.; just as citizens are rationally autonomous in two ways, so are the parties, 74f.; rational autonomy vs. full autonomy, 75; primary goods

introduced to resolve a problem posed by veil of ignorance, 75f.; rational autonomy rests on being moved by the higher order interests, 76f.

Rational intuitionism, xvii, 22; as form of moral realism, 89, 91, 95; four features of, 91f.; can accept argument from original position, 95; 113; relies on idea of reflective equilibrium, 95f., 113; its conception of objectivity, 110–14; kinds of may be heteronomous in doctrinal sense, 113; *see also* Idea of constructivist conception

Rational plan of life, 177, 208

Rationalist believers, 152f.

Raz, Joseph, 135n, 193n

Reasonable, idea of: comprehensive doctrines as, assumed not to reject essentials of democratic regime, xviii; idea of vs. true, xxiv, 94, 116, 127ff., 394f.; two aspects of applied to persons, 48–54, 54–58; three main features of applied to comprehensive doctrines, 59f.; role of in burdens of judgment and argument for toleration, 60ff.; how content specified, 94; idea of reasonable judgment and essentials of objectivity, 111f., 115; relation to idea of legitimacy, 136f, 393, 427ff.

Reasonable comprehensive doctrines, II:3, 58–66: not all are liberal, xxxixf.; how burdens of judgment lead to toleration and support idea of public reason, 58–61; defined by three features, and call on three forms of reason, 59; account of deliberately loose, 59; reasonable persons affirm a form of liberty of conscience, 61f.; this conclusion confirmed by use of original position, 61f.; being reasonable is part of the ideal of democratic citizenship, 62; reasoning leading to toleration not based on skepticism, 62f.; content

Index

460

Index

modus vivendi defined, and three ways such consensus differs: in its object, ground, and stability, 147f., 208; stability defined as consensus unchanged under shifts in political power, 148; toleration in sixteenth century example of modus vivendi, 148f.; depth, breadth, and specificity of consensus defined, 149; contrast with Baier's constitutional consensus, 149f.; *see also* Overlapping consensus neither indifferent nor skeptical

Three points of view, 28; of you and me, 67, 70; how modeled in the original position, 69f.

Tocqueville, Alexis de, 205*n*, 303

Toleration: religious, 8, 196f.; as origin of liberalism, xxviff.; in political liberalism principle of applied to philosophy itself, 10, 154; how burdens of judgment give rise to, 58–62; as a political virtue, 194f.

Transcendent values, as true grounds of political values, 241ff.

Transition, process of and its questions, 17f.

Tribe, Laurence, 359*n*, 422*n*

Truth of moral judgments: in political conception of justice left to comprehensive doctrines, xxii, 94, 116, 126f., 153f.; in rational intuitionism, 92, 111–14; not all comprehensive doctrines must use this conception, 126*n*; in reasonable overlapping consensus, truth of any one doctrine implies political conception is sound, 128f., 153*nf*; truth in the paradox of public reason, 216, 218f.; the whole truth as we see it, 216, 218, 225, 242; politics in a democracy cannot be guided by the whole truth, 243

Two main differences, IX:1, 373–85: first difference, Habermas's view is comprehensive whereas political liberalism falls under category of the political and is free standing, 373–76; Habermas aims to give a general account of both meaning and reference, truth and validity, for both theoretical and practical reason, 376–79; he denies that political liberalism is free standing, 380f.; second difference, original position an analytical device formulating a conjecture concerning reasonable political principles, while Habermas's ideal discourse is used to analyze the presuppositions of rational discourse, 381f.; neither of these devices is monological and both debated from standpoint of citizens in civil society, 382–85

Two principles of justice: stated 5f., 271; first has priority over the second, 6; exemplify content of a liberal conception of justice, 6; presupposes citizens' basic needs are met, 7; three egalitarian features of, 6f; designed to form a social world in which our person is realized and give priority to basic freedoms of civil society, 41; selection of not affected by distinction between two kinds of pluralism, 64ff.; must lead to a social world congenial to citizens' exercising their moral powers, 77

Two stages of the exposition of justice as fairness, 37, 64f., 133f., 140ff.

Unity by appropriate sequence, VII:2, 259–62: developed starting from basic structure, 259f.; contrast with utilitarianism: principle of utility applies equally to all social forms and universal in scope, 260; first principles of justice as fairness not suitable for general theory, 261; idea of appropriate sequence for specifying principles, 262; unity given by structure of such a se-

Index

Unity by sequence (*Continued*)
quence, 262; differences in structure and social role of institutions account for propriety of different principles, 262

Use of abstract conceptions, I:8, 43–46: basic ideas of political liberalism as, 43; answer to combined question of political liberalism: given by three conditions using these ideas, 44; use of such conceptions in relation to breakdown of shared political understandings, 44f.; work of abstraction not gratuitous, 45f.

Utilitarianism, xviiff., 13, 37, 179; its principle lacks simplicity required for public reason, 162; its relation to political conception one of approximation, 169ff.; contrast with contract view, 281; as alternative available in original position to the two principles of justice, 292, 294f.; how specified as a teleological view, 295*n*

Veil of ignorance: defined, in original position as modeling appropriate reasons in adopting principles of justice, 24f., 305; thick vs. thin distinguished, with thick justified, 24*n*f., 273; has no metaphysical implication, 27; second level of publicity modeled by, 70; introduces problem resolved by use of primary goods, 75f., 307; what information excludes and why, 79

Waldron, Jeremy, 391*n*
Walzer, Michael, lxi*n*, 44, 46*n*

Washington, George, 420
Watson, Gary, 212*n*
Weber, Max, 429*n*
Wechsler, Herbert, 191*n*
Weithman, Paul, xxxvi, lii*n*, lvii*n*, 212*n*, 214*n*
Weimar regime, lxif.
Wesberry v. Sanders, 376 U.S. 1 (1964), 361f.
When do objective reasons exist, politically speaking? III:7, 119–25; political convictions objective when endorsed by reasonable and rational persons on due reflection, 119; success of shared practice establishes objective reasons; no defects made good by connecting them with causal process, 119f.; comparison with mathematics, 120; sixth essential of objectivity is to be able to explain failure of judgments to converge, 121; disagreement may allow psychological explanation, but requires grounds independent of lack of agreement, 121; two kinds of facts relevant for political reasoning, 121ff.; distinctions illustrated by slavery, 122–25; constructivist procedure lays basis for idea of possibilities of construction, 125
White, Byron, 359*n*
Whitney v. California, 274 U. S. 357 (1927), 344, 349, 351
Wide view of public reason, lif.
Williams, Bernard, 31*n*, 85*n*, 117*n*
Wolf, Susan, 333*n*
Wood, Gordon, 415*n*
Wright, Skelly, 359*n*

464